ADVANCED MAGNETISM

---·---

OR THE PRIVATE USES OF

EMOTIONAL CONTROL

OVER

MEN AND WOMEN IN EVERY DEPARTMENT
OF LIFE

---·---

TAUGHT BY

EDMUND SHAFTESBURY

ISSUED BY THE
RALSTON UNIVERSITY PRESS
MERIDEN, CONN.
1925

DEDICATED

to all my pupils the world over who have given earnest consideration to the foundation principles of magnetism in the first book of study, with sincere wishes for success in deeper paths of investigation.

EDMUND SHAFTESBURY.

November, 1924.

ADVANCE THOUGHTS

Some persons who possess a shrinking nature regard with fear the presence of a magnetic person. They look upon the study as one of the dark arts.

No greater mistake than this could be made.

The lack of magnetism in the brain and nervous system leads to gloomy thoughts, dark forebodings and fears of some calamity or misfortune that impends; but, in proportion as the brain and nervous system are given the power to develop this natural magnetic condition that goes by the name of personal magnetism, in the same proportion the thoughts and feelings become elastic and bright. The reason is plain.

The conditions that favor ill health, such as the withdrawal of the light, the lessening of outdoor life, the worrying circumstances of the day, and the proneness to see the unfavorable side of every person and thing, are the very conditions that make the development of magnetism impossible; but the things that build up good health, such as light, free air, good cheer, pleasing companions and brightness in general, are all aids to the development of magnetism. How then can any one say that it is a dark or a subtle art?

Thus it is seen that a misunderstanding exists at the very start as to the nature of this power which we are about to examine much more deeply than can be done in a book that is devoted to the development of its presence.

This Course of Training

PRESENTS a wholly separate world of study and practice apart from all other fields of magnetic control, and in so doing proves the fact that the uses of Personal Magnetism are as varied and far reaching as human life itself. Probably there can be no limit to one's constantly growing knowledge of the influences that bind people together in every possible form of association and interchange of interests.

In one course of training the *mind* sways the *mind*; in another course the interweaving of *sex attractions* plays a most important role in the scheme of Nature; in another and very great course the universal and ever present lines of interest extend to all parts of the world and even to the universe itself as holding a destiny for all who live; and here we find spread out before us the most delightful study and practice of the one hundred emotions which, under magnetic training, are capable of swaying irresistibly every class of people from the weakest to the strongest. In fact there is no person living who can defy this power that we are about to teach in this volume of ADVANCED MAGNETISM.

++++++++++++++++++ ++++++++

CHAPTER ONE

MAGNETISM UNITES
ALL THE ORBS
OF THE SKY
WITH HUMANITY AND WITH GOD

++

❧ WAVES AND IMPULSES ❧

++

LL CREATION is connected by natural and not by supernatural influences. There is nothing supernatural. Every law that is at work in the farthest corner of the starry system is at work on earth and within the range of human life. This proposition is the basis of the larger system known as Universal Philosophy. It gives the solution of all problems. If it were not true, there would be no plan, no unity in the purpose of creation.

A natural law is based upon a process that the human mind is able to grasp and to understand. Thus gravity is called a natural law, although it is one of the most mysterious of all the processes at work in the universe. When the mind is not able to apply the right name to a law, it calls it by the nearest term it can suggest. Gravity is so called because it is weight or the quality of being heavy.

But the idea of weight is lost when we connect the same law with the influence of the earth over the moon, and the influence of the moon over the earth.

If you tie a stone to a tower and throw it off, the string holds the stone within leash. This is a tangible hold, something that man can make and control. No natural law is at work when the hunting dog is kept under leash. The nail that binds the board to the timber-joists does not obey a law of man; for, although man controlled it, the real law is that of adhesion which causes the nail to cling to the wood.

If the moon could be chained by a cord tied to the earth, and the latter held to the sun in the same manner, the law of man would be at work controlling the union; but the law of nature would be needed to keep the orbs apart, as their collision would mean ruin.

Here we see three influences. One prevents the departure of a distant body in the sky, keeping it within its system, and not allowing it to go an inch beyond the will of that influence. Another prevents the distant body from approaching the controlling orb. The third causes the material of which each body is composed to adhere and take shape, size, form, and all the qualities of dimensions.

These three laws are attraction, repulsion and adhesion. A fourth law is cohesion, or the adhesion of molecules to each other in chemical elements.

These are all natural processes, not one of them being originated by the will or act of man. But if one object were to be tied to another, as a horse to a post, the process is due to the creative idea of man, taking advantage of the law of adhesion, which makes friction possible. Without friction the knot in the rope would slip and open.

There is nothing more supernatural, weird, strange and subtle than these four laws; yet they are all recognized as natural.

Why a cannon ball, set free from the top of a tower, will come to the ground, is as deep a mystery as exists anywhere in the material or spiritual world. The common mind says it is due to weight; but weight is given to one object only when a distant, free, separable and attracting influence is exerted by another.

It is known to be the same law that the sun employs in keeping the earth within its system; and the same law that the earth employs in holding the moon in place. It is the same law that, more distantly, is employed by the far away systems of stars to maintain the place and rank of our solar system. And, as far as there are heavens, this law of attraction, working in harmony with its sister law, repulsion, is potent and imperious from one end of creation to another.

No orb, no sun, no system, no galaxy, no starry field, is too great or too small for its activities; and, strangest of all, this same law is present in every drop of blood, every fibre of life, every grain of sand in this tiny planet on which we dwell.

What it is has never been explained except on the basis of magnetism. What it accomplishes is partly known. How it works is still a mystery except under the law of magnetism. Enough, however, is known of this magnetic energy to explain the whole process, and also each and every law that is at work on the earth or in the universe.

These facts are admitted as true, and are not in dispute by any person familiar with natural powers.

We thus stand face to face with a series of influences that are as great as the whole creation of God, and that exist in every particle of these bodies of ours. Nothing is beyond the pale of their sway. Nothing is left to itself, and nothing can escape.

The law of attraction holds everything to everything. The only blemish it has is the inability to be interpreted. If we could read its waves of impulse, we might read the secrets of heaven. If the power of such interpretation should some day be acquired by the human race, its revelations need not be regarded as in the realm of the supernatural, for nothing is more natural than the force that is most common and most active in creation.

An endless line of study might creep up on this thought in almost any direction that is assumed. Two orbs like the earth and moon throw out the influence each toward the other, and the effect is readily observed. The attraction of the moon lifts the tides. The attraction of the sun does the same thing. When both the moon and sun are in the same line, the earth's water is lifted to its highest; and, when the sun and moon are separated, as in the first and third quarters of the moon, the earth's water is not lifted so high, and the tides are known as neap, or lowest. Here we have indisputable evidence of the subtle, strange and almost supernatural attraction of one orb for another by a law that is hard to understand except on the theory of magnetism.

Wonders are worked in the sky by this magnetism. The moon once turned on its axis as the earth does now; but the magnetism of the earth has been slowing up that revolution until it has almost stopped, only the librations of the moon remaining to show what has gone before. In like manner the moon and the sun both are slowing up the revolutions of the earth. While a day is the distance from one sun to another sun, or from moon to moon, or midnight to midnight, the length of that day is determined by the time it takes the earth to make one revolution on its axis. If the earth has been slowed up in its revolution, then the day is a longer period than it was. That it has been slowed up and is being made slower all the time, is a proved fact. The reduction is so small that it seems inappreciable, but it is nevertheless the fact that some day the earth will stop making days and nights. What then will be its fate? Seasons will vanish in part, vitality will be differently distributed, and the race will change to suit new conditions.

These thoughts are part of the study of philosophy, which runs them to their full length, discovering the purpose present today in the unfolding of the great plan of creation by following the process of natural laws. All these influences are magnetism.

If you throw a man to the ground, that is not magnetism, although some part of your prowess may be due to such a power. If you compel a man to come to you by using force, as of a rope, that is not magnetism. If obedience is secured by force, threats, fear, or other cause that impels the weak to follow the strong, little or no magnetism is employed. But if the man comes to you, or your will is obeyed without show of resistance, or refusal and resistance are conquered without demonstration on your part, you are employing the same law that has been checking the revolution of the moon and that is making earth's day longer.

The explanation is this:

Between one object and another, on this orb, and in the sky, there is a sea of ether that vibrates with inconceivable speed.

In this ether there is a wave-action that affects the molecules or primary particles of all matter, and that is not hindered by solid masses from exerting its influence on every such molecule.

In the sea of ether, traveling on the waves of action, are impulses, which obey a Supreme command.

These impulses are laws of life that may be employed by the mind of man for his own service.

The human will may set in motion its commands and impel them on ether waves to any distance; although the rule of attraction is that the nearer the object the greater the power of control.

CHAPTER TWO

++++++++++++++++++++++++

THE FIRST VICTORY
IN MAGNETISM
IS
PERSONAL MASTERY

+++

100 PER CENT OF SELF-CONTROL

+++

EVELOPED MAGNETISM must mean something or it cannot be regarded as well acquired. To hold a quality of value is akin to having property of value. If it serves no satisfactory purpose it is not a worthy acquisition. The first book in this series of courses of instruction is devoted solely to the task of developing personal magnetism. That book cannot be omitted in the study of this subject, and this fact has been made plain in every way prior to the announcement of this work. Advanced magnetism is intermediary between the development of the power, and the deeper philosophical investigations of Universal Magnetism.

We are about to embark upon a private consideration of the laws and powers and their uses in controlling other people and checking the silent sway that others may have over the student of this work.

It is assumed that you have therefore mastered the developing stage of magnetism by having graduated from the first book, which is devoted, as has been stated, to the sole duty of cultivating the power.

To test this question, we shall have you pass through several common incidents for a month, and then measure up your per-

11

centage of self-control; for it must be remembered that this kind of mastery is the key to all others. No man or woman could be so foolish as to believe that some other human being could be mastered when the world of self is an unconquered kingdom.

These tests are as simple as any that could be suggested, yet they are more than straws in the breeze. If you fail in any one of them, you should go back to the first book and again seek its aid.

Coughing.—This is a little hacking action of the glottis that grows into an annoying habit. The test is to omit every alternate cough; and keep reducing them until you can control the fault. It is the easiest of all efforts.

Gaping.—This is the vulgar habit of yawning. It follows lack of sleep, loss of vitality, indigestion and other causes. It is not so easy to overcome as coughing; but may be mastered by any person who is in earnest and has some degree of self-control.

Sneezing.—This comes on so suddenly that it is not anticipated, but there is an appreciable length of time between the premonition and the sneeze. The first step is to widen this margin of time; that is, to make it as long as you can. Another consideration is to learn to recognize the approach of the premonition. These two things can be done and with certainty, after a little practice. It is said that more than ninety per cent of the American people possess teeth that are capable of being sneezed out. Many a person on board ship, not having the slightest warning, has sneezed an upper set of teeth to the briny deep. In a street car the other day a nice-looking fat woman who had been unusually meditative, sneezed similar bric-a-brac across the car to the annoyance of the man who sat opposite reading the paper. When she had secured them and was able to articulate, her only apology was that she had no idea she was going to sneeze.

This is true. To get the advance idea is important, not only for practical life, but also as a test of self-control.

Then to hold the sneeze back as long as possible is another part of the evidence of power.

After more trials the time will come when the sneeze will be conquered. There are thousands of men and women who have testified that they have been able to completely suppress it. The result has been a great advantage, for the habit of sneezing easily leads to irritation of the throat, bronchial tubes and lungs; and the easy sneezer keeps at it more frequently than one who does it only occasionally. During the period of rose cold, hay fever, and kindred kinds of malady, the tendency to sneeze on the least provocation and at anything, is so common that it leads to watering of the eyes, and redness of the nose, with running catarrh of a thin nature. When the sneezing can be conquered, all these discomforts can be driven away. Yet it is not an easy task for one who is afflicted in such way.

That the habit can, under those circumstances, be wholly conquered has been fully proved, not in a few cases, but in every case where the patient has developed magnetism under the instruction of the first course.

This fact has been used as a test by us for many years. In one thousand cases where students were asked to suppress sneezing before they passed through the stages of the first book, the result was failure; yet when that book had been mastered, almost all the students could at will hold back the tendency to sneeze, until it disappeared altogether.

Irritability.—This is the most common trait of human nature. It shows uncontrol in the meanest degree; and it may be said that no man or woman can master others who gives way to this habit. It grows with remarkable activity until it envelopes the whole nature, and then everything grows wrong. Yet a magnetic person who assails it in force will soon make it appear foolish.

The first step is to learn to recognize its approach. It comes like sneezing and is in fact merely the temper having a sneeze. If you fail to know when it is coming on, you will give way to it and humiliate both yourself and others. You will say mean things, do acts of violence, or curse something or somebody, either inwardly or outwardly. The girl that you are to marry, if you are anxious to make her think that you are an ideal man, will not see this display, for you know enough then to curb it; but, soon after marriage, and the heart has been won, and there is nothing at stake, you will let loose all restraint, and off will go the bad temper. She never dreamed that you could talk so; she wonders where you acquired that special vocabulary; and, later on, if she protests, her innocent head may be the target for your assault. This is most unmanly, and most unmagnetic.

When you can go one whole month and not show to yourself,

when alone, the least bit of irritability, then you have magnetism to that extent. But the chief victory is in acquiring the power to know of the approach of this sudden feeling, and check it before the cloud has risen in the horizon.

Swearing.—In a man this is generally speaking the word damn, the word hell, the name of the divinity, and terms that are ostracized in decent society. In a woman, it is confined to such words as darn, hang it, oh lord, sometimes vile terms, and often the full masculine swing. The common women of the land swear with as much ease as men, and most of them add filthy terms to their profanity. But we are not dealing with them. The sensible, decent classes are addicted somewhat to the use of these outlawed expressions, and they are expected to master the fault. It runs along by the side of irritability, but there are people who use improper words who do so with each and every emotion, whether there is temper in it or not.

The first step is to master the approach of the action in the mind. Do not let it get shape in thought even. This is magnetism. The more accustomed you have been in the past to swearing or using words that are related to that fault, the greater will be your victory in conquering it.

Drink.—This means the use of alcoholic beverages, and all forms of alcohol whether required as a medicine or not, and especially the patent medicines that create the alcoholic habit in so many millions of lives. If you are of the mental calibre that will believe that such medicines are what they are advertised to be, or that they will do what they are claimed to do, then you cannot hope to hold any influence over other human beings. Your own will power is in the hands of the great corporations that make and sell such medicines.

Also if your health is such that you require alcohol to get well, you are not a candidate for controlling others. Magnetism implies health and wholeness of body and mind.

There is an old idea that drink will arouse the magnetism in a man. This is just the opposite of the truth. It will burn up and drive out all the magnetism that a man has on hand, and leave him weak and empty.

The more alcohol you put into your system, whether in the form of beer, champagne or liquor, the less magnetism you will have, and the harder it will be to acquire that power.

But the present test assumes that you possess this fault, and we wish you to see how readily you can overcome it. When the taste and thirst haunt you, as they will from day to day, then rise above the slavery and appeal to your kingly self for the mastery.

Tobacco.—This is mostly for men; for, while it is true that some females chew and others smoke, they are not students of this or any other line of study. You may not be one of the men who chew; we will let that pass; we feel sure that you are not; but if you are, conquer the vile custom just as soon as you have one ounce of magnetism. You are not wanted in this club, if you cannot do this. If a man were seen lying in the pen with his own swine, one appeal might be made to him to get out and stand with the human species; if one such request did not do the work, he should be left with the swine; and the same is true of the tobacco-chewer.

But the smoker is always at a disadvantage. If he is the fiend of the cigarette, it is the end of all things with him; he will never rise from what he now is; he may hold his own for a while, but he is at the apex of his life; the future is all down hill.

The cigar and pipe smoker uses tobacco to calm his nerves. That is the very thing that magnetism will not allow; for the calmed nerves are cousins to the decayed nerves. The live wire is the current-bearer; not the wire that has been put under an anesthetic. Of all the men who have given evidence of great magnetism, and this does not mean animal cunning, we do not know of one that has been a cigar or pipe smoker.

It is the disposition of men who have not the will power to give up the smoking habit, to pooh pooh the claim that is herein made; but their defence of what they are unable to control does not change the fact. It is important that you master this fault, for it is a fault, although well nigh universal.

Gossip.—This is seemingly a small matter; but, in the study of magnetism, it is a large affair. The gossiper is not magnetic, and for several reasons. One is the fact that neither he nor his acquaintances hold him in respect; and when the public thinks little of you, there is a reduction of your prowess that is felt in the very presence of others. When you fail to respect yourself, you show it in your manner and bearing toward others. Self-confidence is essential, and it must be well founded, not a mere boast.

The individual, whether man or woman, who is a rare talker, and a careful discusser of other peoples' affairs, is always held in greater esteem than the free and easy talker who takes up any subject and forces his opinions on others. Absolute silence is not a merit; but moderate powers of conversation are high marks of good mental quality. What wins favorable opinions from people is sure to give you some control over them.

But on the separate ground of self-control, it is necessary to destroy the habit of gossip. Master these wrong customs in yourself and you will be ready to govern others.

Waste of Time.—Again we have a thing that seems small but that counts up mountains very rapidly. The magnetic man cannot rest; he has no right to have quiet nerves; nor erratic nerves. Employment of the little minutes, the spare grains of time, is the secret of keeping the system on fire and at the same time not allowing it to run itself. In the case of the man whose nerves are wild if he does not smoke them into submission, we see the energy seeking usefulness and yet being put to sleep; an open assault upon the best powers ever given to humanity.

The men and women who have achieved greatness through the development of magnetism, have been time users, never time wasters. They have been surprisingly busy. They have had no time for faults, unless they have been great ones.

In every twenty-four hours there are more than one hundred small periods of a minute or more each in which it is easy to let time wing its flight never to return. Once lost it cannot be brought back. To be constantly doing something, whether it counts value to the mind or to the body is the most virile of virtues.

But on the ground that the habit is a bad one we wish you to correct it. If it is difficult to conquer, all the better, for the Alps are worthy of the Napoleons. Master this delinquency for the sake of proving to yourself that you are not the slave to any habit.

At the Table.—Here the foundation is laid of ill health. The weak stomach is the most potent thief of vitality. Until you have acquired the best powers of digestion you cannot store away the magnetism that is necessary for sustaining the nervous system in its efforts to create the fund of energy that is used in battling for supremacy. On this ground you should not be a glutton, nor should you cater to relish or the likes of the appetite. Certain foods that are plain are known to furnish vitality, and others are known to defeat and overpower it. The system of living that is provided for in the Ralston Health Club is most beneficial to the magnetic person. No man or woman can live up to any of those Vital Laws without adding to the magnetism of the body and nervous system.

But it is to test your ability to master yourself that we suggest the adoption of the rule that foods of the most tempting kinds should be avoided. The odor of the freshly-baked dish, or its appearance, or a clinging recollection of past experience, will tempt you to indulge in it when you know or ought to know that it is not best for you. Here comes the battle between taste as the master with yourself the slave, or yourself the master and taste the slave.

It is beneficial to your powers of self-control to be able to fight down all temptations, whether at the table or elsewhere. The desire to eat something that weakens the nervous system, even though it affects it but little, will cause you to say that this one time of indulgence cannot do much harm; and here is where the un-magnetic person falls down. The feeling that a single indulgence is not a serious breach of rigid eating, leads all good intentions astray. On this rock the entire race is wrecked. Only this evening a guest of good motives ate a meal of sickly pastry, from which she will suffer in the next few days; and her excuse was that, after this one indulgence she would begin in earnest to eat plainer food. And she, as well as millions of others, will go through the world in suffering amidst the greatest proffer of good intentions.

Habits and Régime.—There are scores of good habits and many more bad ones. The good habits are acquired by rowing up stream, and the bad ones come by drifting down with the current, all unmindful of the dangers ahead. One direction requires that you take the oars in your hands and row against the flow of your inclinations. The other course requires that you put the lid down over your finer instincts and shut up the heart that beats for an exalted earthly existence, turn your back on the right direction, and let things go as they will. And they will always go in spite of your belief that you can be right and make progress while the boat of life is drifting with the stream. But the troubling fact is this: there never was a drifting current that was wending its way upland. It is always down and out. Every moving body of water finds its way to the shoreless sea.

Habits and régime are opposites.

The former are fixed methods of doing certain things, while the latter is always a plan by which to live.

Habits may be good or bad; that which is bad is never termed régime. The bad grows by its own impulses. The good must be cultivated.

The adoption of a fixed plan by which to live does much to mold that kind of character that adds to a person's usefulness in the world. It denotes the fact that individual slavery has ceased, and self-mastery taken its place. This is proof of magnetic control.

Excesses.—These occur in marriage. They undermine the magnetism of either sex. They are largely due to the fact that the man has but little control over himself, and he goes about with pale features and a sickly hue over his face attended by drawn and pinched lips, showing that his vitality and the nerve centers have emptied themselves out in excesses.

The history of magnetism shows that the unmarried men and women, if chaste, are less likely to display magnetism than those who are married; but this rule does not always hold true. The exceptions seem to be those found among men and women who use their sex forces in mental work, for the same powers that feed one function feed the other, and this is seen in the impotency of the man when his brain is over-active.

If you are not inclined to deep study, and are not married, you will not become great in magnetism. Marriage takes up some of the force that might go to the brain. No man who has married before his life work was in hand, has made himself great; unless he has left his wife, as young Shakespeare did, when he went to London.

But the law of self-mastery requires that this power should not be used to excess. It preys upon all other powers and weakens all the faculties of brain and body. Non-use, mis-use, over-use are all wrong.

In these tests you should attain a percentage of one hundred before you are qualified to go on with the present course of instruction.

CHAPTER THREE
✛✛✛✛✛✛✛✛✛✛✛✛✛✛✛✛✛✛✛✛✛✛✛✛✛✛✛✛✛

EVERY HUMAN BEING
IS GREATER
THAN HIS
GREATEST ANTAGONIST

✛✛

MAGNETISM VERSUS MAGNETISM
✛✛

 ERY FEW PERSONS are devoid of some power over others; and the ability to determine by analysis the nature of that power, is of service in knowing how to meet it. Nations have very little if any magnetism; the Swiss may be called somewhat so; and the early republic of the United States had some element of this power; but the control of one nation over another is founded in force of arms or the means of effective aggression and defence.

In the old times, the master of a vessel had autocratic sway over the sailors under him; but even the right to flog them did not always make them ready subjects. But there were undoubtedly many captains who ruled with magnetism and had no need of whipping their men.

In the army the fear of death deters most cowards from deserting; but soldiers under magnetic leaders like Napoleon and Frederick the Great had no desire to run away from duty. Force, either physical or official, may compel submission, but it does not imply magnetism, for the latter never measures weapons or comparisons of strength.

The teacher who has no other means of inducing pupils to become orderly than the authority vested by law, or a superior muscle, is sure to have unruly scholars sooner or later. The fighting school-masters of the olden time who could whip the bullies, won respect for supposed courage; but magnetism never strikes a blow or parades official authority. There are little men who hold classes in check and carry the continual respect of pupils much larger and stronger; simply because there is such a law of control as that of magnetism.

Parents have a number of reasons for retaining control over children. Duty, long association accompanied by childish regard, the punishments that have been meted out, and mutual love, are factors in this kind of control; but they all lack magnetism. Those who have this supreme quality never raise children who will one day cause shame to the old folks.

Employers, chief clerks, and heads of departments where others are at work, all have some degree of control, more or less dependent on the fear of losing the position, which fear, being constantly held over the employees, wins obedience, though not honest attention to duties. We have had in our employ a number of colored men, with white superintendents. We paid the colored men. The white overseers had very little control over the negroes, until we allowed them to make the payment of wages directly to the colored laborers. This move resulted in establishing a semi-official authority over the latter apparently in the hands of the white men, for the habit of paying wages seemed akin to the right to hire and discharge. But this is not magnetism.

It may sometimes happen that somebody who is in a position to do you a favor holds a certain degree of authority over you on that account. The law of compensation is a queer one. A pretty miss of sixteen who refused money from a rich man in exchange for sin, quickly yielded when he provided her with a dollar seat to a matinee to witness a play which she had read much about and was anxious to see. She went by herself and became a matinee girl for three years under this arrangement, although his name was never associated with hers in public, until the affair developed into the necessity of marriage. It is probable that she was virtuous with all other men, and that the peculiar power of the favor offered conquered her. But it was not magnetism.

Another girl who resisted both the offer of money and marriage, gave way when her favorite candies were offered; never stopping to think that the money would have supplied a greater quantity of these dainties. She exchanged her virtue for confectionery and afterwards became the wife of her seducer. It does not generally follow that marriage results from such relations.

We have cited the leading classes of control from causes not magnetic; and this has been done for the purpose of teaching you to stop to analyze the nature of the influence that is getting the better of you. One of the duties of every man or woman who makes pretensions to possessing this power, is to take the measure of those with whom they come in contact; and first ascertain if there exists any one of the classes of control that we have named. This will save you from many an embarrassment.

The most subtle and dangerous of all influences is that which is allied to the interchange of favors. It is the one method that dishonest people employ. It is the plan of the demagogue, the politician, the grafter, the wire-puller everywhere; the swapping of favors. Be on the lookout for it. Nine-tenths of all the wrongs in life are committed through this method of winning.

The magnetic person will ask mentally the question, What benefit will accrue to the other party in the proposed affair? If you do not make this inquiry to yourself, you will be swept into some scheme to your disadvantage long before you are aware of it, and it is generally too late to save yourself.

Persons not related to each other, or who do not have at stake some end that will win praise or commendation, are not likely to do any other human being a favor, unless there is a motive of gain behind it. Charity has for its motive the purchase of peace of conscience or of divine favor; it is never free from some spirit of gain. There are in this world today, millions of men and women who cast their bread upon the waters in the hope that it will return after many days; it is the chance for return or reward that inspires the doing of good. And there are other millions who are giving alms, and contributing to the support of eleemosynary and religious institutions under the promise that by doing so the givers will prosper all the more in this world's goods. You cannot name a transaction that confers a favor on another that is wholly disinterested, that is wholly unselfish. The old doctrine of endless punishment and torture after death brought billions into the church; the newer doctrine of eternal happiness is less successful, but nevertheless succeeds well; both are appeals to the desire to gain something, to lessen distress or add to bliss.

We are not making the claim that this motive of gain is a wrong one. Our only position is that it exists and is universal.

This fact being well known, it is necessary for the student of magnetism to be ready for it; to expect it, and to analyze at once the kind of gain that is sought. When you are able to do this, you take the measure of friend or foe. Having taken the measure you are in a position to meet motive with purpose.

Right here we see the principle on which ninety-nine per cent of all success or failure is met in life. Right here is the rock on which you have fallen whenever disaster or trouble has come your way. In this one phase of magnetism a whole book might be written of giant proportions. But other things still more important await us and we must leave the present theme.

Habits are magnetic.

Exercises have no value unless they invite habits.

No man or woman will take rank in the world of magnetism unless the mind and nervous system are trained to act spontaneously and with as little mechanical training as possible.

The habit of reading the purpose, the motive of another, is the most valuable of all acquisitions. But it is a habit. It is formed by separate stages, the first of which is the reduction of all kindnesses and all favors to the plane of a selfish intent. This looks like discrediting everybody that you know. Not at all. There are many kinds of selfishness that are creditable. The mother brings up the child in the most humane and careful manner in the hope that the child may be a noble citizen, and not bring disgrace upon the family. This is selfish, but it is most excellent. The sufferings of parents are often averted by the interest they take in their children; some hope for support in old age; some are affectionate and their love is pained by erring youth over whom they once had control and misused it.

All selfishness is not evil.

Public men, and almost all good people generally, are anxious to see crime reduced, poverty lessened, the poor employed, labor satisfied, health excellent, and the nation prosperous; but why? The opposite conditions breed unrest, danger and feelings of constant apprehension which the good people dislike. Hence many of the acts of charity, of philanthropy, of legislative policy, and of high class citizenship may be traced to the desire to avoid the consequences of adverse conditions.

The man or woman who comes to you and asks your influence or aid in any matter, knows full well that it is necessary to show you the good it will do. But the showing made to you will be such as the other party, if not honest, is able to picture in your mind; the chances are nineteen out of twenty that you will be made to see a larger gain than will really be had at the end. This is the lever on which most people are ruined by schemers.

Learn to hunt for the selfishness in every dealing others have with you. Do not be sentimental and make yourself believe that there is no such motive. The heiress who is ugly will have all the suitors she may desire, while the pretty and poor miss whose mother takes in washing, and whose father is a laborer on the railroad dirt beds, will be passed by as long as the rich girl asks company. And the mental accomplishments of the one will not hold up the balance with the wealth of the other.

See motive in everything.

This is the first step.

The second step is to classify motives, making two divisions; in one class put all those that may be regarded as honest, or emanating from honest hearts. In the other class put those that are not honest. In the latter you will find the inducements and allurements held out to you to be false in fact or in quality.

These two steps are not difficult. The first must be firmly established as a habit of thinking. But never allow any one to break down the habit, even once.

The second step is longer in being acquired, but is brought into a habit by making a record of every instance that arises in your daily life for a while, that is worth noting; predicting the purpose, and then recording the result as it is afterwards ascertained. You will very soon, and much sooner than you now think, be able to discern the character of the selfishness that prompts the acts of others. While changing your mental temperament, as these habits will do in a short time, you should take the stand that all motives are wrong until you have affirmative belief to the contrary. As far as personal dealings with yourself are concerned, this method will save you, will train you, and will show you life as it really is. The plea that you are to give everybody the benefit of the doubt, is a good one, when you yourself or those you love are not involved. The doubt belongs at home until it has shown its credentials and been given free wing.

This is a cold-blooded way of treating humanity. Yes, it is all that, and more. But this line of study is private, and you are schooling yourself to master those who come in contact with you. If the process is too harsh, go back to the old ways and be led by others who will not give you the benefit of anything. If you were to make known to the world the plan which you propose to adopt toward them for a while, it might place you in an unpleasant light. This is one of the reasons why this course should be kept private.

But the process is not as cold-blooded as it seems. Not long ago a business man who had lost more than half the fortune left him because he had given the benefit of the doubt to others, took our advice, and reversed his methods. He said that he trusted no one till he had affirmative proof that he ought to do so; to use his own words, "I assume that every man is dishonest until he proves his honesty." This plan did not hurt him; he is now a very successful merchant; and he has done no one a wrong. He had his choice between this method or poverty.

It is merely justice.

There is another reason why the process is not cold-blooded. It is only a step. The rule requires that you take the benefit of the doubt until you have formed the habit of reading motive and protecting yourself against the wiles of others.

In less time than you would think it possible, this habit opens up the intuitive mind; which is so much dealt with in its peculiar and wonderful operations in the greater course, Universal Magnetism, where it carries one, by other means of help, into the realm of inspiration.

In this present work, the process whereby intuition in one of its most common and most useful operations is developed, is within the reach of every person. Habits that lead to the analysis of human beings are always tending to intuition.

It is true that this form of intuition is not a part of that larger field of attainment which is the climax of Universal Magnetism, but it is practical in everyday things, which means much to the common plodder.

The following rules will assist in formulating the method so that it can be put into use from the very start:

Any analysis of a human being, no matter in what line it is applied, will in a short time result in the development of some degree of intuition.

This kind of intuition becomes more and more acute and accurate as the habits of analysis of human motives are successfully acquired.

The steps in such analysis are two: First, the refusal to credit any act as free from selfish motive, until the contrary is known to be true.

Second, the separation of honest selfishness from dishonest selfishness.

This power is not beyond any person of understanding years. It would be too much for a child or a youth; but not for a man or woman of twenty years or over. It affords a pleasing line of practice, and soon gives one a keen insight into the mind of another to read purpose and to take a decided stand of self-protection.

It is being practiced with remarkable results by the private pupils of the author, and reports are constantly coming in of the greater and still greater success in its use in every relation in life, from the doors of the home to the highest plane of activities.

CHAPTER FOUR

+++++++++++++++++++++++++++++

BELIEVE IN YOURSELF
AND
COMPEL OTHERS
TO BELIEVE IN YOU

+++

ATTRACTION OF CONFIDENCE

+++

T NO TIME in the career of a man is he able to control others if they lack confidence in him. In fact, the first step in the effort to secure mastery is the winning of confidence. There is no such thing as magnetic control without it. Brute force may be employed, or the authority that position and power give may be displayed, but the individual who yields to such influences is forced and not drawn into yielding.

As time advances, there is less and less use made of physical force. Even war depends on mental prowess and skill. The little man and the weak man may plan better and shoot with greater accuracy than the giant or athlete. The fear of authority is growing less every year. In this country one of the greatest problems of today is how to cope with the disposition of the public to disregard the law. Respect for those in authority was never so slight as at this time. This theme has been taken up by those who lead the public thought, by heads of churches, by the President of the United States, and others of prominence.

That which attracts and induces obedience without use of force or superior position, is magnetism. It may be called by any other name but it remains magnetism.

An unattractive thing cannot attract. Hypnotism may invite the sleep known as catalepsy, but it must first find a subject that is nervously diseased. Magnetism deals with normal people in good nervous health. The more it is used the more it awakens the subject and inspires him for life's great work. It is the angel that walks by the side of the ambitious man, while hypnotism seeks the weakling. All magnetic people attract each other. The higher the degree of magnetic power a man or woman may possess, the more easily that individual is drawn to another magnetic person.

This fact was once well illustrated in a gathering of the greatest actors of England and America. The one chief power above all others that is essential to success on the stage, is personal magnetism; let that be lacking, all the gifts and talents of earth piled mountain high could not bring success. Therefore when forty or fifty of the leading actors come together, there is of necessity a volume of power which expends itself in enthusiasm. In the gathering mentioned, the least display of this power was sufficient to set the whole body aflame; small trifles that before an ordinary audience would pass for nothings. And this fact has been many times exemplified in other assemblies of prominent men and women.

When a person who towers in intellect or experience above the people about, is able to sway them one way or another, the power employed may be a weak degree of magnetism.

But for master minds to sway master minds the degree of power must be relatively increased. The attraction must be genuine. It must be a tower of strength, and it must command the respect and inspire the confidence of others. This is a sound principle that you will do well to remember.

A few laws will enable us to understand this proposition in its true light:

Personal magnetism is either an instinctive growth, or is developed by practice and habits.

As an instinctive growth it is natural and powerful; as a developed power it is more accurate and more fruitful in valuable results.

When influences focus toward an individual, personal magnetism grows instinctively in that individual.

Static poise draws all influences toward a person.

That which is useful in the highest degree is practical in the same degree.

Here are five important laws. They should be studied, not only in their own statements, but in connection with the pages that follow.

The last of the five laws is intended to show to the student that we are not treading a land of film. Our work is to be of the everyday and commonplace kind. We shall give you theory but show how to make it bring realization.

The first book of personal magnetism deals with the development of this power as the result of habits and practice. The present work deals with the uses of that power, and to accomplish the end most readily we are seeking to build upon the first book a system of natural or instinctive growth, thus turning the developed form into the natural, without lessening the special advantages of the former.

Static poise is always present in a man or woman who is naturally magnetic. Of a thousand cases or more that were observed by the author and thoroughly analyzed since the first book was published, not one was an exception to this statement. That is, if you find a man or woman who is undoubtedly magnetic, and who attracts a following or becomes successful in life, you will be able to see the principle of static poise fully exemplified.

The third or central law holds the key to this part of our work. When influences focus toward an individual, personal magnetism grows instinctively in that individual. In order to bring about this focus of influences there must be a cause, and this is found in the condition known as static poise, which draws all influences towards a person.

These influences are of every kind. They spring from those about you; from people older than you are, from the people of your own age, from people younger than you are, from youth and children, from those in your employ, from those who employ you, from your rulers, even from your king if you dwell under a sovereign. It is not an uncommon experience for those high in authority to need the aid of those beneath them; in fact, a ruler is helpless except for his assistants. The most successful of monarchs, of generals, of rulers, of employers, are those who know how to choose their aids and helpers. On man can do nothing great alone. He must depend on others, but he is to be the chooser if he would be successful.

The first choice always goes to those who have static poise; and herein the latter succeed because of the mainspring of personal magnetism.

The mighty geniuses of the world have all been born poor, and have grown up amid circumstances of self-denial.

A genius cannot pass from a lowly state to the pinnacle of fame by one step. The first move on the chessboard of life is to attract the great, to be useful to those higher up in position or authority. This has always been the case, and always will be. If you are now an underling, you are in the current that may easily sweep you on to a higher plane, for you are in your natural element. If fate has in store for you a great destiny, your first natural rank is that of holding the confidence of a superior. No unemployed man or woman ever rose. This does not mean that you must work in a store or factory; but it means that you must be useful to others before you can be useful to yourself; and such a line of usefulness may take you in a store or factory or in a household or elsewhere, as accident may determine.

Out of a hundred or a thousand or any number of helpers, the man above you will first select that particular individual who shows the best static poise. He does not know it by that name, but it does not matter. Old things have rarely been truly named. Static is the condition of accumulating magnetism, growing naturally all the time, and yet held without loss. Poise is the mean between two extremes. Poise attracts magnetism. Poise draws all influences toward you.

This opens up the most useful, the most practical, and yet the most sublime phase of the study of personal magnetism.

If you are now an underling; that is, if you are now helping some one else in the world, as an aid or assistant or adviser or in employ; you will rise from that condition in point of speed and height in exact ratio to your rank in static poise. If you are the employer, the one in authority, you will succeed and better yourself in the same exact ratio and for the same reason.

These propositions seem important, but their real value cannot be understood until you begin to analyze the successful man or woman; not the one who has forced success by trickery or unfair means, but who has attracted it by a winning personality. There is no exception to the rules laid down. They bring their wealth of power as certainly as the sun rises in the eastern sky.

Poise, therefore, is an attractive force.

To understand it, imagine a fortress or tower, standing plumb against the view. The solidity of its position suggests strength. Near at hand is another fortress that leans to the right, and another that leans to the left, still another that leans forward or back; all these suggest weakness. You will not seek safety, shelter, or protection in one that is out of poise.

The leaning tower of Pisa may be strong, but it does not look so, and certainly is not as solid in its hold on earth as one that stands in perfect poise. Before it would be occupied by a stranger he would go cautiously about its walls and give them a full test. In the same way a person who is out of poise would excite suspicion on first approach. Greater familiarity might breed confidence, but something that repels *prima facie* is not capable of holding control in high degree over humanity.

There are three influences at work in every phase of poise in man or woman, and they are described as follows:

First Influence.—Poise induces antagonism.

Second Influence.—Poise inspires the highest degree of confidence.

Third Influence.—Poise creates self-containment which is the most potent of all agencies for the development of magnetism.

The antagonist is always on the lookout for an opening that shows the weakness of an enemy. Such an opening is impossible where there is static poise.

Other persons who seek contact or association or dealings with you will yield to you their full respect and confidence if they find you a person of poise in all things.

But this condition reacts upon the individual. It has a trinity of influences; one that repels, one that attracts, and one that works within the person. It disarms enemies; it increases friendships; and it makes the individual greater because of the feeling of being strong and right, of possessing power and having the knowledge of its use.

No other single trait of personality can equal this.

Having said so much on the subject of poise, let us take up its study in a systematic manner.

CHAPTER FIVE

+++++++++++++++++++++++++++

EXTREMES
ARE
NEVER ATTRACTIVE

+++
⚜ ⚜ *P H Y S I C A L   P O I S E* ⚜ ⚜
+++

 AMES AND TERMS are not always understood in their true meanings. The word poise is an example of this fact. It has, in the dictionary, half a dozen meanings, some of them opposed to others. Its real meaning is balance. It implies that both sides, and all sides, are equal in weight. From this comes the meaning of the well balanced mind and judgment. In this life the mental function of humanity is so easily thrown out of poise that when a man or woman appears who can show evidence of the better condition, respect and following are paid as the reward; and this is natural.

In this chapter we will deal with what is known as physical poise, or the balanced body and its faculties.

Poise under all circumstances has relation to three conditions:

First: Excess in the wrong direction.

Second: Excess in the right direction.

Third: The greatest possible distance from extremes.

A few examples will show what is meant. A lady enters the drawing room, and something in her bearing, known as good presence, attracts attention and claims admiration. A man or woman of easy carriage, or commanding presence, is always magnetic to some degree; and the strange fact is that such a presence is always found where there is magnetism, no matter

31

how great. This means to state that either magnetism is the cause of good presence, or else the latter is a necessary attendant of the former. In any event, it helps.

Another lady enters the same drawing room. She is awkward. She stumbles, shows embarrassment at every step, and finally drops like lead into the first chair that will contain her. She is not magnetic, and no lessons can make her so until she overcomes this fault. Analysis shows that she walks, stands and even sits out of physical poise. Embarrassment is a deadly foe to magnetism, and this fault is the first fruit of a lack of poise. But it can be overcome.

Physical poise shows itself in the carriage of the head, of the chest, of the body, of the arms, legs, hands, and all parts. It is not merely the correct balancing of one portion with another, but is the skillful use of the muscles. The dentist who allows the instrument to slip from the tooth and lacerate the flesh, is out of poise; he needs the practice of the dead still exercises in the first book, which is devoted to the cultivation of personal magnetism. In play, sports, work and all uses of the body, this law makes or breaks each individual who essays to accomplish much.

The dancer who carries his weight too far forward pitches and is clumsy, making his absence more attractive than his presence; but if he carries his weight too far back toward the heels, he is even more awkward. Still, perfection of motion, and ease of bearing are all dependent upon exact poise. This is the chief fascination in dancing, and friends are made by it, while the opposite methods invite harsh criticisms. If a party of would-be dancers were to ask for the first and best advice, they should be told to master poise to begin with, and to never lose it.

In walking, if the head is carried too far to the right, it is out of poise; if too far to the left, the same fault exists; if too far front, still the same fault is there; and if too far back, it is also wrong. No person looks so well in bearing as when the poise of the head is perfect. Some persons carry the chest forward, that is out of poise; it is a fault. The critic corrects it and the chest is then carried too far back. That is excess of the right thing.

The length of step is too long in most persons, especially if they are in a hurry. They stride along at an awkward gait, and the critic corrects them by shortening the length of each step.

But many take up this shorter step as a fad, and become

affected; it is an excess in the right direction. Mincing steps are affectation.

The speaker makes straight-arm gestures; they are very awkward and ludicrous, producing laughter and ridicule. The critic suggests the easy curves that nature throws into all motions; but the speaker, in his anxiety to get them right, indulges in over-curves, and the result is silly affectation. You can readily see that the habit that produces laughter and ridicule will defeat all magnetism, and the habit that displays affectation will invite contempt, which is the opposite effect desired. Therefore there is a direct relation between poise and magnetism, between the avoiding of extremes and the attainment of success, for the conditions that give rise to ridicule are barriers in the path of the offender.

A craned neck, or dropped chest, suggests weakness; to overcome it by assuming a bombastic carriage of the body, is even more injurious to the prestige of the person who thus keeps out of poise.

Some persons walk like a stick, no part of the body having muscular play; others swagger and sway; some walk with closed legs and knees almost touching; others waddle, especially if they are inclined to obesity; some throw the feet too far forward with each step; others throw the heels too far back; some turn out the toes too far; others turn them in too far; and there are a multitude of peculiarities, all of which can be accounted for under this law of physical poise. On the one hand, stiffness, awkwardness and clumsiness, interfere with the freedom and ease of the man or woman; and on the other hand, affectation, assumed positions and manners indicate the attempt to fight down the errors without knowing the real cause.

Let the law of physical poise be applied, and error can no more exist than can the ice of the North lie unchanged beneath a tropical sun.

The weaknesses of physical errors carry age into the young body; while the law of poise keeps the old looking young. Vitality is favored in such case.

Remember that weeds are everywhere. If you can find a place on earth where they will not grow, then nothing else will grow there. In every human being where there is opportunity for the development of power, weeds step first into place and seek to hold sway. To fight out these weeds we must study and understand the law of poise; or that middle balance between extremes; on the one hand, the extreme of error through drifting; on the other hand the extreme of correcting the error by excess in the opposite direction, as is seen in the manners of the dude or fop who apes the right without producing it.

Midway between extremes is natural perfection, and this is poise. While it is not easily attainable, it can be approached, and the benefits are at once striking and convincing.

CHAPTER SIX

+++++++++++++++++++++++++

NATURAL
MAGNETIC ATTRACTIONS
BEGIN AT HOME

DOMESTIC POISE

 ONTINUING the study of this great law of magnetism, we come to the conditions that confront members of the family in their own home. All things begin at home. What you are there you will be elsewhere, in spite of all efforts to the contrary. As confidence of others in yourself must precede your control of them, it is necessary that your personal attractiveness shall win them to you at the start. As soon as you repel, others may use you, but will not esteem you.

What you are therefore before the eyes of the public, you must first make yourself in your home. The braggart abroad may be the hen-peck at the fireside; and these are the two extremes beyond poise; they are easily interchangeable.

The qualities that gnaw at a person's power are first formed in the domestic circle. The clergyman who gradually lost his hold on his congregation and was compelled to move away, was found to have been indulging in petty tyranny at home, and this reflected itself in his character before the public. The men and women who are strong in the eyes of the world, are strong in the eyes of their families.

It is easy to get out of poise. There are many phases of this fault, and the most we can do is to touch upon some of them.

Cheapness of manner in the family is one of the most common of examples. Stiff formality is always out of poise; and no really great man or woman was ever guilty of it. Dignity that sits naturally on the individual attracts by reason of its simplicity and genuineness. The geniuses and leading characters that live or that have lived, fill history with examples of gentleness and plainness in their lives; lacking the boastfulness and pomposity that might seem to belong to them.

Thus these two qualities place the individual out of poise. To be cheap on the one hand, or to be pompous and brutal on the other hand, is to be out of poise. Or to be lacking in the good manners that rise from a soul rich in its qualities, is as much out of poise as to be formal, stiff, and austere.

Most men and women win their mates by the exhibition of good manners before marriage, and then let loose all their restraint on the theory that a man may be a boor before his wife, or a woman may be a common jade before her husband; the only time for courteous display being when some disinterested parties call to see them. On the same principle, the reservation of the best room in the house for outsiders often throws the family into uncomfortable and unhealthy apartments. What is good enough for the stranger is none too good for the family.

The member of the household who drops into a lack of good manners is sure to be out of poise in association with the outside world, and this cheapness will follow at every step. The more an effort is made to get in poise, the more lamentable will be the failure. The cure of this trouble is to develop a gentleness, sweetness and kindliness in the family circle, to be watchful of the needs of others, to be generous and helpful to all about you, and to put into practice the plain dictates of good manners before all from the lowest to the highest. This can be done without going to the other extreme, as did the wife who realized that her hard-working husband came home to a cheerless fireside, and she therefore resolved to meet him with a smile. In her excess she assumed what she could not naturally carry, and he was compelled to ask her why she grinned at him all the time. She went off her poise in the other direction.

The cheapness of home conduct saturates the whole being for contact with the outside world. Conversation, address, apparel, and subjects of interest are all lowered.

A wife likes attention. Neglect her and she will seek it elsewhere. But to turn over the new leaf with a bang and shower annoying address on her is to get out of poise on the other side. The man who is so habitually attentive to his wife that she knows it to be natural with him, is her master; she will obey him, and will cherish his leadership. The woman who studies her husband's needs at all times, and does not slop over in her display of affection, will keep him within doors while other spouses are cantering over town for amusement.

Children cannot be neglected ninety per cent of the time, and then caressed to extremes the other ten per cent; they know that the lavish show is an empty bauble. The child that is properly brought up, is given attention many times a day, and a genuine interest is taken in their ambitions, small as they may be. Neglect of any member of the family brings its penalties in the years that ring their mournful cadences over the memories of those that sleep under the sod.

A little girl was run down by an automobile and her leg was broken. She confided her heart to the doctor when she said: "I wish I was a cripple all the time, for then my papa would love me, and take me in his arms." He showed excess of affection when sorrow came. But that was not in poise. An evenness of conduct toward the little ones welds hearts to hearts, and makes the after years of development easier for the parents; for children recall with appreciation the steady interest that clothed their younger years with affection and kindness.

Magnetic control over children begins in poise at home; by which they are made to realize that parents hold them in the deepest concern all the time, and not merely when they are ill.

Excess of good nature when not deserved, should give way to firmness without unkindness; for lack of discipline brings rebellion in time. But ill nature, harsh words, severe temper, the blow that falls on slight provocation: all these are out of poise. The child knows it instinctively if not by process of reasoning. Some parents are soft and shallow in their methods, and then are cruel and hideous by way of making both sides balance; but these are out of poise. One leans to weakness, the other to brutality.

No parent who keeps in poise ever fails to bring up good children.

To be in one mood one day and in another the next day, is to be out of poise both days; for nature strikes her balance with unfailing certainty. How much grander it is to let your family know how to take you, what to expect, and the mood that you will be in for the next dozen or fifty years? This means that your hold on the affections and respect of your family will be made stronger as the time goes by and you will be obeyed because you are loved. The wives of great men watch them at all times to see that they keep as much in poise as possible; for woman's intuition knows the fault and the remedy when a loved one is in her care. God pity the man who is struggling for recognition before the world, who has no wife to inspire him, or whose helpmeet is not in sympathy with his life work!

In your joy and laughter do not run to the silly excesses; in your tears and sorrows do not plunge into meaningless gloom. If you are fond of humor and jokes, let them be within bounds, and hold yourself always in the most careful poise in this regard; for the father or mother who plays the monkey or the soubrette, loses the respect that children pay to those who are their natural protectors.

Do not run to slang, nor to cheap diction at home. Let your vocabulary be as choice as when you are in the presence of strangers. But do not assume a prudish stiffness and stilted selection of terms in either case. A large knowledge of words, and a correct use of them in all their finer shades of meaning will help you to express yourself in the most effective language. Were we to make a suggestion that will help you along faster in the good opinions of others, we would advise that you add one new word each day for ten years to your usable vocabulary; that you actually employ the word until its exact meaning is fully understood; and that you never let go of it. The rule is that the more words you can actually use with accuracy, the more control you will have over the thoughts and minds of others; for words carry the purpose that is in your own brain, and the lack of them makes the conveyance defective.

Some persons talk only in poetical terms and flowery style, even when dealing with kitchen subjects; this is ridiculous because it is out of poise; but the most frequent of faults is the use of cheap talk and slang expressions. They wipe out all good opinions that others might have of your qualities, and you fail in life, unless your mission is to do menial work or run in the stratum of the bar room or race course gamblers.

An interest in the welfare, progress, health, and doings of others of the family should be unselfish, and savor of self-denial. But to make it excessive or impertinent would turn it from its poise and reach the stage of meddling. On the other hand the lack of an unselfish interest would be deplorable, as the social character of the fireside life would at once fail. Thus to be in poise is to avoid the inclination away from the perfect medium. There is no poise that cannot lean either way; on the one side toward wrong, and on the other side toward an excess.

Play, merriment, holiday, vacation and the spirit of good time should be frequent in the domestic relationship to neglect which would mean a dry and unattractive life; but to make the lighter side extravagant or over-done would weaken the usefulness of these functions. Poise is the best power to hold the family together, and the family that is cemented by ties of blood and love is sure to hold a magnetic place in the world. It is wrong for parents to deny the holiday spirit to the family; and it is equally wrong for any one member to seek an excess of it. Thought and careful planning bring the most pleasing results.

Activities should be taught to all the members of the family, young and old; but drudgery and slave-toil are not necessary in this age of advanced living. Children should be taught that all honest labor, from the work of the household up to the highest duties are ennobling; and they should be given their share up to their limit of ability; no more. Poise is best for them, as for the older members.

Laziness is out of poise. Idleness is the workshop of his ill-fated majesty. Waste of time is robbery of life. Rest has its place, but too much is also out of poise. On the other hand an unreasonable amount of work, or too hard labor is likewise wrong. Haste not, rest not, is the philosopher's way of putting things in poise.

Giving way to the feelings, as of anger and irritability, is an error that weakens the influence and control of a member of the family. Some people are not able to hold themselves in check. They fly off their pedestals in a second, make a foolish display of irascibility, and are mentally sized up even by the children. Nothing needs a supreme mastery more than the temper. Yet not to feel, and not to have a sensitive spirit is nervous decadence. Poise is needed; neither extreme.

CHAPTER SEVEN

†††††††††††††††††††††††††††††

MEN TOGETHER
WOMEN TOGETHER
AND MEN AND WOMEN
MAKE UP THE WORLD

††
❧ ❧ *S O C I A L   P O I S E* ❧ ❧
††

VERY PERSON who is not a hermit, or whose mind is not diseased, seeks the companionship of friends, and the relationship of acquaintance. What is known as friendship among men is always on a par with the character of those who engage in it. Most men who meet each other and who wish to make the occasion pleasing, seek a saloon and call for beer or liquor, after which the cigar, and then the women are introduced. A good time, or the friendship of the common run of men, means drinking, smoking and prostitution.

A merchant may say to his clerk, "Show Mr. Smith a good time, he has come to buy a big bill of goods," and the clerk would, if he were up to date, produce liquor, the cigars and the women. Some business men do not have to buy trade by such favors; and others who would like to buy trade, are unwilling to soil their consciences to that extent. But the understood method is that which we have stated. This proposition was challenged by a reader of these advanced pages, and so we left the matter to the first merchant we met who was disposed to tell the truth. He was asked what would be his method of dealing with the purchasing agent of some concern to whom he would like to sell a large bill of goods, and he replied: "I would have my rep-

resentative entertain the buyer, and make him feel at home in
the city for a day or two.''—''But how would he do that?''—
''He would find out what kind of man he was dealing with. If
the usual sort of man, he would let him have what he wanted
to drink. The man would keep his head all right, for the sake
of his position. Then he would have his choice of cigars. Then
he could be shown the city at night. This means the high toned
houses.'' All this was rolled off with an air of usual business
methods. Another merchant was asked a similar series of questions, and replied: ''The greatest problem we have to deal
with when men from out the city come here, and we wish to give
them a welcome, is their persistent inquiry for houses where
women can be had.'' Soon our friend was convinced that most
men are bad.

Then the club man is invariably one who has the opportunity
of using his social connection for the purpose of prostitution.
Some years ago this statement was made and challenged. We
asked ten unbelievers in its accuracy, to become members of the
nicest and most esteemed of clubs in as many different cities.
They did this under pledge to tell the truth and the whole truth.
As a result, after three years of membership, they reported that
the man's club was merely a shelter for prostitution, while it had
ostensibly a dozen other functions, some of them strictly excellent.
One member, a business man of wealth and keen discernment,
says: ''I never believed that men's clubs were organized for bad
purposes, for they make such a showing of good intentions.
But I have satisfied myself that the same club can contain every
grade of man morally that is found in business. What surprises
me most is the good things they profess and actually do, while
harboring the very worst. I am sure that the husband who
wishes to be untrue to his wife and who seeks protection where
evidence is not obtainable, need only join a club and become a
clubman.''

Thus we see the tendency of social environments. They are
the choosing of the man or woman who is found in them.

Social life of today has four divisions. The first is that in
which men only are included. The second is that in which women
only are included. The third is that in which both sexes are
included. The fourth is that in which the means of entertainment are exceptional.

When men only constitute the membership or make-up of the party the means of entertainment are drink, cigars, women, cards, gambling, gossip and foul conversation; unless an exceptional character prevails in the personnel.

When women form the party, the means of entertainment are gossip, cards, drink, sometimes men, and occasionally foul conversation; unless the character of the party is exceptional.

When both men and women form the party, the means of entertainment are gluttony, drink, cheap talk, cigars for the men, cards, gambling perhaps, and a bore of a time until the moment for departure has arrived; unless there is an exceptional character involved in the function. The gluttony consists in the dinner, without which no human being in the social swim would think of trying to please other human beings; and the greater the number of the courses in this gluttony contest, the more éclat the affair will have.

If you can find any other quality prevailing or present in the social functions of this age, from the small fry of society up to the barons of America, we should be pleased to know what it is.

The exceptional means of entertainment are those that omit the cigar, the cards, the gluttony, the gambling, the prostitution, the gossip, the cheap talk, and the foul conversation; but what would be left? Deadness beyond comprehension would close in upon life in the great world of society.

The methods employed by men and women for entertaining their friends are the reflex of their own lives, thoughts and character. For instance, instead of the elaborate and useless banquet or formal dinner, no greater friendship could be shown than the setting of a simple three-course meal. A glass of absolutely pure water, invitingly cool, and a plate of bread with fruits and vegetables, followed by some dainty, would more than fill the needs of a guest, and would leave a healthful and wholesome feeling; but the host who would serve nature's best foods would be set down as a fool, so fixed is public opinion in the wrong direction.

As long as the mind of the public is out of poise, so long will the means of entertainment be out of poise. For these reasons it is necessary for the student of personal magnetism to become an exclusive individual. This you can do without separating yourself from your friends or the public. They are your people, but you must be their ruler. To do this you must rise in a magnetic sense above them, and not be one of them. They are out of poise. You cannot be a hermit ruler.

Association is necessary, but it must be the mingling of the sovereign with the people in the relationship of ruler and subject. Human society must always exist, and its interest in itself is necessary to the well being of the nation. In proportion as it approaches the condition of poise, in the same degree will it benefit the nation and each individual member. But today it is so far out of poise that it would be impossible to imagine a more deplorable state of affairs. All sincerity has gone out of it, and gross selfishness coupled with the love of display have taken its place.

While association and mingling are necessary, the idea of separation and exclusiveness must be kept constantly in mind. This idea is peculiar to itself. In order for you to be exclusive it is not necessary for you to manifest to others this self-containment. If it does become known, its purpose will be seen and the end you have in view will not be reached.

The great minds of the world have always had ways of concealing their methods of dealing with people. To publish the mode of proceeding is to place in the hands of your subjects the weapons of victory, and this is neither good sense nor good management.

As far as social relations are concerned, you should adopt the following plan of getting in poise, and not allowing others to sweep your feet from under you. If taste for the degrading pleasures, or inclination to please others, or a desire to get into the hearts of your closest friends, tempt you to get out of poise, it is necessary to suspend this study of magnetic control.

If, on the other hand, you are willing to place yourself apart from these false pleasures so that you can secure the poise required for mastery, the suggestions to be given here should be faithfully adopted.

First, all the false pleasures must be avoided; not by leaving the environments where they occur, but by not becoming a part of them.

Second, in separating yourself from them you are not to make this separation apparent to others. This requires the most consummate skill.

Third, in your exclusiveness you must appear to be fully in sympathy with the means of entertainment, for it is important that you do not attract attention by a display of exceptional goodness in this age of mockery.

Here is an example: A lawyer of good standing joined a club where over two hundred business men were constantly met. There were other lawyers in the same club. But this particular attorney made himself so pleasing in his manners to all that he became popular. In time he was invited to enter upon certain private escapades with women, but he did not decline; he merely had other engagements that made it impossible for him to do so. When it came to champagne, and other drinks, he did not refuse them, but was not then prepared to take them, as he had some friends whom he was to meet, or other engagements which made it advisable not to drink alcoholic beverages. So, in the weeks, months and years of his membership, he maintained that perfect poise in social relations that gave him standing. He soon found that all his friends respected him. A very wealthy and prominent business man selected him as his counsellor, in place of another lawyer who belonged to the same club, and gave his reasons as follows to his partner: "This man seems to carry himself just right at all times. His judgment seems excellent. He is conservative, careful, steady, of good sense in his personal conduct, inspires confidence, and draws others to him *like a magnet.* I cannot exactly explain it, but there is something in the man that makes me believe in him." What greater tribute to the power of advanced magnetism could be paid to any human being than this? And he was right. The former counsellor whom he gently laid aside, proved to be out of poise more and more as the years went by, and this lawyer who took his place came more and more into poise. He is now a member of the United States Senate. His career has been carefully followed by the author as he was once and for years a student of the works of magnetism, from the first to the greatest volumes.

If you attend a social gathering where gossip is on the tapis, you must not offend by refusing to mingle with the others, but you can talk on the same subject in a different strain, and gradually swing the theme to other matters. If you are invited to attend a smoker, you can have some other engagement; and a student of magnetism has an unending engagement. If you are with men after a dinner who are to smoke, you can remain with them and not smoke; as you can truthfully say that you think your health is better by not indulging too freely in the pleasure. This statement was made not long ago in a group of ten men, and seven of them never lighted their cigars. They happened to remember that their medical advisers had suggested the very same things. To change the temporary indulgence of seven men is not an empty victory. Thus it is possible to keep in poise, not offend, and do good.

To be exclusive as far as the means of entertainment are concerned is not very easy, yet the habit grows so gracefully and firmly that it remains when once established. We would advise you never to give a banquet or formal dinner; for this evil is the most appalling curse in modern life, and you should not be a party to it. Those who seem compelled through custom to give such dinners, hate the function and despise themselves for being slaves to it. We appreciate the wife of another United States Senator who, in the city of Washington, has given elaborate but sensible dinners in which the foods are cooked and served on hygienic principles. There are plenty of plain and wholesome foods to be had to fully supply the table without recourse to the barbarous and uncivilized dishes known as French cooking. It is not necessary for you to become a devotee of gluttony in order to have and to hold friendships in this world.

Poise is the greatest of all principles.

It is the basis of the art of sculpture and of painting. It is the basis of architecture. It is the basic law of every phase of science and physics, in the worlds of art and of mechanics. In the life of a human being, strength, success and triumph come in proportion as poise is sought and maintained.

Not only in social pleasures must you get in poise, but in all social communications. One prevailing idea of sociability is to talk. To not engage in conversation, or to be unduly silent or reticent, is to be out of poise; and, on the other hand, to be too talkative, is likewise to be out of poise. Both extremes must be avoided, and success in life means the escape from extremes. When you are as far away as possible from these conditions, you are in perfect poise.

Do not give advice too freely. And do not deny it when it may do good and will be accepted. The person who has a solution for everything and lets it fall from his lips on the least hint, holds the respect of no one. The same thing is true of those who condemn freely. If you approach a partisan, and most persons are such, all you have to do to start his mind a-whirl is to suggest that something is going wrong in the administration of public affairs; he is soon going, having himself wound up all the time, and never getting wholly unwound; he talks most vehemently, and generally incoherently, on each and every phase of the subject, and his work stands still while his soap-box eloquence steams forth. This is the common type of man found in localities where partisan politics prevail, and where men are not above their party.

This man is out of poise. If you wish the services of a lawyer, you will keep far away from the man who condemns freely, or who has an offhand view on any matter that may be mentioned, or who has decided opinions to hurl at you. If you wish the services of a physician, you will select the one who seems to you to be most in poise mentally and physically as well as socially. If any professional aid is required you will instinctly apply the same unwritten law, for it has come down to us from the remotest ages. The lack of poise repels.

Thus this one principle attracts, and that which attracts is always magnetic.

To have no opinion on any subject is to be out of poise; to have too many and too decided views is to be out of poise in the other direction. "Let discretion be your tutor," said Hamlet to the players, when he warned them not to overdo, and not to come tardily off; showing that the one idea of poise has been paramount in every great mind all through the history of humanity.

Harsh criticism is out of balance; and lack of criticism when good may be done is equally out of balance. The rule is this: if the criticism will help to hold some other person in better lines of action, and is given for no other purpose, it is due and necessary. As long as the world has faults, the people must be held up to standards of excellence in order to maintain warfare against imperfection. But criticism as usually given is wrong, for its purpose is to tear down without offering to re-build, to hurt rather than help.

Frivolity weakens the control which you may have over others in the social world. If you are silly, if you make puns without provocation, if you use funny language or speak in a funny way or cavort for the purpose of being amusing, or guy and kid others, or use sarcasm just because it will subject others to funny ridicule or do similar silly things, you are decidedly out of poise. On the other hand, if you have no sunshine in your nature, if you go about with a coffin-shaped face, saying and doing solemn things just because you live in the vale of tears and are a poor dying worm, you are a nuisance to the world and have no right to be at large.

Sources of amusement often put a person in or out of poise. Your position in this respect can be easily read by the things that please you. If you take your friends to comic opera, or to farce plays, or to senseless vaudeville as most of it is, you are out of poise; and your friends will not enjoy the occasion unless they too are out of poise.

There are wholesome forms of entertainment to be had in most cities; although they are growing less each year, owing to the fact that the general public is out of poise. Still the number of people who are in poise, or reasonably near that condition, is greater than one would think. The trouble is to find them and to get them together. Amusements that leave a bad odor in the memory or a bad taste in the sense of appreciation, are not wholesome. It is in the memory of a thing that the deepest pleasure is found; and there are people enough to appreciate this fact who could be brought together in some way. Magnetism is always a mutually attracting force, and could be employed to this end.

Too much frivolity and silly entertainment weaken the brain, and make it more and more difficult to appreciate the value of the substantial and satisfying forms of pleasure. All work, and all seriousness take the humanity out of a person. Poise is the avoidance of both extremes.

The kind of reading a person engages in indicates the true character of the individual. On a train recently a man who was making his way in the world, was seen to be reading a sensational evening paper. One seat in front of him another man was seen perusing Virgil. Here were what might seem like extremes, but they were not. One was feeding the surface of his brain; the other was feeding his deeper mind. The deeper the foundation rests in earth the stronger the tower stands in its perfect poise.

Shallow minds like shallow walls are unsafe, and never win the confidence of the public.

Religious association is prolific in the formation of character good or bad. The fact that a man goes to church does not establish his religious temperament. Display of religious feeling is a clear indication of lack of poise. Works alone count for value before the world. To give up the varieties of an all-round life for the seclusion of one kind of life is to get out of poise. The brain denotes the many-sided nature of a man or woman, and no one can safely shut up all the departments but one and remain well balanced. Nor will such a person find followers.

People make the mistake of believing that this world is nothing at all, and the next world is all in all. The fact is that each world has its time and place and demands a recognition of the necessity of living the very best in the ever-present NOW. The pilgrim here is making the temple in which he will dwell in the hereafter. To neglect today for tomorrow is to chase the end of a rainbow. There is no tomorrow, and today is eternal.

The individual who keeps in poise is not one-sided in religion or out of it. He has his moral and ethical side; and he has his practical side. He turns his religious creed into a living good for the benefit of all who may be reached by its influence; and he turns his practical life into moral channels because they alone are right. But he does not boast of these deeds, nor of his beliefs, nor of his works, nor of his intentions. People soon grow to have confidence in him, for they see a well-balanced man.

And confidence is the mainspring of magnetism.

Get apart from others while still mingling with them. Do not be one of them in fact while seeming to be in the thickest of society. Let no person suspect that you are trying to maintain a better standard than they, for the knowledge of this fact would place you in the light of one who was thankful that he was not like other men; yet be unlike them when they are below a fit standard of life. The offence is in the boast; and in the emptiness of the boast also.

It is of necessity true that, as long as the world in general is out of poise, the man or woman who would be in poise must be different from the others; yet must not parade the fact. If there were no masses there would be no ladder of success to climb. Take out of life all who live except those that are superior in talents and executive powers, and they would dwell like castles that lack their foundations. The masses are made to climb over. The millions of lives that fail are the stepping ground of the few that succeed. Failure has its causes, and they are as natural and logical as any that ever existed. Inactivity and lack of judgment will explain all the losses that have ever occurred or that ever will occur.

The inactive person is always out of poise. The other extreme is useless activity, and this is out of poise. The only kind that counts is the kind that is coupled with sense and has for its end some useful purpose. To this one quality harness the clear-cut judgment of a well poised mind, and failure is as impossible as that a man shall die before he had existence.

But the masses are led by their tastes, passions, likes and dislikes, and they inherit from the people of Sodom their inclination to ridicule the better phases of existence; and so God has made them masses in order that those who appreciate the talents that are inborn in every individual may have the opportunity of rising in the world.

For this reason you should become a ruler of those about you, and should exclude your methods from theirs in order that you may use them for proper success in the great battle of existence.

CHAPTER EIGHT

AGGRESSIVE CONTROL
AND
DEFENSIVE CONTROL
ARE AIDED BY MAGNETIC POISE

++
PERSONAL HABITS OF POISE
++

 ESPITE ALL EFFORTS to acquire personal power, if you are out of poise in your habits you will fail. In the preceding chapter we spoke of the relation of the individual to others. Now we will refer to the relation of self with self. In private life, as well as in your maintenance of careful conduct toward yourself when others are present, you should understand what is meant by poise, and how to apply it. As you see yourself, or should see yourself, others will see you. What you are with relation to yourself, you will be to others.

The moods and feelings that are transitory in the life of a human being, determine the degree of control that may be exercised over a person; but, inversely, also determine the power to employ that control. If you strike a man, as the saying is, when you find him in a generous mood, you will be able to sway him in the line of generosity much more readily than when he is in a selfish mood. A father who had longed and hoped for a boy, but whose family contained only girls, was the recipient of a telephone message to the effect that the desired boy had arrived, and somewhat unexpectedly. His stern and crabid manner toward his employees at once changed; he allowed leaves of absence, overlooked errors, ceased to scold, and otherwise gave tangible evidence of his pleasure. A lady, hearing of his temporary change of mood, called on him for a subscription for charity that had long been deferred, and was given double the amount she asked for.

This is a type of that fleeting condition of the heart that affects the mind, and through the mind reaches the practical side of life.

A man or woman who knows nothing of the power of moods and feelings over the will, can hardly hope to rule people. This branch of the study of personal magnetism will be fully considered in a later part of the present work. At this stage we will look at its reverse side.

In the meantime we will present several vital principles that govern the whole method:

1. A person out of poise may be more readily swayed than one who is in poise.

2. A person who is in absolute poise is not controlled by any power, human or otherwise, except by deliberate consent.

3. A person out of poise cannot control others.

4. A person who is in poise holds many reins of control.

The foregoing rules relate to poise.

There are others that bear upon the question of moods and feelings in their connection with the laws of personal poise.

5. A person who controls all moods and feelings is in personal poise.

6. A person who does not control all moods and feelings is not in personal poise.

There are still others that are helpful in the understanding of those that precede.

7. A person who does not control his moods and feelings soon becomes their slave, and they control him.

8. In proportion as a person controls his moods and feelings they become his slaves and he their master.

What the moods and feelings are, will be discussed later on in this book. At the present stage we have to do with the personal poise of the student, and refer only in a general way to the influences that throw one out of balance with himself.

It would be well to look ahead to the chapters that contain the system of transmigration, and there analyze the various moods and feelings, in connection with the present chapter. As soon as you have ascertained what they are as far as they have relation to magnetism, you should next learn how many of them are at times dominant in your character. Having done this, make up your mind that you will master them and not allow them to master you.

Take any one of them that you please. While studying it apart from actual experience, you will see only the philosophy of the matter. It is not real. The true benefit arises when you can come in contact with the experience that is involved in entering the mood or feeling. Look at the flippant mood; you know what that is; everybody does; it is the most common of all; but the man or woman who becomes its slave is not respected even by those who give way to it themselves.

It is the one mood that takes away the dignity of a person, that shows the lighter nature with its faults and often its absurdities, and exposes the subject to the full view of those who have hitherto looked up to them as examples of a higher standard. It begins at home, and is due to an unloosening of the restraints that are always a burden to a light mind. Confined to home life the flippant nature does no immediate harm except to cause a loss of that profound respect which the members of a family ought to entertain for each other. If a man is accomplishing anything great in the world, he will not be held in less esteem because he is given to silly exhibitions at home. If a woman has won her laurels in the splendid management of her household affairs, she need not fear loss of prestige because of certain frivolities that are escape valves of a pent up power. But the custom of men and women in the secret walks of life, as at home or with boon companions, of letting go their feelings, either of flippancy or any other mood, does not build character, and this is needed in all forms of control, whether of self or others.

Any mood may be mentioned and followed out in the same way. Hatred, revenge, dislike, dissatisfaction, and many kindred moods are all masters or slaves; they occupy no middle ground. Most of them run into excitement. Let a person give way to one of them, and influence at once is weakened, although the temporary rush of power may be increased.

An illustration of this effect may be seen almost any day. Here is a man who is speaking on a subject in conversation with a stranger; he impresses him for a while, but soon the stranger sees that the man is giving vent to some dislike of another, and the language, the diction, the ideas all swing a little out of poise; just enough to indicate that the talker is not a safe counsellor. Lawyers in addressing juries, sometimes go beyond the line of poise in the way they state their thoughts, and juries lose full confidence in them.

In business the same law holds good. The clerk tries to sell to advantage, and finds himself losing ground the more he talks; but it is not due to the amount of talk. The fault is in the way the ideas are expressed. A man may have goods that are so much needed that they will sell themselves, but this is not the usual case. Talking is advantageous if done in poise, and the more a man talks when there is need of it, the more ground he will gain with another if he remains in poise, not only of ideas, but also of manner of expressing himself. Herein the study of expression is immensely helpful to the man or woman who would be magnetic in conversation or address.

Last Sunday a clergyman became irritated, but only in slight degree, by the coughing in his church; and he asked that those who were coughing would try to avoid it. The same congregation never coughed when a certain magnetic pulpit orator addressed them, and the ability to check all interruptions is one of the tests of magnetism. This particular clergyman had a coughing congregation because he could not hold their absolute interest. His rebuke was evidence of a lack of poise, for it was out of place, ill-judged and ineffective.

Another preacher heard the cars go by at the distance of half a mile from the church. Its noise slightly disturbed him. He gave way to his feelings and uttered a severe rebuke for Sunday travel. This was out of poise in the manner in which it was uttered, the language was intemperate and the effect was the opposite of that which he intended. It led to his dismissal. Even though his opinions were correctly based, the immoderate manner of expressing them put him out of poise.

Still another preacher was interrupted by the violent cracking of peanut shells and the eating of their contents during a solemn evening service. His rebuke was intemperate. Being out of poise it re-acted on him, lead to the sobriquet of the "peanut preacher," and ended in his dismissal.

Immoderate praise or condemnation is out of poise. Lack of praise or condemnation is likewise out of poise. There is a middle ground that uplifts the power of the man or woman occupying it; and this law applies to all departments of life, in mere conversation as well as in the higher uses of speech.

The theatre is often the place where this power is seen. If an attendant is over-enthusiastic in applauding, you may know that there is a personal interest, or else a lack of poise. Perfect dullness is not good taste; for, if the play or the playing is pleasurable, there should be some evidence of approval. Excessive demonstration is never in good taste.

In a great political convention the leaders are passive, but the masses are wild and delirious. These two conditions show the real rank of both classes. The unmagnetic fly off their base on the least instigation; the magnetic hold their poise at all times when the power is present with them.

It is this lack of poise that makes the masses. Take it away and there would be no masses. It is seen in mob rule, when the least suggestion turns a vast assemblage out of mental balance for the time being. They are slaves to their feelings. They cannot be reasoned with. They have no faculties in use, except passion, and they allow it to rule them until they cool off, when the murder committed remains to haunt them during the after years, provided they possess the least spark of conscience. A man who allows himself to get out of poise is a menace to himself, to his friends and to the public. He is the one particular nuisance on the face of the globe, and his name is legion upon legion. He has no limit.

One day he lauds the hero to the skies; then a change comes over his moods, and this same hero is torn and tortured to gratify his whims. In the olden days, two or more thousand years back, the men who did the most for humanity, were those who, after being made idols of love and adoration, were put to death at the suggestion of other minds that put the public out of poise.

Gratitude is a weak quality in public and private life, because the minds of men and women fall from their poise so easily. Republics are ungrateful, and republics are masses. You may heap an enormous pile of favors upon a helpless man, and he will expect more; deny him and he will become your enemy; favor him often and deny him once, and he will do you injury. The debtor hates the creditor, although the creditor has done nothing but favor the debtor. "That man looks at me every time I meet him, as though he wanted me to pay him what I owe him," says the bitter fellow who has received the property of the friend and has not made restitution. The mere glance of the eye is enough to put the debtor out of poise; so easy it is to lose one's balance in feeling. The cause is never adequate.

There are three results from this lack of personal poise:

1. It leads to loss of immediate advantage.

2. It produces a feeling of distrust in the ability and sagacity of one who makes it public as a habit.

3. It destroys magnetic power that is present in the individual who is prey to it.

You would not employ a flippant doctor, lawyer, dentist, or other person on whose coolness of judgment you wished to depend. If you have under you in business or otherwise any person who is flippant, you will find that your affairs will suffer from the fault.

You would not wish to be guided by one who has extreme views of matters of any kind. Radical and conservative methods are not suited to a magnetic man or woman; between the two there must be sought the middle ground of careful but active policies on all questions that come within the range of the person's life work.

We know of several instances where immoderate language has led to the downfall of men both in business and in professional lines. Here are quotations from different cases: One man wrote, "I am acquainted with the party, and in my opinion he is a conceited and irrational fool." Another man wrote, "Yes, I know the man and have nothing good to say of him. I would sooner trust a dog." Another man wrote: "The physician is here and has the largest practice in the place; but it makes me sick to see the fools go to him as though he knew it all." Still another case, that of a woman who applied for a position, brought out a letter in which this confession occurred, "The reason why I wish employment is because I cannot live with my husband. He is a beast in every sense of the word, and I must seek my living in the association of decent people."

All these instances, and they are but few out of many, show the lack of poise in the writer. To disclose a scandal, or confess to private conditions that have no connection with the matter in hand, shows lack of poise; and to give vent to the ideas, if they were permitted, in immoderate language, is also lack of poise.

These are straws, and even weathervanes, that show the direction of the wind. Not long ago a case was brought to our attention for advice and contained the following facts: A woman of exceptional beauty, of rare gifts and accomplishments, applied to an institution for the position of teacher. In her letter she used this language: "I will say, in reply to your question, that I have some critics who do not like me personally but they are jealous. Not one of them is fit to enter the parlor of refined people." The woman was needed in the position, for her qualifications were just what would be most valuable. In the discussion as to the advisability of employing her, the sentence in the letter was referred to as an indication of her character and methods. It was predicted that she would show this lack of poise all through her work, but there were opinions that she was merely excited at the time of writing, and that this mood would not be shown to her classes. She was employed, and it was found that she made confidants of many of the pupils, telling them her most radical views of people she did not like. This fault led to her downfall, and she is still unable to rise from it. A word from a friend might be helpful, but she seems never to have had it as yet.

A young man of twenty-five not long ago was angered by the action of an acquaintance, and wrote him a letter in which he told him many things that were not complimentary. Before mailing it he showed the letter to a man of more experience. The latter said, "This letter may or may not arouse the party whom you attack; whether it does or not, it will not advance your position, and it will have a bad influence on you whenever you give it thought." But the young man thought it best to send it. Later on he was angered by some other acquaintance and indulged in a similar letter. At the end of a year he had written eighteen such missives. The result was the ruin of the young man. The accumulation of small influences will become a mountain.

In hot-headed parts of the country the whole public seems to be out of poise. The malady is an epidemic. It is a most disagreeable place to live for one who is not able to be in poise; but it helps the well-balanced man or woman to hold a certain position of power when ill fortune hounds the lower grades of humanity, as it is sure to do in time. The rule is this:

When a person rises above the masses by any other power than magnetism, each flaw in his conduct is the subject of open abuse and caustic criticism. But, when he rises by maintaining poise, he is not open to any criticism except from the lowest grades of mental or moral humanity, who are always throwing stones at trees that bear valuable fruit.

But this consideration might be made endless. The best plan for the student is to read the full account of moods and feelings in the later part of this book, and then make them ALL his slaves, and not allow himself to become the servant of one of them, at any time or under any circumstances.

History tells us of individuals who have achieved greatness by the power of personal magnetism, and notes the fact that they have been able to conceal all evidence of emotion or feeling, when they so desire. In the same strain Shakespeare makes his most famous character declare that he does not wear his heart upon his sleeve. Christ makes the same declaration in principle, but in different words. It is the noblest of all powers.

Practice does not accomplish the result. It comes from the determination to make all moods and feelings the subjects and not the rulers of the individual. It is more than will power. There must be magnetism to start with, and this first gift is found in the book that precedes this volume. Having that basis, the present course will quickly build the greater structure.

A capable man or woman will know the names of all the moods and feelings as stated in a later chapter of this work. It should be more than memory; an absorption of the many shades of mental and nervous conditions, until names are as well known as such words as week, day, month, hour and minute, all of which come to mind without effort. Having made this a fixed fact, then the approach of any mood or feeling should be recognized before it has made its presence a power, or before it has secured a firm hold like a wave that lifts a ship and tosses it into the vortex of a storm.

To know the moods and feelings by name, to know when they are coming to seize you, to feel their approach before they are within grappling distance, and to rise above them in the instant and command them to fall prostrate at your feet, helpless in their effort to do you or others injury—this is personal magnetism in its highest form.

CHAPTER NINE

++++++++++++++++++++++++++++++

THE
WONDERS OF SELF
ARE
MANY AND MANIFOLD

+++

TRANSMIGRATION OF SELF

+++

IGRATION and transmigration are closely allied in meaning, but neither word expresses exactly what is intended in the line of study that we are now approaching. Migration conveys the idea of moving from one place to another and transmigration refers in its common use to migration from one person to another. This necessarily involves the soul, spirit or essence of the individual. It also embodies the meaning of the passage of the soul after death from the body deceased to some other kind of life.

All these meanings have been dragged into it, and none is what we have in mind.

We take the word for what it conveys on its face; namely, the transmigration of self to another person's self. In place of the idea of soul, spirit or essence, we take the idea of self. Whatever the word self means, we mean. It is not the same as soul, and no attempt is here made to teach the doctrine of the ancients. What of the soul, and of the spirit and of the essential being of an individual may be the constituent parts of a living, thinking, acting self, we propose to include in the word; and it is the power to transmigrate, or pass the self from one person to another that is to be taught.

To pave the way for this method, and to make its usefulness

understood as a part of the system of personal magnetism used in extraordinary effects, we will lay down the following laws.

1. Self is the living, thinking, acting soul, spirit and essential being.

2. Self is not the permanent, abiding soul or spirit of life.

3. Self is the present thought and executive power of life.

4. Self is a transitory or fugitive purpose or personality.

5. Out of the mold of the ever-present activities and thoughts, the character of the soul, the spirit and the essence of life are created and made permanent. Thus minutes make eternity.

6. Self is the channel through which the river of life must pass and be given its character.

The fourth of these laws is the key to the present study. Self is a transitory or fugitive purpose or personality.

The word transitory means not permanent; it is fugitive; it comes and goes; it may abide for a while but not for a great length of time. One type of this meaning is seen in the moods and feelings; they come and go. Too much happiness is hurtful; it is necessarily followed by its opposite nature. No person remains angry all the time; passions die away. The only person who can never forgive or forget is the savage or the criminal. An honest man will find relief in forgiving and forgetting. Revenge is evidence of the barbarian or the criminal. When dislikes have had their time to spend their force, the inevitable re-action is always in the opposite direction, excepting in the case of born criminal or the inherited savage disposition. It is a dangerous condition when this re-action will not take place.

Nature has a purpose in making all the moods and feelings transitory. They weave, and inter-weave, and counter-weave, the strands of the mind and the soul. Habits run in narrow passes, and the soul and mind, as well as the living self are all narrow and limited, when they are the result of mere habits. The grape vine has its habits; the rose bush has its habits; the horse has its habits; but all these, and all else in the world, that humanity allows to run to methods of their own, become useless to themselves and to the world.

The purpose of the Creator is to place every impulse in the hands of humanity. By doing this, most of the habits of the best animals and the best products of earth have been changed so that they are now the slaves of man and not masters of the things themselves.

But man himself has not applied the same law to his own conduct. The horse, the dog, the cow, the valuable animal everywhere, must bend to the will of human control. The rose, the vine, the carnation, the fruit tree, and everything that has favor, is shaped by the direct purpose of man, and cannot run as it will. But man allows himself to remain the slave and willing tool of his own moods and feelings, and so he is lacking in the power and prestige which he compels the lower forms of life to yield to his command.

A few more laws will prove helpful at this stage of the study.

7. *Self expresses its nature only in moods and feelings.*

8. *Self is transitory because moods and feelings when normal are transitory.*

9. *When moods and feelings are not transitory, the mind or the spirit is abnormal and insane.*

10. *Moods and feelings running as habits are the masters of the individual.*

11. *Moods and feelings running as cultivated powers are slaves and willing servants of the individual.*

12. *The actor assumes a few moods and feelings; generally less than five per cent of the natural scope; and really lives in none of them.*

13. *The men and women of power who lead and sway others, are instinctive cultivators of moods and feelings.*

14. *Self is master and self is slave, according as the moods and feelings are cultivated powers or are habits.*

15. *The greater the number of moods and feelings that prevail as habits, the more human and the weaker the individual becomes.*

16. *The greater the number of cultivated moods and feelings an individual possesses, the more magnetic will be his nature.*

17. *Moods and feelings manifest themselves on waves of magnetism.*

18. *Intensity increases the power of magnetic waves.*

19. *Nervous and vocal undulations increase the power of intensity.*

20.   All undulations are developed by practice and become a cultivated power.

At the risk of making this study dangerously difficult, we have laid down a long series of laws which may be studied at a glance, but will not be readily understood.   The danger lies in the approach to a merely technical study.   Our purpose, therefore, is to unfold the explanations so gradually that these laws may be fully understood by the least intelligent as well as by the most studious of our readers.

In order to prepare the way for this solution we will first present the table of moods and feelings.   These are selected with reference to their relation to magnetism.   Some of them are found in the actor's art, but the greater number of them are avoided by actors as being too hard to interpret on the stage.

CHAPTER TEN

++++++++++++++++++++++++++

HEREDITY
ACQUISITION
AND
TEMPER

+++
TABLE OF MOODS AND FEELINGS
+++

 BRIEF REVIEW of the laws laid down in the preceding chapter will prove helpful in understanding the many facts to be presented in the pages now at hand. While those laws will not be fully absorbed in a single reading, they are vital to the subject and should not be passed over lightly. It is more than probable that many of our students will not grasp their meaning even after a number of reviews. It is our duty to make them perfectly clear as we advance.

A human being of normal condition in all respects is composed of a triple nature, and no part of this trinity can be omitted in considering the individual. This trinity is:

1. His fixed native character.
2. His acquired habitual character.
3. His temporary fugitive character.

The "fixed native" is what is born in him, and the rank and quality of his make-up. It is inherited.

The "acquired habitual" is what he has accumulated by his methods of thinking and living. It is added after his birth.

The "temporary fugitive" is the scope of his moods and feelings. It is the endowment of his real self.

A glance at these three parts of the nature of a human being will at once disclose the fact that the required habitual nature is the accumulation of the coming and going of the temporary fugitive nature; and the fixed native nature is the heritage passed down from ancestors who transmit the accumulations of their acquired habitual natures. It all resolves itself into the one primary fact that we are what our ancestors have been building and what we ourselves have been building; but the building process is always in the temporary fugitive nature.

These laws are living facts.

Moods and feelings, therefore, make us and they make the character of the offspring that we bring into the world. It is of the greatest importance that they should be mastered and not allowed to run wild. No study can compare in value with this one branch of magnetism.

We are made up of all the influences that have gone before. It is not at all an improbable fact that a pure and undefiled couple came on earth at the start of the white race. Whether this is true or not, does not matter. If it is true it will account for the present condition of humanity. In a preceding chapter it is stated that a person who is in absolute poise is not controlled by any power, human or otherwise, except by deliberate consent; and this law of magnetism agrees with the theory of the downfall of man. It shows him to be a free agent, able to decide for himself, and left to make that decision as he chooses. Being a free agent, he is the maker of the nature that he possesses and that he passes down to his posterity.

The sources from which he has chosen are many, and the first one will be entitled *heaven,* or the influence of the better powers that wait upon his volition.

There is no doubt that there is in every human being traces of heaven. No wretchedness is so base as to bar out this power in its entirety. It is something to boast of to be able to discover in a fellow being who seems an outcast, the dormant influences of a better nature, and to bring them into the light of culture and improvement. It is not putting it too strongly to say that every man and woman, no matter how degraded, has somewhere hidden away beneath the surface of crime and sin a spark that will burn into flame of brighter hope when once it comes out from under the wreck of its past mishaps.

But the general trend of human emotions is on a high plane of life and here we find the

HEAVEN-BORN MOODS AND FEELINGS.

They are given the following names as a matter of convenience:

1.	RESPECT.	14.	NOBLENESS.
2.	AFFECTION.	15.	PRIDE.
3.	LOVE.	16.	COURAGE.
4.	GENEROSITY.	17.	RESOLUTION.
5.	PLEASURE.	18.	TRIUMPH.
6.	JOY.	19.	PATRIOTISM.
7.	PEACE.	20.	GRANDEUR.
8.	MERCY.	21.	SUBLIMITY.
9.	SYMPATHY.	22.	SOLEMNITY.
10.	SACRIFICE.	23.	REVERENCE.
11.	TRUST.	24.	HUMILITY.
12.	HOPE.	25.	RESIGNATION.
13.	DIGNITY.	26.	REPENTANCE.

Because of the vicissitudes of life on earth there have come into the nature of humanity certain moods and feelings that are known as those of earthly origin. They began as masters of the individual and have held sway for thousands of years. Perhaps in such a realm as heaven, or on another planet where conditions are different, not one of these fugitive influences would be present.

EARTH-BORN MOODS AND FEELINGS.

27.	WORRY.	39.	TRANCE.
28.	VEXATION.	40.	RECKLESSNESS.
29.	PETULANCE.	41.	CHALLENGE.
30.	IRRITABILITY.	42.	DEFIANCE.
31.	INDIFFERENCE.	43.	SADNESS.
32.	FLIPPANCY.	44.	GRIEF.
33.	IMMODERATION.	45.	DISAPPOINTMENT.
34.	EXCITEMENT.	46.	REGRET.
35.	EMBARRASSMENT.	47.	MELANCHOLY.
36.	DOUBT.	48.	DISCONSOLATION.
37.	SURPRISE.	49.	DESPAIR.
38.	WONDER.	50.	INSANITY.

The final group of these influences is of an entirely different origin. Whatever name you may give to the source which we describe does not matter; it serves here as a matter of convenience. Hell itself is fully depicted in the greater work, Universal Magnetism, and its opposite realms are also fully accounted for in that course of study, as far as human knowledge can pierce the unknown with the entering wedge of universal laws.

HELL-BORN MOODS AND FEELINGS.

51.	FEAR.	64.	THREATENING.
52.	SHAME.	65.	MOCKERY.
53.	APPREHENSION.	66.	ENVY.
54.	ANGER.	67.	SUPERSTITION.
55.	HATRED.	68.	LAZINESS.
56.	CRUELTY.	69.	FLATTERY.
57.	REVENGE.	70.	DECEIT.
58.	SCORN.	71.	FALSEHOOD.
59.	ARROGANCE.	72.	SELFISHNESS.
60.	CONTEMPT.	73.	CRAFTINESS.
61.	JEALOUSY.	74.	TREACHERY.
62.	RESENTMENT.	75.	STEALTH.
63.	WARNING.	76.	GUILT.

The Heaven-Born moods begin in respect and end in repentance, after passing through the associations of the other influences.

The Earth-Born begin with worry and end with insanity.

The Hell-Born begin with fear and end in guilt.

No person is so constituted as to be able to abide in any one of these groups to the total exclusion of the others.

Owing to the method of mastering these moods and feelings so that they may be subjugated to the will and service of the individual who wishes to secure freedom from the most exacting of all slavery, it is necessary to compare the process herein presented with what is known as the actor's art. It has already been stated that the latter finds these influences too difficult to depict, and this is true to a large extent. The actor prefers such conditions as the following which we will briefly mention at this stage:

Mirth and laughter are a part of his work; but joy is almost never felt. He loves to enact a dozen or fifty different kinds of merriment, not one of which need contain the least semblance of joy.

The lighter mood of fantastic description, the leaping force of ecstacy, and the power of thrilling tones and manner are attractions to him. Rage, on the other hand, is liked by the heavy tragedian, yet it is no part of the magnetic mood. He loves eloquence, whether in love-making, in mimic battle, in description, in debate, or in the heroics that are suited to his profession. He imitates murder, agony, desperate plunges into fate, deeds of apparent daring, the show of alarm, of awe, horror and frantic frenzy. Youth is a separate realm in his roles, and so is age and decrepitude. He feigns sleep, or fainting, he is wounded, dying and even dead, as far as appearances are concerned.

All these have little or nothing to do with the study of magnetism and the man or woman who would adopt them in the presence of others would at once be set down as unbalanced in mind, unless the impersonating were done upon the stage.

In the lists of magnetic influences there are not many that are attractive to the actor no matter how great his genius or finished his work. He is at home in such moods as respect, sympathy, dignity, resolution, triumph, solemnity, petulance, surprise, sadness, grief, despair, fear, shame, anger, threatening, revenge, arrogance, flattery, craftiness, treachery, and stealth; as well as a few others; but these are less than one-third of the whole number of magnetic influences. Nor does he enter into the real feeling of those that he assumes.

The greatest actors have never been upon the stage, and they have in some instances never seen the stage or sat at a play. Nature has taught them the necessity of assuming the moods and feelings which we have described, not to show them to other people, but to make use of them for the purpose of seizing hold of the personality of others and appropriating it to themselves. This method of obtaining mastery over people in the desperate encounter of life against life, of magnetism against magnetism, is as old as the race. It is subtle, deep and far-reaching; it comes only after years of effort, and generally through natural habits.

But what nature has given to a man or woman through habits based upon culture, she stands ready to give to others by the reverse process of methodical practice.

CHAPTER ELEVEN

++++++++++++++++++ ++++++++++++++++

MAGNETIC UNDULATIONS
SWAY
ALL
HUMANITY AT WILL

+++
⚜ *PATHOS AND INTENSITY* ⚜
+++

IGANTIC STRIDES must now be made by the student who is ambitious. If the way seems obscure, do not get discouraged. It is better to grope in the dark than not to move at all. The work ahead is pleasing and will attract you if you once give it a start. Getting ready is the most difficult part. Do not think that we are seeking to teach you to recite, or to act, or to assume conditions that are not natural. The facts are quite to the contrary. There is not a step, nor a page in this study, that will not assist materially to unfold your powers, if you are willing to take it up with earnest ambition to succeed.

If it seems burdensome to you, or if the process is full of petty drudgery, remember that this is the very kind of work that is most necessary in the art of the actor; but he is compelled to plunge much more deeply into it. What you do he does, and he does a hundred times more. Nor is he acquiring the powers of feeling and of transferring such influences to others at will. His art never leads him in that direction.

As will be seen in later pages, it is necessary for you to be able to depict each and every one of the magnetic moods and feelings, if you desire to acquire the special powers that follow. Before you are able to give the representation of these conditions, you must open the way by adopting the last four laws of chapter nine. These we will repeat at this place, as they are of supreme importance.

17.   Moods and feelings manifest themselves in waves of magnetism.
18.   Intensity increases the power of magnetic waves.
19.   Nervous and vocal undulations increase the power of intensity.
20.   All undulations are created by practice and become a cultivated power.

The first intimation the author ever had of the value of what is here called undulations, was derived from the uniform habit of men and women who are accredited as being unusually magnetic. We had the pleasure of listening to the lectures of Henry W. Grady, the Southern orator, statesman, editor and writer. At first impressions he was in no way above the ordinary run of men of his professional standing. He was not a giant intellect, nor a man of commanding presence. In habits he was affable, gentle, easily approached and kindly. There was a directness and a simpleness in his methods that suggested a sweet and rather womanish gentleman; yet there was manliness in his work. He was virile, strong, persuasive, convincing. After hearing him once, there was a desire to see and listen again.

His critics have referred to him as a man naturally endowed with the highest degree of personal magnetism, which made him a greater man than his birth or other qualifications. In his brief life work he accomplished what few have been privileged to achieve; he taught both North and South the spirit of true statesmanship.

After many conversations with him, the conclusion was reached that he was endowed with the technique of personal magnetism. This included, as its first step, the adoption of nervous and vocal undulations in all his methods, whether of speech or action. Reference was made to this fact in the presence of others who were interested in the discovery of the processes by which power is attained; and a watch was made of the man on all occasions. Comparing these methods with those of men who were known to be un-magnetic, it was found that they were wholly lacking in this one respect.

Years before, such men as Conkling, Beecher, Booth, Spurgeon, Moody, and hundreds of others who were all known to be highly magnetic, were watched as best they could be, and the same quality was noted. In the case of Mr. Moody, it once occurred that he was not in good health, and this quality of undulations was wholly absent, the result being that his address fell flat and he realized the temporary failure. Once or twice Gough experienced the loss of undulations, and had the same disaster. The actor, Lawrence Barrett, made use of the art of undulations to supply a rapidly waning power, and kept before the public for years after his usefulness had gone.

Such an uncertain force as the power of Talmage was wholly dependent on the use of undulations. He could not interest an audience until he swung into this method.

In a list of hundreds of instances, enlarging almost into the lives of the greatest men of the past thirty years or more, there has never been a case of magnetism where undulations were not present and this is true both of public and private life. It is as true of one sex as of another. Being an established fact, the next step is to apply it. The most effective plan is that embraced in the actor's art; mechanical beginnings developed into genuine feelings as far as the twin forces of pathos and intensity are concerned.

In the hands of unskilled novices, these are dangerous forces; but we feel sure of being able to make you an adept in their use if you are both patient and ambitious.

PATHOS AND INTENSITY.

Pathos is neither weeping, crying, snuffling, nor the display of weakness of feeling. These interpretations are too frequently given it by actors. In the subdued sense, it is a wholly concealed method of accord with the feelings of another person. Strictly speaking it is suffering, but this meaning has long since passed out of the world.

Its usefulness is as a stepping stone only in the study of magnetism, for it leads the way to the development of undulations, and any aid to this result is of value. But like all stepping stones it is not to be carried along after the journey is complete.

Intensity is the nervous power of pathos, and this is also one of the most effective of all means of developing undulations along magnetic lines. When these are established, the next step is to connect them with magnetic waves for the purpose of conveying to others the wishes and commands of the mind and heart.

SPECIAL EXERCISE.

Take a standing position. Expand the chest as much as you can without raising it. Keep the shoulders from rising. Hold them firmly down while inhaling.

Put the lips in the shape of a round aperture. Say, oh, or the sound of long O, and make the tone even and perfect for not less than five seconds.

Place the hand on the lower part of the chest just above the stomach, at what is called in anatomy the sternum bone, and press this bone in when you exhale. Allow it to come forward with each inhalation. Learn to locate this bone at once, and to note its movements.

Over this bone place the palm of the left hand. Take the fist of the right hand, and gently strike a succession of quick blows as fast as you can make them, on the back of the hand that is placed over the bone. The blows must be gentle and rapid.

Maintain this succession of blows while the lungs are full of air, gradually expanding the lower portion of the chest. Repeat this for several days until you recognize an increase of lung power at this part. There will be a steady growth of chest-girth there, and it is in this region that the vitality of the body is most rapidly built up, for it contains the lungs, the heart, the stomach and the liver; the four most important of the vital organs.

The larger the girth of the lower chest, the greater will become your power of developing magnetic vitality.

EMOTIONAL PATHOS.

Having spent some weeks in making the lower chest a region of great magnetic development, the next step is to apply the details of the foregoing exercise in the development of what is known as broad pathos or its emotional variety.

This is accomplished by holding the palm of the left hand over the bone at the lower part of the lungs just above the center of the stomach, then rapidly pounding the same for not less than five seconds while a steady tone is coming from the mouth, producing the sound of the vowel O. The fist of the right hand, or the firmly held palm of that hand should be used in making the succession of blows.

The purpose is to make the waves of the voice produce a trembling sound of the vowel O. It will in time come out in perfect undulations, although coarse and crude at first.

The next step may be taken after a week of persistent practice in these crude waves; and this requires you to produce perfect waves of sound without the aid of the hands. They correspond somewhat to the tremolo of the singing voice, except that the latter are executed in the wave-action of the walls of the lower throat, if done properly, while the undulations are made by the rising and falling diaphragm, which is known as the floor of the lungs or the roof of the stomach. The blow of the hand starts the diaphragm vibrating and connects it with the voice. But nature has done this for many thousands of years, and she will take up the action in a very short time, after which it is the easiest of all things for the student to practice it without the aid of the hands.

Having mastered the undulations of the vowel O free of the hands, the next step is to turn the vibrations into a sentence. The common quotation of the actor in the first stage of this work is the following:

"Pity the sorrows of a poor old man. Oh, give relief and heaven will bless your store."

This means that, if you take pity on helpless age, your earthly possessions will be increased. Let the thought as stated enter into the utterance of the quotation, and the undulations will come more quickly into the voice. Actors practice many hours on one sentence in order to produce just the effect that is wanted, and this lessens the future need of practice along the same line; for, when once the power has been acquired, it abides for almost a lifetime.

We therefore recommend that you spend many hours a day on this one sentence, in order that you may establish the undulations beyond all doubt, and your further progress will be so rapid that you will be glad that you adopted the advice. If you curtail the work at the first stages, you will never have fair sailing; there will

be a hitch at every step of the way, and you will be constantly discouraged, finding fault with the method and with yourself. We
have seen examples of both kinds of students. They give a sort
of fling at the practice, then pass on, believing they will come back
to this stage again, and they give another fling at the practice of
later steps; they find nothing going right, and they say there is
nothing in it. You may have one satisfaction in spending time
in this kind of practice; and it is many-fold.

In the first place, while you will never become an actor, perhaps, the work you are doing in this chapter will quickly develop
the powers of acting, and such an education is most useful to all
classes of people. You will be in the companionship of thousands
of students of the actor's art, and it is impossible to waste time in
that line of study.

In the second place you will be developing faculties for feeling
and for expressing your feelings in the most effective manner;
for, while this step is a crude and enlarged one, it is quickly
reducible to the finest uses of the voice and nervous sensibilities
in every contact with humanity in this world. Undulations may
be turned into hundreds of different channels, even though they
seem to be all one thing at the start.

In the third place, whenever there comes to you a natural
tendency to exercise magnetic control over others, the undulations
which are developed in this chapter, will quickly turn into power
without your consciousness of the fact. We learned more than
thirty years ago to believe that the two great essentials of natural
personal magnetism were undulations and purpose; the former
opening the magnetic waves for the latter. Therefore we can
say that, if you do not go another step further than this chapter
in Advanced Magnetism, you will soon find yourself a thousand
times repaid for faithful work at this point.

The inartistic actor, like the clumsy person everywhere, wants
to get results from one effort; he wants to build a house with one
nail. To such a person the whole future means failure, and it is
written in the sky of his fate.

On the other hand, the patient, persistent practiser of these
simple details, as set forth thus far in the present chapter, will
reap a rich and ever growing reward, not only in the study of
magnetism, but in life itself.

We will assume that you have spent about three weeks in

enlarging the vital zone at the base of the chest by the practice first outlined; that you have been able to make the perfect undulations in the vowel O; and that you are then capable of producing perfect undulations without the aid of the hands in striking the blows on the lower chest; and, finally, that you can carry this perfection of vibration into the sentence which we have named.

If at any time you find that the voice will not execute the perfect undulations, you should go back and cling to the early practice until it will do so. Then you will be ready for the

TABLE OF UNDULATIONS.

10.	Intense passion.	Very wide waves of sound.
9.	Passion.	Wide waves of sound.
8.	Suffering.	Magnetic waves mingled with sound waves.
7.	Emotional pathos.	Enlarged noticeable waves.
6.	Common pathos.	First noticeable undulations.
5.	Subdued pathos.	Unnoticeable undulations.
4.	The intense voice.	Intense energy of magnetic waves.
3.	The magnetic voice.	Magnetic waves.
2.	The live voice.	First departure from the dead voice.
1.	The dead voice.	Absence of all waves and undulations.

So important and valuable is the foregoing Table of Undulations that thousands of uses can be made of it in practical life. In the first place it gives us a key to some phases of human character as expressed in the fugitive moods. This will be our first consideration at this time.

We have taught this system in personal instruction for over thirty years, and have had the opportunity of noting the success which can be attained where the pupil is patient and persistent in practice. We have found that, in the beginning of each course of lessons, no student is able to catch the distinction between the different degrees of the Table. But few fail, and none need do so.

In a class of forty-five ladies and gentlemen, thirty-eight were able after three weeks of practice to catch each degree of the Table, no matter whether the tones were made as practice, or were found in the life about them. In another class of sixty-one pupils, fifty-eight were able to do as much, and they reported that they could quickly catch the magnetic undulations of any voice in real life; that is the life that teems about them. They could take the measure of the magnetism of any man or woman. This actor they found to be most magnetic, that speaker they learned was of low magnetic degree, this lady was very magnetic, that one was most affected, and so on; they had records of their observations covering six months of advanced study in magnetism.

You can readily acquire the same power of reading people.

The most important thing to do is to train the ear to catch the different degrees of undulations; to know what voices lack them, and are consequently dead; and to know when they are artificial, genuine, empty and full.

In order to secure this knowledge, you should be familiar with the tones of your own voice, and should develop all ten of the degrees of undulations. We will show you how this is to be done.

Look at the human nature in the voice.

The lowest degree is the total lack of all undulations. It is the common voice about you. If you meet men and women with such voices, it is important to know the fact, for then there is no magnetism in the brain, nerves, or heart, and your control will be secured without any other effort than the use of plain, convincing appeals to the earthly born moods and feelings of such people.

Out of a thousand persons whom you meet not more than fifteen will be free from the dead voice. You will then see what is meant by the masses; the crowds of drifting, almost aimless humanity that pave the way of progress for active, earnest people by allowing themselves to be walked over in the march of success.

A dead voice lacks undulations, yet it can assume the tremolo in singing, though without any real feeling. Nothing so jars on the sensitive and sensible ear as such a mechanical vibration, coming out of the throat and not from the seat of vitality, the lower chest.

A dead voice lacks undulations, yet can assume any of the upper five degrees in the Table of Undulations. It is an old saying that still waters run deep. It is a well known fact that the person who feels most deeply gives the least outward evidence of it. A hen when *hors de combat* can emit more noise in proportion to her size than any other kind of life; yet she does not exhibit depth. A coward will yell the loudest when in danger. The shallow minds make the greatest disturbance in the world. Bravery, depth, fullness of feeling tend all toward stillness or the least outward exhibition of feeling.

It is for this reason that there is a leap from the first degree in the Table of Undulations to the upper five degrees; jumping over the four intervening degrees that mark the voice of power. The reason is this: The dead voice is the common, lifeless, indifferent voice of humanity; it has no connection with mechanical or magnetic waves. It is like the tones of the crude singer that either are lifeless or else yell in their vociferation; there is the leap from nothing to the over-doing. Poise is not always the exact midway between the extremes of a table, but the adjustment of the individual to the middle ground between the extremes. It is not measurable in inches or numerical order.

The auctioneer possesses the first degree, or dead voice, no matter how much noise he makes with it; and the same is true of the street vendor. Yet the newsboy who wants your sympathy has in some way taught himself to use the undulations, and he passes from the dead voice to that of the seventh degree. Noting his vibrant tones, which suggest some kind of distress, you buy his stock, and he goes off to get another supply for the next party who looks as if he could be misled.

The pleading wife moves the stingy husband by the same ruse. Vibrations are less than weeping, and tears hold a tyranny over the husband. When the pleading tones will not suffice, the wife passes into the ninth degree, which is weeping, or the mechanical passion of the diaphragm. She has been her own teacher, and what wife is not able to weep at will? The bonnet or hat is the stake, and she wins in any event.

The eighth degree is genuine suffering, for there is some true feeling in weeping or pathos or emotional display, even though the rule runs that still waters run deep. The child always weeps or cries in the eighth degree if it is really suffering. So clearly marked is this degree from the sixth, seventh, ninth and tenth, that the ear will very soon learn to catch it. The eighth is genuine. The child may have colic; and it will use the eighth degree. The hand may pain, the heart may be torn in its sorrow, and the eighth degree will be used. Its waves are remarkably distinct from all others, and note the mingling of genuine feeling with the shallowness of mechanical emotion.

But when the child is angry, it will use the ninth or tenth degree, and the mother's ear has been trained by nature so that she knows at once if the passion is in a case of wilful resentment in the child, or real suffering. Nurses lack this facility for distinguishing between the ill-natured baby that yells, and one that is truly suffering. It is the chord of instinct between the mother and the child, but this has never brought the nurse and its charge together, except in rare instances.

If we were again on the threshold of this study and had the knowledge of human nature that comes through making a specialty of this line of investigation, we would be most thankful to any person who would compel us to stay right at this stage until practice, observation and analysis had made us perfectly at home with every degree of the Table of Undulations. So the student ought to be willing to be guided by the suggestion that this is as important as any study that can benefit a man or woman. To under-estimate its importance is to lose the greatest of all opportunities for winning success later on.

The peculiar movements of the voice from the sixth to the tenth degree should be noted. The sixth is that of common pathos. The ear is able to catch the undulations as waves, for they are noticeable. But the seventh degree introduces emotion, and this is the common work of the kind of actress that was seen in such plays as East Lynn, Camille, and others of that stripe. The sixth degree is used much by the preacher, who wishes to impress unduly, by the woman who has sympathy for animals, by the pretender, and by those who seek to condole when they have no real feeling or care in the woes of others. The world is full of them, and they use the first degree at all other times.

The dead voice may belong to a shrewd, sharp, designing man or woman, who knows how to leap to the sixth degree in order to produce effects that are not legitimate; and you, as a student of magnetism, should know how to pick them out and to master them at will.

In the ninth and tenth degrees, passion is present; but passion is always a flying away of the nature even if it is genuine. The anger and ill-conduct of the child, or the excess of display of feeling by the widow at the funeral of her husband, when she has a successor already waiting the lapse of time, will appear in the ninth degree, and turbulent anger or violent exhibitions of suffering will appear in the tenth. These are as often genuine as they are assumed but they are nevertheless the wild display of a shallow feeling.

Passing the house where an Irish woman was making her cries heard far and wide, and asking a friend what he thought of the case, we were told promptly that her suffering was transitory and would soon pass away; and this proved true. Passing another house where a child was crying in violent tones, we asked the same question, and the answer was that the mother had neglected the child and had allowed it to develop the habit of yelling for no cause whatever. This proved true. The friend did not know how to analyze the voice, but his ear knew enough of genuine suffering to be able to distinguish between the shallow feelings and the real anguish. In the cases named both voices were in the tenth degree.

Passing another house where a child was crying in the eighth degree of undulations, we asked the same question, and the answer came that the child was sick. A few days later we passed the same house and the voice was in the fifth degree. Next day there was crepe upon the door.

These experiences are common the world over. The sympathetic doctor has great advantage over other physicians if he will train his ear to recognize the difference between the degrees, for then he will be able to add greater intelligence to his work for saving life and relieving suffering.

There must be learned at the same time the difference between the outward sound of an undulated voice and the effect produced. Thus the first degree, or dead voice, is soon recognized; but the second, third, fourth and fifth degrees are only caught in their effects. We have seen teachers giving examples with their own voices of the ten degrees, and pupils are quickly taught to catch the effects between the second, third, fourth and fifth degrees, although there are no undulations that the ear can detect.

An example of the dead voice is merely a reproduction of some person who is trying to recite or act, who lacks life in the tones; and it therefore appeals to the sense of the ridiculous. In immediate contrast with such tones the second degree would attract attention; but when given by itself, it would be hard to analyze until the ear and nervous system has mastered the various changes in the voice. Once recognized it will always be familiar.

The third degree is magnetic, and the fourth is intensity, while the fifth is subdued pathos. All four, from the second to the fifth, inclusive, are within the scope of magnetism; but the eighth is too natural and too shallow to be useful to the student of this science; for, although it contains genuine tones, they are made so by the realism of suffering which demands other attention than that of seeking control over one who is so unfortunate.

The pathos of the sixth degree is assumed; that of the fifth degree is genuine. If you hear the sixth degree, look out; some one is trying to work unduly upon your feelings who will have no use for you after the point is gained.

The sixth degree undulations are an open book; no one need be misled by them; they are distinct enough to be caught by any ear. The undulations of the fifth degree are too fine, or too close together as waves of sound, to be caught by the ear. They will never be used by a person who is not magnetic. Therefore you should be able to recognize them, not by their sound effects, but by their magnetic effects, in order that you may know the nature of the influence against which you must contend. Likewise you can use them with safety, for no human being who is not an adept in magnetic study is able to analyze them. They wield a powerful influence that cannot be securely withstood unless you know what they are and how to meet them.

The undulations of the fourth degree are the sweeping, commanding forces that carry all things before them. In the life of Andrew Jackson, of Bonaparte, of Clay, of Calhoun, of the elder Booth, of Salvini, of Forrest, and of thousands of impetuous men and women, they have been towers of gigantic strength that seemed impregnable. The best type of this degree was that of Bernhardt, the French actress. Let one such actor or actress appear on the stage in this era, speaking English to English speaking people, and the success of Garrick, of Siddons and of the first Booth would be immediately attained.

The undulations of the third degree are found in the women who rule their homes, their friends and all who come in contact with the sweet influence they give forth; and in the men who, like Grant, say and do things that count the highest value. This degree is prevalent among the merchants, the bankers, the financiers, the professional men who win at every turn, and in the quieter victories of humanity.

The undulations of the second degree are merely the difference between the dead voice and one that has some life in it, but not enough to accomplish much in any direction.

Strange to say, the dead voice does the most talking in the world, and the live voices in the second, third, fourth and fifth degree do less talking in proportion as they rise from the second to the fifth rank. The voice of the second degree talks more than any of the others except that of the first degree.

The first five degrees are known as those that present no undulations that the ear can catch. The last five contain undulations that are easily recognized.

This distinction must be borne in mind at all times in your effort to analyze the tones that you hear about you every day.

We are now ready to extend practice into the adoption of all these degrees, and then apply it to the analysis of all voices for the purpose of measuring the control that may be exerted on either side. A few laws will prove helpful.

1. A dead voice indicates a nature that cannot control others, but that may be easily controlled.

2. When undulations are noticeable to the ear, they belong to a person who can control those who are un-magnetic, but who cannot control those who are magnetic. This distinction always proves true, and should be at all times fully understood.

3. In the practice of developing the magnetic undulations, progress can be made rapidly by mastering the highest degree and reducing them to the lower ones.

4. It has never been possible to increase the undulations from the first degree to those above, as the voice invariably jumps from the dead voice to the sixth degree.

This last law is somewhat of a surprise, and can be accounted for by the fact that the pupil is being guided solely by the ear, and the first step from the dead voice that the ear can recognize is that of the sixth degree. These are not arranged in the order suited to the actor, because the latter aims at artificial effect from necessity, although he is supposed to seek the natural. He cannot produce natural death on the stage, nor natural sleep,

nor any of the natural conditions, unless nature is wholly substituted for his art. His thrust to kill does not kill. His
laughter lacks joy; and it would be a waste of this heaven-born
gift to spill it upon the un-swept stage.

You are now to acquire the ten degrees of the Table of Undulations, and you will be pleased with the rapidity with which you
do this, provided you have been faithful in the early exercises
of this chapter.

By this time you are able to speak the quoted sentence in an
undulated voice. As we wish you to acquire the flexibility which
the top degrees will afford, we now substitute another quotation
with which to do this.

"Reputation, reputation, reputation! I have lost my reputation!"

In order to bring this into the tenth undulation, it must not
be attempted until the former quotation is fully mastered, and
can be rendered off-hand with a fullness of vibration. Then
pass into the present quotation, while making a marked increase
in the undulations. To do this with success, it is necessary to
unloose all restraint and plunge into the work with a determination to bring the result.

This will give you flexibility. While the tenth degree is not
an everyday affair, it is common enough in life. Having made
sure of reaching the tenth degree, try the same quotation in the
ninth degree, and compare the two by many days of review
until you are sure that you can distinguish between them whether
in your own case or in the experiences about you.

The eighth degree must then be sought by a light reduction
of the force or size of the waves, and here a new feeling is
attained. The loss of the violent waves is such a relief that the
voice seems to come into a naturally easy rendition, provided
the two top degrees have been mastered.

The seventh degree is that of emotional pathos, and we suggest
the two following quotations as the best to aid you in the development of that step.

"She loved me for the dangers I had passed, and I loved her
that she did pity them."

"He cast me forth into the night; and yet, my heart, you
throb still."

One of these will suit the man, and the other the woman;

although it is well to be able to render any emotional sentence in perfect harmony with the rules of acting. Both these sentences require the seventh degree when acted before audiences; and any other interpretation would make them fall flat.

The sixth degree is the common pathos of everyday life, and is met with at every hand where people wish to secure sympathy or impress others with their misfortunes. Yet it has phases of genuineness as may be seen in the following quotations:

"Claude, they are coming. Have you no word to say to me ere it is too late? Quick, speak."

"And yet within a month,—let me not think on't. Frailty, thy name is woman."

Carry any of the foregoing quotations into the lesser degrees and the result will be the development of magnetism, except that the fourth or powerful degree is not so attained until another line of practice is introduced. That will be the scope of the next chapter.

Thus we pass from the work of developing the moods and feelings in order to secure the means of so developing them; and now we pass from the full work of this chapter in order to step aside to secure the means of developing the fourth degree. There is no other way.

The third degree and the fifth should be compared by the following test: Give the sixth degree with the finest waves of voice that are noticeable to the ear; then shade them off to those of the fifth degree making waves that the ear cannot detect but that seem almost as full as those of the sixth degree.

Then pass to still finer waves, and adopt them as the ordinary tones of conversation; remembering this fact, that there is no man or woman living on earth who does not use the third degree at all times in conversation, no matter what the subject under discussion or the character of the affair, whether business, social, professional or otherwise. If you can find a magnetic man or woman on the face of the globe who uses any other degree of voice than the third we will pay you a very handsome reward.

Still reduce the voice until it seems just barely alive, and finally pass into the first degree or dead tones by practicing the following quotations in imitation of some one who is trying to recite and who has not a particle of life in the voice.

"Caesar paused upon the brink of the Rubicon. What was the

Rubicon? The boundary of Caesar's province. From what did it separate his province? From his country. Was that country a desert? No, it was cultivated and fertile; rich and populous. Its sons were men of genius, spirit and generosity.''

You will not have to try hard to make this impersonation a great success, as all you have to do is to speak it in a dead voice, in which there is no undulation whatever.

CHAPTER TWELVE

+++++++++++++++++++++++++++++++++++++

THE POWER OF
MAGNETISM
IS INCREASED BY
INTENSITY

+++
DEVELOPMENT OF INTENSITY
+++

 O PERSON ever lived who was gifted with the power known as personal magnetism who did not show a greater or less degree of intensity. That this quality may be acquired is easily proved. The process is built upon the plan set forth in the preceding chapter. We have come in contact with so many persons who have changed their natures from the commonplace to the intense, that we have come to regard this training as the most successful in all this line of work.

Before any attempt is to be made to acquire intensity the first step is to master all the degrees of the Table of Undulations except the fourth. That may wait on this chapter. If you fail to develop the other degrees you will find this part of the course ineffective.

With the understanding that you now have acquired the ability to render all such degrees of undulations, we will proceed to give instruction in the methods whereby intensity, the greatest of all magnetic forces, is attained. Its basis is the flexible voice of the Table of Undulations.

That is the foundation.

The next step is to memorize a number of extracts that are calculated to arouse the intense nature in you. This is not at all difficult. It is a very pleasant line of training. The extracts are those that have done the work many hundred times before, and are consequently not experimental. Let each one be thoroughly committed to memory; not almost memorized, but thoroughly. The first relates to the stalwart power of defiance and personal prowess under adverse circumstances.

"THE SEMINOLE'S REPLY."

Blaze, with your serried columns! I will not bend the knee! The shackles ne'er again shall bind the arm which now is free. I've mailed it with the thunder, when the tempest muttered low; and where it falls, ye well may dread the lightning of its blow! I've scared ye in the city! I've scalped ye on the plain; go, count your chosen, where they fell beneath my leaden rain! I scorn your proffered treaty! The pale-face I defy! Revenge is stamped upon my spear, and blood's my battle-cry! Some strike for hope of booty, some to defend their all,—I battle for the joy I have to see the white man fall! I love, among the wounded, to hear his dying moan, and catch, while chanting at his side, the music of his groan. Ye've trailed me through the forest, ye've tracked me o'er the stream; and struggling through the everglades, your bristling bayonets gleam; but I stand as should the warrior, with his rifle and his spear;—the scalp of vengeance still is red, and warns ye,—Come not here! I loathe ye in my bosom! I scorn ye with mine eye! And I'll taunt ye with my latest breath, and fight ye till I die! I ne'er will ask for quarter, and I ne'er will be your slave; but I'll swim the sea of slaughter till I sink beneath the wave.—*George W. Patten.*

Having committed the foregoing to memory, it should be recited aloud at times and places permitting you to be alone. If there is the least disposition to make light of any part of the work, you might as well give it up until you have come to the contrary conclusion. The one great quality of the masses is flippancy; of the successful men and women, earnestness. Some one may disconcert you, or may make fun of your efforts at self improvement; but this has been the history of the world from the beginning of progress. If you are too weak to endure the flippancy of others, just read back to source of that influence in the preceding chapter, and let the matter drop; as magnetism is not in your line.

The great men and women of the world, as far as known, have been reciters in solitude of the powerful extracts of great writers. Thousands of instances of this habit have been collected by the author. The love of intense thought, and intensely worded language, is inherent in every great soul.

This short selection, known as the "Seminole's Reply," has fired many a boy and girl in the early days of school life. It cannot be properly rendered in a dead voice, although some pupils have done so in order to fulfill the task imposed upon them by doubting teachers. Still the same dead-voice students would be awakened by it in after years, if the ideas were properly absorbed.

Slow rendition is best for all forms of intensity. Rapid speaking turns intensity to excitement, one of the faulty moods. Let the lines be spoken aloud always, and never to oneself, or in silence; for the tones of the voice arouse the nervous system in the reciter, just as they do in any other listener. If you go to a theatre and have before you a very magnetic actor whose voice is completely drowned, you have no enjoyment in the play. His voice will arouse you; and so the sounds of your own tones will have the same effect upon yourself as upon your audience. In fact, the power you produce on yourself is the measure always of the power that you will be able to produce on others.

Mental pictures are helpful to the development of intensity, but that work is included in another course, and there is not room for it in this volume.

Do not add action to the delivery, unless you know what is required. It is better to seek a glimpse of the Seminole who uttered these lines, as he lived in the fancy of the composer of the poem.

Action mis-applied will deter the result sought. Much action is evidence of a shallow nature. Violent action may serve the actor who wishes to impersonate a character suited to it, but is always out of place otherwise. For these reasons it is much better to stand as the Seminole would stand if he really were to say all these intense things. Think of him and let his conduct be your example. In proportion as he is great and powerful, he will remain dignified and grand.

He defies the white man. He tells him to blaze with his serried columns; fire, kill, exterminate, if need be, but the Indian will stand as should the warrior, with his rifle and his spear. Get this picture fixed in your mind, and repeat the selection hundreds of times until the power that inspired it shall have passed over into your own nature. It is sure to do this.

We recall a number of cases that at first seemed hopeless, where students who possessed dead voices were unable to develop the fourth degree after having passed into all the other nine. But constant repetition brought the results, and then they would not have exchanged these for any other gift in the world.

The following embodies the spirit of liberty or self-sacrifice in the cause of country:

"MAKE WAY FOR LIBERTY."

In arms the Austrian phalanx stood, a living wall, a human wood; impregnable their front appears, all-horrent with projected spears. Yet, while the Austrians held their ground, point for assault was nowhere found; whene'er the impatient Switzers gazed, the unbroken line of lances blazed; that line 'twere suicide to meet, and perish at their tyrant's feet. It must not be: this day, this hour annihilates the invaders' power! All Switzerland is in the field—she cannot fly, she will not yield, she must not fall; her better fate here gives her an immortal date. Few were the numbers she could boast, yet every freeman was a host. It did depend on one indeed; behold him—Arnold Winkelried! Unmarked, he stood amid the throng, in rumination deep and long, till you might see, with sudden grace, the very thought come o'er his face; and by the motion of his form, anticipate the bursting storm. But 'twas no sooner thought than done—the field was in a moment won! "Make way for liberty!" he cried, then ran with arms extended wide, as if his dearest friend to clasp; ten spears he swept within his grasp. "Make way for liberty!" he cried, their keen points met from side to side; he bowed amongst them like a tree, and thus made way for liberty. Swift to the breach his comrades fly—"Make way for liberty!" they cry, and through the Austrian phalanx dart, as rushed the spears through Arnold's heart, while, instantaneous as his fall, rout, ruin, panic seized them all; an earthquake could not overthrow a city with a surer blow. Thus Switzerland again was free—thus death made way for liberty.—*James Montgomery.*

This, more than any other selection, impressed the author when he was in his teens. Switzerland has always been the representative country of freedom, the first republic since the days of Rome, and its handful of soldiers on the occasion, now held as memorable, stood as the embodiment of the uneven struggle between liberty and tyranny.

The fighting was done with spears, and these had long handles. The cordon or circle of Austrians were so placed that they completely surrounded the Swiss soldiery, all the spears being turned toward a focus at the center of the position held by the latter. There was no means of escape. To seek an outlet meant to fall upon the spears of the Austrians and die. The end was in sight from the beginning.

All Switzerland was in the field. If she fell then, there were no defenders at home to take up the struggle and prolong it. She cannot fly, for there is no way that escape is possible. She will not yield, for her men are willing to die for their country, not go to prison for it. She must not die, because her better fate is at work behind the event, looking for the future of the little republic. One patriot, through immortal self-sacrifice, saves the day, and causes rout, ruin and panic among the enemy.

When once the feeling of these facts is aroused, there will come the disposition to throw action into the delivery. This will ruin it. Attitudes almost invariably tell the story better when the power of intensity is involved than action or gesture. The deeper the feeling, the less it is shown in voice and movement, as far as demonstration is concerned. In competitive tests of reciters to ascertain who would produce the most magnetic results among audiences, it has always been found that those who are quietest in tones and in action have had a very great advantage. Still this does not mean that you are to stand like a stick or look like one who had no life. The whole face lights up, the eyes flash, the attitudes become eloquent, and the voice is filled with the irresistible power, when intensity takes possession. Sarah Bernhardt was the ugliest of actresses when her face was in repose, and the most fascinating when she was intense. Talmage, the homely orator, passed through the same change as his powerful sentences took possession of him and lighted up his whole being.

Another selection of the same kind, but suited to modern efforts, is useful in its way in developing this power.

"KOSSUTH."

Rufus Choate, on being asked what, in his opinion, was the most eloquent passage in all oratory, replied: Kossuth's appeal to an American audience for aid to carry on the struggle for liberty, when, remembering the glorious armies he had led to battle, the tears filled his eyes, and bowing his head for a moment to conceal his grief, he suddenly raised it, his face shining with God-like eloquence, and exclaimed: Pardon me, but I thought I saw the thousands of my comrades pass again in review before me, and I thought I heard them shout once more: "Liberty or death!"

This follows naturally in order after that of the Austrian deliverance. It possesses the stirring power that few quiet pieces can acquire. In most cases its hold upon the feelings is secured only after many repetitions.

There is one brief extract from the play of Richelieu that has never, as far as our experience goes, failed to instantly arouse the fire within man or woman. It is the scene where the cardinal defies his king. Richelieu was not only the head of the church, but also the prime minister. There was a deeply laid conspiracy against him that almost failed. To bring about the dislike of the king for his prime minister the enemies of the latter sought to produce circumstances that would lead to friction, and a girl, Julie, the ward of the cardinal, was made the subject of the dispute. The king was desirous of possessing her for immoral purposes. Barradas undertook the task of bringing her to his majesty.

Richelieu, after listening to the message from the king, said: "She shall not stir."

To this Barradas replied that the cardinal was not her father, but that he was merely her guardian, and intimated that she was merely an orphan. Richelieu now rejoined:

"Then her country is her mother." If this were true, he, the prime minister, was entitled to retain charge of her. But Barradas, wishing to provoke the cardinal into a declaration of treason said:

"The country is the king's."

If this statement were denied by Richelieu, it would be an act of treason, and would be so reported. The cardinal, however, remembered that many centuries before all persons, no matter what their offence, who reached the doors of a church and passed within, were free from arrest; and he now launches forth this doctrine in the most intense words that are recorded in any dramatic composition:

"Ay, it is so? Then wakes the power that in the age of iron burst forth to curb the great and raise the low. Mark where she stands. Around her form I draw the awful circle of our solemn church. Set but a foot within that holy ground, and on the head, yea, though it wore a crown, I'd launch the curse of Rome."

As he speaks the words, "Around her form I draw the awful circle of our solemn church," he pretends to build the walls of the church about the girl, and thus places her within its protection. The effect on Barradas is so great that he drops to the ground, crosses himself, and gives up the battle.

We have repeated this extract aloud for thousands of times, and it has been helpful during the many years that we have maintained the practice. We have letters from more than two thousand successful men and women, many being old students who assert that they have never allowed their practice of intense selections to be neglected, as it keeps the nervous system strong and its fire alive.

Do not forget that power rests in the constant repetition of the great thoughts that you are absorbing. The language itself will have a beneficial effect upon your diction and style of conversation, although you may never use the identical thoughts or arrangement. Daniel Webster had memorized Milton, and other works, and his diction was much more elevated in conversation, as well as in oratory, on that account. The purer and loftier styles uplift the trend of the mind, even if they are not actually copied.

The greater the number of quotations that you imbibe and appropriate into your own mind, the richer will be the run of your thoughts; and the richer your thoughts become, the more they will attract others. For these reasons, aside from their value in teaching intensity, these extracts are of the highest importance and should be made a part of yourself. You will enjoy the vigor and sparkle they give to your speech.

The next selection, or part of one, is suited to a more impetuous nature, and will prove much more cyclonic that any thus far given; although it still keeps within the fourth degree.

"THE GYPSY FLOWER GIRL."

But when I heard Egypta's cursed kiss, and saw her snaky, coiling arms around Don Jose's neck, and heard him swear by Egypta's gods that he was her's alone—"Sic, sic! upon them Zhock!" I cried, with all my wild-cat nature boiling, seething, hissing hot, through all my veins, hissing through my lips and brain, "Sic, sic! upon them Zhock!" I cried, and urged my Afric lion on. Zhock sprang and bore Don Jose to the ground. "Back Zhock! back Zhock! back to thy mistress, back! In vain I cried, I cried in vain through the glare of the storm. Lo, Egypta has seized Don Jose's dirk, quickly it falls across my Afric lion's eyes. Zhock reluctantly releases his weakened hold, and sneaks away with hurt, blood-blinded eyes. Now Don Jose and Egypta fly toward the sea, thank heaven they reach the cliff, now disappear. "Help! Why Zhock how you startled me; why Zhock, how you glare; how you stare. Down, shame, shame!—Ha, I know now, Zhock is mad. Hungry with the taste of Don Jose's blood, my Afric lion now returns, eager for mine own. Where shall I flee? Back, down! sic! upon them Zhock, yonder Zhock, down by the sea. Zhock, how dare you, peace Zhock, I am wild Zingarella, thy mistress, fair boy, down, back, away, down, down." I feel his thorny claws around my neck, his hot breath on my throat, thrice with my stiletto do I cut the monster down. Backward toward the cliffs of Malaga I fight my horrible way. I near the cliffs, keeping the frenzied beast at bay, backwardly fighting, parrying, evading with supernatural strength, I hold the treacherous wretch at bay. At length I reach the cliffs. Twice, thrice my good steel pierces the raging, foaming lion's side. Then with a prayer to the Christians' God, I plunge far down in the roaring tide. Zhock's eyes like crackling gypsy camp-fires shine, or twin-danger signals out on a sea, with a roar of rage far out he leaps: but the Christians' God was kind to me; for e'en as Zhock sprang some hunter's gun spake, and Zhock from the sea will never awake.—*E. L. McDowell.*

The foregoing is part of a selection which describes the power of jealousy in a young woman of tropical blood, and of the wandering class. Zingarella possesses a lion that is a little less tame than herself. She sees her lover, Don Jose, embracing and kissing another woman, whose name is Egypta. In her frenzy she urges her lion against the couple. Zhock tastes the blood of Don Jose; this maddens him; the lovers have escaped; he must have more blood, and now comes back upon his mistress, and they fight till the cliff is reached. In desperation the girl leaps far out into the sea, and the lion after her. But some hunter kills him in his wild flight, and the girl is saved to tell the story.

This will set your whole nervous system on fire if you study it in the right way; that is, master first all the work set down in the preceding chapter; then follow out the selections in this. Once or twice reciting it will do no good; it should be repeated aloud for hundreds of times. No matter if it takes years to do this. No matter if this year you have all the magnetism that one person can acquire in a twelve-month, and an increase next year, and another increase each and every year to follow. Time counts for nothing if you are progressing always.

Again allow us to warn you not to ruin the effect by grotesque action. If you do not know what to do, then place yourself in the position of this girl who is telling the story and tell it as she might do to her chance acquaintances.

Another selection of the most intense character, and suited to men, is given here to match the last one, which is better adapted for women. What is familarly known as Sheil's Peroration, is one of the most stirring things in speech. It is full of meaning and fire, from the very first word to the last. The scholastic movement of the style is also an influence that counts for great value in one who absorbs it and makes the diction his own for the time being. This extract should be so thoroughly memorized as to become a part of the very mind and feeling of the reciter. Such memorizing is not always given to quoted language, but the great reciters and speakers acquire it as a habit. To be compelled to grope for thoughts while undertaking to put power into the rendition, is sure to weaken the latter.

"SHEIL'S PERORATION."

Whose were the arms that drove your bayonets at Vimiera through the phalanxes that never reeled in the shock of war before? What desperate valor climbed the steeps and filled the moat at Badajos? All his victories should have rushed and crowded back upon his memory,—Vimiera, Badajos, Salamanca, Albuera, Toulouse, and last of all, the greatest.—Tell me,—for you were there,—I appeal to the gallant soldier before me, from whose opinions I differ, but who bears, I know, a generous heart in an intrepid breast;—tell me,—for you must needs remember, —on that day when the destinies of mankind were trembling in the balance,—while death fell in showers,—when the artillery of France was levelled with a precision of the most deadly science, —when her legions, incited by the voice and inspired by the example of their mighty leader rushed again and again to the onset,—tell me if, for an instant, when to hesitate for an instant was to be lost, the "aliens" blanched? And, when at length, the moment for the last and decisive movement had arrived, and the valor which had so long been wisely checked was, at last, let loose,—when, with words familiar but immortal, the great captain commanded the great assault,—tell me if Catholic Ireland with less heroic valor than the natives of this your own glorious country precipitated herself upon the foe? The blood of England, Scotland, and Ireland, flowed in the same stream, and drenched the same field. When the chill morning dawned, their dead lay cold and stark together;—in the same deep pit their bodies were deposited; the green corn of spring is now breaking from their commingled dust; the dew falls from heaven upon their union in the grave. Partakers in every peril, in the glory shall we not be permitted to participate; and shall we be told as a requital, that we are estranged from the noble country for whose salvation our life-blood was poured out.—*R. L. Sheil.*

The foregoing is an oratorical description of the battle of Waterloo. The oration was delivered in the English Parliament at a time that was much nearer to the era of that battle than the present. The orator can point to some of his audience who were there. He is an Irishman and is defending his country from the charge of being aliens, a term applied accidently by the Duke of Wellington in the House of Lords not long before. The words, "All his victories," refers to all Wellington's victories. "The last of all, the greatest," is Waterloo. The reference to Napoleon is first made in the words, "When her legions, incited by the voice and inspired by the example of their mighty leader." The words, "and the valor which had so long been wisely checked, was, at last, let loose," refers to the body-guard of Napoleon, every man of which was a proved hero in some previous conflict; a mass of fighters that had never known defeat.

The peculiarity of this peroration is its fullness of thought; you cannot repeat it without finding some new idea cropping up, no matter how many times you make the review. It is to get as many ideas as possible that you should give hundreds of repetitions all aloud.

All the extracts of this chapter ought to be mastered by each student. While some are more suited to one sex than the other, they are nevertheless all effective whether recited by man or woman. Do not practice them before others, for there is a lack of edge when two or three persons are listening and gaping at the efforts of a reciter who lacks faith in self.

Intensity is fire. It burns in the nerves, in the brain, in the heart. It sets in motion the magnetic waves that are everywhere waiting to bear messages of influence from one individual to another. Without intensity there is nothing in the person, and no means of conveying or reaching the feelings and thoughts of others. You may look at the successful actors, and there will not be one who remains long upon the stage if intensity be lacking. Indeed it is a very difficult thing for any man or woman to rise from even the lowest ranks, when there is no intensity; and history fails to record a single star who has been lacking in this quality.

One of the foremost managers in this country, a man who has developed hundreds of unknown people into actors of prominence, says that all he wants is evidence of some personal magnetism and a reasonable amount of good sense; and he will develop both voice and business in the candidates. But, let magnetism be lacking, and there is no hope. The same thing ought to be true of every man in every profession. It will prove true in your own case.

In the business world, and in the social world, the lack of magnetism is a weight about the neck of every one thus afflicted. The race is uneven.

We are not teaching the use of intensity in marked degree or as an impetuous force. It should be acquired because of the fire which it arouses in the nerves, and which communicates to all the faculties and powers, making them more acute, much more attractive, and far more influential in the battle of life.

No person can accumulate too much intensity. It feeds the vitality to such an extent that the loss of sleep will hardly be felt, and the decadence of the physical powers will be checked. It is said that sleep is essential to prevent the breaking down of the mind and of the nerves; but, against this statement, is the fact that no man or woman has ever achieved a great life work unless the wee small hours of the morning have been employed; or, in other words, unless work has been done night and day. Let intensity be lacking and this practice of working sixteen or eighteen hours out of every twenty-four, will soon make sleep impossible, and lead to a complete breakdown of the health. Those who take such chances should know on what ground they are standing.

The possession of intensity rather than its use, is what is herein taught. There will come times when you will have unexpected demands for its use. Nor will the professions alone require it. There is no man or woman who would not be much more powerful, even in the quietest walks of life, by reason of the possession of intensity.

A more direct reason is the connection it has between the individual and the power of transmigration which is to be taken up in later pages.

CHAPTER THIRTEEN

✠✠✠✠✠✠✠✠✠✠✠✠✠✠✠✠✠✠✠✠✠✠✠✠✠✠✠✠✠✠✠✠✠✠✠✠✠

LIFE'S EXPERIENCES
ARE ALL
THERE IS TO
LIFE ITSELF

✠✠✠

QUOTATIONS FOR MOODS AND FEELINGS

✠✠✠

 VERY MOOD and feeling is a distinct and separate phase of the nature of the individual. Some of the moods last longer than others, and some abide for weeks, months and even years. From the state of temporary fugitive they are all the time seeking to establish the acquired habitual character. A mere feeling may come and go in a brief time. A mood may last for almost any length of time. One is the larger form of the other, and for this reason the terms are interchangeable.

There are twenty-six of the Heaven-Born Moods and Feelings, and they are listed in chapter ten. They should now receive a brief description before attempting to adopt them for the purposes for which they were introduced. The reason why the consideration of them was interrupted has been stated.

All the Heaven-Born Moods and feelings should be acquired; for it is true that the same individual lacks a majority of them. In the study of character it is the custom to take account of stock of yourself to see where you stand and what you have, each matter of doubt being put in the balance against yourself. The same rule might be applied here, but that is for you to decide.

RESPECT is the first. It may be a temporary feeling; if so, it should be increased and cultivated until it is ever-present.

It is hard to assume respect, if the quality is not a part of your nature. All motives, all persons who seem to you to be your inferiors, and all efforts made in earnest, invite respect in the true man or woman. The following quotation is the key to this mood.

1

RESPECT.

"No man is my inferior in my own eyes. All who live are made by the same creator, and He alone has the right to judge between us."

2

AFFECTION.

"A lady, the loveliest ever the sun looked down upon, you must paint for me."

This quotation is from "An Order for a Picture." It might seem to depict the feeling of love, as the lady is the mother; but such feeling is that of affection. Love is regarded as confined to the passion that leads to marriage, although many other moods go by the same name. There are many kinds of affection, and the following quotation will show what is meant:

2

AFFECTION.

"I see the same old look in your eyes, Tom, that shone there when we parted many years ago. Not a day has passed that I have not asked about you, and wanted to be with you again."

This is the affection that one man has for another man.

3

LOVE.

"And when night came, amidst the breathless heavens, we'd guess what star should be our home when love becomes immortal."

This is part of the address made by Claude Melnotte to Pauline. The whole speech is charged with the same feeling, and would make an excellent bit of thought for regular recitation.

4

GENEROSITY.

"What is mine, is thine. Naught that I have will I keep from thee, and this shall be my guide through all our lives."

5

PLEASURE.

"The seasons come and go, and all are full of exciting pleasures to me. I never long for something not at hand, but give the full bent of enjoyment to each blessing as it comes."

6

JOY.

"I am overwhelmed with this unexpected good news. Give me breath, for I can scarcely realize the good fortune."

7

PEACE.

"How sweet the moonlight sleeps upon this bank."

8

MERCY.

"The quality of mercy is not strained. It droppeth as the gentle rain, from heaven upon the place beneath. It is twice blessed; it blesseth him that gives and him that takes."

9

SYMPATHY.

"Tears, my boy? What's them for, Joey? There, poor little Joe, don't cry."

10

SACRIFICE.

"There's yet a world where souls are free; where tyrants taint not nature's bliss; if death that world's bright opening be, oh, who would live a slave in this?"

11

TRUST.

"The soul, secured in her existence, smiles at the drawn dagger and defies its point."

This is from the play of Cato, and represents the abiding belief in immortality.

12

HOPE.

"Ah, well, for us all some sweet hope lies, deeply buried from human eyes; and, in the hereafter, angels may roll from the grave its stone away."

13

DIGNITY.

"Sage he stood, with Atlantean shoulders, fit to bear the weight of mightiest monarchies."

This supreme description of dignity by Milton reaches the climax of superlative diction.

14

NOBLENESS.

"There was no mark of fear upon his manly countenance, as with majestic step and fearless eye he entered. He stood there, like another Apollo, firm and unbending, as the rigid oak."

15

PRIDE.

"Behold it! Listen to it! Every star has a tongue; every stripe is articulate."

Pride, in its true sense, is a just recognition of some good quality, or some grand achievement. It is never haughty or arrogant. Were it not for this feeling of pride, there would be no reward for the results of life's struggles. In this case, the American flag is referred to; but any other quotation, bearing upon anything that excites pride, may be substituted."

15

PRIDE.

"England, with all thy faults, I love thee still."
The foregoing, from one of the great English poets, is familiar to every native of that country.

16

COURAGE.

" 'Make way for liberty,' he cried.   Made way for liberty and died."

17

RESOLUTION.

"They'd rob me of my daughter, would they?   Let them try it."

18

TRIUMPH.

"I have re-created France, and from the ash of the old feudal and decrepit carcass civilization on her luminous wings soars phoenix-like to Jove."
This is the boast of Richelieu, referring to his life work. But, being a summary of the facts, it is not an un-warranted claim. Therefore it is not idle boasting, but genuine triumph.

19

PATRIOTISM.

"Thou, too, sail on, O Ship of State! Sail on, O Union, strong and great! Our hearts, our hopes, our prayers, our tears, our faith triumphant o'er our tears, are all with thee, are all with thee."

20

GRANDEUR.

"Roll on, thou deep and dark blue ocean, roll. The armaments which thunder-strike the walls of rock-built cities, bidding nations quake, and monarchs tremble in their capitals; the oak leviathans, whose huge ribs make their clay creator the vain title take of lord of thee, and arbiter of war—these are thy toys, and, as the snowy flake, they melt into thy yeast of waves, which mar alike the Armada's pride, or spoils of Trafalgar."

21

SUBLIMITY.

"Hast thou a charm to stay the morning star in his steep course? Thou first and chief, sole sovereign of the vale! Who sank thy sunless pillars deep in earth? Who filled thy countenance with rosy light? And you, ye five wild torrents fiercely glad, who called you forth, from night and utter death, from dark and icy caverns, called you forth down those precipitous, black, jagged rocks, forever shattered and the same forever? Who gave you your invulnerable life, your strength, your speed, your fury and your joy, unceasing thunder and eternal foam? 'God!' let the torrents, like a shout of nations, answer."

No attempt is made to confine the quotations to their original words. The only purpose here is to bring out the thoughts that portray the moods and feelings to which they are attached.

22

SOLEMNITY.

" 'Tis midnight's holy hour, and silence now is brooding like a gentle spirit o'er the still and pulseless world."

23

REVERENCE.

"King Robert, who was standing near the throne, lifted his eyes, and lo! he was alone! but all apparalled as in days of old, with ermined mantle and with cloth of gold, and when his courtiers came, they found him there kneeling upon the floor, absorbed in silent prayer."

24

HUMILITY.

"I pray you believe me, I am humbly at your service."

25

RESIGNATION.

"If I should live to be the last leaf upon the tree in the spring, let them smile, as I do now, at the old forsaken bough, where I cling."

26

REPENTANCE.

"While yet I hold the power to make restitution for all the wrongs I have done, I will undo them and seek forgiveness from God."

We pass now from the moods and feelings that are born in heaven, and take up those that are due to the conflict of human nature with the vicissitudes of earthly existence. These are born as our masters, and never as our slaves.

The moods and feelings that are born of heaven, while they should lead us, are not to be our masters; they are good steeds that we should drive; and all others are devils to be put behind us. Yet the sad spectacle of men and women being hurried along through life yoked to all that is bad, is the most common experience of today.

27

WORRY.

"I can see no way out of the trouble. Whichever direction I pursue I feel sure I will fail. I am always unlucky and nothing I can do will make me successful."

28

VEXATION.

"There it goes again. I wish I had never moved into this place. I cannot bear the sound of a crying child, and that old piano is enough to drive me wild."

29

PETULANCE.

"Get out, you fool. I'll knock you down if you come near me again."

30

IRRITABILITY.

"I cannot get this on. The collar was made too small and the laundry has got too much starch in it. There, I've dropped that button. Where, in the name of Dickens, is it?"

31

INDIFFERENCE.

"I never had a sick day in all my life. Those bottles? Oh, those I got to have on hand in case I needed something. I never pay the least attention to my health, and I think it a great bore to talk about it. My brother died of typhoid, but I did not, and as long as I am alive I'm not bothering myself about the water I drink. It won't make any difference in a hundred years, anyhow."

32

FLIPPANCY.

"Give me the Sunday paper, and let me get the sensations fixed up before I take in the solemn duties at the church. Oh, I enjoy dropping in there, for the hats and dresses are worth seeing."

33

IMMODERATION.

"I borrowed five dollars from him, and he has pestered the life out of me ever since. He has the meanest nature I ever met. I do believe that he would rip up a cement walk to find a nickel."

34

EXCITEMENT.

"Away on a hot chase down the wind. But never was fox hunt half so hard, and never was steed so little spared, for we rode for our lives."

35

EMBARRASSMENT.

"Oh, you here? Yes, I was expecting you. Yes, I was helping myself. That is, I knew you were coming."

36

DOUBT.

"I am; how little more I know? Whence came I? Whither do I go?"

37

SURPRISE.

"Gone to be married? Gone to swear a peace?"

38

WONDER.

"O, a wonderful stream is the river Time."

39

TRANCE.

"I was half awake, and yet half asleep. I knew everything that was going on, and I had no power to prevent it."

Trance refers in this instance to the condition of the mind in which the thoughts lapse, or cease altogether, and the individual permits anything to be said or done. It is a condition in which the brain is emptied of its own thoughts and is merely a witness of the doings of others.

40

RECKLESSNESS.

"And there are times when, mad with thinking, I'd sell out heaven for something warm to prop a horrible sinking."

41

CHALLENGE.

"Lay on, Macduff, and damned be he who first cries hold! enough!"

42

DEFIANCE.

"Avaunt! My name is Richelieu. I defy thee!"

43

SADNESS.

"We parted in silence, we parted in tears, on the banks of that lonely river."

44

GRIEF.

"I have been patient with my Maker, but this grief is too great for me to bear."

45

DISAPPOINTMENT.

"I never loved a tree or flower, but it was the first to fade away."

46

REGRET.

"But the tender grace of a day that is gone will never come back to me."

47

MELANCHOLY.

"Seems, madam? Nay, it is. I know not seems."

48

DISCONSOLATION.

"Tomorrow, and tomorrow, and tomorrow creep in this petty pace from day to day to the last syllable of recorded time."

49

DESPAIR.

"Down, down I go, with no power to hold me from the gulf of black despair."

50

INSANITY.

"You are not afraid of me. I would not harm you. They say I am not well here."
In this last remark the hand is placed upon the forehead.

All the foregoing moods and feelings can be kept out of your life, and they should not be allowed for one instant to hold the mastery; for, if they do, the legitimate end of it all is the last.

The final group of moods and feelings are those that are born in hell; perhaps not the hell that is understood by the superstitious people of the past and present, but the hell that is described in Universal Magnetism.

51

FEAR.

"Whence is that knocking? How is it with me when every noise appals me?"

52

SHAME.

"To be now a sensible man, by and by a fool, and presently a beast."

53

APPREHENSION.

"My God! Can it be possible that I have to die so suddenly."

54

ANGER.

"And darest thou then to beard the lion in his den, the Douglass in his hall?"

55

HATRED.

"If I can catch him once upon the hip, I will feed fat the ancient grudge I bear him."

56

CRUELTY.

"Ha! Bind him on his back! Now, bend him to the rack! Press down the poisoned links into his flesh, and tear agape that healing wound afresh!"

This kind of selection is a classic and is regarded as the highest art by dramatic critics. It is the story of Parrhasius and the Captive.

57

REVENGE.

"Front to front bring thou this fiend of Scotland and myself. Within my sword's length set him. If he 'scape, heaven forgive him too."

58

SCORN.

"I loathe you in my bosom. I scorn you with mine eye."

59

ARROGANCE.

"I have no brother. I am like no brother. I am myself alone."

60

CONTEMPT.

"Thou slave! Thou wretch! Thou coward."

61

JEALOUSY.

"I do mistrust thee, woman, and each word of thine adds truth to each suspicion heard."

62

RESENTMENT.

"Not what you have said and not what you have done, but what you would say and do, make me sorry for having known you."

63

WARNING.

"Beware! Lay but a finger on her or what she loves, and thou shalt know what 'tis to have Ingomar for thy foe."

64

THREATENING.

"If thou dost slander her and torture me, never pray more."

65

MOCKERY.

"The old man walks like a bent grasshopper. See! This way he goes; and hear him munch his words."

66

ENVY.

"Why should he have power and wealth, and I be left to plod along in the lower ranks? I'll none of this plain living. I'll steal or worse, to get me fortune."

67

SUPERSTITION.

"If we enter this way, some dreadful calamity will befall us, and if we sit down with others that make the number thirteen, all will die ere the year has sped."

68

LAZINESS.

"Why should I lift a finger for myself when others will care for me? For what use is wealth if not to keep the opulent in ease?"

69

FLATTERY.

"Such eyes were never seen before. Such lips and sweet beauty never graced a maiden fair."

70

DECEIT.

"I never sell what is not perfect. These are the same through all the lot. It is useless to look at them, for here you see what they are in every part."

Deceit refers more to action than to language, and the pantomime of this quotation will assist in making the mood clear.

71

FALSEHOOD.

"I swear by all the saints and all that is sacred and holy that I have never given my love to another but you."

72

SELFISHNESS.

"I am entitled to it, for I am the elder."

73

CRAFTINESS.

"This plan will force them to seek a loan, and we are the only parties who can supply them. In giving them the accommodation we can compel them to accept our offer in the other transaction. They have no means of slipping out of our clutches."

74

TREACHERY.

"When thou liest down by night, my knife is at thy throat."

75

STEALTH.

"In slowly moving steps we came upon them, and ere they could make cry we had taken them by force."

Treachery implies an abuse of the confidence that one may place in another; while stealth is the method of action or thought employed.

76

GUILT.

"Oh! God! That horrid, horrid dream besets me now awake. Again, again with dizzy brain the human life I take."

Chapter Fourteen

++

PROGRESS
NOW BECOMES
EXCEEDINGLY
RAPID

++
⚘ MASTERY OF THE MOODS ⚘
++

HE GREAT FINAL step is now to be taken prior to the actual practice of transmigration. This step is based upon all that has been taught and suggested in the six preceding chapters, from the eighth to the thirteenth, both inclusive. If you wish success in this study, you must go back to the beginning of the eighth chapter, and make yourself familiar with every word. You cannot catch the ideas in one reading. Many reviews will help you. The progress that you are to make is wholly dependent at this stage on the grasp you have secured on those six chapters.

The Moods and Feelings that were listed, and then laid aside until the power of pathos and of intensity could be developed, have been further developed in chapter thirteen. There they appear with quotations suited to their nature. Where two or more seem alike or closely allied, an examination and analysis of them will disclose the fact that they are widely separate. The meanings are secondary to the feelings.

If we were to teach men and women to take a high rank on the stage, we would include only those moods and feelings that have been referred to as suited to the actor's art; and these we have successfully taught to some of the foremost men and women

110

during the past thirty years of the drama in this country; and so great a genius as Wilson Barrett, the leading actor in recent English history, was willing to become our patron. This success was due to the deep analysis that we have made into human character, motives and methods.

But if there were to be a supreme stage, one in which no actors were to appear except those who had reaped the harvest of success in the worlds of finance, of business, of business and social prowess, and the audience were capable of reading and understanding these powerful men and women, we would lay aside all other arts and take up the seventy-six Moods and Feelings that have been elaborated in the preceding chapters. These would train loftier characters than those that the stage invites, for the stakes are greater and the processes of winning them are far beyond ordinary grasp.

Then we have the perfect stage.

The methods by which the man or woman learns to act and to keep as close to nature as circumstances will permit, are worthy of imitation in mastering these greater Moods. The first thing that the actor must learn is to conceive in his mind the person he is to portray. The second thing is to know what that person is to say and do. The third thing is to ascertain how he is to do it, and in what color he is to say it. The latter is called vocal color.

Vocal color is the native value of a Mood or Feeling. It comes from the inmost sources of oneself. Once established it never leaves the nervous system. But it may require thousands of repetitions to secure the true color. Most persons say all kinds of things in the same color. Try that with the quotations of the preceding chapter, and see what havoc you will make with them. The beginning of versatility is the first step in securing colors suited to each Mood; and versatility is the actor's genius.

This gift is attained by endless repetition. In proportion as you are artistic you will be willing to repeat the same short extract an endless number of times. Edwin Forrest undoubtedly stood at the head of his profession for thirty years, and he was willing to make these repetitions. In one case where he wished to secure the color of great terror he repeated a short sentence five hundred thousand times, putting all the feeling and voice into it that he could command; and, when he spoke that line to the audience, they were moved beyond description. This acquired color attended him all his life, for the color never leaves the voice. Edwin Booth in a similar way made himself the most versatile actor before the public during the last twenty years of his life.

Having obeyed the instructions as set forth in the six preceding chapters, you should begin to memorize the seventy-six quotations of chapter thirteen, so that you may render them aloud whenever the opportunity affords. You should know them so well that years will not drive them from you. Be content with a little progress day by day. Memorizing will make the brain strong and give you a new power of memory. Let each of the Heaven-Born Moods be known by number, and their quotations also be connected with them in your mind, so that, when you speak the lines, you will know the names and numbers of the Moods they represent.

Then master the Earth-Born Moods in the same way; and, finally, adopt the same methods with the Hell-Born Moods.

The way to begin to acquire the color of each is this:

The first part of each day's review should be given to stating the number, and the name of the Moods in their order; then to the vocal rendition of the quotations; thus assuring their entire review once a day. This will take five minutes or more; and you waste many times that portion of the day in idle talk or useless reading. Success in magnetism is based on having more to do than any other individual in your neighborhood.

After the review, you must allow yourself to be attracted to one or more of them that seem to you to be most readily depicted in the tones of your voice. Do not be afraid of the tragedy lists, as they are only classic. It is a rule of acting that what you can best do on the stage you are least likely to be swayed by when off the stage. This is known as the law of re-action. Thus the heaviest villains on the stage are the gentlest in private life, and the funniest comedians before the public are the most solemn owls in the bosoms of their families. This is the balancing of nature.

No actor or actress that has played insanity for many years on the stage has gone insane; and this fact can be proved by investigation. But nearly all those who have suffered mental breakdown in this profession are the comedians. We can name nearly two hundred such cases. Their brain seems to suffer from paresis.

These facts are stated to allow you to become calm in the presence of some fearfully gloomy lines in the preceding chapter.

In the first week of practice after you have memorized the lines and can connect them with their names and numbers, you will be attracted to one or two only; in the next week you will find half a dozen that appeal to your liking. Later on more will be added until you find that you can render them all, giving each a different color.

In order to separate the colors and become versatile, and therefore a genius, the old plan is still the best. This consists in exchanging colors. Take, as examples, the two following quotations:

22. SOLEMNITY.—"'Tis midnight's holy hour, and silence now is brooding like a gentle spirit o'er a still and pulseless world."

55. HATRED.—"If I can catch him once upon the hip, I will feed fat the ancient grudge I bear him."

It is useless to attempt to interchange these, or other colors, before they become properly rendered. It is the variance between one color and another that makes the interchange show the difference. When you have mastered Solemnity so that your whole being is filled with a sensation of the solemn, and have also mastered Hatred so that you realize just how a person hates, then you can exchange them, giving the words of Solemnity in the color of Hatred and the words of Hatred in the color of Solemnity. When these colors, thus turned around, seem to you to present fearful discords, then you are becoming their master.

It is not possible to develop color unless you use your voice. To think of the color will not do. Your own voice is your guide, and you are to make it interesting to yourself by being your own listener. If you produce upon yourself the same effect that a versatile actor of great ability would be able to produce on you, then the victory is complete.

Do not be discouraged at the passing of time. There is no hurry, and no need to hasten. Were you not making the effort to progress in this direction, you would be drifting somewhere else. Weeks may pass into months and months into years before you have created all the seventy-six colors; but some will appear in a very short time. To these you will add one or more every week, and so you will be gaining ground all the time.

Pitch in, and do your best to produce the right color. Take a few minutes each day. Arrange your engagements so that you will be alone part of the time, for the presence or knowledge of another person will disconcert you, and some flippant remark will turn you from the trial. If you were really studying for the stage, the amount of practice that you would be required to indulge in each day would compel you to seek solitude as the means of fitting yourself for your chosen profession; for the successful actor is the sum total of a tremendous amount of private practice.

Make a resolution that no week day shall go by without your using a few minutes of this practice; and summon enough will power to carry out the plans that you make.

Throw yourself heartily and fully into the color that you are striving to acquire; no other method will succeed. Thus if you are endeavoring to render the color of respect, think of what this mood is, to whom you do and should show respect, and in what way you would display this conduct. Then let your habits lead to a greater exhibition of this quality toward others, whether your superiors or your inferiors. When George Washington, on returning the bow of a colored servant, was accused of fawning to a negro, he replied that he did not propose to be outdone in politeness by a colored person. That was the true spirit of respect. You can repeat aloud the words in the quotation, all the while keeping in mind the nature of the quality they stand for.

If affection is the mood that you are to depict, think of something in your past experience that arouses now this feeling, and let that control you while reciting the words. Repeat them over and over again, ten, twenty, thirty or more times, but always have the mind on what is meant by the color of affection.

Love is the passion of sex for sex, and your own knowledge of that sensation will be helpful; otherwise you will be obliged to pass the color.

Generosity is the mood of giving something to another that requires self-denial; a parting with an advantage, maybe, or some property, or attention, or effort. There are in the course of every day many scores of opportunities for showing generosity to others, and habit should be cultivated to the highest degree. Out of it grows the best estate of manhood and womanhood.

Pleasure is an abiding satisfaction with the conditions in which you are placed. Joy is a more fugitive mood. Peace is the settled content of mind and heart. Mercy is the willingness to give the offender good for evil. Sympathy is a genuine interest in the ills and misfortunes of others. Sacrifice is much more than generosity, but in the same direction. Trust is a settled belief in a thing that cannot be proved. And so these different colors are variances from each other for the most part, each requiring an intelligent interpretation.

The rule always is that the bolder the color the easier it will be to acquire it. Thus you can do much more at first with courage, resolution, triumph, patriotism and the decided moods than with the less vigorous feelings of peace, dignity, hope and the like. We recall with pleasant memories the many discouraged pupils who could not for some weeks start even the semblance of color in the quiet moods, but who launched forth with right good will on challenge, defiance, anger, hatred, revenge, scorn, contempt and others of that sort; and these were selected as the colors to be first developed if there was a preference for them. The voices of the pupils would ring out in those vigorous quotations, and soon they found that other colors could be added one at a time until they had gained the mastery over all of them.

Some of the colors you will not take any interest in at first. This is due to the fact that they have never lived in your voice. If you have been in the habit when younger of reciting a certain style of selection and have had a liking for that style, the fact can be discovered by the colors that first attract you here. The past is often read in this way, and we do not recall ever making a wrong guess in such a case.

An all round benefit will accrue from the development of these colors. It is hard to make this fully understood at first; but you will be more of a personage after a few weeks spent in this practice. You will have more power in conversation, a better mind with which to address yourself to others, and greater fullness of heart and humanity in your make-up; even if you never apply these steps of development to the practice of transmigration.

CHAPTER FIFTEEN

PRACTICE
IN
TRANSMIGRATION
MADE USEFUL

✦ ✦ ✦ APPLIED CASES ✦ ✦ ✦

MMEDIATE STEPS are now to be taken to put into practice the principles of transmigration. Success will follow in every case, provided the suggestions already made in preceding chapters have been adopted. The suggestions and methods therein stated are not difficult. Any man or woman of intelligence can readily adopt them all, and no person can fail except one who wishes to get results without practice. It is not a question as to the length of time. The nature of the practice is exactly the same as that adopted by the actor.

In reply to inquiries as to whether or not this system will make actors, we will say frankly that it will quickly develop the very best of actors, because it will produce only natural ones. This is not to be looked upon as a drawback, for there will always be better actors off the stage than on. Every great personage in every era of the world's history has been a consummate actor. This does not mean a pretender or an artificial character; but one who knows every phase of human nature and can step at once into the mood of another. Such skill is evidence of the highest of powers.

The ability to step at will into the mood of another person is transmigration of self. It is not new to the world, but has been

116

the art of supreme control of other human beings for thousands of years. Proof of this fact can be drawn from every nation on earth, and from the history, literature and creeds of every people.

In order to step into the mood of another person, it is necessary to know what mood such person is in, and to recognize the mood as one over which you have attained mastery.

In order to attain this mastery it is necessary to develop the mood in your own self, and to express it in perfect color. The mood is said to exist when its color is rightly depicted in your own voice and manner.

If the mood comes and goes at will, it is your master; if it comes and goes by your command, it is your slave. The actor has trained himself to simulate any of those moods that he chooses to adopt in his profession and has had time to develop; but his work does not reach into the deeper feelings. It is largely superficial. On the other hand there has been no great genius in history who did not have the power to throw himself into a score or more of moods and feelings to their very depth. The complaint has been from many sources that they are too keen in their sensibilities and take on themselves too much the moods of others. This fault is due to the development of a limited number of moods without giving attention to those that predominate in the first list.

There are people who are sympathetic in the highest degree; they have, by mere habit, developed the feeling of sympathy; and, if they had no other department of acting than that one, they would be world-geniuses on the stage to that extent. Lacking versatility, they feel too much the one sole mood which they have fully developed.

There is a class of people who have given encouragement to still another mood to the exclusion of all others; this is stealth. They deal toward all others as if they were to be injured by them. They suspect everybody. Good and bad motives alike are the subject of their ill will. By using this method they save themselves loss, but at the expense of friendships and valuable associations in life.

Then there are persons who have learned to falsify to such an extent that they cannot speak the truth. The mood of falsehood is in them as a fixture until an awakening comes.

Some persons at certain periods of life are generous to the

exclusion of all other impulses. Some are the very epitome of courage, and often without the judgment that should direct it. Some are run away with by their patriotism. A few are humble, and give themselves to the mood of humility at all times. Dignity sits enthroned on many men and many women as their chief attribute. Some are fond of peace, of deepest quietude, of seclusion and rest. A few are solemn. And so the whole list is found scattered among many different individuals, but no two of the moods are paramount in the same person. This is the difference between the ordinary individual and the one who possesses power.

It can be safely asserted that, in proportion as there is ability to step into any mood or feeling, in the same proportion will a person be master of that condition; but, more than this, he will also be master of the circumstances which are involved in the possession of the mood or feeling. Here we have the great law of transmigration.

If your house is on fire, and you are able to master that fire, you will also, of necessity, be able to master the source of the fire, and all the circumstances are under your control.

If there is a thief in your house and you secure him, you will also secure what he has in his possession. Control of the effect is control of the source that is present in the effect.

Moods balance each other.

When you have found it possible to portray one of the better class, you will find it easy to portray one of the meaner class that is as near as possible its opposite. The nerves re-act from one side to the other of the moral nature; and also from one phase of feeling to its opposing phase. Thus the practice of the color of love gives way most readily to the practice of the color of hatred. An actor who has a part in a play that gives him opposing moods to express will make them both greater if he follows this law of re-action. Time is saved, and a much more powerful color is acquired in each mood. To be all on the better side, will not protect you from the wiles and tricks of the world.

If your whole nature is given to generosity, you will most likely become the prey of schemers and tricksters. Moods come and go. The face of Andrew Carnegie showed clearly the miserly and money-making disposition, involving envy and craftiness; yet, at a time when life had passed high noon and the amassed fortune must slip from his grasp by the decree of death, he was seized with the desire to exercise control over much of his wealth before the inevitable ruler should assume the receivership; and generosity began making its inroads in his character. But he had a large number of other traits which proved that he was a successful reader of men all his life.

Here are two opposing moods exchanging places in the same person; craftiness having held its sway, and then given way to generosity.

It is often true that, when years have been absorbed in one kind of mood, its opposite will be invited into the life. A joyous nature has many times been succeeded by one of sadness. Humility of position is sometimes the quality of a poor girl; knowing her penury, she makes the least display in life; but, let such a girl become the wife of a wealthy man, and the opposite character will soon come to the front. She will be arrogant. This has occurred so often that it is current knowledge. ''I will marry a girl born of poverty, and one who is humble in her wants, so that she will not become extravagant and waste my accumulations,'' said a rich man. He found such a girl. She was demure, simple in her habits and humble in all matters; but, soon after they were married, the opposite tendency began to develop and she showed no trace of her former nature. This is a common illustration of the law of re-action from one mood to its opposite.

What is true in life, is true in any phase of life, and is also just as forceful in the assumption of the moods that make up the portrayal of life. The comedian at home is the best tragedian on the stage, and the gloomy fellow in private life is the best comedian on the stage.

For these reasons it is best to acquire all the moods and feelings, so that they may serve as a complete balance for one another. Personal power will be greater, and the scope of control will be wonderfully increased.

The third degree of undulations must be used at all times unless there is the minor or sad side to be portrayed, in which case the fifth degree should be used, but never the higher degrees, for they are theatrical. This is one of the great differences between the actor and the man of personal power; the former must move by claptrap, the latter by the subtle art.

The rule then is that the sadder, gloomier colors are to be set in the fifth degree undulations; that all other colors are to be set in the third degree; except that those representing impetuous energy are to be set in the fourth degree.

An actor would master all the degrees as a mere method of attaining a flexible voice. To him it would be a source of pleasant practice to become adept in the ten degrees of undulations.

As the practice, even if nothing more than mechanical, is sure to make the voice flexible, rich, expressive, easily colored and full of attractive quality, there is every reason why the time should be taken for the development of these ten degrees to a nicety. Let the description given in preceding chapters be read and fully understood, and all the suggestions adopted with a determination to show an artistic temperament in acquiring each degree of the undulations.

We urge this because we wish to know that you have become successful in the art of transmigration, or throwing yourself into another person; and success is sure to attend a careful development of these degrees.

PROCESS OF TRANSMIGRATION.

With the basis established in the most perfect manner, as already set forth, the process of throwing your own self into the personality of another is as follows:

1. All thoughts, feelings, plans, purposes, intents and methods of one mind or nature, that are directed toward another individual, must employ magnetic waves.

2. Magnetic waves travel with the same speed as light, but penetrate any substance no matter how solid or thick it may be.

3. The fifth degree undulations coincide with the magnetic waves in the minor moods, or those that are akin to the darker side of life.

4. The third degree undulations coincide with the magnetic waves in the positive moods or those that are on the vital side of life.

5. The fourth degree undulations coincide with the magnetic waves in all the impetuous moods, or those that are stronger than the commonplace conditions of life.

6. When one person feels a mood that is not felt at the same time by another person, the waves of magnetism will not convey impressions from either of such persons to the other.

7. When one person is able to assume the mood that is felt by another person, if that mood is the master of the latter, the former person will be master over that mood in the latter person to the same extent that he is master over it in himself.

8. As humanity is swayed in practically all matters by moods and feelings, the mastery of these influences is equal to the mastery of the individuals themselves.

"What is the explanation of your wonderful control over your husband?" asked one wife of another.

"I first find out what mood he is in, and I favor it."

"Well, I oppose my husband when he is not in the mood that he ought to be, and I have no control whatever over him."

When two persons are in the same mood under control, and not controlling such mood, both are without power to influence the other.

This fact is seen illustrated in the case of two men who are angry at each other, or who are both angry at some third person; although, in the latter case, one is less likely to be mastered by that mood. The following experiment is one of hundreds that have been successfully made where irascibility was to be overcome. We cite one instance only, but it is sufficient to make the idea clear to you.

A man who could not control his anger when aroused by the stupidity of any one of his employees, had in his office a clerk who had submitted mildly to abuse. This clerk caught the idea that there was a cure for the trouble, and took up the study of acting for the one purpose of learning to portray anger. He selected the parts of the noted characters of the drama where irascibility was feigned, and then came down to the diction of his employer. The next time the latter flew into a passion the clerk also did the same, not crossing the employer, but aiming his shafts of abuse against some mild-tempered employee who had not given offence. The employer stopped, listened, then burst into a fit of laughter. This ruse was continued for several weeks, on an average of twice a week until the employer was nearly cured. He soon learned that, whenever he got angry, he might expect this clerk to fly in a passion soon after, and the peculiar connection between the two events struck him as ludicrous in the highest degree.

In another case a wife who found her husband growing more and more morose over his affairs, adopted the practice of showing the same mood over hers, as soon as he would start in on his.

In these cases the party using the moods is always making them servants of the will, and not submitting to their tyranny.

A use of this art, which is most familiar to the public mind, is the disposition of the wife to cure her husband by adopting the same tactics that he employs. Here is a husband who flirts with women, and the wife is jealous. She pretends to flirt with men. If she does so in fact, the home may soon be broken up. But she has control of her feelings and wishes simply to torture her husband in the same way that he has made her suffer; so she carries on some pretence of flirtation in a way that he cannot help noticing it. The more he investigates it for the purpose of making a case against her, the less evidence he finds; but the awful fact that she may be untrue to him is rankling in his bosom. He may be one of those men who intend to go to the bad on learning of the actual unfaithfulness of the wife; but this fact never looms up. The result of this campaign is the cure of the husband unless the wife lacks some other quality, or overdoes the ruse.

It is not improbable that this kind of acting has been tried a million times in this country or in any country in the past twenty years, and that it is adopted by mere intuition.

There is hardly any fault that cannot be cured if the proper method is adopted under these laws.

Even so common a mood as that of flippancy is easily cured by some companion who adopts it as an assumed color. This is not at all difficult, as flippancy is a common trait of today. As an illustration of this method of cure we cite the following incident:

A young lady was indulging in a series of fresh or flippant remarks, in her walk one evening with a young man who had loftier ideas, and did not relish her treatment of every subject that he took up. He was trying to approach a favorable opportunity for proposing, and she had an instinctive feeling that such was the case.

"I enjoy such an evening as this," he said.

"It is a jolly nice night for mosquitos," was the reply.

Later on he said something like this: "How fragrant the air is!"

And her reply was: "I guess somebody has spilled something."

He could not stand it any longer and so took up her style of conversation; but not in a vexed tone that showed that he was slave of some mood; for he knew that this would lead to a lack of cordiality between them. He simply assumed the color and method.

"I see where they spilled it," he said after looking along the ground for a moment.

"Spilled what?" she asked in surprise.

"Why, that fragrance."

She burst into laughter, and both had a better understanding of each other from that time.

It is recorded of a queen who had a spendthrift husband, that she made a great show of wasting money and property, until he came to his senses and was cured of the fault, although she had not in fact wasted anything in the ruse.

There were two sisters who were in the habit of quarreling on slight pretexts. It seemed that the elder lost her calmness on the least provocation and would give way to a spell of excitement which annoyed the other. The latter feigned the same mood of excitement at each subsequent incident, and the elder sister soon discovered, as she thought, that her own conduct was unbalancing the mind of her younger sister. The cure was complete.

There was a young man of about sixteen summers whose father had developed the habit of swearing at home. The mother and the son agreed together to effect a cure, after the best efforts at suasion had failed. One evening, when the minister and some friends of high standing were present, the son met with an accident purposely planned in the next room, and uttered in one volley all the profanity which was included in his father's vocabulary. The father heard it, and rushed from the room to see why his son should thus disgrace the occasion. The latter gave as an excuse that he had hurt himself, and that what he said came from him so suddenly that he could not help it.

"It is your own language, father."

The father never again allowed himself to use profane language either alone or in the presence of others. He saw the effect that it might produce in the life of a loved boy.

There are men who have stopped the habit of going into saloons on finding that their sons were forming the same habit.

If you flatter the flatterer you will soon cure him, provided your offence is as frequent as his. We know of a number of these people who realize that it is not wise to use flattery in the presence of certain persons who have taught them this lesson.

Threaten the threatener, is the advice given in Shakespeare; and it has been good advice ever since the world had human beings on it. This law is so universal that the animal kingdom takes it up, and makes it the basis of all society between the fighting species. The tiger and the lion rarely come together in conflict, as they know the aggressive nature of each. One wild animal fears another wild animal for the reason that they know the danger in approach.

In ten thousand women, and in ten thousand men as well, there are not ten who are free from some past errors or episodes that are best left unmentioned. Many enemies have been silenced by the threat to expose them, and nights and days of unrest and worry have followed the warning. There is today, in the city of Washington, a clergyman whose past career is known to a few, and possibly to one person only, who would probably go insane if the merest suggestion or hint were made that publicity would be given to it.

Several New York editors of the sensation-sheets of that city, have learned this phase of human nature, and work upon the motto that most men have something they wish to keep from the public; and the hint from a reporter that that scandal will be printed, is sufficient. It is not necessary to state what the scandal is. The man who is thus warned will begin to think and ponder, and recall everything that might come to light, finally hitting upon something that he believes is known to the paper, while the editor may not have the slightest knowledge of any scandal.

But the use to which this law may be put is not to levy blackmail, as that adds a crime to a sin. The individual who improperly seeks to intimidate, may be overcome by a quick and effective aggression, either in warning or threatening; and this is a proper use of the law.

A member of a family who worries, is easily cured of the fault by the assumption of the same habit, provided it is not based upon a genuine cause. The subject of the worry must be something that is wholly foolish and that seems so on its face to the other, while the imitation must seem to be genuine suffering. This allows a side view of the lack of sense displayed in worrying, and causes a re-action in the real worrier.

Thousands of cases of the use of this power will come to you during the next few years, if you are observant of the conduct of others. Many principles are recognized by the careful student of human nature, that would otherwise be lost. Much is going on all about you that escapes your attention because you do not know how to analyze the doings of men and women.

The remarkable fact is this: After you have become an adept in the use of this power, and are able to recognize in the conduct of others their purpose and intentions towards you or themselves, you will say that this has always been going on but that you have never recognized it. You will think, "How easy!" as you carry on the analysis of humanity.

To one who has not yet practiced the training that leads up to the use of these laws, the thought will come that it is not possible for every person to acquire the power; that it is a gift with some and is denied others. This is not true. It is within reach of every man and woman who is not abjectly lazy.

Let us review the main facts as a means of ready reference.

In the first place transmigration is the power of stepping into the personality of another individual. This has not yet been fully taught in this volume, but will be carried on to completion in the next few chapters. We have partly covered the ground, and the training has been thoroughly given as far as it has gone.

In the second place the means of stepping into the personality of another individual is acquired by using the only channel by which magnetism travels, the ether waves.

In the third place the ether waves are used only through the undulations of the human voice; for these, while much larger than ether waves, are of such a character that they coincide with them.

It is one of the easiest processes known to any branch of training to acquire the several degrees of undulations; no person need fail, and very few do. So readily are they employed that it would seem a disgrace to not succeed in mastering them.

In the fourth place the acquisition of intensity is easily

attained by any one who is in earnest. This power is necessary in order to give vitality to the carrying power of the feelings, and it exists not only in the voice, but also in the whole nervous system, and finds use in every sense. It quickens each sense and seems to give them all renewed energy and youth.

In the fifth place the moods and feelings are the only means of expressing human life. Every person is at all times, sleeping or waking, in one or more of the moods. Analyze them and ascertain if this is not true. Being true, they are life itself and humanity itself; therefore they are the only avenues of passage from one self to another self.

In the sixth place, the moods and feelings, being the personality, are capable of development to their full nature. They are so readily transferable that the art of acting has been the foremost art of the past five thousand years. In the greatest days of ancient Greece and Rome, there were but two forms of education: Acting and philosophy. The tendency to the drama is due to the fact that there are moods and feelings and that they are capable of being transferred from the genuine to the simulated form.

In the seventh place there has never been a successful man and woman on earth who has not depended on personal magnetism as the means and method of winning success. Call it by any other name you will, the cause is within our definition of personal magnetism.

In the eighth place there has never been a magnetic person who has not been master of all the magnetic undulations of the voice. You may study humanity for the next fifty years and analyze all who come before you, and you will never find one exception to this statement.

In the ninth place there has never been a magnetic person who has not been master of intensity. This fact is as readily provable as any fact in the universe.

In the tenth place there has never been a magnetic person who has not been able to simulate a number of the moods and feelings. The cases cited in this chapter are a few of the most common, and are introduced for the purpose of showing our students how much of this law is in actual use at all times. People who have used it have been their own trainers in most cases; and the idea of using it has occurred to them as the result of common sense thinking.

The practical and the commonplace side only has been put before you, as we do not wish to lead you to depths where you must drown if you are not equipped with the means of baffling the sea in the lesser depths. What ought now to be done is to close this book, and not read another word until you are positive that you have given the proper amount of time to the training up to this stage. Or, better still, if we could hold back the next few lessons until we were assured that you had mastered the work up to this juncture, we could then guarantee your full success clear through to the end. But, at the beginning of this book, we had you make a test of your ability to master yourself, and we feel certain that the greater majority of our students will be able to hold back as an act of the will until the lessons may be thoroughly worked out as stated.

If you do this, you will succeed in the greater things that are to follow. If you do not choose to obey the suggestion, or if you lack the power to do so, then you will fail and will of course charge it to the inadequacy of this course rather than to your own weakness.

CHAPTER SIXTEEN

+++++++++++++++++++++++++++++++++++

MAGNETISM
REACHES INTO
THE THOUGHTS
OF OTHERS

+++

♣ TELEPATHIC MAGNETISM ♣

+++

TILL PURSUING the study and adoption of transmigration, we come into its advanced steps one by one. There is yet much to be considered, and the main purpose in view should be to keep the training within the reach of every student. A line of instruction that is to be adopted only by a successful few after years of the hardest kind of plodding, is not practicable. It is possible to make this very course at the present stage such a difficult matter that the fruition will be far away and evanescent.

This undesirable end might be brought about by carelessness in the arrangement, and without any intention to make them obscure.

We desire the opposite result.

We realize that the work is not the easiest on the side of patience, but the most tiresome part has been gone over. What is ahead from this place will be much more interesting and more readily adopted, provided there has been a thoroughness in the past lessons.

Telepathic magnetism is a mental form of transmigration, and is an important and a necessary part of the advance in the progress of this study. The next step beyond this will be a nervous form of transmigration, and a most logical one also.

It has been discovered that, when a person is able to master

128

any mood or feeling, and to simulate it with perfect portrayal, any person who is a slave to the same mood or feeling will be unable to conceal such condition from the other person. This is the whole law in a nutshell. There is a disadvantage connected with this method, and it lies in the fact that, when an individual has mastered but one or two or a very few of the moods and feelings he is super-sensitive to the moods and feelings of others that coincide with those he has acquired. It is this super-sensitiveness that make actors take kindly to all opposites in their work; that is, they welcome and quickly enter into the practice of such moods as are directly different from those they have been hard at work upon. This seems to sustain the view that actors have but a very few real moods under control. If they were to master a large number their super-sensitiveness would pass away.

Normal sensitiveness is necessary, and this is acquired only when a large number of the moods and feelings are mastered. We advise you to maintain the practice until all are conquered. These ideas are not new in our work. For more than a generation we have taught them to classes with success. We have seen pupils whose voices were dead and whose powers of control over others were at zero, come out bright and powerful through this line of training. We have seen them acquire the needed colors in one hundred emotions, and as many in mental versatility; the result being a complete change in manner and gifts. It is our candid belief that there is no other kind of training that can make a man or woman practically successful.

The difference between super-sensitiveness and normal sensitiveness should be understood. The former will haunt and trouble you, and become a positive nuisance as well as injury in your life; while the latter will be helpful in many ways.

One of the reasons why persons become nervous and take on the habit of worrying, is the fact that they have one or two or a few only of the moods developed as habits, always from the bad lists or groups, and they respond to the feelings of others against the will of both perhaps, but surely against their own will. This is telepathic coloring, but not magnetism. Nothing can be regarded as magnetism unless there is control over the mood by the individual, and not the reverse.

Telepathic coloring, then, is the forcing into your own nervous system of the troubles or moods of other people. Sometimes they are of the better class, in which case the results are positively beneficial. As there are many people in every part of the civilized world who have made themselves keenly desirous of attaining certain qualities in life, some powerful person is able from any distance to reach them by the right kind of energy in the use of magnetic waves.

This is called telepathic magnetism because it involves the reception of right moods, even though they are few in number. A right mood uplifts a person, no matter how limited it may be.

Charles Spurgeon was so magnetic and had such an impetuous control of the fourth degree of undulations that he could send out influences in any mood at will and reach thousands of persons who were in a condition of nervous sensitiveness. His greatest mood-use was that of generosity, and he reached hundreds of thousands of people by the intensity of his magnetism. To him it made little difference whether the people to be reached were present where they could hear his voice or not.

Any man or woman who has mastered any mood so as to be able to portray it in perfect color, can wield a wide influence over almost any other person who has become receptive in that mood. But this subject will be considered under the head of distant control later on in this book.

Telepathic coloring is now to be discussed. This properly relates to super-sensitiveness in the receiving of the bad moods. It is due to a perfect development of the color of such moods in small number only, and the inability to throw off the influence that some person is unconsciously sending toward a person. A few instances of this law will be given here.

A clergyman was unable to sleep at night, but had no trouble in getting sleep by day. In order to save his mind from breaking down he changed his habits on all week days, and got along nicely for a while. He sought the solution of the peculiar condition and the case reached us. In reply to inquiries, he stated that he felt a strong power hanging over him; that he had been in the habit of retiring at about ten o'clock every night; that soon after he got in bed this peculiar power impressed him with such a weight of feeling that he felt like getting out of bed and looking all through the room, in the closet and everywhere for some fiend that was lurking near.

We at once assumed that he had an enemy, and that this

enemy was engaged in some work of revenge. To test the matter we met him by day, at a time when he was perfectly free from the weight of feeling, and we then recited in the color of revenge a strange incident that embodied the meeting of enemies to plan and work out a campaign of malice. As we entered upon the color, using no art greater than that common to the direct and simple form of stage portrayal, this man began to shake and cold drops of perspiration stood over his face and neck.

"This is the same feeling that I have at night," he said.

"You have been torturing your mind with the fear of revenge from some enemy," we asserted.

"Not for the past twenty years," was the reply. He said that at that time he had taken an active part against a gang of gamblers who were leading young men and boys astray, and they retaliated by threatening to burn his house at night. He was so full of the idea of this revenge that his nervous system had become sensitive to it. A color, once acquired, will stay with a person till death. So he had carried the susceptibility to the color of revenge all these twenty years. But he knew of no enemies that he now had, and the peculiar weight of feeling at night was inexplicable.

With this much as a basis, the next step was to find the source of the trouble; for we were satisfied that it was due to the night conspiracy of enemies. But he knew of no one who had a malice intent toward him. Perhaps some old enemy had come within his locality and wished to square accounts. Even then he could not name one. The peculiar feeling came on at about ten o'clock every night and abided with him for an hour or more, after which he could not get asleep, although the weight grew less. When once the regular time for falling asleep has been passed, it is not easy to fall into slumber. The terror of the sensation was of itself enough to keep him thinking for hours. He had laid it to the possibility of losing his mind, and thought that this might be the fore-runner of that malady. But in this he was mistaken; although many a misled man or woman has allowed such a condition to run on for months or longer, and then have actually succumbed to the tyranny of the haunting spirit ending in insanity. We believe that most forms of insanity can be averted by mastering all the moods and feelings and making their colors perfect in rendition.

Taking as a clue the fact that the hour of ten at night was the time of beginning the weight of oppression, the suggestion arose that perhaps some man or woman who had leisure at that time, might be at work upon a conspiracy to harm the clergyman. A hunt was made for all persons who might be thus free at that hour. This did not avail anything. Then a detective was employed to watch the house of the minister to see if any persons were hanging about. This did not bring results. The next suggestion was to walk the streets to see what men were out at that hour. In the course of a few nights the detective reported that a saloon-keeper was in the habit of going from his place of business to a small house where he was met by another man, who was afterwards known to be proprietor of another saloon. Soon after ten o'clock a third party entered the same place, and there they remained for one or two hours. This they did every night for about two weeks, when the watch was shifted. The meeting seemed to correspond with the conditions described, but the detective declared that there was no connection between the clergyman's mental depression at night and the secret meeting of these three men.

The next step was to get at the third man. This was done by the detective under our advice. We also told him to make a bold move by declaring to the third man that we knew that he was hired or to be hired by two saloon-keepers, naming them, to do injury to the clergyman, naming him. This was a decided position to take, and the detective demurred because he saw no connection between the parts of the claim. It was, as he thought, sheer guess work to connect the meeting of the two saloon-keepers and the third man, with the supposed revenge on the clergyman. The third man, however, was told all these things; and, to the surprise of the detective, he made one or two remarks that confirmed the latter's belief; then he became silent and refused to go further until other pressure was brought to bear upon him. The detective recalled some previous episode in the man's career, then connected him with it, and there was a hastening on the part of the old criminal to get under cover as the saying goes. He confessed that these two saloon-keepers were laboring under the belief that the clergyman was at the bottom of an attempt to prevent a renewal of their licenses; they had been told so not long before, and seemed to credit the statement; and, wishing to secure revenge, they had been at work upon some method to reach this end. But their meeting was not for that purpose; the plotting was incidental only. They had met for an entirely different purpose, as they were political heelers and had to make plans for the coming campaign. It was, however, at some of these meetings that they had conspired to do harm to the clergyman, but there were nights when that matter was hardly broached.

"What shall I do?" asked the clergyman. "Shall I have the gang cleaned out, or punished, or notified that I have had nothing to do with the matter of the license?"

"You make their fears warranted, and we will guarantee that they will not do you harm," was the reply we gave him. He did not seem to have enough confidence in himself to carry on an aggressive policy against them; but he overcame that weakness and took up the matter with zeal and vigor. The saloon-keepers actually planned the murder of the man. The third party, an ex-criminal, was made to act the tool of the conspirators under the threat that, if he played false to our party, he would be given a punishment that he most dreaded. A fourth man was brought in to help him, and he was kept in the dark as to the treachery of the third party. A final meeting was planned at a place where three officers were in hiding, and the conspirators were all bagged. The third man was set free after the others had been convicted in court. More than this the discovery that another planned murder had been carried through, put the saloon-keepers where they will remain for life.

If an aggressive policy had not been adopted by the clergyman he could never have freed himself from the haunting fear of the revenge that had so oppressed him.

In another case that came to our knowledge, that of a wealthy woman who had terrible loads of lurking fear hanging down upon her soul, as she expressed it, we found that her mood was that of melancholy. It came on at about nine o'clock at night. We found that we could bring on that mood in her by simulating in the day time the color of melancholy, and she responded to it at any time when we made the experiment. The information was given her that some person was suffering from melancholy and that they were most seized with it at the hour of the evening when she found the weight over her mind the greatest.

As a basis for her super-sensitiveness, it was learned that she had been subjected years before to the same feeling, and it had grown into a habit then, but had since entirely left her. It was natural to conclude that some person now connected her with his or her ill fortune, and this was the theory on which the investigation proceeded. Why the mood should come over her at about nine o'clock every evening was the most peculiar part of the mystery.

The first search was made among her relatives, but there were none within a thousand miles. She had a sister who was the mother of six children, and the family was wretchedly poor. The husband had struggled against odds for many years and had finally died. His life insurance yielded a temporary fund, but this had gone. The widow was too proud to write to her wealthy sister telling her the circumstances; but every evening at eight o'clock she and her children had family prayers, and each prayed that the heart of the well-to-do sister might be touched. This was followed by a period of thought, ending in melancholy and depression.

The woman whose nervous system had been so weighted down by the same mood years before, was influenced by a family more than a thousand miles away. It was not during the prayer period which lasted only a few minutes, so much as in the after moments each evening that this influence was set up. It may be argued that it was the result of prayer. Spurgeon so declared; but, admitting such to be the case, it only goes to prove that prayer employs natural processes for attaining its ends, and that the Creator has set up these laws as a means of carrying on His plans and purposes of dealing with humanity. We have never believed that there is a supernatural, although it is often referred to as such when the open laws of nature are not in evidence   God may create and employ these methods of carrying on every kind of work and conveying every kind of influence, and this fact would only seem to draw us closer to Him. The feeling that He is far away and that we are separated from Him by a gulf so wide as not to be passable, keeps many away from the full realm of faith. This is not as it should be.

In the case referred to, the wealthy relative had the family brought East and the children put to school as they grew up. She saw to it that there was no more suffering. The weight of fear passed away as soon as she knew the cause and had resolved to remedy it.

That such influences are not always connected with prayer, is shown in the following case:

A man on every Saturday afternoon was seized with a fit of jealousy involving his wife. At all other times he was free from the feeling. It had been his custom to spend that afternoon away, and his wife had likewise been left to herself. He had once before had the mood come down upon him, but not in relation to this woman. Years had passed, and he had outgrown it as unmanly. When the mood would envelop him now he became so restless that he determined to follow his wife and see if there was cause for the jealousy.

In his quiet pursuits which were carried on in disguise, he at length came upon the wife and found that she was engaged in the same enterprise, having been told that he was not faithful to her, and seeking to ascertain the facts for herself. In the conversation that followed she confessed to having had the feeling of jealousy for several weeks, but had kept quiet in the matter until she could decide what was best to do. No person was taken into her confidence, and she was free to manage the affair as she deemed best. This proved to him that the initiative was taken by her and that his mood was a reflection of hers, not hers of his.

The greatest generals on the battlefield are those who have had this power of magnetic telepathy. Instances are cited of both Grant and Lee in the use of such power, and the subsequent success attained by its aid.

It seems that the training schools that turn out military men seek to develop in them the keenest sensibility to such moods as fear, apprehension, threatening, warning, deceit, falsehood, craftiness, stealth and kindred influences, most of which are taught under the name of strategy.

Generals are sometimes Christian gentlemen, but they are as quick to make use of any of the hell-born influences as of any other, on the plea that war is hell, and the use of a weapon of the devil may shorten the war and save other lives. Thus murder is called killing, and no nation punishes its men-killers. Deceit is the one chief element in the mental campaign, and craftiness determines the ability of the greatest generals.

If a man is to succeed at the head of a mass of men in war he must be sensitive in the highest degree to these moods. Grant was never known to fail in his guess of what the enemy would attempt, and Lee had the same keenness, probably in greater fineness. All the foremost generals of the world in the many wars that have served to develop these powers, have been thus gifted. It has long been said that a successful general must be born with the gift of war, whatever that means. Napoleon never failed to guess the purposes and plans and deceits of his enemies. He could map out all their possible moves, but he always made his first plan in accordance with the chief estimate he placed upon his foes. In his mind he could see the Russians marching day by day along certain roads, reaching certain places each night, camping there and starting the following mornings to resume their journey; and he saw the Austrians in their forward movements; he knew at what point they would join the Russians; and this gave him the ability to overwhelm each army in turn before their combined forces could swoop down upon him.

But in the intricate maneuvers of battle he saw each turn and shifting of both armies, and told his generals what to expect, as well as what to be prepared for.

Magnetic telepathy has been used for centuries, and probably since the world began to be populated. It is based on the law of moods. Grant tells this story of himself: In a campaign against Lee he had made plans for a certain movement in surprise of the foe. After he had perfected the details, he and his generals retired for sleep until about four o'clock the next morning. He could not sleep. It was eleven o'clock when he retired in his tent. He at once got up and sat down before a fire that had died into embers and thought for a full hour. Suddenly he exclaimed to the guard, "Call my staff. Don't lose a minute." They came in looking bewildered. "Lee has taken the initiative. He is on the move," said Grant.

"How do you know, General?" was the inquiry.

"They have not been to bed. They have been at work with the map and a blow will be struck before we get up. A battle is close at hand. Have every one ready."

That was all; but the feeling was confirmed. The battle did come on and Grant was not surprised. The key to the discovery was the period of reticence that followed his retiring that night. He felt that his enemy was at work and wide awake.

No general would be a safe leader who followed solely his own feelings, unless he knew them from past experience; nor would any general succeed who was dead to such influences or who could not interpret them.

It seems that success and greatness are born with these developing moods, and they become a source of immense responsibility. To carry them all requires broad shoulders and wonderful courage. The first phase of their development is in the information they seek to convey to their possessor; and the second phase is in learning how to interpret them.

In true magnetic telepathy words are absent. Moods and feelings existed long before words were coined or spoken. The child knows as much as the adult, but his little vocabulary must come out year by year, and it develops only by contact with earthly experiences. His mind is incoherent if his experiences are such; his physical activity is likewise incoherent under the same conditions; and he passes for a fool or an imbecile because he lacks the power to express himself in words and action. Yet we all know that the wisest sayings have fallen from the lips of fools and jesters.

In sizing up the brain and gifts of a human being we must not link past human experience with a standard that has not been attained; for the former is the measure of both mind and action, either in the individual, or his ancestry.

Back of the child's undeveloped brain, back of the mind of the idiot, is the genuine being, the personality that knows no words and no diction. What that is may be far different from what the estimate may be of the individual.

This much is known to a certainty, that magnetic telepathy knows no words. "What am I thinking? What words are passing through my mind at this moment?" are questions that cannot be answered; but the mood and feeling can be interpreted to a certainty by any person who has developed the power of feeling such moods and feelings in their own past.

It has been stated that generals who are trained in strategy at schools organized for that purpose are quick to detect the same kind of strategy, deceit or whatever it is known by; and this keenness becomes a gift of the most extraordinary character. But it is rare to find one of these great generals who is a good business man or a good administrative officer. Grant failed in both. Napoleon was a wonderful architect, a superb jurist, and a poor administrative officer and poorer business man. In his domestic relations he had neither judgment nor wisdom of policy. In times of peace he was always out of his element, and fate forced him to encourage war in order to give him control over his followers.

This shows that the limited power of detecting and interpreting the moods of others makes life one-sided and unsuccessful except in its narrow scope. The dismal weakness of Grant after he ceased to be a fighting general was evinced in his two terms as President, and in his business career afterwards. The reason is in the fact that a President deals in words, and a business man deals in words; the real success of either avocation depending on skill and wisdom in such use, as the basis, and of course upon the magnetic faculties as aids. The general who wins his battles is almost always reticent, except to advise or to be advised. Grant was noted for his laconic speech and his want of words. Napoleon was likewise a man of few words, and Wellington, the Iron Duke, was given to the same habit. Lee had very little to say when a battle was being planned or fought. The necessity for reticence is due to the fact that the language of moods and feelings tells the full story, while the language of words and sentences has nothing to do with the art of successful war.

In an avocation where words are the vehicle of communication, as in most of the professions, also in political life and in statesmanship, the winner must know how to couple moods and feelings with the language of speech. But he labors under the difficulty of having to use speech as a collection of words, and moods and feelings as aids to such words, but not as interpreters of them. It is useless to define fear, or apprehension, or any of the seventy-six moods which we have set forth; for they have no synonyms in any language on earth. Each has shades of feelings and divisions of themselves, and so they make up a most intricate vocabulary which the magnetic individual soon comes to know by heart in its full measure. But he cannot put them in words. He does in fact build language about them and makes them felt by those with whom he comes in contact, but they still exist in his own mind and heart as separate conditions.

The general in war has need of only the moods we have named; and, in proportion as he has developed them in advance of his military career, he will be able to make use of them in his profession. When the war is over he is helpless until he develops power in new directions. This has always been the history of great warriors, and always will be to the end of time.

Moods peculiar to a business or profession are developed to keenness as experience sharpens the wits; and the man or woman who is not all the time making such moods deeper and more useful is falling behind in the race. It is for this reason that some people stand still while others go forward in life. The salesman, especially one that travels and has to create his clientele, or hold his trade against odds, has much greater need of this keenness of moods and feelings. He steps into a place of business and says nothing until he sizes up his man. He takes in the full situation at a glance; or, after a few inquiries or remarks, knows the mood his customer is in. In some cases he changes the moods to suit his own purposes; in other cases he goes away and returns, offering some excuse that makes such delay seem advisable to both parties.

But the drummer who, in this age of mental acuteness, depends on argument will not win from his best fields of operation. Argument is very little employed in the higher grades of trading acumen. It has its part to perform in the whole transaction, but the convincing part of the business is in the personality of the drummer. This fact has been demonstrated countless thousands of times. One man may come along with the best argument, and sell nothing; another may come along with bits of an argument and secure a large order. It is a common occurrence to hear a merchant say: "I like to do business with that man." Another will say, "This drummer always rubs me the wrong way; that man seems to agree with me." This is the secret of stepping into the moods and feelings of the person with whom you are talking.

The commonest use of this power is to study the mental and nervous phases of the other party; to know in advance what are the moods in which a man or woman may be found; and then interpret them from outward signs.

The practice of this art makes one keener the more it is indulged in. It should be increased until it is as much a habit in your life as it is in the careers of great men and women. There is a satisfaction in knowing that each interpretation you have made has been correct. To look a person in the face, or to stare in studying another, is wrong, as it often irritates and leads to the belief that you are impertinent. The more successful observers of human nature never spend much time in the searching glance.

The eyes can be trained to catch forms and expressions at a side look. This was the power of the Indian, to see three-quarters of a circle without moving the head. It depends almost solely on practice. The eyes need not be brought to a focus in order to see what is on the face of another person. A movement of the eyes, quick and unnoticed, may take in the refractions on either side, and the astonished friend may wonder how you have been able to see so far around. We have a relative who has a habit of walking behind us, and of moving his fingers in his collar. Not wishing to offend by criticism, we simply turn about quickly when the hand is raised to the neck. A few repetitions of this movement sufficed to effect a cure of the habit, and still he wonders how it was possible to see so far about.

To see and not be seen looking, or to appear not to have seen, is an advantage; for it enables one to study another when the latter has no suspicion of being observed. The eyes catch looks of dislike on the face or certain movements of the features that leads to the moods within, but not through magnetic waves.

WHAT THE EYES MAY DISCOVER.

The eyes may learn on which side of the range the moods are tending, by construing a few of the incidents of human nature.

The corners of the mouth show this tendency to perfection. Each person has a normal carriage of the lips; based upon fixed native characteristics, or acquired habitual personality. This normal is the average height of the corners of the mouth in a man of the balance of George Washington, or Speaker Randall, this average is what is known as the level mouth. It is likewise seen in the faces of actors who play many kinds of parts. No great actor or actress has any other normal or average mouth-position, as their photographs will show.

This shifting of the carriage of the mouth is a most notable fact. If you will take the trouble to look up the portraits of these people when they were in their teens, or before they took up the profession of acting, you will find thick lips in nine out of ten, and also a downward drooping of the lips if they are born for heavy or all round parts; and a rising carriage of the corners of the mouth if they are born for comedy parts.

Out of three hundred actors and actresses whose portraits were obtainable when in their teens, as most of them have been, we were able to select with certainty all who were destined to become comedians and all who were destined to become heavy acting people. It is a common fact that the face of the miss or the youth does not coincide with the face of the same individual as an adult; so that old photographs of the years preceding the adoption of the profession do not lead to the identity of the future personage.

As an example of this law, we commented on the face of the younger Sothern, when he was a comedian; it being clear that he was built along the lines of heavy acting, for the corners of his mouth in his youthful pictures show the downward carriage. At the time of this comment, we were told that we were wrong, as Sothern was a successful comedian. Since then he has dropped comedy, has played Hamlet, the Proud Prince and similar heavy rôles.

The face of Stuart Robson in his youth was that of the reverse character, all the pictures revealing the uplifted corners at the mouth; and his after attempts to play heavy rôles were not successful.

But the fact most worthy of attention is the change that comes over the face after the study and practice of acting has been going on for some years. Most faces in their teens show the down position of the corners of the mouth; and these very faces gradually lift the corners to an average level position as the years go by. In the three hundred cases to which we have referred, there has not been one exception to the statement, and the privilege of observing this rule is open to all persons who have books or sketches of these men and women, where the pictures of their younger days are to be seen. The down corners are brought to a level in all cases where the profession has given them a variety of characters to play; and the raised corners are lowered to a level under similar influences. The mouth of Henry Irving, of Ellen Terry, of Booth, of the two Barretts, of Salvini, of Mary Anderson, of Otis Skinner, and of all those men and women who have had many years of experience along varied lines of rendition, are pictured in their photographs representing them out of their characters, as level.

The peculiar straightness of the mouth of George Washington at once attracts attention. He was not only a warrior, but a surveyor, a student, a statesman, a farmer and an all-round lover of life. Napoleon never showed the level position of the mouth, although the depression was slight.

In the temporary fugitive moods all joy and bright feelings raise the corners of the mouth. A glance of the eye will tell you how this is when you meet another person. If the corners of the mouths are depressed, they come so either from past habits, which you can discern in a minute or two, by the range of movement; or else they are positive evidences of dislike which is possibly to be aimed at you.

If the corners of the mouth have already acquired the habit of falling, the act of raising them in any attempt to be polite or pleasant will not carry them above the level position.

A man who seeks as a wife a woman who has the habitual habit of depressed corners of the mouth, will find one who lives on the dark and discontented side of life. If, to this, she adds the contraction of the brow over the nose, she will be a scold and most disagreeable. The same rules apply to the man.

If the temporary mood is the cause of the lowering of the mouth, then you must throw your own mood into the dark side; for you will not wield an influence that opposes such a condition unless you do it by an appeal to the eternal selfishness of humanity. Positive good news, or some pleasing surprise, will waken the better condition because of the love of advantages. This appeals to selfishness. This method is about all that is now employed in advertising matter to get the attention of the reader. Something is offered free; you reply; you get something free that is worth what you pay for it, nothing; and perhaps no attempt is made to sell you anything; but your correspondence is turned over to another branch of the same concern that may be thousands of miles away; and then some one will seek to sell you something for money. The first appeal was to selfishness.

This is the king mood if the claims can be substantiated. If you can make the public believe that you are really desirous of selling a gold dollar for sixty-nine cents, you will find responses.

But the keen mind of the public is aware that this mood is to be played upon and worked, and so used have some people become to the proffer of something for nothing, that they cease to bite at the bait, except in bargains at the stores where trading is necessary at almost all times of the year. The bright business man or the superior woman is driven farther away by an attempt to play upon the mood of selfishness.

We make these remarks, as we would advise you to be on the lookout for such methods under some other guise. The shot is generally a double-barreled one; the other party has some advantage to secure and seeks to influence you by proffering you an advantage of some kind as the entering wedge of the transaction.

Next to this worn out mood, the use of flattery is now becoming the most common. It has been the weapon of the ill-disposed for thousands of years, and always will prove useful. Few persons are really exempt from this power. There is not one man or woman in ten thousand who is not susceptible to the good opinions of others, and this is both natural and wholesome. A peculiar characteristic of flattery is the fact that the smaller the mind the less power is achieved by employing praise, whether merited or not; and the greater the mind the more power is wielded by flattering it, provided it takes hold at all.

If you praise unduly a small mind, the party will either look pleased or will resent it. If it is pleased, it will be depressed if, at any time in the future, you omit the praise; and if, on the other hand, after once giving the praise, you censure, you will awaken all the vicious nature in the person. Some of the most malicious acts of harm, including even poisoning, have grown out of censure after excessive praise of a small mind. It is well established that the lower grade of servants and employees should not be praised. Let some acts of quiet appreciation be substituted. The more you separate your personality from that of such a mind, the more influence you will wield.

As a person advances in the world so as to become conspicuous in the public eye, whether in the narrow circle of a small acquaintance, or in the broader glare of fame, there is a desire to know what the people have to say; and the declaration of personal friends that flattery is obnoxious is not to be believed. The very nature of the position occupied is warrant for the love of praise and compliments. The woman in the drawing room, the lawyer who has tried a case, the preacher who has delivered his sermon, the statesman who has introduced a bill, all are open to the wiles of this mood.

We recall the case of a poor young man, about twenty years of age, who found himself coming to the end of his means, and who placed all his hopes of getting up out of his lowly rank by the use of this one mood. He had intuitive sense, and this is what he did and did not say: He went to a United States Senator, and did not say "Your friend Senator ———— told me to come to you. He said that you were very busy and that you nevertheless had time to help all young men, that you were most generous and philanthropic, etc." Had he said that the Senator would have seen the purpose of the talk and dismissed him as soon as he could; for this is a palpable effort to play upon the feelings of a man who is too old to be mis-led by hints. Nor was it flattery. A senator is not flattered and certainly not pleased to be told that he is generous and philanthropic.

The young man knew this.

Any thoughtful person would have reasoned it out, had he taken time enough.

But what he did say is real flattery, and let us see why: "I am ambitious to show my people at home that I can make my way here in the city. I want to learn to talk well, and to teach and influence the people. I went to Senator ———— and he said he was no talker. He told me to come to you, for he said that you were regarded as the most successful debater and orator in the Senate, and that you would some day and very soon sweep the whole country with your popularity as a defender of the rights of the people."

"Did he say that? Well, well, I am surprised. He over-estimates me. Do you think he was in earnest?"

"I know he was. He put his hand on my shoulder and said to me, 'Young man, mark what I say, he is the most feared of debaters in the Senate, and he has the real power to sway the people.' "

"Well, I should be glad if I merited a tenth of his good opinion. Come back this afternoon, and I will see what I can do for you."

Not a word was true of what the young man had said; for the Senator was a conceited but weak speaker. He did not dare, however, to probe the other Senator to find out if he had made the remarks, for he did not see how the young man could have made up the story, as he would have no object in doing so.

But the incident proved the starting point in the career of this offender; who, having got in the good graces of the man, fed him on well-tuned flattery as long as it paid to do so. He is now a man of wealth and affluence, as well as possessing much political power.

We do not cite this case as a guide to those who wish to gain rank by lies; but to warn all people against submitting to the use of flattery.

Almost every society woman will favor another woman of intelligence who hangs about her with praise. A good opinion of the gown worn is the most effective of all weapons in this respect; and next in order is praise of the complexion; while the charming form brings up the third phase. Women also like to know that others look up to them in good opinions as to their wealth, and social influence. To be envied is also the goal of the existence of a large army of women in the upper class.

Now the indiscriminate use of praise is not flattery. Some women know the difference. To tell a bulky female that she has a graceful form, or a butcher-neck, that she is shaped from the shoulders to the cranium like a fawn, will not reach the mark; she knows it is a lie, and praise can never be passed current as flattery when the stolen chickens are peeping out of the crevices of the hat.

To drop the pleasing remark by accident, is more successful, provided there is a basis of truth for it. In the case of the Senator there was no basis in his mind for the assertion that he was generous and philanthropic, and he did not care if he was; but he believed that he could orate some, and this moved him because it touched the most tender spot in his professional anatomy.

To make the praise seem to come from another is more pleasing than to have it come from the speaker; and the higher the rank of the supposed flatterer, the more force the praise will carry. "I heard the Governor ask Mr. ——— if he had seen you lately, and he whispered that he wanted to see you, but did not wish to let you know it," was once worked off on a politician of wealth, who was swept off his feet by it. The person concocted the bit of flattery, but stood so low in the estimation of the politician that the latter would not have cared for the good opinion from such source; but the Governor, that was different! People believe what they want to believe, more readily than the opposite.

These two moods are used a great deal to shift the condition of the party who is found with the mouth drawn down. The selfish mood has had its day, and does not catch many, unless there is apparently no purpose in the talker telling something that is not so. Good news will revive a man in most instances.

Here is the way a drummer got a large order; using the selfish mood to shift a very disagreeable facial expression of his customer:

Before entering the private office, he talked with the head clerk, and ascertained that the proprietor was out of sorts because he had money tied up in stocks that were down. All the drummer now wanted to know was the name of the stocks. He then glanced at the paper, and noted the quotations of yesterday's market. In accosting the customer he started in this way, after a casual greeting:

"I am probably on my last trip, as I have saved up a few thousands and want to stay at home with my family, instead of going all over the country as a traveling man. My uncle is connected with the ———— and has advised me to buy heavily. He has inside information that the stock will rise thirty points in the next few weeks. I could not have found out in any other way, and might not have got the chance to invest. The bears have forced the price down to 69, in the hope that they could scare weak holders to unload. I suppose you never invest."

Had the corners of the mouth remained down the drummer would have needed further ammunition. He had enough knowledge of human nature to know that, as they rise, the customer was getting into another mood.

An all-round character possesses a level-shaped mouth, and this rule is always true the world over.

The character that carries the mouth-corners raised, is free from care or has just entered upon a specially pleasant mood.

The character that carries the corners of the mouth down can be influenced only by appeals to selfishness or by the use of flattery; unless the law of transmigration is employed under the method yet to be stated in this course; or the ALTER EGO is projected.

The level-mouthed character is the aggressive in the lines in which certain moods have been developed, and is not swayed in those lines; but must be approached through moods that are not included in the habits of that individual.

When once the corners of the mouth can be changed, though but a trifle, from the position in which you find them, you are on the road to securing influence.

Now counter laws come into play. The mouth has several positions, as follows.

One with the corners down.
One with the corners up.
One with the corners level.
One with the lips relaxed.
One with the lips firmly closed.
One with the mouth open.

As none of these can act alone they must appear in combination, and the nine positions in combination are as follows:

1. Corners up, firmly closed.   "Satisfaction."
2. Corners up, relaxed.   "Pleasure."
3. Corners up, mouth open.   "Laughter."
4. Corners down, firmly closed.   "Discontent."
5. Corners down, relaxed.   "Grief."
6. Corners down, mouth open.   "Horror."
7. Level mouth, firmly closed.   "Absolute control."
8. Level mouth, relaxed.   "Ease."
9. Level mouth, open.   "Astonishment."

These positions blend and cross, but their basis can always be detected; and the habit is soon formed of reading the face without attracting attention or taking your mind from other thoughts. In fact after a little practice in observation, it would be difficult not to read the face at a glance, so accustomed does the mind get to the position of the muscles.

The firm mouth is the most difficult of control, either in the combination with the level position, or with the corners up or down; but the level mouth occurring with the firmly closed lips is master of all moods. If you cannot change it in the party who sits before you, or in your dealings with others you will not succeed in making any headway toward securing influence over the individual.

HOW TO TELL OF CHANGES IN INFLUENCE.

It will be noticed that the mouth is firmly closed for satisfaction, discontent and absolute control; which means that the last named is the ruling position over all.

It will also be noted that the three main positions of corners up, corners down, and level mouth run a gamut or scale from the other positions of being firmly closed, relaxed or open.

It is in this gamut that you can tell what influence you are exerting over another person; for, in proportion as you are resisted or set at naught, the lips will remain firm in whatever other main position they may be. If you were able to assume absolute power over a person in the darker moods, or any one of them the mouth would take a wide open position and there would be abject fear or horror. Of this fact there is no doubt. A photograph of persons on a car when it was being robbed, showed this facial condition wherever the revolver was placed close to the head; and criminals read the faces of their victims in the same way, though by native instinct. Animals know very well the resistant and fearless face, and hesitate to attack until either horror or relaxation is depicted.

If you can assume absolute power over an individual whose face is on the bright side, and remains so, the result would be laughter, for that means uncontrol in that position.

If you could obtain absolute control over the level mouth, the result would be mere astonishment, and this is common; but it is seen as the wide open mouth of the ordinary carriage which results from the fixed habit. If it is the habit of a person to carry the corners down, not as a temporary mood, but at all times unless moved otherwise, then the mouth of astonishment would open from the position of the corners down, and would drift nearer to that of the level wide open mouth; and the same thing is true of the habitual carriage of the corners up. The tendency is towards the round mouth in any event.

Men and women who carry the mouth level, rarely ever give way to the open mouth; but it is possible to so influence them that they cannot refrain from the change.

If you are changing the condition through the exercise of power over another person, you are to the same extent securing control over that person. As long as the mouth remains firm, you will be powerless though not lacking in the possibility to overcome that setness of expression. Many cases have been cited of this use of influence. In one instance, a man wished to please another who was downcast; the drawn lips and firm closing of the mouth told the story of his feelings. He knew his friend was a lover of good stories, and he told some of his best, but the firmness never gave way. At length he reached one that happened to suit the listener, and the first indication of interest was the relaxing of the teeth which held the jaws together; then the lips showed signs of parting, though but slightly, and finally the mouth opened. As it did so the corners came up to a higher position, indicating pleasure, and a hearty laugh followed.

In another case a man had success in the darker mood, as his story was of sorrow. As soon as the interest began to grow, the jaws relaxed, and the mouth opened.

Whatever the condition, if the mouth remains firm, you are making no headway.

The rule is that, when the party whom you are addressing has the lowered corners as a fixed habit, you are to look to other sources for your information as to his temporary mood. This source is the thumb. In the case of a normal condition of the mind and nervous system, the thumb is carried level; by which is meant that it is on the same plane as the first finger. If you will hold the hand on edge, with the little finger side resting on the table, and the fingers all relaxed, you will see that the thumb has three moods, the first is level, or on the same height or plane as the first finger; the second is depressed, or in toward the palm under the first finger; and the third is raised or away from the first finger.

The hand is not generally held on edge; but, whatever its position, the relative shape of the thumb always follows the mood of the whole body. That is, the thumb is under the first finger during the dark moods, is open or away from all the fingers during the bright moments, and is normal or on the plane of the first finger when the feelings are normal.

The first part of the hand has also its meanings. When the fist is clinched, with the thumb over the second finger, the purpose is that of strong will or determination. When the fist is clinched with the thumb at the side of the first finger, the meaning is that of mild resolve. When the fist is clinched with the fingers spread apart at the second joints, the meaning is that of uncontrolled hatred. Here then are the three meanings of the clinched fist.

The fingers have three moods.

When the fingers are relaxed or almost touching each other with the hand open, the meaning is normal. When they are straight and spread apart, the indication is that of excitement. When they are apart and crooked, they depict horror or abject fear.

The fingers, fists and thumbs run gamuts or scales of meaning from one to another as they gradually drift in their changes.

Combining, as all humanity does, the expression of the hand with that of the mouth, we look to the thumb to ascertain if the downward carriage of the corners of the mouth is a fixed habit or a temporary change. If the former, the thumb will be level or on the plane of the first finger. If the mouth is in a temporary depression, the thumb will be under the first finger and toward the palm of the hand. In case of the combination of the lower corners and depressed thumb, the voice and brow will participate, as the mood will be so decided that any person will be able to interpret it.

These matters seem complicated to the novice; but so quickly will a student take them up that they soon become second nature. It is no tax to read the mood of a person by the hand or the mouth. The painter or sculptor is always true to these laws. An investigator went among the hospitals and collected during many years the records of twenty thousand cases, and found no exception to the rule that, where death is approaching, the thumb seeks the palm under the first finger. He also found that meanness, treachery, gross selfishness and all the darker moods had the same influence over the thumb. It is most natural for the thumb to fly out and away from the fingers when a bright mood comes on. The carriage of the fists and fingers is also true to nature. A man said that he would never be afraid to strike his adversary when the latter had his fist closed but his fingers open at the knuckles, for a man so angry as to hold the hand in that position cannot strike a powerful blow.

The position of the head has much to do with the mood of a person. Like always draws the top of the head slightly towards the person or thing that excites that like, although the movement is but a trifle. Dislike or disbelief always draws the head away from the person or thing that excites such mood. A normal head, or one that neither inclines to or from an object or person, is the carriage of normal interest, free from like or dislike. The elevation of the head means arrogance or a feeling of superiority. The depression of the head means humility or some kindred mood. These elementary indications make nine combined meanings as follows:

1. The elevated head inclined toward the person or object means lofty regard.

2. The elevated head inclined from the person or object means lofty disregard or arrogance.

3. The elevated head without inclination either way means a feeling of superiority.

4. The level head, which is neither raised nor depressed, means ordinary regard when inclined toward a person or object.

5. It means ordinary disregard when inclined from a person or object.

6. It means a neutral mood when it has no inclination.

7. The depressed head when inclined toward a person or object means humble regard or worship.

8. It means low disregard when inclined from a person or object, such as is seen in jealousy and similar moods.

9. It means three things when depressed without inclination either way.

a. Shame when the eyes drop.

b. Scrutiny when the eyes are fixed on some object outward on the same height or at any elevation.

c. Meditation when the eyes are not focussed on anything, or when the gaze is what is called parallel.

These are all natural meanings that are read the world over by all tribes, nations and peoples. Herein there is a universal language.

The eyes may see much.

It is well to be an adept in the knowledge of this form of universal speech, for you can tell to a certainty what is in store for you in any part of the world when you come in contact with other folks whose tongue may be wholly obscure. More than that you may become a very accurate reader of people who say one thing and mean another. Even your own family may not talk as freely as you would like, or they may be in moods that they try to force down. They can smile perhaps, but they cannot falsify all these three great realms of the heart and mind. They may talk as if there was nothing the matter, yet they are talking much more plainly with their twenty-seven lettered-alphabet, the nine moods of the hand, the nine of the head and the nine of the mouth.

It is most gratifying to be able to read them by this kind of world-wide language; a tongue that they cannot interpret and that they are unable to hide. "I am feeling very well and happy this morning," says the bride, as she assumes a face of pleasure. She does not know that her thumb is at the palm under the fingers; and all she can do and say will not hide that frank confession.

How is this art to be acquired?

Simply by learning what the twenty-seven positions are; what they mean; and how to read them. This requires a little memorizing, but not much. It also makes it necessary for you to observe people without permitting them to know that they are observed. Here some skill is required, but no unskillful person ever succeeded in anything.

All magnetic men and women are close, exact, constant and unremitting observers of their fellow beings.

But they are also skillful enough to know how to conceal their methods of observation. This has been thoroughly discussed and need not be further dealt with at this place.

Learn then these two things:

1. To observe others.
2. To conceal the fact.

Having memorized the twenty-seven positions and their meanings, *apply* them in your observations.

Learn to separate your mind from an interest in the sayings and doings of others, so that it will be free to carry on these observations. If you say as did a lady the other day, "I was so engrossed with what he was saying that I could not think to observe the positions of the head, mouth and hands." This was proof of the fact that she was magnetized.

The same rule will apply to you also.

If some person so engrosses your attention that you cannot

separate your interest in what is being said and done, from your purpose to observe the positions, you are also being magnetized. You are not hypnotized, for hypnotism puts to sleep. Magnetism wakes you up, but in the wrong berth.

Think this over and be on the lookout.

The practice of mental separation is one of the most beneficial that you could adopt, for it teaches you to carry on two processes at the same time. If you find that you are able to perform it, you may be sure of having a strong brain and a clear mind. It also brings unusual keenness into the powers of thought.

These directions are the result of many years of careful experiment. The rewards they will bring are sure and have been thoroughly proved.

The actor has to learn these positions and many more, for he takes in the scope of the standing attitudes of the legs with their many meanings, the attitudes of the torso, and the indicated expressions of the arms and general action of the body, of which there seems to be almost no end. What you are studying he also has to study, but for other purposes. He does not observe other people; you do. He never applies his knowledge to the investigation of the plans and purposes of those with whom he comes in contact; you do. He portrays characters and in a narrow limit; you feel and live them but in the widest realm of application. You have much less work to do to accomplish results that are worth a thousand fold more.

A review of this chapter will show that it contains enough matter to make a large volume were the information worked out into full explanations and examples. Enough has been taught to make it all clear to you, and your intelligence will do the rest. If we had made this chapter a whole volume of hundreds of pages, you would be deluged in a sea of printer's ink in which you might be swamped. Still great volumes are built on less information than is presented in this one portion of the present course.

It will be seen that there are several kinds of magnetic telepathy. These should be carefully considered, each by itself. We have included all kinds in this chapter so as to clear up this part of the study under one division of the course.

What the eye sees is the part that relates to the twenty-seven positions; and they are keys that unlock any doubts that may attend the use of the more subtle form of magnetic telepathy, as in the susceptibility of a person to the moods of another.

This branch of the study should be often compared with the line of instruction that precedes it in the present work, and also with the uses of the moods that are yet to be taken up. The greatest power of transmigration is yet to come, and the next chapter will go more deeply into it.

Every suggestion made is practical and capable of serving the highest usefulness in the life of every person who chooses to adopt it. Nothing is left to the peculiar powers of a few individuals. All that is taught is within the reach of every man and woman who owns this work.

Quick progress will be seen if there is a slow and conscientious plodding through the minutest details of the instruction. Be patient and persistent, placing the greatest value on the smallest suggestions, and you will come into a greater reward than you anticipate. It is a grand acquisition to be able to harmonize your mood with another's either close at hand or at a distance. It is also the best test of skill in handling humanity to be able to observe each and every detail of conduct and expression, and not be seen so doing.

With practice, there is immediate progress, if you begin at the first stages of development, obeying every rule and bit of advice laid down herein from the first page of the volume to the present stage.

It is not possible to make progress ahead unless it is connected with the present and the past chapters.

Assuming that you have given due heed to these points you are ready to enter upon the deeper problems of transmigration.

CHAPTER SEVENTEEN

++

STRONG MINDS
BEND
TO THE POWER OF
MAGNETIC USURPATION

++
⁂ ⁂ ⁂ SUBSTITUTION ⁂ ⁂ ⁂
++

OVING ONWARD step by step we come to the next phase of transmigration. The most common form of this power is that which is trained by nature. By looking back to the preceding chapter it will be seen that a magnetic person is subject to the unconscious and generally the unintended influence of others. We doubt if any person would be subjected to such power if there were no susceptibility, and this condition makes a person the prey of another. The illustrations given, such as the case of the clergyman who was being hounded by the plans of saloon-keepers, and the wealthy woman who had poor relations, are selected from a crowd of common incidents which you may have experienced in other forms but without knowing the cause or being able to interpret the meaning.

This is the negative side of magnetic telepathy.

All that is magnetic is electric, and all that is electric has two sides, negative and positive.

This fact should be kept in mind in order to avoid running against supposed contradictions.

We have seen that generals in war are able to feel the strategy of their opponents, and the most successful leaders of armies are not caught in traps set by the enemy. They cannot know, and

155

depend on a more subtle method by which to secure their information.

A keen business man uses his years of accumulated experience for the purpose of knowing the intentions of those with whom he has to deal. If a young man can start his career with such keenness of susceptibility of the motives of others, he can launch almost at once into the deep waters of success; and there are rare instances of this power being used at a very early age. When it comes as a gift the long years of waiting are reduced to months. Caesar, Napoleon, Alexander the Great and others who have stood out more prominently in the world's history, were as mighty in their thirties, or late twenties as at any other time of life. Byron, Poe and countless others had their full power while yet in their twenties.

All this is on the negative side of magnetic telepathy.

It means that you may receive the mood of another person and may be so influenced by that feeling that you realize what is being transacted in that person's mind and nervous nature. It has been stated that susceptibility in a few moods leads to annoyance and unrest; but that a large variety of moods balance each other and allow you to take in at will the feelings of others, rather than the intense mood of one alone.

In explanation of this sensitiveness as to one mood, it may be further stated that many persons suffer from their inability to throw off the influence that another person is throwing over them, even from a great distance. Night is most favorable for the exercise of this power, for all magnetic influences are greatest at night. The actor and the orator dislike the day time for their heaviest work, and they are types of the most used forms of public magnetism. But a person of strong magnetism may do well in the day time if all conditions favor him. His battles of mind over mind and magnetism over magnetism are best fought, however, in the waning of the year, as in the winter months, or else at night. The brightness of day especially in the vital hours of summer are not conducive to the best displays of human power, as there is the counteracting influence of the sun's energy.

It is then at night, or in the winter period if at day, that you carry the burdens of others and not know the source. A feeling of weight, of heaviness, of depression, comes over you, and some apprehension or fear of future days, as of coming misfortune or poverty, hangs over you. This is unpleasant, and sometimes unfits a person for the sterner duties of life. It takes the vitality and iron out of the heart and soul.

When a person is in the crisis of disease, if will-power is not strong, it is much better to be unconscious, so that the mind may not fail by reason of its fears when under the influence of those about. The sick person feels keenly any suggestion, even if not expressed, of discouragement as to his condition; and this depression lowers the tone of his own will-power. A feeling about him that he will recover has a strong influence over him, and those who carry approaching calamity in their faces have a still stronger influence in the other direction. What the eyes can read added to what the nervous feeling experiences will prove the strongest combination either for better or for worse.

To be haunted with the moods of another is to be influenced by that individual. It is not only unpleasant but decidedly worrying and depressing. It means that the other person is throwing his or her self into you, and that you are carrying burdens that do not belong to you.

This influence is exerted generally in the ordinary case without the willingness or knowledge of the other party, that is, of the party who wields the power. It is hap-hazard, but so common and so effective that it has much to do with the health of body and of mind of the party so influenced; since worry and loss of sleep are factors in such conditions.

As has been stated the cure is in opening the mind and nervous system to a large number of moods and feelings; this can be easily done by the development of the colors, stated in a previous chapter.

Yet it is all on the negative side; and the better plan is to build up the positive forces of magnetism along the same lines. This will be better understood by the law of substitution, which may be described as follows:

1. A person who possesses control of powerful magnetic waves is able to throw out positive influences that will overcome the moods and feelings of others.

2. Such control is secured by the positive use of colors both mental and nervous.

The development of the colors of the moods and feelings has been throughly taught in this course, and the control of powerful magnetic waves is the scope of the Exercise Book, which is the first course in the study of personal magnetism, and which must in all cases precede or accompany this course in Advanced Magnetism. That course is always necessary, and no person has been allowed to procure the present course who has not had the first work.

Having laid the basis of both lines of development, our work now is to turn to the positive uses of this double power; namely the power to develop magnetic waves, and the power to use the color of the moods and feelings on the positive side.

A few examples of this positive use will be necessary.

When Sheridan was twenty miles away, his troops were discouraged and labored under the fear of capture or slaughter. They, with almost one accord, were on the run. An ordinary individual would not be able to shift their mood of fear. It required one who could inject into them his own magnetism. Here we find another law.

3. The numbers influenced by the positive magnetism of another do not weaken the power of that person, as a hundred thousand feel as keenly as one person the waves of control.

This fact has been demonstrated so many times that it is now a self evident truth. It is thought that it may be due to the rapid increase of the power as it is taken up by one person after another and transmitted to a crowd or mass of humanity.

Sheridan started on the wild ride to meet his broken army. They did not know of his coming. Other leaders less magnetic had tried in vain to turn them about. Sheridan had more magnetism than the officers under him; that was the reason why they were under him and he was above them. Rank is almost invariably determined by the degree of magnetic power and its judicious use.

When this great general met his retreating soldiers, not alone the sight of the man, which was magnetic, but also the sound of his voice, served to drive from them the moods which had been in control; and it is hardly necessary to speak words under the circumstances. All his soldiers needed was the power of his own purpose which he projected into them at a glance and in the very impulse of his presence. It was not the power of position, for there were many generals who held as high a position who could not have exerted any influence whatever over the stampede of excited men.

The stern, determined face with sharp, clear-cut lips, and fixed purpose visible in every feature; the excited horse charged to the full with the magnetism of the rider; the fiery flash of the eyes; and the wild dash forward were all legitimate exhibitions of the influence which was destined to turn about the army now in confusion, and change the fate of battle. Words are only incidents of magnetism. Spoken by some persons they fall flat, but the identical words spoken by a certain voice arouses to the highest pitch those to whom it is addressed. The entrance of a magnificent woman in a drawing room, even in plain attire, makes its magnetism felt without words. Moods and feelings command more than language. This was the case with Sheridan's return to his army. He had one mood and his soldiers had another. He substituted his for theirs and they were willing tools in his service. For him, as much as for the cause he represented, they plunged into the thick of the fight and the day was won. This is substitution, or the affirmative side of magnetic telepathy.

Andrew Jackson had the same power. He had a variety of moods, as the art of war in his scope of action was so small in his day, and his armies so few in numbers that he had time to study humanity in many phases. He had domestic troubles to deal with, and domestic scandals to train his emotions. He had literary enemies, although he was not literary himself. He had political enemies and political ambitions, and a variety of home enterprises and interests that kept him busy in mind as well as active in body. These opened up many avenues of development. When he assumed a mood he held to it until every human being within reach of his presence or influence whom he sought to control, fell in with his way of thinking. His was a master mind in the use of magnetism.

It is asserted of him that he knew no will but his own, which means that he allowed no one else to have leadership over him; and when the policy of the people against a third term prevented him from being elected President of the United States for three

times, he was at the helm during his life, even though not in
office. He was in private the President of the United States.

The familiar episode related of him, where he compelled a
desperado to surrender to him, although he himself had no
weapons and the criminal was armed and able to kill him, is
but one of many examples of Jackson's power of substituting his
own mood or will for that of another. The desperado could not
give a reason for his quick yielding to Jackson except that he
saw in his face that he meant what he said. Animals and human
beings are ruled by this excessive firmness of face and manner.
It is tantamount to saying, "I have my will. You have yours.
Mine must take the place of yours." This is substitution.

The typical juror who had, previous to sitting in the box to try
a term of Choate's cases, expostulated with other jurors for
bending so servilely to the magnetism of that great lawyer, was
as ready to give his vote for Choate's clients; and, when his
friends called for an explanation, he said, "The evidence was all
Choate's way." This meant, when translated, "I had my views
of the case. Choate had his. Choate made me substitute his for
mine. Choate was right." This kind of convincing method of
dealing with men and women is everywhere prevalent. And the
wonder of it is that the parties so swept off their judgment are
satisfied that they are right.

Some persons are so skillful in the use of substitution that they
begin with opposing the mood of a person who is on the right
side, though weakly at the start, and then swinging round to
the views of the other party, leaving the impression that the
magnetizer has been magnetized.

Here is a familiar illustration of the use of this influence:

A man who stood at the head of a business house, hated to be
"squeezed," as the expression is; that is, he could not bear to
think that somebody else was getting the better of him. He
thought that A. was doing this. A. did not wish to lose his
position which was then close to the rank of partnership, and he
knew that it would be useless to argue the matter. He then
planned to take advantage of his employer's suspicions; which
he did successfully. He selected, after days of observation, some
individual who was in fact taking too large a profit from the
employer. This had been going on for some time and might not
have been discovered but for the extra diligence of A. The latter

made a show of fight, as though he were extra zealous to defend the interests of his employer and this won with ease.

In another case an employee made a mistake and lost by it. He was eager to make himself appear vigilant in the business, and so he tried to make too low a contract price with a certain dealer who had been selling goods to the firm for years. This employee, whom we will call B., made a show of forcing down the price to be paid, and the following interesting conversation was the result:

Employer. "I am told by C. that you have refused to buy goods of him unless they are sold for ten per cent less than he has been getting for them. How is this?"

B. "C. says that he will sell them for that price."

Employer. "But he tells me that he cannot make any profit if he does so. What is your purpose in crowding the price down to that basis?"

B. "I did it for your interest. What he takes off his prices adds to your income."

Employer. "But that is a cold-blooded way of robbing a man. Give him his usual rates, and hereafter when you want to start a crusade to send honest men to the poorhouse, let me advise you before you start."

Here was a man who was willing to live and let others live. The moods are consistent. The very same employer may wish to escape the toils of those who try to reap unfair profits from him, and yet may be glad to pay a reasonable profit in every case. Some day this high standard of business ethics may prevail to a larger extent than at the present time.

Here is another case where an employee turned a double table at one stroke. He had an employer who disliked falsehood. On one occasion the employee whom we will call D. had made the mistake of creating an impression with his employer of having told an untruth. He was at the point of being discharged. Over him in the business was a tricky and unreliable man who stood high in the estimation of the employer, so adroitly had he avoided suspicion. This man was pressing home the charge of falsifying against D. The latter went to the employer's wife and stated the case. She agreed to help him. It was arranged that the employer should be in a certain private office at his place of business, when D. would come upon the man who was seeking to injure him. We will call that man X. The following conversation was heard:

X. "I may report you to the boss. Do you want me to do so."

D. "For what?"

X. "For the statement which you made. It is not true."

D. "I think it is true. If it is not true, then I will get it right. I have no intention of stating an untruth."

X. "Of course you and I know that, but you can't convince the boss."

D. "I do not want to convince him of what is not right. Any man may make a mistake or get the facts wrong. If I have done this I will face the matter, and you are free to tell all you know. But be sure that you do not get the facts mixed as you have done many times of late. The difference between you and me is plain. You mix the facts up purposely and I never do. I will face all my mistakes and you run away from yours. That case you had before you came here is being investigated and you will have to meet it and the law too. So look out."

X. "What do you know about that case? It is none of your affair."

D. "I did not hunt it up. The officers have done the hunting."

X. "How much do you know? Tell me, and I swear that I will never report you to the boss, no matter how much you may lie."

D. "I never knowingly have told him any lie, nor anyone else. My mother taught me differently."

The wife had brought the employer as if by accident into the private office, and seems as much surprised as he was to hear the conversation between the two employees. The result was the saving of D. and the discharge of X. The hint about his previous life was explained to the wife by D. as follows:

"I never knew anything against him. But from the kind of man that he showed himself to be during the year or more that I have seen him, I felt sure that he had something wrong in his past, and the guess was so covered that it might have referred to almost anything. No one is exempt from small troubles and enmities, and I did not feel that I would miss some mark. I happened to strike the bull's-eye."

The energy of this young man was of the kind that forges to the front. He could not fail in anything that he undertook. In his method of shifting suspicion or anger against himself for a supposed untruth, he substituted the same feelings so that they operated against X.

This kind of power is dangerous to use.

It may seem a bit of practical joke; but it is far from it.

If you undertake to use it except in a crisis, as where your reputation or property, or rights are at issue, you may bitterly repent it.

It is a kind of power that should be kept as secret as the thought and motive that impel it. That there is such a method of meeting the wrongs that others would do you, must be kept concealed, or the opportunity will fall flat.

So astute a man as General Benjamin F. Butler made greater use of this plan of dealing with his fellow beings than any other person whom we have ever known. He employed it at all times, and for the mere purpose of making some one feel uncomfortable. As a rule he was feared and hated by his opponents in law trials, while the people sat by and enjoyed his smartness, as they termed it.

His first purpose was to ascertain if his position as the leading lawyer of England awakened fear in the opposing counsel or the witnesses he cross-examined. If he saw that it did, he increased the fear as much as he could, and rendered his opponents from doing their best in the conflict. Many a time some lawyer would say, "Oh, I am not afraid of Ben Butler, and I'll show him the stuff I am made of when we come to the trial." But when the case was on, and the bold courage of this lawyer who had no fear of the giant, was being projected into the trial, it took but a single stroke to substitute fear in place of bravery.

When this was not effective, as against an older lawyer, Gen. Butler would substitute flippancy or ridicule; but he always waited until he saw a clear opening; as the recoil would not be pleasant. There is no human being who has not some fault that will creep out on the proper encouragement, and it requires an astute observer of the frailties of mankind to detect them at the exact moment. They then become self-accusers which makes the weapons for an adversary.

We are not advocating this method of worrying an antagonist and thus taking away his ability to do justice to himself. It is well to see to it that such a weapon is not used against you. In the social and business as well as in the professional vicissitudes of life, you are strongest when you are making your plans for meeting others; and you are weakest when in the heat of the meeting. So many accomplish untold and marvelous achievements in their boasts to their friends, who are on the border of collapse when the real test begins. Yet they are made of the stuff that succeeds; for the brazen, tight-skinned, heedless fellow who lacks sensitiveness, is not impressionable enough to receive or wield magnetic power. The man or woman who is magnetic is always sensitive, susceptible, impressionable and easily affected by moods and conditions. No other kind of person can acquire the powers of control over others. But in order to be powerful it is necessary that you maintain mastery over the moods and feelings; and there is no school or preparation equal to the development of the colors of these moods and feelings, as taught in the preceding chapter. To be impressionable and to show it to others, is weakness.

The more sensitive you make yourself, not merely in one or two of the colors, but in all of them, the more power you will develop if you control such moods and feelings.

This is a two-fold law. It refers to the development of extreme sensitiveness of the colors and then to the control which must at all times be exercised over them. They are like strong and swift steeds, useful and mighty when they are driven with care, but dangerous when they are allowed to run wild. The horses that run away are not as useful as those that are kept under management. Any power is thus good or bad. It all depends upon the control that is exercised over it.

The question now arises as to how the colors may be developed to the greatest degree of sensitiveness. Repetition in practice is one of the most potent factors to this end. But it is not enough. The mind must be on the work, as you practice.

Even this is not all.

The innermost mental force must be thrown into pictures of the scenes which are involved in the quotations that are appended to the moods and feelings. This is enhanced by the development of intensity and pathos in the degrees named; for there is no mood that cannot be made far more keen and vital by such aids. On the whole, there must be the picture-making faculty of the fancy.

Let these be understood and failure will not come to the student who is really ambitious to succeed.

In direct substitution, the process is simple and effective; and there is rarely any failure when time and patience have been properly expended in the preparation. Where only a few weeks of practice have been had, the progress is certain as far as it goes. The student is always becoming more and more successful.

Who fails?

The reader of these chapters will fail if the interest taken is only devoted to reading. Reading will not make the piano player or the swimmer. If you buy an expensive piano, you will not become a player of its keys because you have read all about the art and the science of the piano. You cannot learn to swim and actually swim if you never go into the water.

In the same way you cannot wield a power that you have not drawn into your being by actual indulgence in the methods by which alone that power is to be created.

We have repeated the requirements in this chapter, and they will be found stated over and over again in preceding chapters in this book; our purpose being to show the things that have to be done, and how they are to be done. There is, therefore, no reason why you should not know what to do and how to do it.

Take at random any of the moods and let us see how they are substituted in other persons. In the first place you must have been made an adept in the use of magnetic waves, and this skill comes from the practice of the lessons in the first book, the name of which is the Exercise Book of the Magnetism Club, or the Cultivation of Personal Magnetism. That course is sure to develop magnetism and the use of the magnetic waves.

The rest of the work is to be done in this book; the application and manner of using personal magnetism.

With this preparation, and the progress of the preceding chapters added to it, you can make many hundreds of remarkable experiments. We suggest that you try the mood of PEACE. It is one of the easiest. If you have behind it the power of magnetism, which comes from the first course, and the pathos and intensity in the degrees required, and also have the color of PEACE, you can substitute that color in any person, at will. The exceptions are generally those who lack brain and standing in the scale of humanity. A cur will rant and shout and grow wild, despite all your efforts. Magnetism requires brains to work upon. Hypnotism has its success on subjects who lack mental force; but the reverse is true of magnetism.

In the great mob in New York City at the time when Lincoln was assassinated, no one had power to curb the on-moving mass of excited humanity. It seemed as if every moment would be the last for the safety of the enemies of the republic. Standing on the balcony of a building, Garfield, who was afterwards destined to be struck down by the hand of the assassin, looked forward over the surging thousands whom others had tried in vain to subdue. Raising his right hand he stood there with uncovered head and face full of power. One by one and then by tens and hundreds the populace calmed down. All was the stillness of a deathly silence. He spoke and they heard: "God reigns, and the Government at Washington still lives." He had substituted PEACE in the wildly raging breasts of countless thousands.

We have seen schools thus brought into quietude by certain teachers where others had failed to control them. Let the color of PEACE be fully developed in yourself, and the very moment you enter the room it will be felt by all who are present. This has been so many times demonstrated in our own work, and in the presence of so many other persons that it is hardly a matter of any difficulty to quell the unrest of intelligent people.

In the mood of peace the face shows the presence of the color; and, next to this, the voice is certain to convey the influence. The parent and the teacher need this mood at times when nothing else will effect quietude in the family or among pupils. We recall the case of a mother who had the gift in an unusual degree, and it added a sweetness to her presence that was most fascinating. There is no charm in all the range of womanhood that is so effective.

If we were to advise the lady or young lady what would most attract lovers and admirers, either before or after marriage, for love is the bright light of wedlock, we would suggest the mastery of the mood of peace. The single quotation given in a preceding chapter is enough to establish the color; but other quotations and extracts from the drama may be added if this color is to be specially developed; and then transfer the color to conversation and manner of meeting and dealing with people. It can be more readily transferred than any other color we recall; though perhaps this statement is made because we have seen it practiced more than any other color.

When in the color, your voice is particularly gentle though not a bit lower in tone or lacking in its usual force. It is possible to shout in the color of peace, despite the fact that noise and this color seem to be contradictory terms. But Garfield could not have employed quiet tones when he addressed the thousands of people in the New York mob. We have seen many uses of the tones of peace in loudness, still preserving the right color. It is done by first establishing the color in the quietest tones, then gradually adding to the force until the sound is as loud as the voice will make it.

There is the greatest charm in a voice in the color of peace. It lives not so much in the gentleness as in the color, which is peculiar to itself. Once it is heard it will never be forgotten. Because of its attractiveness we advise that women and girls cultivate the color until it has become a second nature with them.

Not only does it give the charm to the voice, but it imparts a most decided influence to the whole body, the methods of movement, of walking or sitting and standing, and to each motion however great or small. It is far the superior of gentleness and gracefulness; and it all comes from the practice of the color of peace until the very nature of that mood belongs to the personality. Such a personality had Bishop Phillips Brooks, Wendell Phillips, Queen Victoria, and many others of lesser rank. It is not found in actors and actresses except as an assumed color. What we would teach is its fixed nature at all times.

It suits the lady and the young lady far better than the man; as it is not so virile as most men prefer. They may assume it for special magnetic purposes. Sometimes under the stress of a great emotion a man may find it suddenly born in him, and it departs as quickly when it has served its usefulness.

In the case of the lady, or the young maiden, its charm is so in harmony with what is most to be desired in them, that it at once enhances their powers of attraction over the opposite sex. It seems to shut off excessive volubility in speech, and frothy manners and frivolous ideas in thought. The influence of peace is to make all departments of the being at peace with all mankind. Yet, while it lessens the virility of the man, it does not weaken the power of woman's presence. It seems to give an increase of the womanliness in the fair sex. Nor does it deaden the energy and sprightliness of either sex.

Too much stress cannot be laid upon this mood as the greatest of all that may be cultivated by man or woman; to be used whenever the occasion fits in the life of the man, and at all times by the woman. Grant said, "Let us have peace." The Savior said the same in effect. The theme on which the Gospels are written is, "Peace on earth and good will to men."

It is a color that calms all angry moods, that drives away all unrest and worrying, and saves the loss of power through irritability. In the quieter periods of the day or evening when you are alone, this color makes you a power to yourself. You feel its over-mastering sway in what you read and what you think as well as what you do and say. It is not possible to find its superior in toning down the nervous tossing about of a mind or body that is suffering from discontent and ill nature, due no doubt to the conspiracy of events which make your life a daily failure. Once the mind and nerves are calm, the thoughts will take new strength and the faculties will better execute the duties assigned to them.

SELF-CONTAINMENT.

This is the greatest quality of personal magnetism. It is made the subject of a treatise that has been held in the highest esteem by those who have practiced its rules. As a basis for the work, it has been found that every man and woman who has personal magnetism is noted for habitual self-containment. How to acquire this habit, has been the problem for years. It comes from the color of peace, and in the manner we have described; but so much preliminary work has been needed to make it teachable that this course was really required in order to provide the steps to its acquisition.

It is not conceit, although it seems to the novice to pass for that quality. It is not the quietude of inactivity; for the first essential of self-containment is power in excess. This is seen in the comparison of the human being to the locomotive.

The engine may hold a tremendous accumulation of power, yet be still when not moving, and move with steadiness when called upon to travel along the rails. In contrast with this repose of power is the restless, fidgety individual.

A few illustrations will suffice to explain what is meant. Here is a woman who is quick-motioned when walking, and when at work. This would do no harm if it saved time, but she makes mistakes through her carelessness and her ill-considered haste. She slams things about, slams the doors, bangs everything she touches, drops herself into a chair, rocks violently, snatches whatever she takes, hurts children in combing their hair or dressing them, and makes everybody nervous by her excessive restlessness. She is the very opposite of self-containment. If the case cited is an extreme one, it is well to remember that there is a long gamut of degrees between her and that of the equally active woman who accomplishes more and is perfectly self-composed in every act.

Self-containment does not mean listlessness, for that is self-emptiness. There must be action and purpose, but no wasted motion. What would you think of a locomotive that stood at the station ready to haul a great train to a distant city, and yet turned a driver every four seconds, jumped a half-inch on its pony wheels, joggled its smoke-stack from one side to another, rung its bell when there was nothing to ring at, played with its throttle in place of a handkerchief, swung its cab around, scratched its cylinders, wiggled its piston-rods, rattled its eccentrics, and went through a large number of little motions that were useless from every point of view? Yet men and women are constantly losing their vitality by faults that are much worse in degree. The stately engine, when it comes to do its work, giant as it is, moves with the grace of a fawn and rides as composedly on the rails as if it were afloat in some quiet lake. It is an example of power and self-containment.

We have seen lawyers lose good cases because of their restlessness. We have seen doctors who irritate their patients instead of gaining their confidence. In one month we heard eight different ministers preach as many sermons, and we saw why there were empty pews. One clergyman winked his eyelids all the time, and the more earnest he became the faster he winked. Outside of this one fault he was qualified to meet the requirements of his profession, but a would-be magnetism fell flat ere it took on power. Another preacher had the common fault of saying "uh" hundreds of times in every sermon. Another had jerky, restless, meaningless gestures. Another stepped around as if the floor were over a hot furnace. Another had but one kind of gesture, and this tired the eye to see it. All these clergymen had some qualifications for their work, but they lacked self-containment, and could not, therefore, win the full confidence of their people. They were failures in the pulpit. Had some kind angel whispered to them the secret of power, and had their bandages fallen from their eyes, they could all have developed themselves into successful preachers. Church members are driven through the prickings of conscience into houses of worship, and this compulsion cannot be credited to the clergymen who may have full churches in spite of their preaching.

All persons can learn self-containment in its ordinary sense. Why not do it? It will add vastly to the usefulness of every man and woman who adopts the habit. More than this it will add to the vital fund within the body. It will increase the health. It will command the respect of others. It will lead to magnetism.

A few directions may be serviceable at this place. Self-containment begins with the habit of observing yourself, and the omission of your faults of person. Then it proceeds to drive away all habits of restlessness, physical, nervous and mental. Then it enters more deeply into your life and checks all exhibitions of feeling except when you voluntarily permit such exhibition. We do not mean to advise you to be heartless; but, on the other hand, deep waters are still. Satisfaction, malice, triumph, pride, revenge, joy over another's misfortune, displays of gloom and disappointment, and all outward evidences of what is transpiring within the body, should be held in perfect check. The face that pictures every mood is weak. Its action is large and soon becomes coarse; thus preventing the mind and heart from chiseling their finer lines over its surfaces.

A person who is always giving vent to joy or despondency, is not likely to secure the confidence of others in more serious crises. Sympathy is most appreciated when it comes up from a great depth. A keen listener, an attentive observer, a full thinker are leaders of others when the time comes to shape a policy. People who are squirmy or fidgety are always in somebody's way and never out of their own. If they have an opinion on every subject, small or big, their views are shallow. If they must discuss every point that comes up during each day of existence, they have very little to offer.

One of the most common traits of prevailing human nature is the willingness to believe everything that is heard or read, and the readiness to express an opinion one way or the other. Harsh criticism generally follows. The morning paper brings news on a hundred subjects, and each reader thinks, feels and talks as if the statements were true, and many angry moods flit through the mind. It is the design of the paper to make the laboring classes hate their employers, and the employers to hate the unions; and malicious articles that fire the anger of both classes are constantly published in order to sell papers.

It is the duty of self-containment to believe nothing on any hearsay evidence, and especially not on the evidence of a newspaper. The mind must be kept cool, calm and unruffled; for, when it is of a cast to be easily disturbed, its magnetism flies out and is lost. The art of not believing is a great one. It is not the practice of disbelief, for that is another thing. If we affirmatively doubt a statement we are setting up a claim that it is untrue. If we do not know it to be untrue we have no right to believe it so. But non-belief is an unwillingness to accept a statement as true. Self-containment is non-belief when the evidence is lacking. "I do not believe you are telling the truth," is equivalent to saying, "I believe you are telling an untruth." But, "I do not know that you are telling the truth," is an expression of neutrality, a desire to let the matter pass as though it had not been uttered.

Credulity is opening the mind to matters that, in ninety-nine cases out of a hundred, have no right there. It is the weakness of the public.

If the person who uses the power of magnetism to control others, were unable to secure their belief, he would at once be at a disadvantage. It is for this reason that the user of the power should select the materials for his belief. He will be controlled by others to the very extent of his belief in the assertions of others. The magnetic person must of necessity make his mind neutral by adopting the habit of not accepting as true any statement that is not of importance to him. This requires care and judgment. Carelessness in permitting all kinds of material to enter the mind places the person in the category of being influenced rather that of controlling others.

The meaning of self-containment is the containing of self; and what is held in the mind and heart should be of the highest value and the greatest importance. If you have a clean and beautiful house, will you open it to filthy tramps and wandering vermin? You cannot give out better than you take in. You cannot throw about the lives of other men and women influences that are nobler or stronger than the material which you admit into your self and allow to become a part of yourself. Self-containment therefore must control what you take in and store within your heart and mind.

Now what is the material that you admit? It comes from gossip, from sensational newspapers, from novels, from light-weight magazines and other periodicals, from ill-advised discussions, from self-formed opinions, from political demagogues, and from all sorts of people who seek to use you to their own advantage. A stream of this bad material is constantly flowing toward the mind. Do you admit it? The highest exhibition of personal power in this world is in the art of selecting what you allow to enter your mind, and in rejecting all else.

The habit of self-containment is one that can be cultivated without practice. As far as that branch of it is concerned that prevents unworthy material from entering the mind, its adoption is best begun with a determination to hold the belief neutral in all matters that are useless to your stock of knowledge. This habit brings results that are of immense importance. We have not the space in which to explain it, but will say in a general way that the body is nothing but a collection of cells—each cell has a dormant center within its nucleus in which there is electric life held in abeyance; some of this life is aroused by flesh-tensing; some of it escapes in the act of living; some of it feeds the nerve-centers; and all of it, as far as it is not actually asleep, is whipped about by the brain impulses. The person who hears a bit of news or gossip and gives it credence, is more or less aroused by it. You may have an employee concerning whom some remark or hint has come to you; at once you believe it, and then it leads to other possibilities, and you believe them because they are possible; when, in fact, you have no right to believe them even if they are probable. This leads to a change of manner toward that employee. You have acted upon a belief, and the belief has grown up out of a hint that stood for nothing tangible. Had you suspected the employee, the proper course to have taken was to investigate thoroughly before you acted.

The same kind of influence is constantly assailing the brain. Some one seeks to lessen your regard for a friend or for a business acquaintance. You allow a belief to get seated in your mind. You worry. Your thoughts lose their power of controlling others, because you yourself are controlled by the suggestions, suspicions, hints and straw-evidences that float in upon your mind at every turn. The power of swaying other minds does not come into play until you have shut off all possibility of being tossed about by the beliefs that would sway your mind.

You must be able to say with decisiveness, "I do not choose to accept this, that or the other as facts. Whatever I wish to believe I will elect to believe. I will invite matters into my brain, not let them invite themselves in." To a person who thus controls the thousand incidents of occurring life, *nothing ever goes wrong*.

The man who says, "Things have gone wrong in my business today," is not magnetic. The woman who says, "I have been much worried of late, for so many things have gone wrong," is not magnetic. Things may be going wrong, and undoubtedly are, in every life; but that is the time for action. When they "have gone" it is too late. Worry is justified only when you could have prevented it; and if you could have prevented it you were very unmagnetic not to have done so; if you could not have prevented it you will not worry if you are magnetic; and if you are magnetic you will prevent it; hence the magnetic person never has cause for worry.

Thoughts that hamper the soul or depress the mind are serious barriers to the development of personal magnetism. They come through habit; or they stay away through habit. They are mental tramps; if you like one of them you ought to be sufficiently in control of your own castle to invite it in; as things now are these tramps enter of their own will and roam about wheresoever they please, while you stand aghast and fret over their escapades.

Habit shifts from year to year. You can, by the smallest attentions, change the whole course of your life. When thoughts, beliefs and worries are allowed to come as they please, the habit of fretting over everything, and of being depressed in mind, will grow apace. When you make yourself the guardian of your own castle—the mind—you will allow no tormenting suggestions to find entrance; and then you will not worry. A new habit will be formed.

This habit will of itself develop magnetism. We do not mean that inattention to the vicissitudes of living is commendable. Indifference is weakness. It is of Negro descent. Its parentage is Ethiopian. The man or woman of power, no matter how obscured the little life may be, is the one who plays the game of existence as though the moves were being made on a chessboard; each act is seen far ahead in its consequences. The game of chess, applied to human operations, is an excellent method of training, for it makes "today" provide for many "tomorrows." It enables every person to live so that no heed need be taken of the morrow. Life's opportunities and faculties are "talents," to "bury" which is a sin; they should be active and thus provide so well for the future years of this life that no heed, no worry, no anxiety need exist for any morrow.

It is well known that a guilty conscience destroys magnetism. The successful person in the use of this power is the one who is bold, determined and aggressive through lack of fear. A steady self-reliance is an anchorage from which the bolts of influence may be hurled in any direction without danger of recoiling. This condition is attainable by every person.

The purpose of self-containment is to keep out all distracting thoughts. Worry is a distracting thought; it works counter to the purpose of a magnetic thought. The two are like trains going in opposite directions on the same track. Take worry out of the mind, prevent the will-power from going over to a state of indifference, and magnetism grows as the natural fruit of these conditions, just as vitality is the natural fruit of certain ways of living.

Fear as to the happening of something is a distracting thought, and works counter to the purpose of a magnetic thought. Any weight upon the mind or conscience is likewise a distracting thought. The admission of gossiping news, the reading of sensation, the submerging of the mind in the plot of some exciting novel—all these are distracting thoughts and they run counter to the purposes of magnetism. On the same principle the habit of believing what you are told or what you read, is hurtful to the mind, except where you choose to select what you wish to believe and to remain neutral as to all other matters. The imperturbable mind, the calm and unruffled nervous system, the complacent mood and the mastery of all the affairs of life as far as they have relation to yourself, are marks of self-containment.

Never allow yourself to get excited; but, on the other hand, do not withdraw from the causes of excitement. Try to find them. Try to get into the thick of the battle, and court all the influences that may tend to stir you up or create in your mind feelings that ordinarily you would be free to display. In the actual battle of war, the commander who has the situation well in hand is he who knows everything that is going on and who sees all the dangers that surround, yet sits upon his horse placidly and calmly, white it may be, but strong and determined, with jaws set in purpose, and yet never disturbed as the news comes to him thick and fast of the dismayed troops, or the wavering lines, the mad rush of the enemy or the stubborn resistance of his own army. When reports of disaster reach him, he issues his orders without nervousness or anxiety, as far as his face shows; and when the moment for the final assault has arrived he is still calm and unmoved; not a distracting thought enters his mind; he admits no belief, no fear, no misapprehension; he has no room for any idea except the one fixed purpose of the hour; and as his army, like a rolling sea driven by the irresistible impulse of that purpose, throws itself upon the foe, he sees the overwhelming tide rush before the impending storm and sweep all resistance away in one mighty onslaught; yet is he still the same calm observer of these stirring events and the same controlling power throughout them all.

This power of the mind is of itself magnetic; and may be acquired by every earnest man and woman. It is habit, good or bad; good when you study to be calm; bad when you let things go as they will. There never was a time when things went right, if they were allowed to take care of themselves. It is contrary to the law of nature and the law of life. We do not therefore preach indifference; but we teach the art of paying no heed to matters that ought not to command attention, but all the time selecting such details as you wish to give entrance to the mind. Can this point be made clear?

Things left to the care of themselves go wrong; they never go right. They will come in upon you when you do not wish to receive them; and, being left to run themselves, they will also run you. These thoughts that come and go as they choose, are sure to distract your attention from the main work before you in each day of your life. You should be able to select what thoughts and what cares you wish to enter your mind; and you should acquire the power to be wholly neutral as to all others. This may at first sight seem like a contradiction; but it is not. Neutrality as to all matters that you do not wish to receive in the mind, is simply shutting the door of your house against all tramps, and ignoring their demands to come in. The admission of some visitors is an act of choice, in which you are the party who determines who are to come in and who are to stay out.

This same principle holds true in allowing no distracting thoughts to bother you; in remaining calm and undisturbed in the fray of life; in showing no feeling or emotion when nothing is served by so doing; and in refusing to take in the stuff that is passing before the eyes and ears all through the long hours of the day.

You may have all the faith you desire in your fellow-men and yet not believe one per cent of what you read and hear. A mind that has faith in the remarks of gossip, never can be magnetic. A mind that has faith in the statements seen in the newspapers, can never be magnetic. These two sources of falsehood supply all the bulk of mental intrusion that exists today. The fact that some of their skeletons have truth in them does not justify giving credence to the general drift of them. One item of truth in a mass of lies, is not reason for believing the mass.

We make this point as strong as possible in order that the mind of every reader of these pages may be cleaned out and may take a new start, with the resolve never to admit to the chambers of belief anything that is not needed in the performance of the great duties of life.

This new condition comes from habit. It is one of the easiest things to cultivate. It is the easiest of all the principles of the law of self-containment.

Self-containment, as a whole, is hard to acquire; but the habit of selecting what matters shall receive credence in the mind, and rejecting all others, or remaining neutral to them, is quickly invited by a determination to do exactly what it demands. Every person can do this much, unless the will-power is mere slush.

The difficult part of self-containment is that which requires the even carriage of the disposition, the lofty purpose in everything, the ease and strength of all the faculties, the unruffled calmness of the feelings and the superb quality of mind which refuses to come in contract with the meannesses of life. This does not refer to the arrogant pride that makes some men and women detestable; but it means that, even when you are associating with the lowly, you are not to mingle with the evils that often environ them. No person is too unfortunate for the care and help of those who are better favored; but misfortune is generally the fruit of wrongs committed by the parties who are made to suffer. We know that this is not supposed to be true, for investigators have not as a rule gone back to the days of the wanton neglect of the opportunities of life to find the cause of poverty and ill-health. It is the spirit of these neglected opportunities that is contaminating, and that must not be given contact and association.

Meanness in any form is degrading. Rise above it.

The really great magnetism comes from the highest degree of self-containment. We cannot describe it, for no language has words that mark its true character. The nearest we can approach it, is to say that it is perfect imperturbability of body, mind and soul accompanied by full life within these three departments of existence. This gentle drawing of life into the body, and the lighting of the quiet fires of electricity will affect the whole system in a very short time. Under the feeling of this kind of imperturbability one of the conditions of self-containment will be acquired. On the mental side it is helped by the plan we have given of allowing no thoughts to enter the mind unless they are selected as desirable, all others being rejected, and all beliefs being likewise chosen.

Any reader of this chapter must, by this time, see that personal magnetism is life in the midst of calmness; and action that moves out of repose. Let the essential—life—be lacking, and calmness becomes indifference, while repose becomes laziness. The magnetic men and women of the world have possessed great vital energies, great volumes of mental-life, soul-life, or animal electricity, while yet they have held them in the stillness of perfect control so that they might be used at will.

As may be said by many who are thoughtless, that such forces are natural to those who possess them, we have taken the pains to introduce methods of habit-culture whereby they may become natural to those who do not possess them. Let us look at the three great magnetic energies at a glance:

1. Soul-energy is stimulated by an aggressive purpose in living.

2. Mental-energy is stimulated by the selection of beliefs.

3. Animal-electricity is aroused by the habit of carrying the flesh firm at all times, without the use of the muscles in so doing.

This is intensity in the nervous system and always accompanies the fourth degree of undulations as we have already stated in a previous chapter.

The importance of developing intensity to the highest power is now seen, and the value of the several quotations will be grasped. They are the longer extracts furnished for the purpose of generating intensity in the mind and nervous system. Humanity at times is hungry for just such quotations. We saw the magnetic Mary Anderson a number of times take up a book of such extracts from the thrilling literature of the world, and throw herself into the feeling of oral reading, memorizing the text as fast as she could read it and re-read it once; and then letting the energy of the thought seize upon her mind and nerves until she was a mass of fiery intensity. We saw Modjeska do the same thing with several cuttings from the review of a new play. We have seen both Lawrence Barrett and Wilson Barrett awaken their fiery powers by the same method. It is said that not only actors, but men who go to battle, and men who transact business, or men who engage in professional life, almost invariably have some love of such intense thoughts, if they are in any degree magnetic.

This power is necessary and should be cultivated by the methods that have been the common trainers of the greatest people of the past and the present.

You can see the infinitude of the mood of peace.

See where it has led us in our consideration of the study of self-containment alone.

If it is clear to you that this power is the presence of the greatest energy combined with the greatest calmness, we have achieved success in our explanations.

What a wonderful influence a man or woman of self-containment must wield in the world.

That it is worth the effort to win is admitted on all sides. How difficult is it of attainment? Every step of the way has been shown. You cannot certainly discard the practice of the exercises for developing intensity, for they bring quick rewards, and are always enjoyable. We have found nothing in all the world so gratifying as the exhilaration that follows the practice of this form of rendition.

The mastery of the degrees of undulations will prove inviting to you, we feel sure, for it is easily and quickly attained.

Then, with these two preliminary steps taken, you cannot fail to enjoy the short quotations that open up the coloring of the voice and nervous system in the portrayal of the moods and feelings. Having made headway in this line, you are then invited to spend more than the usual amount of time upon one above all others, the color of PEACE.

This is the key that unlocks the realm of self-containment, and people turn instinctively to you in wonder at the imperial calmness of your nature which seems to be all afire with energy while under the perfect control of a fixed and steady purpose.

This one quality alone will draw people to you, and make you their leader. Try it. Not in a small way, but in all its opportunities for making you great.

The reward is yours for the asking.

Chapter Eighteen

HUMANITY
IS A FRAIL REED
WHEN SWAYED
BY MAGNETISM

✛✛

❧ METHODS OF INFLUENCE ☙

✛✛

 E NOW COME to a further advance in the process of transmigration. The moods and feelings open the way to almost every line of development, and this should not be wondered at, for they are all there is of human life. When there are no moods and feelings left, there is no longer any life itself remaining. We saw in the last chapter the force that one mood, peace, may wield in the world. It is not our purpose to follow them all out; for, if we did, it would take volumes to cover the whole ground. New vistas of thought and training open to the view in an almost infinite variety of experiences, of which the study of peace is but one. Persistence in this study will yield a rich harvest.

Substitution is in advance of all the processes that preceded it, and is not the full journey nevertheless.

By substitution is meant the ability to project your own mood at will into another person, and so drive out the latter's mood. To do this you must hold control of a mood that you select by design. Some power is attained at hap-hazard, as has been shown; but it is not scientific, nor can it be depended upon; while the mastery of a selected color is more likely to win for you.

Perhaps the most useful of all the acquired moods is that of peace. It accomplishes the greatest volume of victories, from the least to the mightiest. Let that be made the first goal of your special practice.

To take a further step in the art of controlling by this method, let us look at two laws:

The person who can assume and thoroughly feel any mood at will, is able to recognize the mood that any other person is in.

The person who can assume and feel any mood at will is able to transfer any mood to another person.

The first of these two laws is highly important. It may be doubted at first; but we have shown all the stages of magnetic telepathy, and this is the most practical use of a power that is given to humanity for well understood purposes.

If the success of this course of study depended only on the accuracy of this first law, it would have no chance of failing. In the first place any woman who has lived for years with a man is able to tell the mood he is in, and she does not require lessons to teach her that power. A mother who could not detect the mood of the child would have to be separated from the latter, either in distance or in sympathy. These are common illustrations of a God-given faculty, that may be developed by the practice we have outlined, until it may be applied to strangers and all persons whom you may meet.

It might be thought that the actor would have the same power; but in his profession he seeks only to depict the moods and not to make himself the recipient of them. And his line of moods are not the same in most respects as those used in the development of magnetism.

The eye can help, but it is not required as an aid. It serves to settle doubts and to hasten conclusions. It is always used by those who are within seeing distance, and it is natural to employ it.

A person who has made himself sensitive to a large number of colors will feel the moods of all those who are about him. They seem to stand out like so many signs that are ready to be summoned out of their owners at the will of one person. When the wife realizes that her husband is depressed, melancholy, discouraged, or whatever else may be his mood, she does not try to cheer him up, if she is skillful; but will seek to put herself in accord with him, and thus be his companion in the mood.

She will not, if shrewd, mention the mood, but will get fully into it and make it a part of herself for the time being. This puts a controlled feeling in companionship with the same feeling not under control. The influence of the controlled feeling is to master the uncontrolled, and soon the two moods are mixed and give way to mastery over that which is not under control. The husband will feel the change, and hardly know how to explain it. The wife still is silent except to reply to his inquiries, and he eventually has a desire to talk to her. Being somewhat ashamed of his mood he passes into most any other feeling of his own choice.

Here is another case: A young man has what is called the dumps or "pouts." He is hurt in his feelings and is silent. He may be about the house all day and say nothing. The more you try to get him to talk or to drive the blues away, the more pugnacious he will remain. That is not the course. Say nothing. Get in the same mood with him but be ready to show him ordinary attention and to reply freely and pleasingly to any inquiries or remarks he may make. Do not do the mean thing of shutting up and refusing to be social. That will not cure him. But your silence and your assumption of the mood he is in will shift his and drive it away. In a remarkably short time he will brighten up and even forget that he has been in the dumps. This experiment has been tried with success many scores of times to our knowledge.

Flippancy is the most distasteful mood with which to combat a person who is out of sorts or who is in one of the unworthy colors. Here is a wife who has been hurt by some remark of her husband. She resents it by being silent. He had no malice in what he said, and she realizes that fact, or will do so as soon as she gets her thinking faculties back again. He thinks he will jolly her, as the saying goes, and he is flippant or even flip. She is still more angered, and the mood becomes fixed perhaps for a day or more. Wearied with her nonsense the husband now gets angry and this mood is the wrong one. She may go home to her mother, and so the romance of the wedded life will end.

What should he have done?

If he apologized, she might not have accepted, and his pride would then have been wounded. If he was at fault, he could say so, but the chances are that she would not care whether he was at fault or not, as her mood does not do much brain-work while it is on. It seems in the run of cases, as far as we can get at the facts, that the best course is to take up the mood that the other party is in, and let matters work out their own climax; always standing ready to be courteous and normal in word and deed. "Moody" persons are soon cured of their habits. But this word is taken to mean the disagreeable state of mind that some people enjoy tumbling into when they get their feelings hurt.

But the real mood is the life pulse of every individual, and this is always something; and never nothing.

The most practical of the hard moods is that of deceit. This is so often the mood of the person who seeks to deal with you in business, or who may pretend to be your friend, when there is no actual fondness for you on the part of that individual, that it is an advantage to be able to detect the pretense or deceit.

This involves a peculiar line of practice. The color of deceit must be mastered, and then it should be fully felt as a part of the nervous system. We have shown that the general in war and the financier in business is keen to scent deceit in an opponent, or in the party with whom he is to deal. So acute does this color become in the skilled banker and the shrewd business man, that even so strong a magnetic personality as the fascinating and convincing woman, cannot pass for something that she is not, nor make her story of wealth seem a truth. The more persistent she is in her assertion, the less faith is placed in her word.

To tell when a person is lying, and to feel the untruth, is high art in magnetism; yet it is not at all impossible. Of how much value is it to the student of this book? What will you gain by being able to feel the lie before it is uttered, or afterwards? If some one is trying to deceive you, do you wish to know it?

Some remarkable results have been obtained in this line of practice. The process whereby success is secured, is the same as in the development of the color of peace. Read all that has been said in the preceding chapter; only remember that, when once you have laid the foundation for one color you have laid it for all; and there is nothing further to do but practice in the color until you are skilled in understanding it.

When the elder Booth, the greatest of all American actors, wanted to depict the color of the Jew in the manners and style of talking in Shylock, he lived all day long in the family of some leading Hebrew whom he knew. On the same principle if you wish to get color of deceit, take up the story of fraud in as many phases as you can come in contact with, and master the atmosphere of deceit. Then find some plays where there are lines that portray falsehood and learn to throw yourself thoroughly into the rendering of them. Try to be the deceitful man or woman. This does not require you to deceive any person; for that is the mood acting as your master. Be the controlling power over the assumed mood. In proportion as you imbibe the feeling of deceit as a piece of acting, you will not be likely to use it in actual life; for the actor's art goes by opposites.

The business man who is not able to feel deceit, as in the case of one who is all honesty and knows nothing of the wickedness about him, will not remain long in business. If he is innocent to that extent he will be fleeced by a hundred different people in the first year of his enterprise. The best weapon with which to fight down fraud and deceit is the knowledge of what these wrongs are, and how they operate. Do not avoid knowledge of any mood that may select you some day for its victim.

It has sometimes been asked, shall the young woman or the young man be kept from all knowledge of the sins and wrongs that are everywhere prevalent in the world, or shall they be allowed to get in the mire of sin and crime in order that they may learn how to avoid disaster? Both extremes should be avoided.

The best way to fight down the evil that lurks about on every hand is to know it by study and practical operation in the lives of others, but not by mingling with it as the guilty party. The latter may go on for years and not be able to free himself from his condition. You cannot be the boat that sails in the water, and the water it sails in, at the same time. Young men and women will be our theme later on in this volume as far as they may be helped by magnetism; but, in a general way, it can be stated here that the boat that sails the water is the master of the waves, while the water is the vehicle of transfer from one port to another, and may be the very sewerage of a nasty city.

Now suppose that you have mastered the color of deceit so that you can feel it in your own nervous system, just as the keen financier can feel the falsehood that is spoken or written to him; and suppose that some person seeks to lead you into some transaction where you will be subjected to loss or disgrace; what shall be the process whereby you are to offset that effort? You cannot tell him to his face that he lies, for you may feel it and yet lack the proof. The courts still cling to tangible evidence, which means that they demand proofs that are available of examination before they will allow a verdict or judgment to be rendered; and feelings are not such proof.

What you feel is for your own mind and not for others to know.

What will be the best method whereby to avert the disaster?

You have made yourself sensitive to all efforts to deceive; and this verdict is in your own heart. Throw yourself thoroughly into the mood of deceit. Once there you will be like the keen merchant; he knows the lie before it has fallen from the lips of the falsifier. As he is skilled in the study of deceit, so he is a correct judge of the deceiver. If he chooses he may, in a few questions, throw open the deception. A lawyer who knows how to cross-examine for the truth, would not be long finding out the facts. There are always a limited number of incidents that open the way. You may not know how to find them, and so you could not indulge in cross-examination. The shrewd business man of long years of experience would be an instinctive cross-examiner.

But as you are able to throw yourself into the mood of deceit, you will be in accord with the mood of the party with whom you are dealing. This harmony will be felt by him. He will soon see in his own mind that his scheme is open to the light of day, as it were; and he will seem to realize that it cannot be concealed. Then he will show his shame or whatever mood you choose to swing him into. This is not only not an uncommon experience, but is actually being transacted daily many thousands of times. This we know from careful investigation.

Thus we see again how close to the facts of life are the moods and their characteristics. It is like getting down into the pit of the battle of humanity, to study these various moods one after the other.

Absurd and arbitrary uses of this power are not taught, for the reason that they are not probable. We must keep as near to the actual life about us as is possible. In the study of deceit we see the method by which the mind of the deceiver may be made to feel that his whole scheme is laid bare, whether it is or not. A young man who had concocted a story to his employer in order to be allowed to take an afternoon off, was confounded when his employer looked him all over in a kindly way, and then said,

"Why did you not tell me this an hour ago? I would have sent an ambulance."

But the employer had been taking in the situation and saw in the young man's manner that he was afraid of being exposed for falsifying, and so he turned the subject into another channel. He assumed anxiety in behalf of the young man, and proposed to take the initiative in having help afforded the unfortunate person whose mishap was the cause, in his mind, of the youth desiring to attend that game of ball. So urgent was the employer to be of service that the young man gave up the effort to maintain the excuse. Yet there was not the slightest danger of doing an injustice by being anxious in behalf of the youth; if the story were true the help would be welcomed; and if it were not true, the proffered assistance would break down the fabric of invention, as it in fact did.

This was much better than telling the young man that he lied. It effected the end without risk of being mistaken. It does not pay to be too aggressively suspicious, for a deep wrong may be done by one who thinks it not possible.

Look over the lists of the bad moods and feelings, and see if there are any that you think are present in the personality of some party with whom you are conversing or dealing. Having made yourself sensitive to all of them, try to catch, by feeling your way mentally or in your nervous system, the condition of mind or nerves of the party who is present. In the best class of tests that have been made, the results are somewhat astonishing. A large number of individuals have been able to feel the mood without seeing the party who was present.

In a dark room two men were brought near to each other, but not so close that they could touch. One was an adept in the expression of nearly all the moods. The other had never heard of the work in any way. In less than ten seconds, the former said:

"This gentleman has had some good luck, for he is in a most pleasant mood. He feels joyous."

This turned out to be the fact. It was not mind reading, for there was no attempt to peruse the words that were passing through his mind. It was merely feeling the mood.

In another case a woman was placed in a dark room and twenty persons passed in front of her, all in the dark. Not one was blindfolded, and the room was not light enough to see more than the merest outlines of the body. The lady, who was not in any sense gifted with special powers and who had no clairvoyant sense, but who had taken up this line of study as a pleasure, made the following remarks as the twenty persons passed before her:

"Nonsense, is it not? That is the way you feel, and you and you. This gentleman has lost his courage and is depressed. This one is suspicious. This one is making fun. Here is one who is good-natured but not in the same way as the last. You who come next, would deceive us if you could. This one is flip, or full of nonsense. This one is respectful and kindly."

And so the different veins of the people were tolled off as they went by. Those who had the more serious moods confessed that the facts were correctly stated; but the flippant people denied the accuracy of the judgment, even while exhibiting the very nonsense and flippancy which were described.

Such experiments are not satisfactory, as they seem to have nothing to disclose. The best use of the power of detecting the mood of another is in the serious and important transactions of life, and not in tests made for the amusement of doubters.

You arise in the morning and meet some member of the family. In what mood do you find him or her? If it is necessary to maintain good fellowship, it is well to know just the bent of mind of each person who is met during the day; otherwise the matter does not concern you. The teacher meets the pupil as an individual; and the knowledge of the mood of the latter is helpful in the government of the school, for the individual makes up the whole. In meeting the class, what is the mood of the assemblage as an entirety, and as constituent parts? A keenness of discernment cannot be taken as useless, for it helps in the success of the instructor.

Then the teacher must account in one way or another to the parents and to the committee. The mastery of moods, and the ability to transfer your own self into the self of another person at will, must at all times help to win good opinions and influence, and these you will need. Some teachers call it tact, but tact is mental only, and belongs to the school of diplomacy, which is most excellent as long as it avoids deceit. Diplomacy is compelled to depend largely on flattery and falsehood or simple misrepresentation. The transfer of self leaves the feeling that all has been done for the best interests of the person so influenced. There are teachers who have been so careful to study the moods of all persons with whom they come in contact that they are loved and respected. They never need to look for other friends. This is one of the most desirable victories in life. In its place the efforts to parade genuine ability will not succeed half so well. Of course there must be qualifications for the position of teacher, but you know of scores of instructors who are counted able and skillful in their professional duties, who are not hated. To be qualified and repellant in manner or mood, is not the rule of success. The candidate may say, ''I will show them that I really know all that can be required, and that I am the best qualified of all applicants for the position, and they will then be compelled to employ me.'' But is his logic good?

If a teacher wishes to remain long at one place, or to be called to higher positions, due preparation is the first essential in order of time, but not in order of importance. To know how to deal with pupils and their parents, with the school board and the public, must take prominence over all other considerations. Smartness and commanding talents may set the pace, but magnetism is all that will maintain it.

We recall the case of a man who had received the best education that money could buy in this country; and who had added to it a four years' course in Europe. He knew more than any other school principal in his State, and he was given the best place to be had; but he failed to hold out. Pupils took a dislike to him, other teachers were out of harmony with his method of accosting them and planning their work, and the parents soon reflected these feelings. Mere diplomacy could not have saved him.

In the pulpit there is more need of the power to read moods and to transfer the better ones for the drifting or set feelings that are sure to prevail in church bodies, than in any other profession. The greatest of pastors must be keen readers of humanity. Christ knew what was in the mind and heart of each person in the throng of thousands that stood before Him. He so declared in unmistakable terms.

Let it be acknowledged that special powers were delegated to

Christ, but do not forget that all divine laws are but enlargements of the principles of human conduct. God makes use in more effective form of the laws that are given to man to employ. This fact may be seen in every miracle in the Old and New Testaments. Take, for instance, the frequent reference to the knowledge which Christ had of the thoughts and moods of men and women about him; this keenness of sight or feeling was only an enlarged form of the natural law that millions are using today in all parts of the globe, though in lesser force. Christ used a natural law, not a supernatural one.

Let any person enter into the study of this law of transference of self into self, and the same power will be increased until it approaches the divine perfection. On earth nothing is really perfect, and no human being could hope to attain that condition; but men and women have lived and do live who are able to feel the mood of any other person at will, to make known the fact, and to substitute the better or stronger mood in place of the lesser.

The difficulty arises in the lack of language to interpret the meaning of a mood. Words are not synonyms for feelings. Christ could read the hearts and minds of men in any part of the globe, although He had before Him only those who talked Hebrew or Greek. To the individual who depends on words as means of influence, the absence of a knowledge of the French tongue would be a barrier to the exercise of authority over a Frenchman; but the language of moods and feelings, like that of music, is world wide. Even more, it is as broad as the universe itself.

A word is an attempt to preserve or convey an idea that relates to some thing, condition or action on earth, or that has association with such thing, condition or action. Words serve no other purpose. But humanity is not as narrow as the life on earth. There are elements of a broader existence that are all the time making themselves felt in the mind and soul, and words do not express them.

If there should ever be established in this world a language that can be understood everywhere, it must have as its basis the synonyms of moods and feelings, and the notes of music; for these cannot change. In the hereafter the same language would of necessity be adopted, for life beyond the earth is made up of the perfected moods and feelings, with song in the hearts of everybody.

A clergyman who could increase the Christ-like power of reading the minds and hearts of men, would rise rapidly in his avocation until at last he stood close to the divine teacher; as near as it is possible for humanity to come. To him this course of training would mean greatness and a giant-like success in saving others. His usefulness would be almost without limit.

In the first place he would draw people to him. He would not be misled as to their intentions and purposes. If they possessed hell-born moods, he could drive them out, and here again we see a law that is useful in lesser degree, but of the same character as that employed by Christ, who drove out devils. A devil is a bad mood. There may be no other devil in the universe. A bad mood is enough to carry all the charges and odium of any devil. Look at the hell-born moods of a preceding chapter, and note how many of them are devilish. Here you have the answer to the question, what it was that the Savior drove out of men and women?

They fled into the swine.

Still another law comes into play that will be considered in later pages of this work.

Our purpose is to show that there are no supernatural conditions in the universe. All is natural, but not recognized. The powers that are called supernatural, and therefore miraculous, are larger uses of the same laws that are offered to you and to each and every human being.

The first law that was enlarged was that of knowing the thoughts and moods of men. This law you know is at work in lesser degree in your own life and everywhere; the only difference being in the greater sensitiveness of the person who perceives the conditions in another. We have cited many instances of the everyday operation of this principle, and these cases are known to you, for you have witnessed them in other people in one way or another.

The second law of the supposed supernatural is that of driving out the evil dwellers that possessed certain men and women. By transmigration the same operation is going on in this and every age. Let us see if we can make this clear.

Self is the individual. Self is composed of moods and feelings.

Another person possesses a Self, and that consists of moods and feelings. Assuming that that self is weighted down by the presence of hell-born moods and feelings, and you can project into him your own Self which we will suppose to be possessed by heaven-born moods and feelings, you transfer the better dwellers from your own body into his body. The evil is driven out and the good takes its place.

When devils are cast out it is not essential to the working of the law for better moods from the master personality to enter in their place, for some mood will follow. The mere casting out of devils would be sufficient to get rid of them. Christ may or may not have brought people to His own standard. The operation of the free will may, on the other hand, have been the plan, which would leave each man and woman to act without being subjected to the superior power.

In your own case, assuming that it is your purpose to control some other mind, you will transfer such Self as you have summoned, which means such mood as you have brought within yourself, to the individual over whom you seek control. His own mood may stand in the way. That you cast out. How are you to do it? Suppose it will not leave, what then?

Here magnetism comes into play. If there were to be no obstacle, there would be no need of magnetism. The possession of power over the magnetic waves is readily asserted in every such case. In the first place, there is the magnetism which has been developed in the practice of the exercises in the first book. Then the development of intensity and undulations, will put that magnetism into the waves that pass between you and the individual over whom you seek mastery. The next step is the ability to know the minds and hearts of men; which knowledge you gain by the colors that have been built up in your practice under the exercises of the preceding chapters. They make you sensitive and susceptible to all moods and feelings of others.

Finally comes the decision on your part to assume a certain color or mood which you wish to make prevail in the person before you.

Good dwellers have been driven out of people by the influence of others. The resolve to be honest and honorable has been swept away by the magnetism of others. They may never have studied the art, but the fact that they can drive out the good and substitute the bad is proof of the possession of this power in its dark phases.

You have this influence over others for good or evil; and it rests with you to determine which way you will sway the lives of those with whom you come in contact.

If you have given average attention and interest to the instruction up to this point, we are positive that you will be able to exert whichever side of the list of moods and feelings you choose, in the life of any person, unless you meet someone who is your superior in the use of magnetism. Even then there is a defence available in your behalf and in most cases an opportunity to overcome the greater influence which may operate against you.

Perhaps you seek to take advantage of another person, not to do him wrong, but to make your own position better or stronger. In such case you must substitute your own Self in place of his Self. Maybe you are a wife, and do not receive enough attention at home from your husband. He no longer is charmed by your presence and voice. You have grown unattractive and annoying to him. Your method of scolding him, nagging him, or picking a quarrel on the least provocation, has made it all the more desirable in his opinion to spend his evenings away.

Is it worth while to win him back? No, he is too ugly, too conceited, too boorish, too much of an animal, and too everything for you to waste time or money trying to get back what you are sorry you ever got in the first place. This is the mood of most wives who have seen the romance go out of wedlock, day by day, until nothing but the mire is left in the pen.

They hate the kind of man their husband is, although they may not dare to say they hate him personally; they hate themselves for having made such a mistake; and they hate the bonds of wedlock. If they are young and attractive, they begin to cast about to see if they have fascinations for other men, and the door is ajar for scandal and divorce. If they are too old to charm another man, they look up the business opportunities for women to support themselves; and all day long their thoughts are disloyal to home and husband.

What is the better way?

Not particularly the moral way, or the Bible way, but the method that, in their case, will bring the most substantial reward?

There is but little cost required to make themselves actually pleasing and charming, even in their maturity. Some effort is necessary, but it is the part of wisdom to waste less time in cheap reading and cheaper gossip, and put more time into self-improvement. We believe that the husband is the reflection of the wife, and the wife is the reflection of the husband. It requires two parts to make a reflection; and the couple that is so widely estranged from the first months of wedlock as not to be interested in each other is the exception and not the rule.

Here is a wife who writes us in all confidence that her husband is so offensive to her that she hates to know that he is in the house. She poohpoohs the idea of trying to make herself charming for him, and starts to quote the saying, ''Cast pearls before, etc.'' It certainly is a hopeless case to begin work with.

Let us cite a case that has been worked out since our very last book was written.

Just such a wife wrote that she wanted to try to make a swine a human being, and was willing to degrade herself in the experiment upon her husband. He was foul of speech and foul of manner. He had been going lower ever since they had been married. Now he chewed tobacco, and even spit upon the floor of the house. He talked in nasty tales, and had epithets that were vile. His teeth were a sight, his breath too realistic to be mistaken for a flower garden, and there was not one good word that could be spoken in his favor.

But she was willing to degrade herself.

She seemed surprised to be told that the first improvement must be in herself. She was all right. She needed no improvement.

Still she agreed to reduce her gossipy engagements, and in a short time she postponed them, or, as she put it, adjourned them over until the experiment had ended.

She also agreed to pay more attention to the kitchen and the cooking. Indigestible articles gradually disappeared, and the stomach complaint of the husband went with it. This made him feel better and his irritability was lessened. He had been fed with cake, pastry, and all kinds of troublous things, in addition to some plain food, and the latter assumed a majority without his protest. In fact he said that he liked his meals better than ever before.

She took up a line of useful reading. He was a reader of the news and had magazines about him, behind which he hid himself when she had curtain lectures by the hour; then he sought solace away from home at night. She ceased the lectures and stopped criticizing his fearful faults. He began to remain in on stormy nights; and things were so comfortable that he lost most of his inclination to go out at all. His wife seemed to take an interest in having him at home.

When things went wrong, he abused her as before, and used vile language, and was most offensive, but she kept her temper under restraint, and his manner and diction gradually changed.

The color of PEACE she mastered. It pervaded her voice, her manner, her presence, and filled the home with its fragrance. One day, as she was sitting at the window, two men going by were heard by her husband, who sat at another window obscured, to say: "There is a beautiful woman." A week after a friend of this husband, said to him: "Henry, you have a very sweet wife. I am surprised that you and she do not appear more in public." He said nothing. But once more a third party made the same assertion, and he began to think. He looked at his wife, when she was not looking at him. He noticed the tidy and neat appearance of her attire; he had never heeded that before. Her eye was bright. There was a sweetness in her face and manner. She had changed, but so gradually that he had never noticed it. Now he felt that he was once more in love with her. He paid some attention to his dress and manners. Words that he used to shout out, he felt were offensive to the very air, and he omitted them. Soon he began to assume an attractiveness that she admired, and her old hatred for him vanished.

This case is a fact, not merely a polishing up of a basis in fact, but a straight report from beginning to end, in its minutest details.

Which was the better course to pursue?

Is it, or is it not true that the wife reflects the husband and the husband reflects the wife?

If it is true, then you are what your mate has made you, and your mate is the result of your making. A responsibility rests on both of you.

To say that the subject is not worth the trouble to improve, is equal to saying that your reflection is too bad to be made better.

Let this principle be fully understood, and unhappiness will depart from wedlock. The main cause of the trouble is the unwillingness of one party to bend and crawl before the other. They cannot see that the bending and crawling are done before themselves. Nothing is ever lost that begins with self-improvement.

We cannot see where the servility comes in when you make up your mind that you will cast pearls before swine. The pearls are your better value, created and developed by pure will-power, and the swine is the reflection of yourself in the life of a person who has been associated with you. Look the matter squarely in the face, and see if this is not so. Humility is a heaven-born mood; adopt it. Through its leavening process you will brush away the cobwebs of your own conceit. But humility is not servility. It is a tearing down of the monuments of evil that hold you to a bad resolve.

Our first advice to a man or woman who seeks to re-build the nest in which fate forces them to live, is to aim at self-improvement, and take the chances.

The oft repeated history of human struggles in the privacy of life shows one fact above all others, and it is this: The better mold in which daily character is built gives shape to all who come within the radius of the uplifted personality.

Confidence is an opening key to all good opinions, and helps to make it easy to transfer your Self in place of another Self. To first gain the confidence of the person whom you would control is half the victory. Let us see how this is to be done, and apply a few general suggestions to the method.

Many things begin in confidence; but the confidence is not perfect. What is called "a sure thing" is not absolute; for it would upset the laws of probability and possibility, and destroy the element of chance that belongs to every train of circumstances. Yet the person who is controlled in a magnetic sense, never has any defect or doubt in the confidence which is bestowed. There the kind that belongs to personal magnetism is perfect, and differs in this respect from all other kinds.

A few illustrations of what is meant may be given here. Take as the first one the case of the minister. In order to be successful in his profession he should win and hold the confidence of four classes of people: First, the members of his church who are sincere in their protestations of goodness; second, the insincere members of his church; third, the sincere people of the general community who are not of his church; fourth, the insincere people of the general community. These classes all have their eyes upon him; or at least a representative number of them do. His earnest pleadings in the pulpit, his emotional prayers, his tearful solicitude for souls, his zeal in his churchwork, and similar exhibitions of what may be an acquired art, are not what secures the confidence of any of these classes. Nor will his spasmodic efforts in behalf of reform suffice. The people look at the man, both in and out of the church. Is he a true man? Are his protestations genuine? Is he a man of good judgment in all departments of life? Is he trying to improve himself every day of his life? Is he progressing? Does he mean it when he expresses his belief in dogmas, creeds, and certain phases of theology, or is he acting a lie in order to please those who hire him to preach? What kind of a man is he when calling, or in trade, or on the street, or under special circumstances? The people want to get at the *man,* and thus learn of the preacher. When the sincere members of the church find him to be an earnest, honest, dignified, courageous, cool-headed, self-improving, progressive, highly intelligent man, with sense enough to make each sermon "the greatest effort of his life" by means of careful preparation in matter as well as in manner of delivery, they will flock to his standard and believe in him. The insincere members of his church will then thin out and leave, or will become penitent and join the ranks of honest worshipers. Those of the community who are churchless will be attracted to the place where he preaches; for a sincere and capable minister is a rare jewel these days. Capability in this profession means the ability to speak better than any other person in the community. Oratorical grandeur is not only attractive, but is also wanted. The masses of the people wish true oratory to stir them to action; but the narrow minds that control the church declare that the minister is good enough for them and so the church stands still, nursing its moral weaklings one week and lashing them the next.

Ability inspires some confidence. The good sisters and sluggish male drones of a church who think the minister is good enough, are millstones around his neck; for their praise ruins his chances of acquiring ability. They praise his weak preaching to please him, not because they believe in him. It is customary to praise inferior ministers; no one dares to extol a capable one.

The lawyer must have ability, judgment, dignity, earnestness, honesty, and untiring studiousness, in order to win the confidence of the public. A really great lawyer is not an extortionist. Most lawyers are extortionists. When the public gets the opinion that attorneys think more of fees than of justice, then these men are hired as ferrets are employed—always with a fear that they will turn and bite their employers. A true lawyer wishes to see justice triumph, and as speedily as possible. The attorney who fights with technicalities to throttle justice, never holds the confidence of the public. There are three things that bring discredit upon the legal profession; the law's delay, its technicalities, and the extortionate fees that are charged. A lawyer who takes a firm stand against all three; and who is a true man on all occasions, in public and in private, will soon win the confidence of the people. He must be a man of dignity, of solid character, of sterling honesty and of studious habits. Such a lawyer would soon be at the head of his profession.

Judges are too often weak men. They lack courage, and people withhold confidence in them. Of all classes, the judiciary ought to most readily win the trust of the people; and yet in this country the intelligent public distrust the judges from the highest to the lowest. Election of judges is wrong in principle, for the products of machine politics are never capable of reaching that standard of excellence that comes from nomination by the executive. The latter takes pride in his selection for a life-office, and his mistakes have been few compared with those made by political machine election, and more particularly those in such a State as New York where party judges make party decisions in many instances. The moral and mental weakness of judges is seen in the decisions which they render; many of their reasons being nothing but slavery to technicalities. In Missouri the Supreme Court reversed case after case in the convictions of the bribe-takers of that State. In Delaware a negro who ravished a girl, cut her open, tortured her and murdered her, although proved guilty by overwhelming evidence at every trial, was sent back and forth for years between the Supreme Court and the trial court on technicalities until at last he was set free by action of the Supreme Court, and is living today. In the same State, another negro who had ravished a girl and been set free after a term of imprisonment, laid in wait for another girl, outraged her, cut her open to make entrance, then cut her throat because she would not promise to keep silent after he let her go; and the public, viewing her dead body and remembering the technicalities of their Supreme Court in a similar case, resolved to take the law in their own hands.

It is because of the slowness of justice, the long dragging of trials, the quibbling of lawyers and the swarm of technicalities that everywhere abound, making courts and judges the most unbusinesslike examples of modern times, that the public lack confidence in the judiciary. Brave judges are rare. For fear of adverse criticism many of them cater to the sensational press, and mold their decisions to receive the claptrap praise of the latter.

In order to win confidence the doctor should study disease from the standpoint of the habits of his patient, and he should awake to the fact that food and régime are the sole causes of every malady. The skilled doctor will get at the cause as well as the remedy for sickness, and will treat for prevention as well as for cure. He must possess personal qualities that are in harmony with his profession, gentleness, sympathy, earnestness, studious progress with the times, and a high standard of health in his own body.

The business man must win public confidence because of his integrity—a quality that is very rare in business; but this is only a beginning. He must be awake to the fact that most lines of trade are full of fraud and adulteration; and his excuse that he buys the goods in the belief that they are honest, does not win the confidence of the people in his ability. It is a part of his business, and should be made a part of his education for entering business, to know how to find out whether goods are pure or not. Here are two druggists on the same street in a city. One sells over two hundred articles that are shoddy and adulterated. The other sells over three thousand such articles. The latter knows very well that the goods are not honest; and he has no right to be in business if he does not at least guess as much. A church elder, a real honest man, told us that he sold only honest goods; at least he did not know it if they were not; and yet we went through his store and almost emptied his shelves in discarding articles that were adulterated. How does an honest man feel when he has a half-belief that he is cheating the public and does not intend to do it?

Ignorance is no excuse. When a man enters upon a business career he owes a duty to his customers; and that duty is his fitness to be in business. In these days of consummate fraud in all directions, and especially in selling adulterations, the man who is to deal in goods should prepare himself in advance by a line of education that embraces the knowledge necessary to buy honest goods of all kinds. Instead of doing this, he thinks he is qualified if he can purchase low and sell high, and thus make a profit. That kind of a man can never win the confidence of the people. Honesty is the first great element of success in trade; but honest weight and measure are not enough. There must be a stirring about, an aggressiveness that will drive the fraudulent manufacturer and wholesaler out of business, and a determination to protect the public without being asked or required to do so. What sort of a heaven is there for those religious men who profess to be God's own and who in business do as the grocer, who tries to sell us poor goods part of the year, and yet holds a high position in church? The agent of the wholesale house of which he buys showed us his order for goods; and every item was the cheapest and shoddiest grade. The agent said: "This man is like hundreds of others. He won't pay an honest price. We carry shoddy goods for that class of merchants. They know there are several grades better in almost every line before they get to the first class goods; but they won't touch anything but the shoddiest and cheapest." So this man stocks his store with fraud and pretence to save a few cents here and there. What kind of a heaven is there for him? If he would win confidence let him protect his customers. There are many ways of doing it, even with financial gain to himself.

The clerk, maid, or other employee, who would gain the trust of his employer has a splendid opportunity of doing so. Of course honesty is always essential; but stupidity is honest; and many non-progressive persons are honest in the sense that they are non-criminal. More is needed. The employees should have no limits of responsibility. They should keep within their lines of duty, and should be ready at all times to be generally helpful in every way. It is not enough to perform all necessary work; they should do it in the best possible manner, and should study all other opportunities of being helpful. They should hunt up all the little duties that may pertain to their employment; and should study their employer's interests in preference to their own. The fear of giving more value than they receive makes them desire to be on the safe side by giving less value than they receive. Most employees are eye-servants, and dodgers at that. They acquire the art of pretence so as to appear to be doing all that is expected of them, when in fact they are not.

As the people who are employed are by far the most numerous of all classes, let us take the time to present two typical cases. Here is a young man who is given charge of a small department of business in an office or store. He is on time, but rarely ahead of time, morning and noon. When the hour comes to go at the end of the forenoon and afternoon, he shoots out of the building at the exact second of time. His employer, who knows something of human nature, is convinced that the young man will give never a thought to the duties of his employment from the moment he leaves until he returns, so he watches him. He gives the young man several letters to answer on the typewriter; and suddenly enters the room a while later. The typewriter is quickly closed with paper in it. The employer lifts it and exposes the paper; it is a letter to some other young man regarding their last "smoker" at the club. That ends the employment. The incidents are merely straws, but they are typical of the millions of similar cases where, in one way or another, employees are unfaithful to their trusts and are unsuccessful in their chosen paths.

To the same employer there came another young man. After the newness had worn off, this young man was still coming to his duties ahead of time; and, when the hour of leaving arrived, he was never in a rush to go. He did his work as well when not watched, as when he was observed. He hunted for things to do. He asked for more work but not for more pay. When at times he did not have enough to do to keep him busy, he took an interest in putting things to rights, filing away papers more neatly, and verifying some of his past work. This done, and yet there being moments of leisure from time to time, he asked permission to study up his grammar, his rhetoric, and other useful lines of knowledge; and so he plodded on, making use of the little minutes, the diamonds of time, until at length he found himself on the road to rapid promotion.

He had won the confidence of his employer. Beginning at a meager salary which barely supported him, he took as much interest seemingly in the business as did its owner. He was in real earnest, in deadly earnest. He is a type of employee that is rare in this country. Honesty is necessary, but it is only the beginning. Ability is not everything. Honesty and ability are not all. They must exist. But the employee must have a genuine interest in the employment, must give it thought outside of business hours, must be progressive, must be self-improving, must be willing and in harmony with the position, and must accomplish all that is possible. If you receive ten dollars a week, do not be afraid to make yourself worth fifteen or eighteen dollars a week. The employee who says, "When I get more pay I will give more value," rarely ever rises. Nor will the underpaid person go along without reward. More than ninety per cent of employees are routine workers, glad when the day's duties are done, and sorry when they begin. It is because of the prevalence of this indifference to their employers' interests that salaries are kept low. A man at the head of a department store said, "I keep watch over the methods of eight hundred girls, although they do not know how I do it. I am sorry to say that most of them are unworthy of their places, and that is the reason they are paid so little." He then called in a woman of forty and said, "Tell this gentleman what your salary is,"—"Thirty dollars a week," she replied.—"How many years have you worked for me?"—"Nearly twenty-six years," she said.—"What did you first receive?"—"Six dollars a week."—And she went on with a description of many other girls who had been selected for promotion, solely because of their interest in their work; and the salaries of all such were exceedingly high. "A girl who is faithful is sure to be promoted; and all others stay down." This is true in nearly every place of business. The successful employer keeps watch over those he hires, and has a way unknown to them of finding out what interest they take in the duties assigned to them. No work is well done that is disliked.

What have all these facts to do with magnetism? Very much. The one underlying principle is the ability to gain the confidence of those who can be helpful to you or who can assist in making your life a success. Magnetism cannot exist for itself. Its very nature implies two or more persons. If you were the only person living you could not rise in the world or win success. You need the help of others. Absolute loneliness in earth or heaven is suicide.

No person can acquire magnetism who is a drifter, or who leads an aimless life, or who follows a routine line of duties without a specific purpose to accomplish deeds that require the surmounting of difficulties. We have seen thousands of men and women who are more or less magnetic, and we have never yet seen one such who was not bent upon doing something that was of general or of specific value to the world, or to some other people than himself or herself. This fact may seem strange to students of this art. It was a surprise to us. At first we thought it a coincidence in a number of cases; but after careful investigation we found that it was always true where genuine magnetism was present.

A certain law is at work in this disposition to accomplish something that is difficult; nor does it indicate a desire to be cranky or eccentric. The peculiar methods that some persons adopt are always handicaps to their success and magnetism. The rule is that you must be in harmony with the drift of conservative public opinion, and yet take the lead in something. In taking the lead do not pull away from those you wish to follow-you; keep back with them close enough to be of them; for if you pull away too far to the front you will be alone; and to be alone is to fail for the time at least.

These considerations show that personal magnetism is a talent that is bestowed upon men and women to make them useful to the world or to some part of it, however small. Crankiness and eccentricity destroy confidence, or make it hard to gain. Dishonesty, flippancy, insincerity, frothiness in sentiment, and indifference to self-improvement are barriers to all efforts to gain public confidence; yet if a person undertakes to be ultra-honest to the extent of parading it, or if he puts a stiff dignity in the place of flippancy, or if his sincerity becomes a graveyard seriousness, or if cant takes the place of his frothiness, he is still a failure; for success lies in the middle ground between extremes of self-exhibition.

Personal magnetism is built upon thoughtfulness. The mind must be trained to great activity. As magnetism is a bolt of purpose hurled from a fund of purpose, the determination must have origin in the fullness of the mind, for there can be no purpose where there is no deep-seated and burning thought. It is necessary for you to keep thinking. Choose the kind of thoughts that enter your brain. Get your inspiration for thinking, not from the news and editorials of newspapers, nor from the opinions of the people who feel more than they think. Acquire the power to disbelieve in these sources; for the masses are weak, and they believe what they hear and read. It is a sign of inferiority to believe in such cheap sources of information as newspapers and frothy talkers.

Base your beliefs on proven facts.

Having learned the art of belief in selected sources of information, and the art of disbelief in other lines of statement, develop the power of thought in the spare moments of the day. Have no idle seconds in your mind. Thought is the mainspring of magnetism. This power is not an empty affair, but is substantial and full of valuable composite parts. The thoughtful person is not always magnetic, but the magnetic person is always thoughtful. These laws should be well understood. Magnetism is so great a power and is capable of accomplishing so much for its possessor, that it must in the very nature of things be built of something real.

It is true that many persons are naturally gifted with magnetic fire, but that is only one of the corner stones of personal magnetism. Like a flash of lightning, it runs away with itself. This misuse of the gift is seen in the ignorant actor, orator, politician or woman flirt. Each has power, but no control. The ignorant actor is often very magnetic, but his art is a series of explosions that fracture his hopes. He starts with no fund of promise except magnetic fire, to which he couples a love of dramatic expression that is inborn in every normal life. If he is wise enough to become studious, thoughtful, self-improving in his mental department, he is sure to rise; but if he places no value on such studies as history, language and rhetoric, he will fail, for he can no more drive his powers of magnetism and dramatic expression than a child can drive the steeds of a Roman chariot.

Thought, then, is the mainspring of magnetism, and must be cultivated. It should be constant, deep and diverse; not wavering, shallow, and in one channel. Weak thinkers, or those who keep along one line, are never magnetic. While thoughtfulness should be founded upon selected sources of information, it should run off into the daily inquiry, "What use can I put this idea to in my own life?" And the use must be such that the thinker will not get too far in advance of the people whose confidence he hopes to win.

It is at this very juncture that the work of real magnetism begins. There must be the thought, there must be the advanced idea and the work to be accomplished, and there must be the methods that win public confidence. Keep these three laws in mind.

By public we mean any person or persons of your association or meeting that you wish to lead, whether one, two, or a thousand. Numbers do not count in any one effort, except where the nature of the effort implies many followers. You may be the leader in your own home, or in your office, or in your society, or at the bar, in the pulpit, in the drawing-room, or out in the wide world in some one line of achievement.

The habit and power of valuable thinking cannot be acquired at once. They take time. Start them slowly and do not get discouraged. They will begin to grow if you really wish them to, and try to make them.

The best advice we can give at this time, is to get control of the little moments of the day. They are abundant. Disuse of the brain for even one minute, weakens its magnetism. As long as there is variety of thought there can never be too much thinking. Many of the headaches that attend brainwork are due to the emptiness of the stomach, for the mind does not endure long tasks with the stomach foodless. This is a physical consideration.

As the brain must be sustained by nutrition, so the mind must be fed by purpose. Every magnetic man and woman has been constantly busy with some mental purpose; something in progress of planning or to be accomplished. It is impossible for magnetism to exist without such purpose at hand; and the eagerness to win any achievement of the mind is of itself a great developer of magnetism.

Here is the first law of the personal power without practice. It comes by habit. Every life runs to some kind of habit, and either in one direction or another. It requires no more time to develop a good habit than it does a bad one. It is a matter of choice.

Not only must the mind live in one or more constant purposes, but it must adopt a new method of receiving information. We have made a study of magnetic men and women; and this study has covered a very long period of time. One fact that has surprised us as much as any is the celerity with which such persons grasp ideas. So marked has been this trait, and so uniformly general has it appeared in all lives that have succeeded through magnetism, that we were at one time almost convinced that it alone was the cause of personal magnetism.

To ascertain the truth we took advantage of our wide acquaintance with these men and women, and asked them point-blank such questions as were likely to bring decisive answers one way or the other. Observing a man reading a book of history, we asked him if he knew what was on a page that he had merely glanced at. "I know every fact on that page that is of service to me at this time." "But," we said, "you were about five seconds in reading the whole page. How can you know anything about the facts that you did not see?" "I saw them all in a glance. I learned to take in all the contents of a page by a quick movement of the eye; and any fact that needed closer study could be reviewed, while all else was passed by. At first I could not do much with this practice, but the more I tried it the easier it became." "Why did you ever undertake it?" "An old lawyer, a friend of my father's, and a judge of court, advised the practice, telling me that it would make my mind quick and alert. From the time I began it until I had acquired it in full I steadily improved, if results are to be considered." "How did you begin the practice?" "I was told to take a short paragraph and read it with the eye as quickly as I could, then recall the fact that most impressed me. But I could not do this with a paragraph. I began with sentences of single lines, having from five to eight words each, and then I succeeded very well. I allowed but one glance of the eye, a quick flash across the line, to tell me the fact that was recorded. The mind grew into new habits right away. Longer sentences came in turn; until a paragraph of a hundred or more words was as easily absorbed. Then pages were read by glances. I told this to a clergyman, a young fellow who was struggling along in obscurity, and he took up the practice. Today his sermons are winning victories in the pulpit, both for their literary value and for their substance." The more alert the mind is, the more it secures of the knowledge of the world, in the past and present.

An alert mind is quick-acting. It is not the dull mind of a student or bookworm whose brain is weighted down with volumes he has read, for such a mind is slow to act. When the brain is quick to receive and flexible to assort a mass of facts, it is magnetic; and that is just what the practice referred to will make it.

We saw a young man rise out of the ranks of the laboring classes by the aid of this practice; and he began it in about the same way as that which was adopted by the man whose experience has been so amply stated herein.

We also recall the case of a clerk who wished some way in which to attract public attention so that he might be sought after; but he did not wish to enter politics. We suggested this same practice, as we were then experimenting with it, and wished to know what it could do for others. He began slowly and was quite a time in getting hold of the essential power by which a fact could be picked quickly from a line. But he succeeded, as any and every person may. He came to possess a mind that was wonderfully quick to catch ideas and ready in the assortment of them, selecting the potent ones and letting all others go; and he rose out of his position as clerk into that of partner in a very prosperous business. He has told us many times that he owes his success to our advice and the method which he adopted.

In many court trials we have watched the methods of successful lawyers. They are always magnetic; but some of them possess personal magnetism and others have only mental magnetism. We have sat hundreds of times close to lawyers of the highest magnetism, and have assisted them in much of their work, and therefore know the facts of which we speak. One thing that has struck us as peculiarly forcible in its suggestive meaning, is the facility with which some lawyers read a page of a book or letter. We have in mind a number of instances where some attorney has gained a material advantage by a quick glance of the eye. It is not in one case but in many that this gift has led to a signal victory. Of the several instances referred to, one may be cited as an example of what the eye may be trained to do. A lawyer wished to compare a signature to a letter with another signature, but did not wish to show the contents of the letter, nor was it necessary to do so; but in turning over the page he allowed the opposing counsel a glance that could not have exceeded a fourth of a second in time, yet the trained eye of that counsel took an instantaneous photograph of the page and caught a most important fact. Not one person in a million could have done the same thing, but it was the one in the million that did it and reaped the advantage. We had noticed the incident and followed the matter very earnestly for several months, and at last found out that the lawyer had devoted himself to the practice of catching the contents of a page by the quick use of the eye and mind.

The catching of the contents of a page consists in the use of the eye by a sweeping glance, accompanied by an alert brain that has been brought by practice into the habit of perceiving any one or more facts that may be sought, while all others are allowed to pass without attention. This, at least, is the ultimate purpose of the practice. In the period of developing the habit, it is necessary to retain all the ideas; but later on the important ones are to be sought and all others let go.

The purpose of taking in the principal facts at a glance is to save time in reading, and to be able to secure the needed or useful facts and not be burdened with the others. By this practice a person will have the opportunity to read hundreds of books where now he reads but one. He can take in all the news of the paper each day, and leave the mud out of his mind, consuming not more than five minutes in the duty. The person who spends more than five minutes daily in reading the news, except where there is some great event to be perused, is a waster of time, and is moving backward in the world.

This quick reading is preparatory only: for it is to be used to give the reader nothing but a general idea of the contents of a book or periodical. When a fact of real value is reached, then the time for study has arrived. This study should be slow, deep and thorough. No person of sense would think of studying the novels and papers or magazines of the day; they may be read by the glancing practice, and any facts that need careful consideration may be given full attention, but they need not be studied. There are some lines of information that are great enough to be made guiding rules in life, and they cannot be studied too much. Every person should have a certain number of books that possess this rare value, and should make friends and intimate companions of them.

If you can take into your mind twiæ as many important facts today as you did yesterday, you have gained twice the mental vitality. The brain is stimulated and not wearied by this excess of work. It is an easy task to form the habit of doubling your store of facts that possess real value, and to do it in a short time; but the limit is not in doubling them once. When you find that you can as readily get one hundred per cent more knowledge in the brain today than you could a few days ago, you will then proceed to double that; and so continue until you have acquired the ability of taking in facts by mere glances of the eye. Then the vitality of the brain will have grown accordingly. There will be real value there; and real value in the mind is of itself a thing that commands attention from others and also wins approval and even a certain kind of worship, for the public have a great admiration for a man or woman who is in fact brainy and substantially wise. It is the pretence that fails.

The alertness of the mind is of itself a great magnetic stimulator and excitant. Magnetism is a sort of suppressed excitement as opposed to the usual deadness of interest that is present with unmagnetic people. Alertness must be real; and the only way to make it real is to adopt the method of training the eye and mind together to catch facts from a page of print or writing. There are two ways to proceed. One we have already given in the experience of the man whose words we have quoted; the other is as follows:

Take a page of very coarse handwriting, containing about one hundred words, and have not less than five ideas in that page. Hold the paper up before the person who is to go into training, and withdraw it in a half-second. The person should have not quite time enough to see what is written. Previous habit will make a long and steady glance necessary. We refer to three seconds as a long time in which to glance at a page of one hundred words. The matter should be new to the person, or the training will not progress. After the glance of about a half-second of time, the person who glanced should state how many ideas he caught. The teacher should have four sheets of paper all written on in the same handwriting and of the same size, but each of the four pages should have one idea taken out and another that is entirely different substituted.

By this is meant that the five ideas of the first page should all appear but one on the second page, and the five ideas of the first page should all appear but one on the third page, and the five ideas of the first page should all appear but one on the fourth page. This will preserve the five original ideas all through, so that those that are used as substitutes will take the place of one only of the first five, and two new ideas will never be present in any of the pages that follow. If a substitute were to be put in the second page for idea number two of the first page, then idea number two would have to reappear in pages three and four; and so on.

Hold up page one to the person to be trained; then in half a second withdraw it; and ask what idea was caught. Then hold up the same page and ask for two ideas only. Now hold up the second page and call for one idea; then hold up the same page and call for two ideas; then the other pages in the same way. Having used all four of the pages, hold up the first and call for three ideas; then the second and call for three ideas, then the third and call for three ideas, and likewise the fourth; then go back to the first and call for four and so proceed all through, and finally call for all the ideas on each page.

This is practice, and we promised to present a system that did not require any practice at all. This we will do. The plan by which the eye and mind are trained to quickly grasp many ideas is shown in the foregoing method; but the very principle, now that it is understood, may be utilized by busy persons in their daily habits. If you do not have the time to practice, you have at least the time to form different habits, and life is merely the making of one kind of habit or another. It does not require practice but determination to teach yourself a very effective system of mental alertness. Try it in reading the morning paper, or that of the evening if you so prefer, and it will save you time. Take a paragraph and see how quickly you can gather up its ideas. Or, if you select the Sunday science columns of the great (?) editions of the day of rest, you will be able to secure the idea in each article in one fell swoop, and you will never find two ideas there to bother you, even if you study very hard in your search for them. The trip to the North Pole is far more productive of discoveries, and not a bit harder.

Business men teach themselves this art by the law of necessity; and they do not set aside any time for special practice. Letters come in by the thousand every month, and the pith must be seen at a glance unless some salient point is at hand; then the letter must be studied. We do not teach neglect of important matters. A man who is compelled to read one hundred letters a day will stay up all night the first time he tries it; for his mind will not work fast enough to get the contents and feel that he has made no mistake. At the end of a week he will be proceeding twice as fast, and may be able to read one hundred letters in twelve hours. At the end of a month he will do the same work in six hours; and at the end of a few years he will do it in one hour. These things are facts. We have done this, and have also dictated answers to more than one hundred letters in ten hours, although the mind ought not to do so much work of opposite natures in so small a space of time. Severe neuralgia is the penalty.

The point we are making is that habits and not practice may bring the alertness of the brain that leads to magnetism. Any alert brain is magnetic.

CHAPTER NINETEEN

+++

THE BEST STUDENTS
ARE
THE BEST
REVIEWERS

+++
⚜ TEMPORARY SUMMARY ⚜
+++

VERY EARNEST student of these pages will stop to get breath at this juncture. Much has been presented that calls for special consideration now, before proceeding to the further application of the principles of control. The things that must come most prominently before the mind of the reader will be stated here as a sort of temporary summary; from which further progress will be made to higher ground. What are the facts that seem to hold the attention?

The first, and perhaps the last great consideration of the chapter just closed, is the fact that magnetism is not an empty power. It cannot be built on itself alone, nor will it avail the crude mind or the worthless character. A low moral condition cannot employ it without genius somewhere. The combination of immorality and genius makes it most dangerous; and we regret to say that the world presents more such cases than it does of the combination of high morality and genius.

But the man or woman who is successful in the scope of a bad purpose aided by magnetism, would be much more powerful under better impulses. Some of the greatest preachers and statesmen the world has ever known have been graduates of villainy; by which is meant that those who have shown ability to tempt people into bad paths, have had greater ability to invite them into good paths, if only the bent of the purpose is changed.

The first deep impression, then, of the basis of magnetism, is its need of something real in the character behind it.

Then it must be busy. Idleness is the devil's workshop, does not mean that doing nothing leads to evil; but that avoiding the worthy duties and allowing the mind to drift, will end in ruin. This is true. It is true of everything that grows. Our oft repeated illustration of the garden left to drift by its own nature, is always to the point.

Every magnetic man or woman who has come within the range of our observation has been active; more than this, there has been excessive activity in such a life. We have not met all the great personages of the present and recent generations; but we have met many of them; and those we have had the privilege of analyzing by an intimate knowledge of their habits, have all been unusually busy.

So potent is this characteristic in the life of a magnetic person that some years ago, a writer promulgated the one law for the development of personal magnetism: "Be busy. Be very busy. Be so busy that you have more to do than you can accomplish, and keep on the rush with a variety of duties."

There is truth in this law, but it is only the result of the study and development of magnetism. Being busy will help to create the power, but the incentive to be busy does not arise unless there is magnetism to arouse it. Many thousands of men and women are busy, but they allow their power to run wild because of habits of nervous unrest and a sameness of duties. The housewife has many things to do, but she works all in the same strain and under one idea, that of getting her housework done. She does not seek time, and therefore does not have time, to cultivate a garden, flowers, books, history, language, music, and a hundred things that ripen and enrich the faculties and make one duty balance the other. Variety is required, and it must be of the kind that will change the mental interests.

With this amendment the rule laid down is a valuable one, although it runs along the natural side only.

To be intelligently busy, and to love the work you are doing, will help on very much; but variety of duties and variety of mental interests must be maintained at all times. Then turn on the steam, and let the pressure of crowding duties run very high.

It will pay. All the faculties will grow. All the mind and heart, health, energy, alertness and other qualities will be brought out.

This means business.

Success cannot be bought by the will, or by resolution, or by any fancied subtlety hidden away in the supposed genius. This term, genius, is only a synonym for a great love of a great amount of hard work. Anything else that is called genius is bastard.

The next great fact is the needed quickness and alertness of the mind, the perception, the faculties and the whole being. Perhaps, as has been claimed by one of our students who has risen to the very highest rung of the ladder of success, the way to get this alertness is to make your duties for each day greater than you can meet, and then plunge in to do all the most important of them. This ought to bring alertness and the sharpened faculties.

The lazy, slow, idling, easy-going man or woman has no hope whatever of making life a success. People who appear to take things the easiest are under a fearful strain all the time. They cover up all evidences of it, however.

Is this plan injurious?

It has been in vogue all the thousands of years the world has been rolling around the sun. With variety for the mind and for the faculties, we believe that it is just the opposite of being hurtful. It is the most wholesome of all methods.

Power carried at high tension and so skillfully concealed that it seems to slumber, is the greatest outward exhibition of magnetism. It comes to those who are in earnest.

We are firm in our opinion that the human body was made for great efforts, not for the supposed enjoyment of ease and luxury. Wherever a people has given itself over to the lap of luxury, it has grown weak. It is useless to review the ground that you are perfectly familiar with, showing this fact to be true. You know the story of every nation, people, organization, church, and other collection of humanity, in lesser or greater degree, and also the story of every individual who has invited ease, luxury, rest and comfort; all have fallen to rust and ruin. There is no life that can rest. Life itself means to live, and this means to be active.

In the body itself we see the constant effort of nature to keep every function active. We may sleep, but the heart, the respiration, the circulation, all keep going. Once they stop and we are dead. Not only is every part of the body active, but every cell and fibre is all the time changing.

This natural condition must pervade the whole life and all the faculties, or we grow dead while living. A wise man once said, "If you wish to be at your best you must let no faculty rest." Sleep is not rest; it is the period of repair, for the body is active all the while we are wrapped in slumber. The mind is called from its management of the body long enough for the great repairer to take charge and put things to rights. Too much sleep will make you sleepy, and too little sleep, under normal conditions, will sharpen the mind and wits of a healthy person.

Intense activity, with the outward appearance of being calm and self contained, will make you useful to yourself in the highest degree. If you are not well, then these rules will not apply.

We have never seen a magnetic idler.

We have never seen a magnetic man or woman who was not at all times tense in every part of the body, unless the work of the day had been accomplished, and then the respose of slumber was invited. The ability to shift from the habitual tensed condition to that of devitalization, so as to bring on quick sleep, has been displayed by so many persons that it seems to be an easy habit. But it is not effective unless it comes in contrast. The great physician of Philadelphia who could, while waiting for another patient, or while keeping another patient waiting, throw himself into a sound sleep, was always highly tensed, and this contrast was bound to induce instant slumber, provided the tensing could be laid aside.

The difficulty with most people is the inability to untense. They go to bed and strive for hours to get to sleep, trying every scheme known, not thinking that it is necessary to learn how to untense; and their minds may break down for lack of repair.

As this relief from the strain of magnetic activity is as necessary as anything else in life, we wish that all our students would learn the art of relaxation, not merely of the muscles, but particularly of the whole nervous system. If this art is not acquired, the vitality may run away in sleepless nights. All who are excessively magnetic, and who acquire the ability to untense, get sounder and more refreshing sleep than those who have no magnetism at all.

This form of relaxing is a letting go of all the muscles, of the nerves, and the mind at the same time. The color of peace, once established, will bring on the condition in a second, and sleep will follow if needed. Peace of itself does not invite relaxation, but the latter, with the letting go or collapse of the muscles and nerves, will bring sound slumber.

We have never seen a person who lacked magnetism who could not acquire it by practice, or by habits. The only difference between practice and habits is this: the former is the result of a resolve to imitate nature, and the latter is nature herself. As both employ the same methods, the students who practice are as skilled in the power as those who depend on habits. Even more. Our experience is that the practicer is more careful, more scientific and more conservative of the energy that makes magnetism, than the individual who depends on nature's help alone. Culture, founded on natural principles, is the master of nature.

Where a person possesses the power of influencing others by magnetism, the power has come to that person in one of three ways:

1. Either as the result of certain inducing causes,
2. Or habit-culture,
3. Or by practice.

When acquired by practice, some complex system must be employed, such as that which appears in the Exercise Book of the Personal Magnetism Club.

When acquired by inducing causes, the latter must be modes of living and of conduct that tend to create magnetism, and the results are then popularly supposed to be a natural gift.

When acquired by habit-culture, the plan of procedure is simply to adopt the inducing causes that have been at work in other lives. Nothing could be plainer. We have made the most exhaustive investigation possible into what we call the inducing causes of personal magnetism where that power is present supposedly as a gift. No examination could go further. In our desire to get at the truth we have spared nothing, neither time, money nor effort; and we have proved the fact that this power, when it comes as an apparent natural gift, is the result of certain known causes that have induced it. These are properly called inducing causes. They have come into the life of each person as the natural processes that attend certain ways of living.

If Mr. A. is a man of special characteristics which induce the accumulation of magnetism in his body, and if Mr. B. is not such a man, and is not magnetic, then we are led to search far enough in other lives to ascertain if the possession of those characteristics leads to the accumulation of personal magnetism; and, if it does, then we proceed to give the unmagnetic B. the characteristics of the magnetic A. On doing this we find that B. has become magnetic. He has done no practicing. He has simply formed new habits. He has adopted characteristics that he never before possessed. The great question was, would they fit B. even if he were able to acquire them? Experiment comes into play at this juncture and shows that B. is able to acquire the characteristics of A., and that they fit him perfectly. He becomes magnetic.

One important characteristic in the life of every magnetic man or woman is the tense walk. If you know what this walk is, you can select your magnetic people by a glance of the eye. We had a class of students on observation tours in a great city, and we called attention to the people whom we passed on the street; some having the slipshod walk of indolence, some the walk of muscular energy, and others the walk of magnetism. In the last named cases, there was a firmness and yet a total lack of stiffness in the way the body was supported and moved.

It being true that every magnetic person has this tense walk, the question now arises, why should it not be made a habit with those who are students of the power?

Let us make an effort to have it clearly set forth in your mind.

If you set your muscles as if to lift a weight or to strike a blow, or to run or walk, to kick or jump, or for any physical purpose, the effort is muscular; but if you have your muscles in readiness for any of these without setting them, the effort is what is called vitalization. In the latter the flesh is very firm and the muscles are given a full degree of life. It is a very easy condition to assume.

This vitalization is always present in the life of every magnetic man or woman. It is a characteristic of which they may not be aware for the reason that they have never given that part of the subject any thought. Many men and women are totally ignorant of the fact that they are magnetic. They seem to have supreme control over those with whom they come in contact and they account for this by believing that they are persons of greater judgment and care and therefore their advice is always followed, whether they are the gainers or not. This is seen among merchants who have succeeded in gaining the confidence of the community in which they live. It is also seen in the case of many a woman who is looked up to by all her neighbors and friends as a leader in every social or other event.

The important fact is that this vitalization is never absent in the life of a magnetic man or woman. It gives a strong and easy bearing to the body in walking, and a commanding presence at all times, be the person small or large in stature. A single step is enough to show the characteristic, and we can at all times detect the magnetic man or woman by a single step if taken without premeditation. There is a peculiar elasticity, yet great firmness, in the legs as they walk, and in the whole body as it stands or moves. The flesh is held firm and solid, without the slightest straining or setting of the muscles.

This combination is not by any means easy to understand, but it is very easy to do when understood. As a rule we find that only one person in a hundred catches the true idea, while the other ninety-nine ignore either the directions or think they have them when they do not. We will try to make them clear.

The thing to avoid is firmness of the muscles as in making a strong muscular effort. This is muscle-setting and is just the opposite of what is needed.

The correct practice is that which makes the flesh firm without any attempt at physical strength. It is thus both an affirmative and a negative condition.

Every person walks every day if in health. It requires no more time to walk in the way we have suggested than it does to walk in the way that is already established. Thus it will be habit-culture, and not practice, that turns your common walk into a magnetic developing power.

Owing to the fact that it simply improves your usual methods of walking, there can be no loss of time or of effort in adopting the magnetic walk, provided it can be understood. We are frank to say, however, that it is not easy to understand.

Do not try to adopt it all at once, for it cannot be so acquired.

Let the first change be very slight and very gradual. Success is much more likely to come in this way than by attempting too much.

While walking as usual, make the flesh a very little firmer in the legs, but not appreciably so. Do not allow the muscles to get any firmer or to make any extra effort. It is the first fault of the student to do this. It leads to stiffness and straining. Stiff walking is not attractive, and all stiffness is a useless waste of vitality.

The habit of walking with firm flesh, if begun very lightly, will change the entire life of the body. It is that kind of vigor that arouses countless millions of electric-cells throughout the entire body. You cannot vitalize even a little finger without setting on fire the whole battery-system from the brain to the feet. This experiment, small as it is, is very valuable, for it illustrates what is meant by magnetic firmness. Try it by raising the little finger, opening the hand so as to spread the fingers apart, and make the flesh of the little finger as firm as you can without setting the muscles. This firmness is very slight in fact, yet it influences the whole body. We have spent weeks in training a pupil to accomplish this much, small as it is, and at the end of six months it had changed the whole expression of the face.

The reason for this is easily explained. The making the flesh firm arouses the life of the whole body; not the physical or the muscular life, but that finer vitality that creates magnetism. On the other hand the setting of the muscles for physical exertion causes a loss of magnetism. Laborers or hard physical toilers of any kind are not magnetic as a rule. Physical prowess may establish fear or admiration, but its zone of influence is very limited, and it affects only a certain class.

The same gentle firmness that gives life to the little finger, is used in magnetic walking. Instead of being stiff it is supple and elastic; each step is buoyant and light; yet this very kind of step is sluggish and lazy if it is not magnetic. Buoyancy might be the descriptive word, if it were not for the fact that there are many kinds of buoyant dispositions that are not magnetic.

Our various attempts to explain what is meant by the magnetic walk show the difficulties under which we labor. If the person who sought to acquire it would only think of the one fact that there must be no decided change in the walk, the progress would begin much more auspiciously. The rule for the beginning is that there must be only the slightest change in the style and **manner of walking**; and this change must be as delicate as possible. The flesh of the legs must be firmer without permitting the muscles to participate in the firmness. It must be so slight a difference in the kind of walk to which you are accustomed that it may be said to be no difference at all.

One of the first indications that you are doing the correct thing is seen in the face. The features are the result, not of what the muscles of the body do, but of what the will-power does as expressed in the nervous organization. Any person who is familiar with the laws of the face will at once see that the right kind of walking has been adopted even when the person has been absent all the time. This fact was nicely illustrated in the case of the class of pupils, consisting of ladies and gentlemen, all adults, who were very anxious to be instructed in this particular thing. We spent a week showing what was meant by the magnetic walk, and all the pupils thought they had acquired the habit, and so they all went away for seven days. On reassembling they were in as many different stages of progress as there were pupils, for no two had made the same advance. Eight of them were at once recorded as having done nothing at all, although they were told that they had been trying hard; and they wished to know in what way we could tell before we saw them attempt to walk. The ninth had changed somewhat in face, and we at once made the record that he had been fortunate in his understanding of what was required. The tenth had changed somewhat more in face, and we made the record accordingly. One lady in particular had acquired a more beautiful and more finely-tempered face, and she was placed at the head of the class in her progress. Even the first eight had done something in mere practice that counted for progress, and had gone far enough to have reached the first stage in magnetic walking. We went over the ground with them first and showed wherein they were at fault. When the class again assembled after another lapse of seven days, there was improvement marked in their faces, and not in any instance did we fail to ascertain the exact facts from the features.

Why?

Because, when men or women are magnetic from what is called a natural gift, which means from previous inducing causes due to their acquired habits of living, they show this magnetism in the character that lives in the face. It is not stubbornness, for that is the opposite of magnetism. It is not muscular firmness, for that is physical and not electrical. It is not solidity of features, for that may come out of the accumulation of flesh or the animal propensities of the individual.

The face is the key to the mind, and the mind is the master of magnetism. What the mind and the heart think and feel, the face reflects in its fine and diversified nervous structure that responds to these two sources of influence. Magnetism is a quiet fire of the mind and heart that traces its purposes in the features with lines so small that they have no existence to the eye even when it is aided by the microscope.

Some of these changes may be described. One evidence of the lack of magnetism is the projecting lip. The thin lip is not an indicator of magnetism, but the projecting lip is evidence of the contrary. The change of the face from that condition in which the lips protrude forward, to that in which they are firmly set, each against the other, may be accomplished by the study of articulation and enunciation; and the training is of the highest value; but it does not necessarily prove that the individual is magnetic. Yet the opposite position of the lips is a certain and never failing sign that the person is unmagnetic.

How do we know this?

In the first place we have observed many hundreds of men and women who possess this great power, and there are photographs of many hundreds of others available; and never in a single instance have we seen one where the lips protrude. Who that has looked upon the faces of Daniel Webster, Rufus Choate, Henry Clay, John C. Calhoun, Andrew Jackson, George Washington, Patrick Henry, U. S. Grant, Robert E. Lee, Edwin Booth, Edwin Forrest, or any of the hundreds of famous personages whose magnetic power has been the mainspring of their success, can fail to see the chiseled mouth in which the lines of the lips are draw with sharpness and clear-cut decision? There is no firmness and no decision in protruding lips.

While this fact, being universal in the faces of all those who have possessed the great gift, may not quite prove that it is necessary to the acquirement of the art, yet, on the other hand, the protruding lips are never seen in the face of any individual who is thus endowed. Imagine Napoleon Bonaparte with projecting lips!

Further proof is seen in the progress of all who attempt the development of the power, and who proceed in the right direction. We recall many cases of private pupils who have had ugly and unattractive features, with mouths that had projecting lips, and thick ones always, who have entirely changed the condition by the right kind of practice, or such as leads to the development of magnetism. You may think that thick lips are not changeable; but they are thick from the use made of them. No part of the body is so easily trained to alter its size and shape as the lips. This you can prove in many ways. Let the rule be observed that the center of the upper lip should always touch the center of the lower lip when they are together, and you will get started in the right direction. This position is, in the study of articulation, called center to center. At once the lips seem to be thin, when they are just as thick as ever. Another rule is that the mouth should be so shaped that the finger can form a straight line from the under part of the nose to the chin. This will compel the projection to remove itself.

As an illustration of the gradual change that comes over the face, we will cite one of many cases. We had a lady as a pupil who had the projecting lips to excess. She thought that she had already some magnetism; but we assured her that she possessed none at all. "How do you know?" she asked. We did not tell her. She was quite an intelligent woman, and we had no trouble whatever in showing her the way to make the flesh firm without setting the muscles; and she caught the art almost from the very start. As we watched her practice, we saw that she brought the center of the upper lip against the center of the lower lip, and we made the record that she would very soon be an adept in the art. Some persons change the lips at all times when they are trying to do something that requires determination and will-power. We had the pleasure, during the many hours that she was our pupil in the first year of her lessons, of seeing her at work seeking to learn what was meant by the magnetic habits of the various parts of the body, and week by week she unconsciously drew her mouth into what is known as the ideal shape, until at last the face had changed completely, and she was counted as a beautiful and highly attractive woman. It is now a well established saying that all magnetic women are attractive and beautiful; not in the sense that a doll or an empty face is pretty, but in the nobler and more exalted meaning of true womanhood and womanly beauty.

All pupils who start in this line of development, having projecting lips, will find that these will shift about and become the finely shaped lips such as are seen in the pictures of the successful men and women of all ages, so far as we have evidence at this time. The strength of character will not be reflected in the face if it does not exist as a matter of fact; nor will the rich qualities of mind and heart become pictured in the features unless they have a living reality in the individual. Beauty, character and nobility cannot be assumed. What we refer to is the mechanical reconstruction of the face; and this is not a dream, for it can be seen by anybody who cares to take the trouble to observe it. There is no secret in its existence.

What is herein described is the open evidence that you yourself may obtain in your own life, if you will take the pains to understand what is meant by the magnetic walk, or the magnetic firmness of any part of the body. It is a fact that is not generally understood for it is taken up too quickly and too earnestly in adoption. It is understandable, and you ought to catch the idea without any trouble; but we fear that you will go ahead with a great determination to win, and will therefore use the muscles and not the flesh.

The change from your accustomed methods to the condition known as magnetic firmness, is exceedingly delicate. You will know it as soon as you get it, for a phosphorescent fire will be lighted in every nerve-fibre of the body. Magnetism is nerve-glow. There is no doubt about that. We have taken the following experiment as a proof of it. Ordinarily in a dark room a human being has no fire in the eyeballs, such as is seen in animals of intense vitality, of which the cat is a common example. The cat is able to halt the attention of a bird and then to charm it into a state of yielding that costs the bird its life. All animals of intense vitality possess the same power in other uses, and all such animals have glowing eyeballs at times.

Men and women do not, as a rule, possess glowing eyeballs. There are exceptions to the rule as you may prove. We have followed the matter for many years and have become familiar with every phase of the question from the least incident to the greatest. We do not claim to have discovered everything, for much was known before we took up the work, and much yet remains to be ascertained. Others have accomplished much, notably the French scientists who were able to attract the magnetic needle of the compass out of its course by tensing the flesh of the arm, which is exactly what we mean by the magnetic firmness of the flesh.

When students of this power have used the present habit long enough to be able to arouse nerve-fire at will, they are generally far enough advanced to cause the eyeballs to glow. In the light this warmth shows itself in greater brilliancy of the eyes; but in a perfectly dark room, where the students are widely separated, the glow may be distinctly seen by all who are present; and non-magnetic persons observe it more readily as they have none of the fire in their own eyes to intervene. Let a class in a very dark room or hall separate themselves so as to be at least twenty feet apart, and let each have a numbered chair arranged as much out of order as possible so that there will be no consecutive responses; then call on the students by numbers, one, two, three, four, etc., asking each to tense the flesh of the body in turn, but without previous knowledge as to where they are located. When the experiment succeeds, a pair of faintly glowing eyes will be seen somewhere in the hall. Of course the students are to be formed in a large circle so that each faces a given center. When number one has been called upon, and has succeeded or failed, let number two be likewise called upon. After time has been allowed sufficient to overcome the tendency to frivolity which lies at the root of failure, and after repetitions enough have been made to give the matter a thorough test, then if there are two who have succeeded or who have been especially fortunate in arousing the eye-glow, let these two be placed at random in opposite parts of the hall, and then allowed to tense the flesh simultaneously, to see if they will be able to discover the positions of each other. We recall the names of more than fifty persons who have done this. They have succeeded in bringing the flame into their eyeballs to such an extent that two persons could walk across the hall to each other, having no other light to guide them. You have undoubtedly entered a dark room or cellar and seen the glowing eyeballs of a cat at some remote distance. We remember the case of a brave boy who was sent down to the basement to get a cat. He took no light. He went and returned in about two minutes. When asked how he found her without a lamp he said that he saw her eyes shine and went right to her. The experiment with students was based on the same law applied to human beings.

These facts are mentioned to show the change that takes place in the body. We do not ask you to enter into any special practice in this Course. If you desire to proceed with this great study, which is undoubtedly the most important in human life, you should devote yourself to the complete systems of the other works. As a means of education and self-protection this training outclasses all others and will do so to the end of time.

Having said this much on the subject of magnetic walking, have we given you the necessary help to enable you to acquire it? Try it a few times each day when you take your usual walks. Throw a feeling of firmness into the legs as you walk; and, if you do it in the right way, a glow of faint, delicate fire will come back and travel all through your body, even setting your heart to fluttering, as is done by a piece of good news.

We sincerely hope that you will succeed in understanding what is required, for the doing of it is very easy. Be on the constant watch to avoid setting the muscles. As soon as you once get it, the future progress is very rapid, and there will be no delay in seeing results.

We are often asked what the feeling is and how it may be recognized. There is some such feeling, in coarser degree, that is occasionally experienced but not always, when a person who is languid from too much sitting, goes out into the fresh air and inhales a good breath while stretching. Any person who has ever felt the glow of pleasure that comes for that brief instant, will know what the truly magnetic man or woman feels at all times when the mind so wills. The sensation is ecstatic.

Inhaling pure air and stretching at the same time will set the millions of cells on fire throughout the body; and that is why nature, through instinct, teaches it to animal creation. It develops magnetism; but it is an exercise and we promised to present a system that did not require practice. Then, again, if one is willing to practice, there are scientific exercises to be had in our "Cultivation of Personal Magnetism" to which you are referred and which you may already own.

Stretching is nature's method of arousing life in the inmost parts of the body, especially the magnetic centers, and no person is thoroughly healthy who does not have at least one good stretch a day. If this be true then it could not be called practice to do what ought to be done as a part of the duties of life.

The magnetic walk may be made a habit by adopting it at all times after once it is acquired. Every step may be taken with firmness of flesh. No more time will be required, and no practice will be necessary. Habit-culture is not practice; it is merely another way of doing what you must do. When the right kind of walking has been adopted, then let the same principle come into the whole body; let the neck, the arms, the torso and all flesh be vitalized by a gentle firmness that is free from muscle-setting.

Never before have we tried so hard to make a fact clear as we have done in this matter. We believe that if you avoid muscular effort, you will succeed in producing the tense condition that is so necessary to the development of magnetism. We have never seen a man or woman who possessed this power, who did not have the whole body slightly tense at all times, and quite tense when special use was being made of the art. On the principle that a result, by adoption, will create a condition, the constant employment of tense flesh will fire the whole body and charge it with a wonderful vitality which is of electric origin.

When it comes it will come to stay. It will grow fast and keep on increasing without limit, if the habit is maintained. It will prove to be a power that must have a wise governing engineer, and that is good judgment carrying out some mental purpose as stated in the first part of this treatise. The brain must think, must plan, must govern, if this enormous energy is to be rightly used.

We come now to another habit; and it is even more difficult to explain; but we feel certain that we can make it clear. It is called the habit of self-containment.

Before this can be understood, it is necessary to impress upon the reader the need of a constantly unruffled disposition. This is a stepping-stone to self-containment. The unruffled disposition is a rare quality in these days, except among those who are counted great. It is a habit.

The beginning of this habit is in the perfect control of the body and all its parts. If you lack grace, ease, good poise, polish and the traits that outwardly mark the lady and gentleman, try to attend some school where expression is taught, or seek a graduate of such a school and obtain all the training possible. It would require hundreds of pages to teach it by book, and that kind of teaching is not effective. The schools of expression are everywhere increasing in numbers and they are doing a grand work. They teach the best use of the faculties, which is so essential to success. Among these are the development of rich and pleasing voices, the mastery of the art of modulation, and the attainment of perfect self-control under all circumstances. Thus expression and magnetism go hand in hand.

We have now reviewed all the leading general principles of magnetism, covering the ground that precedes this course, as much as a bird's eye glance may do so in the few pages at our command. The preceding chapter has also repeated and summed up the work of this present course so that the two chapters may be said to end the technical part of this volume. More pleasing experiences will now open to the student.

The pages yet un-turned are based upon all that has preceded, and your coming success will depend on your faithfulness in the past lessons. If they have been read only, then the coming lessons may be read only. If they have been studied, adopted and absorbed until the laws and the practice have become second nature with you, all that is to be stated will be quickly acted upon and drawn into your life.

Let us now go still more deeply into the work.

As we do this, it is well to lay aside the idea of mystery and supernatural surroundings in this study. Pupils sometimes declare that the very name and feeling of magnetism are suggestive of the strange, deep, dark powers that lurk in the sky and that seem to come down at night to parade the earth. This tendency is due to the inherited taint of superstition in the blood.

Difficult problems arise in the treatment of such subjects as transmigration and the ALTER EGO; but these are reduced to the very simplest propositions and language in order that the ordinary mind may have no more trouble understanding it than in catching the meaning of a newspaper article.

The first set of illustrations, or examples, are taken from common occurrences, and they are seemingly unscientific. The purpose is to avoid clothing the subject with mystery, and dark habiliments.

The dark side of the matter is its relation to the wickedness that is practiced by men and women who are magnetic. This is not a reason why it should be cast aside. If you have children who are being made the victims of the wrong influences of others, it is your duty to throw all the protection about them that you can command. If you yourself are being taken advantage of by some designing persons, is it fair to you and to those who are dependent on you that these influences that are stripping you, should be allowed full sway?

Good judgment tells us that the opposite course should be pursued.

Learn what the influences are, whence they arise, who wields them, and by what process they are directed against your welfare. Then you will soon be in a position to thwart them and free yourself.

Defense is a legitimate use of magnetism.

Of every thousand of our pupils, fully eighty per cent study the art solely for the purpose of looking after their own interests against the intentions of others. They care nothing for the use they may put it to against friends or enemies.

The complete, or two-sided art, serves as a means of defense, and as an agency for aggressive activity towards other persons. In the latter capacity there are three divisions.

First, the use of magnetism directed toward a friend, the purpose being to uplift that friend and increase the power for doing good.

Second, the use of magnetism directed toward an enemy, the purpose being to compel obedience and submission, or to secure proper advantages.

Third, the use of magnetism toward persons who are neither friends nor enemies, the purpose being to hold your own in transactions, or in social relations, or otherwise.

There can be no harm in any of these uses of the power. We would advise every person to develop it for the good they can accomplish in many walks of life; uplifting others and spreading the principles of a higher moral code and a better plan of living.

This world is so constituted that some persons are actively engaged in plotting the ruin of others, or else in planning to get advantage by fair means or foul. They do not take into consideration the suffering they may be able to inflict on their victims. They think only of themselves, and take chances even on their escape from the criminal law. If they can cheat in a bargain, mislead and rob under false pretenses, deprive a girl of her chastity, or do any one of a thousand contemptible things, they seek only their own safety and never look to the consequences of their acts as far as the others are concerned.

From this numerous class we hope that you and yours will ever be safe and free.

There are others who intend no wrong but who propose to get as much advantage as they can out of their fellow beings. And there are still others who merely seek to make all people think as they do, and suit their actions to the whims and notions of a conceited or imperious mind.

Then some persons believe that they themselves are always in the right and that all those who do not agree with them are in the wrong. They become nuisances unless they are curbed at the proper time and kept in the background. The fractious child or pupil, the hesitating or uncertain employee, the followers that are attached to almost every one in some way or other, these and numerous others are needful of salutary influences which you can exert, and not prey upon the honesty of man or woman or do wrong to any person.

CHAPTER TWENTY

+++++++++++++++++++++++++++++++++

RICH AND WISE
MEN AND WOMEN
ARE
EASILY SWAYED AT TIMES

+++
❧ BRIGHT-MINDED VICTIMS ❧
+++

OTH EDGES OF THE BLADE of magnetism are capable of cutting. The victim of one edge may be the wielder of the weapon. So it is true that bright minds everywhere may fall prey to the influence of the power of a lesser mind. The common case is that of the man of wealth who has mental acuteness to protect himself in business, to meet and overcome all mercantile adversaries, and yet falls down in abject defeat at the knees of a woman. The first questions that arise are these:

Is it the sex of a woman that gives her the power over the man?

Or is it her intuitive nature?

Or is it her magnetism?

We take the last word in its usual sense. Our definition of magnetism is anything that will attract. So, if the sex attracts, that is magnetism. Or if intuition attracts, that is magnetism. Or if any quality that enhances the power of a man or woman, is capable of winning favors, that too is magnetism. If these definitions were not all true, then the meaning of attraction would be lost.

Here is a case in court where a man worth millions has been compelled to sue his wife for divorce. The evidence shows that he is yet in the very prime of his mental and virile powers; that she was a prostitute long before he married her; that she has been untrue to him; and that he is entitled to a legal separation. The wonder is that she could have so deceived him prior to the fatal step, and thus plunge him into public scandal.

Here is another man, one of the four greatest creative geniuses in the industrial world, worth perhaps a hundred million of dollars, of the same name as the first mentioned millionaire, who has a similar wife, if the court records tell the truth. Why was he misled? Astute and gigantic in business, he rose to the top crest of success only to be dashed into the vortex of scandal and heart-breaking disaster.

Here is another case; that of a woman, perhaps pretty, but of advanced years, and of an age when the wiles of sweet womanhood fail to enchain man; securing a vast fortune on worthless commercial paper. The bankers who were duped by her have nothing to offer in explanation.

Here is still another case, freshly in the minds of the people. A man who has so large an income every month that he could erect a great business block every four weeks, is enticed in Paris by the sweetness of a girl not sixteen years of age; is followed to this country by her; is hounded by a lawyer until suit is threatened; settles the suit on threat of exposure; and is then sued by the girl's attorney for his share of the fees.

This man is a king in his business. He did not amass his fortune by mere good luck. He worked it out, and knew how to make it count up fast, and how to preserve it. He could start over again, put the same genius into the effort, and win the same great fortune, for he is endowed with the power to do that.

Did his mental astuteness take a vacation when he met this pretty girl in Paris? On what principle of common sense, to say nothing of morality, did he allow himself to be dragged into circumstances that were sure to be weighed against him? Magnetism does not allow a man to fall into a trap. It sees the trap and shows him the opposite course.

The reason is generally that the man or woman who wields a two-edged sword, may cut on the outward stroke and be cut on the recoil.

This man thought that the girl was pretty. He thought that his wealth would give him standing in her favor.

We do not know the facts in the particular case cited, but it is true as a general rule that a man of high position or great wealth, thinks girls and women who are fascinating are his legitimate prey. We recall the visit of Charles Dickens to this country, and his voracious appetite for girls wherever he went. The name and fame of Dickens made him a demi-god in the minds of the public, and some girls did not have the resistant power to refuse his advances.

It is said that Napoleon had innumerable opportunities to take advantage of girls who had hitherto been pure; and it is likely that he did not avail himself of the chances thus thrown at him. We base both these statements on evidence that has not come into print, but that seems to be trustworthy. The glare of fame and high rank is likely to sweep a woman's judgment aside and draw her to the abyss of ruin in one single flash.

The man who thus uses whatever power he has in the degradation of the other sex is cutting with a sword, one edge of which does harm to another, and the recoil brings the other edge dangerously close to himself. Of course any man is likely to become the target of blackmail or unfounded malice. The whiter the light in which he lives, the more conspicuous he becomes for the shafts of others. But such methods, resisted, fall to the ground in time.

We can imagine a man pure enough to be able to make himself a mark for the intrigue of the other sex; but not shrewd enough to coin millions of money and be led to the alter in marriage by a prostitute, unless he is cutting with the two-edged weapon. Nor will a millionaire be made the tool of a pretty and confiding miss unless he is cutting with the selfsame sword.

He begins with insincerity, and ends with a blackmailing suit.

We do not believe that the man of business shrewdness is without blame in his entanglement with women. He simply has allowed his own schemes to lead him into deeper water than he intended to find.

But the fact remains, nevertheless, that he has been outgeneraled by the woman. Had he been wholly innocent, he must have been too weak to have carried on a successful business. Being keen and strong in his magnetism, he has used it for his own satisfaction with the opposite sex, and the woman has gone deeper.

The question arises, on what principle can a woman secure power over the shrewd merchant or banker?

The answer is in the sex, more than in the magnetism; or rather in the fact that sex is a strong magnet that draws a man to a woman, and more subtle and powerful than the same influence coming from a man.

This law should be borne in mind by every man who would play with the two-edged sword.

He has in his make-up the natural craving for a woman, and he longs not only for the wrong use of it, but especially for the glamour of the companionship and presence of a woman. This feeling sets up a fine edge in his nervous system and he is on it ere he is aware. The humdrum repetition of each day's affairs in business is dull to him unless he has some goal in view. Fame is empty if there is nothing to it but fame.

A man needs and seeks some goal. Heaven is not attractive to a business man or a banker, and it is too far off. The coarse pleasures of men's society are not worth the stooping of character that they cost. The club room is only a flitting butterfly, in the evening's life; unless there is a woman to be had; and she is generally the adjunct of club methods.

The successful man when he sees that there are no new worlds to conquer that require the concentration of his powers, will instinctively turn toward woman, and will need her companionship. If she is promiscuous, he does not care for her. He is in that frame of mind that will permit love, as it is usually termed, to fill his whole being if she will come and assist in the process. He may have a wife, but the tinsel of a neglected love has long since shed its soul, and he cannot find romance where there is no risk and no adventure. To him it is a glorious thing to be able to impress a woman; and he does not look deep enough to see that she is being impressed to order, making her manner toward him suit his aggressiveness toward her.

Now comes into play the artfulness of nature. She knows that the race needs offspring, and she blinds the man to the wiles of the woman, until it is too late to escape when he has awakened. In all nature it is the female that does the steady work, while the male is hung on the spit of solicitation or wild yearning. The male elephant runs amuck, not the female; and he does not even do this unless there is no female to be had. The animals are led on by the females in their own species, and the male awaits the mood and decision of their mates. When the latter are ready, and not at any other time, will the males dare to respond. If they presume to advance when they are not wanted, they soon retreat in dismay and hang their heads in shame.

In the human species the female holds the key when mere brute force is not used. There are no bad houses where men wait to serve women at so much an engagement. It is always the women who have the favors to confer and who receive the reward.

Unless a man is excessively busy and rushed with a variety of duties which tax his powers and draw his sexual energy into his brain and nervous system, he is unable to resist the attractions of womankind. He must have her; but, after using her, he ceases to hold respect for her sex until there comes the imperative demand for further use of her. The oftener a man goes to a house of prostitution, the less respect he will have for the fair sex. The oftener he mis-uses his powers, the less manhood he will have. The more conquests he makes of women the less inclined he will be to marry her and pay devotion at her shrine. To him she is so much beef, so much animal, so much meat to be worked upon.

The successful business man, in nine cases out of ten, is not a rake. He is too busy. His fashionably dressed clerk plays the rake for the house, and does the honors at the shrine of fallen women.

If a man has made money by severe application to his affairs, he has turned the energy that lesser men spend with women, into the labor of building up a great establishment that shall produce him a steady income. He therefore has no time and no waste vitality to put into this form of evil. This makes him the more ardent lover of woman when he takes a rest from business and is free for the vacation period of his life; for his natural respect for the fair sex has not been destroyed by an illegal indulgence of a promiscuous kind.

Such a man will throw himself into the lap of a female with the same enterprise and hustle that has made his business a great success.

There is a feeling of fine sensibility which seems to devour his will. He thinks he loves this particular woman, even if he has a wife at home. A novel adventure to him is romance of the sweetest kind. As he is taking a rest from his business, he is also taking a rest from his accustomed shrewdness. She is to him the impersonation of all that is pure and particularly all that is ingenuous and naive. He is blinded, and the fine sand she flings in his eyes completes the work of shutting out all vision.

At that particular moment when he wakes up, she has some letters and a few incriminating circumstances hanging from her belt, and the scalp naturally follows.

This is the oft-repeated story, too old to be told except as a souvenir; but it holds the interest at all times.

When he wakes up it is too late. She will not return the letters, and he becomes indignant. They quarrel. If he yields to her wishes, he must compromise himself further, and then she has a tighter grip upon him. The result is either open scandal or years of blackmail. He is allowed his choice.

In the case of the banker who allows a woman to secure a vast sum of money on worthless security, there is not the sexual attraction. The relations between the two are purely financial. The basis of the transaction is confidence. The woman has so conducted herself that she seems really to be immensely wealthy, and her public reputation is in line with this assumption. So cleverly does she maintain this estimate of herself that the banker would consider it an affront even to doubt the fact.

With the show of wealth in her favor, and the belief of the banker added to it, she needs only conduct herself in a strictly business-like manner in asking for loans, in order to get them. But now comes the kind of security she brings; it could not possibly be accepted except on the theory that no security is necessary. Her magnetism now helps her overturn the traditional and well-established usage of all bankers, and the mind of the money-lender passes into a lapse, during which he makes the mistake which after events compel him to cover up by continuing the error in the knowledge that it is the only way back to first conditions.

This lapse of the mind is a very common occurrence.

It is based on the principle of ALTER EGO.

This is the throwing out of all moods and feelings from the party influenced, and projecting another self into that individual.

This is so important a phase of magnetism that it will be considered in another part of this course, a few pages later on.

The result of the ALTER EGO is a lapse. This is the non-existence of Self in the party affected. The personality goes out and another takes its place.

During the lapse there is no choice of conduct.

The disposition is paramount to do what is told, yet it is not in any sense related to hypnotism. The latter is a sleep and a dead obedience to the will of another. The lapse is a full waking period, but not even the will of another is in operation. There is no blind obedience to some suggestion. Every outward evidence is that of the bright, full-witted man or woman of affairs.

A hypnotized person goes about in a partly dazed condition, and shows full stupidity between the adoption of one suggestion after another.

A person who is in a lapse appears to be the same as usual, and has no semblance of either stupidity or lack of judgment as far as conversation is concerned. The face is the same as usual, and the eyes are bright.

Under the head of the study of ALTER EGO we will discuss all the phases of this form of magnetism. It is not an acquired kind, for it is so common that it may be said to be the first form of loss of self-control in dealing with others. Habits and often necessity invite its use; and it must always form a part of man's dealings with man, and woman is even more in evidence.

CHAPTER TWENTY-ONE

TO BE BESIDE ONESELF
IN ANY MOOD
IS A COMMON
EXPERIENCE

ALTER EGO

SINCE EVE TEMPTED Adam, the world has been the victim of the power of the ALTER EGO, or other self. This has already been referred to in the chapter next preceding, and is now our subject at this stage of the course. In the use of this influence the mind and faculties seem to stop thinking and yet all the operations of a skillful thinker are at work, making plans and executing ideas. In moods and feelings the particular mood of one person is made to give way and be displaced by the chosen or projected mood of another person. Of course the mind feels and is the seat of mental feeling, as it is said the heart feels and is the seat of nervous feeling.

A mood may have its origin in the brain, or in the nervous senses, and it may be created by the thought of the brain.

A lawyer may so work upon the idea of chivalry when a man shoots to death the violator of his home, that the jurors can see nothing but justification, and in this mood they discard all evidence and all law. On this ground in some parts of the country it is impossible to convict the slayer of the man who ruins a pure girl, or the murderer of the villain who commits rape. Even among the most enlightened conditions of Christianity there is a feeling that such crime should be summarily punished and that the violation of the law is a mere technicality, especially where there is a Supreme Court that deals out justice on the forked spit of technicalities instead of using common business sense.

We cite a common case to show how easily the mind may arouse the feelings.

If at any time you can drive out sense and substitute feeling in the mind of another person, you have used the power of transmigration. But if you can drive out one form of sense and put in another form of sense you have used the power of the ALTER EGO.

This is based on the principle that a person is what he thinks, and that thought makes the self. There are uses of the lapse where the feelings are largely involved, but they soar to that realm where we deal with what is familiarly called the supernatural, although that is a term invented by people of earth with which to describe what they have not yet come to understand. If we refer to the supernatural, we do so to be in accord with this definition, although in fact there is no supernatural.

The ALTER EGO therefore is the substitution of another self to do the thinking for the real self, when it is confined to merely mental conditions. But when it takes on wings of speculation and touches the mysterious, the feelings and moods are laid aside in a normal mind and the thinking powers are lifted out of earth to the realm that hovers over this planet. The wonder-struck individual who sits in contemplation of some fact or belief that has the garb of the supernatural hanging from its limbs, is not in any mood that serves the man or woman of earth. If the nerves are unstrung, it is fear or awe; but we are to deal with normal beings only.

From the time that the mind was swerved from its belief in the plain methods of doing things, as in the first use of supernatural suggestions, down to the present day, when solid banks will loan money on empty securities, the use of the ALTER EGO power has been constant and at most times cruel. It will rob a man of all he has, and a woman of what she most needs to hold sacred. As its use has come into the world through the laws of necessity or the law of crime, the first thing for every man and woman to do is to learn to recognize it, and to avoid it, when innocent people are its intended victims. The next step might be to learn how to use it for legitimate ends.

As has been said it produces a lapse in the mind and being of a person, and, during this lapsed condition, another mind or self does the work without loss of identity as far as the individual is concerned. To think is to live. To do your own thinking with your own brain, is to be yourself. To allow someone else to do your own thinking with another mental function, is the ALTER EGO.

Insanity is ALTER EGO. It started with the phrase that the person was beside himself. Still another term was that the man or woman was out of his or her mind. The old meaning, as we see it given in the time of Shakespeare, was the same, although expressed in the Greek word, *ekstasis,* or in its English form of ecstasy. Not until recent years has that word meant excess of pleasure. Hamlet is accused by his mother with the charge of ecstasy, and he refutes it by showing that he is as sane as she is.

Ecstasy means to be besides one's self, or out of mind. He is out of his head, is a familiar translation of it. Yet, with the modern meaning of excess of pleasure, we have the Greek words of standing from or aside or beside oneself. In the asylums for the insane there is always a ward for those who are called subjects of ecstasy, and in this use of the word, the attempt is made to designate those who are insane on the happy or laughing side of the diseased mind.

To be beside oneself is to step aside and be possessed by another self. This meaning is thousands of years old, showing that the experience was part of human history in the remotest ages. Some students of the New Testament have construed the casting out of devils to mean the driving out of the possessors of the mind.

The present disbelief in witchcraft has made it impossible for the people to be misled at this age in their notions of this peculiar power which was once described as the possessing of another person's mind with the witch-being that was carried about by some one who had the gift of influencing others. That men and women, and in some cases, children, could be put to death because of this fearful crime, seems to us today to be most strange; yet if you will visit among the ignorant negroes of the South, and in some of the remote districts of Europe, notably in the Scandinavian peninsula, you will come across the full belief in witchcraft, and will find actual living witches.

We personally have met not only those who believe in this power, but we have been introduced to witches and have had the opportunity to test the question whether or not they believe in themselves. It is rare to find one who is insincere. They wield a strange and genuinely potent influence over those with whom they come in contact. Not long ago a friend of ours discharged a cook because she practiced witchcraft to such an extent that she was looked upon as a sort of demi-god; and it was only by accident that the fact came to light.

The explanation of belief in witchcraft is the sincerity of those who give it credence. With this as a basis, and the added power to impress the fact on such believers, the whole fabric is complete, and it would require but little stimulus to rehabilitate the world with the old scare.

In other words belief is the chief factor.

This is not hypnotism.

The latter depends solely on the power to throw a person into a cataleptic sleep, and therein to offer suggestions which seem real to the subject, all the while the latter is in the sleepy or stupid condition. It is a form of nervous disease.

But the lapse that attends the use of the ALTER EGO, is not in any sense a sleep; it is a change of self; an introduction of a new form of belief for the time being. If you come upon a hypnotic subject you will at once tell the condition. If you see a banker loaning a fortune to a woman with no adequate security, you will see a man who is able to loan you a thousand dollars and insist on iron-clad and gilt edge security. He is under the ALTER EGO of one person and not of all. The hypnotic is dead to all and alive to only the suggestion that the controlling mind puts into him.

The banker will simply be satisfied that it is right to loan the million to the woman on worthless security; and he will at the same time and in the same moment, think it a wrong to his bank to loan you a hundred dollars unless you can enforce the application with a mountain of certainty.

And we see men of the highest standing, makers of the greatest period of American history, governing with a clear head and stern hand, framing laws that are destined to live for thousands of years, yet believing in witchcraft.

We see the millionaire tightening the screws whereby he outwits keen minds in his commercial transactions, yet being led about by the blackmailing female whom he has allowed to put the noose about his mental neck.

We see teachers of divine sweetness and holy peace, love, mercy and forgiveness, taking white-faced maidens and innocent old men to the rack or roasting them alive on the heaps of fagots their bigotry has piled up. Many a time and oft, the priest and church official, rising from prayers in which they have implored pardon for themselves, have sent out orders that have put men and women to torture and agonized death for no other reason than that some word has been misunderstood, misstated, or misapplied, or some belief has not been accepted. This is the cross-grain of the human mind.

Coming down to commonplaces, we find a merchant of sound ability, trudging home with some worthless trinket or book that he has bought from a peddler, at the time thinking he was getting value and helping a worthy individual. The reason why so many people will not give audience to the traveling peddler, or book agent, is that there is a fear that something will be sold that is not wanted. To get rid of the persistent, pestering fellow, the price is paid, so the excuse goes; but it is easy to send the agent away if one has the disposition.

Today the ALTER EGO method is the most employed. It seeks first to get an audience, and this seems to be nine-tenths of the victory.

To approach in the dress and paraphernalia of an agent or peddler is fatal to the issue, unless the man is a dealer in the regular store goods. Traveling dealers have an almost endless clientele who take pleasure in waiting for his coming and looking over his bargains. He is a moving merchant.

But the peddler who has no store, either on wheels or otherwise, and no rents or other expenses, must conceal his purpose. He must make himself welcome to start with.

Here is a good example: a Brooklyn life insurance agent found it difficult to gain admission into the offices and homes of his prospective patrons. He had tried the dodge of presenting a visiting card, so as to leave the impression that he was some old-time schoolmate or friend; but this soon wore out. He then conceived the idea of getting the names of all persons on whom he intended to call. He had a similar name reserved for himself.

If he was to call on John Smith, his own name was Frank Smith, and he had the genealogy of the Smith family in preparation, reaching back to the time when Peter Smith came over on the Mayflower.

He was right when he assumed that John Smith would be glad to know that his ancestors, in a direct line, without side-track or switch, had come down from the first of those Smiths that found room in the famous Mayflower.

If he was to call on Jones, say William Jones, he took the name of Jones, say Charles Jones, although the Jones are not partial to the name of Charles, and he had the Jones' family tree rooted in the same Mayflower. This was his method. He kept a system of books for the purpose of not getting mixed in the genealogies, and his plan worked for a while. We were calling on a friend one day who was working out some family-tree information to supply to this life insurance canvasser, and our attention was called to the first steps in the correspondence. We said, "It would be strange if this should turn out to be a new method of getting into the good graces of our friend." He was shocked to think so, and would not believe it. The ALTER EGO was at work.

Later on this canvasser wrote to the man that he was to be in his city the following week, and asked at what hour he might call. The man set aside a whole evening. They talked genealogy for a while, and it leaked out by pure accident that the Brooklyn man did not have all the time he wished to devote to the work of following up the genealogy, as he was not in the best financial circumstances. This lack of wealth compelled him to take up the work of soliciting life insurance. Before he got through the evening's conversation, the first steps were taken for insuring the life of our friend, and the result was a very satisfactory transaction along that line.

The peculiar fact was that the agent had a card bearing the name of our friend, the first initial being different. He had a card for each of his would-be patrons, changing the name to suit that of the party on whom he was to call.

Nothing more was ever heard of the genealogy except the brief statement that, as soon as he had more leisure, he intended to push the search and thus connect our friend with his ancestor who surely came over on the Mayflower. There are times now when the belief is fixed in the mind of our friend that the agent was a genuine relative; for, said he, "Every man must have some occupation if he is not rich, and why should it be strange that this distant relation of mine should be a life insurance canvasser?" So the ALTER EGO hung on for years. The operations of the man were afterwards discovered, and did him no injury. The law has no penalty for this form of shrewdness, as there is no robbery in it.

The far-reaching force of the ALTER EGO is seen in the recent bank affair in the middle West, where the United States government stopped the mail, and undertook to wind up the affairs of the bank. The founder of the latter sent letters and literature to its victims in which he succeeded in many instances in impressing upon their minds that he was in the right and was being persecuted.

By a peculiar lapse the hordes of people who sent their money to him in the first place, were made to believe that the transaction was a safe one; and, later on, many of these people still maintained the same view.

The following dialogue is an actual fact, as we engaged in the part of it marked B. A man called, presented his card and announced that he was pushing certain scientific investigations in which we were interested. We will call him A for this purpose.

A. "I have been a school teacher for the past forty years. I have recently resigned in order to be able to take up a special line of work in which I am much interested."

B. "What is it?"

A. "I will tell you. My father was a poor man and I had no choice in the matter when he decided that I should be educated for teaching."

By this time we knew that the man was not what he had announced himself to be; but, as he seemed ingenious, we allowed him to go on.

A. "I did not resign because I wished to stop work. The political party to which I belong was in the minority at the time. They could not hold their own. The other party wanted to get me out to make room for their own fellows. So I was told that I was too old to teach. I took the hint and sent in my resignation."

B. "Well."

A. "I had nothing saved up after forty years of teaching and I had to do something. I do not wish to be looked upon as a peddler, and if I am intruding just say so, but say it kindly. I do not wish to be abused or driven away, but told that my offer is not favorably received."

B. "What is the scientific investigation that you have been making?"

A. "It is this. I have found that pans, pots, kettles and other utensils, when placed on a very hot stove, are likely to get too hot, and I have thought for a long time that asbestos might serve to protect them. You know, I feel sure, that asbestos is a non-conductor of heat."

B. "But asbestos has been used for some time for the purpose you mention."

A. "Ah, then you have been investigating that question, too? It is very gratifying to me to know it. I have brought with me," etc.

He took from under his coat, where he had held them hidden, a set of eight disks made of asbestos and bordered with tin, which he called English metal, but which he could not locate in the accepted list of geological metals, and so we had to let it go either as tin, or English metal.

No simpler case could be cited than this. The man knew that it might be difficult to gain an audience if he came announced as an agent or had on view the evidence of being a peddler. He sought the ALTER EGO in its most frequent form, that of appearing to be something that he was not. The difficulty under which he labored was the turning point in the conversation. It became necessary that he should make known the real object of his mission. This he bungled and failed.

In order to have carried the ALTER EGO in the above case he should have produced some real proof of being interested in scientific research and should have carried this far enough to have established a relationship of genuine interest. Shifting so suddenly, even if gradually as it seemed to him, from the guise of one person to that of another, he invited suspicion and dislike.

Still the dull mind will not note the change, and will be led to the very end, believing in the sincerity of the man. It requires a lapse to effect this, and it is done every day in countless thousands of cases.

The prevention of deception is to keep in mind the EGO of the person talking; that is not to let the assumed guise drop without knowing it at the time. To wake up when it is too late will not do. The waking may not be pleasant.

The clever Yankee dealers who succeed in making their patrons believe anything they please, are types of this power and of the waking up too late.

Perhaps the best example of the same clouding of the mind is seen in the man with the twenty dollar bill who called upon a dozen merchants one evening and succeeded in making money fast. He laid the twenty dollar bill on the counter where it remained in full sight of the merchant. He then asked for the accommodation of change; preferring one ten dollar bill and two fives. He placed the ten dollar bill on the twenty; and, as he was folding it to put it in his pocket, he asked if it would be too much trouble to let him have five ones for one of the fives. This the merchant did, not noticing that he had not taken the twenty dollar bill. The result was that the man got away with the forty dollars. After he had gone the merchant would come out of the lapse and detect the transaction. In talking with six men who had been victimized in this way, we found that they all had the same experience. They seemed to half realize that there was something wrong, but did not locate where it was, and the man would get away before they woke up, although there was no hypnotic influence at work. The whole affair might occur in ten seconds or half a minute, so there could be no opportunity for hypnotic manipulation.

A blind consent to the influence of another, is the real definition of this power.

The borrower of money is sometimes very skillful in its use. He may live on his wits if he is able to wield this power among his friends. Some men are professional borrowers and are never in want. They succeed in increasing the loan where it is first placed, and do not suffer from chagrin at facing those to whom they are already in debt.

At the theatre it is worth while to sit in a box and look over the audience when a magnetic actor is on the boards. The hundreds of people present, if they are held in his power, will sit with mouths wide open and live in his very thoughts and emotions. They are wholly unconscious of all else about them for minutes at a time. If this actor could meet any one of them in private he would be able to convince his subject of anything that he could propose with equal power. But the actor who speaks the lines of some great author with fire and magnetism, may not know how to frame his own speech for any purpose, and so would fail.

There are magnificent lovers on the stage who are clumsy in private conversation and who make no headway off the boards. The case of Garrick, as shown in the play, may suggest some of the power on both lines.

A thrilling thought, couched in language that gives it a full carrying power, is often irresistible; but, in crude form, may be less attractive. Thus we have four agencies of the ALTER EGO, as follows:

1. The thought.
2. The diction.
3. The color.
4. The sex.

In more extended form, we have the same agencies stated as follows:

1. Every important thought is magnetic.
2. Every effective use of language is magnetic.
3. Every use of the moods and feelings within the third, fourth and fifth degrees of undulation, is magnetic.
4. Every sincere sexual feeling is magnetic.

Under one or more of the above circumstances all persons who seek to gain advantage or influence over others, employ their energies and purposes. It is easy to take lessons from nature when we see these efforts being made to gain something from some other human being. We see the power of the idea more often than the power of the feeling, and both more often than the power of the diction. But, in the average of years, the sex influence is most in vogue. This phase of magnetism will have full attention in its proper place in this work.

Nothing is more frequent and more effective with an ordinary mind than to see the quick and complete effect produced by the ALTER EGO in an idea only. You can go among your fellow beings by the score in the course of the day, and find most of them swayed completely by this process. It is the first rule of advertisement writing; to catch the public by the idea. The second rule is to catch the public by the diction, or the way in which the idea is presented. The unskilled merchant who knows more about his business than about the English language has come to the conclusion that persons who are trained in the use of words can do more for him than he is able to do for himself in making the advertisement effective, both in ideas and wording.

To get a pleasing glimpse of human nature evolving itself through these two processes, study the written advertisements of any concern; and in a little while you will be able to tell those that are composed by experts and the others that are in the old style. Many great establishments now have ad. writers in their exclusive employ. They are more valuable when so retained, for then they are in the very atmosphere of the business and can get better ideas; whereas the ordinary ad. writer who composes the matter for many business houses, has less potent grasp on the thoughts to be brought before the public, and the result is an attractive diction empty of vigorous ideas of a business status.

The first step is to attract the eye; the next is the mind. The advertisement that catches the eye has taken its first stride toward victory. How to secure this sense is the study of thousands of ad. writers at this date.

If it is too beautiful, it is proportionately less virile, and excess of beauty defeats the purpose of the advertisement.

Virility, or strength of value, must stand out as soon as possible if the more thoughtful public are to be swayed. We saw the other day, what we have seen many hundreds of times, an exceedingly rich and expensive coloring that contained an advertisement; and it had gone through many hands to be admired, without once being read. The beauty drew full attention from the facts presented.

Cheapness may appeal to the common and half-ignorant mind, and accomplish good in that direction. In such case the word FREE will have to do the work of holding the attention, for the classes that have the least to spend are most allured by the liberality of the advertisement.

To get something for nothing is the ALTER EGO of this class of mind. But, like every other ALTER EGO, there comes the turning point when the something for something must be suggested, and this is the crucial factor in such business. We looked into the home of a very poor family where the postman was unloading an armful of mail, and saw the room littered with past deliveries. We asked of the postman:

"How is it that this poor family gets so much mail?"

"Ask the woman there," was the reply.

On renewing the inquiry we were told that she had sent for everything that was free and had continued the practice for several years; but had never invested a cent. This is the experience of thousands of people, and possibly of millions. The question arises, does it pay? The answer comes from the concerns that adopt the method, and they tell us that there are many poor people who do spend money, and they make a profitable patronage as they are more easily convinced. Once they get an idea in the mind they hang on to it until dynamite displaces it, and this is not an uncommon bit of human history.

The middle classes are about through with the practice of sending for things that are FREE, for they are bothered with mail matter that is positive burdening. But the advertisers got the idea that the word FREE would convince the public that there could be no swindle where nothing was charged. The public, some of them, have come out of the lapse and now know that nothing is really FREE, if it is advertised.

The great diversive advertisements of the department stores are all based on the idea of BARGAINS. Here the woman is visited with the ALTER EGO in a form that experience shows to be most effective. She goes, she sees, and, if she has her money with her, she is conquered. Bargain days are regular epochs in her life, and she lives in a waiting or desultory manner between them. They frame the past and the coming limits of each phase of her life. So well settled in her anatomy is the belief in the bargains they offer, that she will ride six miles across a city to get a thirty cent ribbon for twenty-nine cents. She does not stop to realize that there is method in the plan of giving advantages to buyers; and the chances are one hundred to one that she has never reasoned out the fact that, what she gets for less than she ought to pay for it, she makes up in some other way on other goods.

Take the gift enterprises that sell breakfast foods and other food stuff; much is given away in the form of trinkets and prizes, and an enormous amount of money is spent in advertising the goods. The purchaser is compelled, in the long run, to pay for all the prizes and for all the advertising. One concern sells fifty thousand dollars worth of breakfast foods in a year and spends forty thousand dollars a year in advertising it. What is left is ten thousand dollars in the difference. Some one pays fifty thousand dollars for ten thousand dollars.

To be entirely free from the ALTER EGO on the mental side, it is necessary to extricate the mind from the idea that clouds and occupies it. This idea is that for fifteen cents, or for ten cents, that amount of value, less the natural profit, is being given to the purchaser; when, in fact, the latter is paying for all profits and all advertisements, and all prizes.

Here is an opportunity to test how much power you have over the ALTER EGO of the manufacturer of food articles. God has made them grow so freely all over the civilized globe, that nothing that is really wholesome and good for the body need be advertised. To end the lapse in which you are plunged, take this for a rule:

Never under any circumstances buy any food that is advertised.

How would this rule work? You can get all the fruits, all the vegetables, and all the staple grains, meats and other articles just as easily without knowing of any advertisement, as you can by reading and following the advice of advertisements. In fact these foods are never advertised. We do not refer to the retailer who has his general notice in the papers and elsewhere; that is very proper, for he wishes the public to know where he is and the nature of the business in which he is engaged.

But the millions of dollars that are spent in this lapsed country making known the merits of package goods, are to come back from the pockets of the people, and the goods advertised will not stand the test of analysis if it is made apart from the employ of those who set forth their claims. There are thousands of families who keep from their homes all advertised package goods, and they have better health, for they are free from an enormous quantity of preservatives and chemicals that have been put into the goods so that the stock of 1920 will not be stale in the year 1924.

Such families are not under the yoke of the ALTER EGO of the advertisers of package foods.

What about the users of patent medicines? There can be not

one man or woman who is using or has used an advertised medicine who is not under the ALTER EGO of the makers of that medicine. And every such man or woman should take a decided stand at once to stop this slavery to the influence of the controlling party. It is a bad sign. It shows the lack of self mastery, and the bending to the belief that the medicines are helpful, coupled with much extra-belief in their efficacy when they are being used.

It may be set down as a rule from which there is no variation, that the person who uses such medicines is to be the victim of the next schemer. Straws show the direction of the wind, and this kind of person is carrying the straw of being duped. A little reasoning will convince the clear mind that patent medicines are not suited to any use, and are the very danger they have proved to be. The long train of ills they have brought on humanity is their natural goal; there could be no other. That there are yet millions of people under the power of the ALTER EGO, may be seen from the fact that carloads of such medicines are all the time moving through the land. It is interesting to note the sincere belief which people have in them.

No wonder there are so many lines swinging over the heads of the public with bait hung to be nibbled at. It is ever thus and will be the same for thousands of years to come.

When a trader can completely blind the judgment of the person with whom he is dealing, it is a case of mental ALTER EGO; the use of an idea.

But the beggar and the friend use another power, as they do not always find the idea as valuable as an appeal to the heart. On the street a lady stops and listens to the piteous tale of the boy who is the sole support of a family of ten, although he has yet to turn a dozen years himself. The lady never doubts him, and she contributes to the needs of that large family. It is not the idea with her, but the picture which is aroused in her emotional brain, showing this little fellow hard at work from early morn till after dark, pinched with want, barefooted, hungry, half clad, out in all kinds of weather and compelled to struggle to his shabby hut with only seventy-five dollars in his pocket each evening.

A merchant or a banker who would appeal to another merchant or business man on the ground of want, suffering, need of sympathy, or would otherwise make use of the nervous system, would be pretty sure to fail. The idea only is useful in such dealings. Yet we have knowledge of several cases that were adroitly managed on this department of magnetism.

In one case a man trying to sell goods would subject himself to a pretended spell of fainting, and this would arouse inquiry which led to the disclosure that the man had been discouraged by his lack of success and was unable to sleep or eat because of it. The result was an unusually large sale at every place where he worked this plan. It had to be carried on so skillfully that all suspicion of fraud was absent, and this is complete ALTER EGO. This shows the possibility of projecting into another person a mental state so clear as to be accepted and adopted; for the time being the other party is as much in the thought as the person who projects it.

It is on the mental side only.

Most men would be misled by this appearance of weakness, verging on fainting, but there must be an unshaken confidence in the scheme, for the least suspicion would re-act at once and lead to complete disaster.

Business dealings are so free from this use of the emotions that they may be classed wholly apart from it. The mind, the thought, the idea there prevails. The law of need and supply is the first principle of mercantile transactions; but one man may often make another think he needs what he never can make use of, and so the judgment is weak. Many dealings have accumulated in the lives of some merchants, until the pile at the end is more of a burden than they can carry, and failure in business is due to a breach of the Franklin motto, ''Never buy what you do not want, even if it is cheap.''

CHAPTER TWENTY-TWO

✦✦

WORDS AND THOUGHTS
OCCUPY A GREAT
COMPARATIVE PHASE
IN MAGNETIC CONTROL OF OTHERS

✦✦
✦ ✦ *MAGNETIC DICTION* ✦ ✦
✦✦

 HERE ARE WORDS that are called beautiful, and a beautiful mind will employ them when a special effect is sought. There are other words that are called grand, and the mind that seeks to impress a thought or feeling of grandeur on others will make use of such diction. There are words that are virile, and they deal out thought with a master effect when employed by a master mind. And so classes of words go on, each with some mission of its own, holding a certain grade of power over the minds that receive them.

Ideas may arouse the emotions, and then it is not the ideas they present, but the pictures they compel, that holds sway. If you tell your friend that he can make a profit out of a certain transaction, he may be induced to venture in it. If you tell him that a brave man will not see a helpless child drown, but will plunge beneath the waves and rescue it, the appeal is to his emotions. A reference to the flag is a similar appeal, but to another kind of emotion. The thinking part of the brain may not leave its realm of reasoning; but the emotional section knows no reason.

It is on this basis that the lawyer, finding the law against him,

251

and the judge against him, and the evidence against him, will in one sweep of the will discard all appeals to the reasoning faculties of the jury, and plunge into an attack on their sensitive emotions. He has no use for their reasoning powers, for he knows that the more they reason the darker his prospects will grow.

It is a very fine piece of experimental analysis in human magnetism to listen to a trial in court where some clever lawyer who is very magnetic, is running away with a bad case. Rufus Choate has been called the Ruler of the Twelve, because he could win about all his cases from a jury. When he stood before a Supreme Court he adopted tactics that were just the opposite from those that he used before a jury. No lawyer is bold enough to employ an emotional appeal to the great courts, unless he has the adroit skill of a Daniel Webster. The very idea of trying to work on the sympathy of judges, especially a bench of them, is ridiculous and would not be entertained for a moment by a self-respecting lawyer or jurist.

But the following account of Webster's address to the Supreme Court of the United States is furnished us by so excellent an authority as Hon. C. A. Goodrich, and is supported by the history of the times. It will be remembered that Dartmouth College was the Alma Mater of Webster, and that an attempt had been carried through the courts with success to end its career. This success was reversed by the United States Supreme Court, and a new legal principle was born, under the general rule of the common law and the provision of the Constitution relating to the contract and its protection from legislation that may impair its obligations. The law itself was old enough, but the extension of its principle to a grant under which the existence of this college was secured was unexpected, and the question now arises as to what effect the breakdown of Mr. Webster may have had on the emotions of the Supreme Court and through them on their minds and judgment.

"WEBSTER'S PLEA FOR DARTMOUTH COLLEGE."

The argument ended. Mr. Webster stood for some moments silent before the court, while every eye was fixed intently upon him. At length, addressing the Chief Justice, Marshall, he proceeded thus:—"This, Sir, is my case! It is the case, not merely of that humble institution, it is the case of every college in our land. It is more! It is, in some sense, the case of every man among us who has property of which he may be stripped. Sir, you may destroy this little institution;—it is weak, it is in your hands! I know it is one of the lesser lights in the literary horizon of our country. You may put it out. But if you do so, you must carry through your work! You must extinguish, one after another, all those great lights of science which, for more than a century, have thrown their radiance over our land! It is, Sir, as I have said, a small college. And yet, *there are those who love it—*." Here the feeling which he had thus far succeeded in keeping down, broke forth. His lips quivered; his firm cheeks trembled with emotion; his eyes were filled with tears, his voice choked, and he seemed struggling to the utmost simply to gain that mastery over himself which might save him from an unmanly burst of feeling. Every one saw that it was wholly unpremeditated, a pressure on his heart, which sought relief in words and tears. Mr. Webster recovered his composure, and fixing his keen eye on the Chief Justice, said in that deep tone with which he sometimes thrilled the heart of an audience,— "Sir, I know not how others feel (glancing at the opponents of the college before him,) but, for myself, when I see my Alma Mater surrounded, like Cæsar in the senate-house, by those who are reiterating stab upon stab, I would not, for my right hand, have her turn to me, and say '*And* thou, too, my son.'"

The foregoing is a masterpiece of magnetism carried into fields of triumph where such influences are supposed to have the least weight. Had there been a clumsy outburst of feeling, it would have proved fatal to the occasion, and even the minds of the judges might have been given another light by which to guide them to a decision. No man is so wise, or grave, or dignified as to be divested wholly of the human element that dwells in him.

In the preceding chapter we spoke of the many uses of the "idea" in swaying others. Here we have to deal with the "words" that are employed, and the appeal to another department of the being.

To be able to make a picture in the minds of others is the most telling of magnetic uses, but requires consummate skill. Webster, in a few words, drew a picture of the old Roman era and placed before the court the assassination of Julius Cæsar, with his dearest friend, Brutus repeating stab after stab; and as he fell, he spoke the words that have come down to us through these centuries, *et tu Brute!* And history tells us that Cæsar offered no further resistance to his murderers.

Here the words suggested the idea of the falseness of close friendship. The same picture was made to apply to the case of Dartmouth College in its effort to resist the assault made upon it. The institution still stands today, while its enemies are forgotten.

Webster's plea won!

Diction fails when the words are not fraught with thought or suggestions of feeling. One of the most common of mistakes is the use of words of beauty when no beauty is being described, or of grandeur when nothing is grand within a radius of a hundred miles. We do not refer to the slang use of great words, like the awfully sweet color of a piece of cloth, or the splendid plate of oyster stew, or the magnificent flavor of the glass of soda water, etc., etc. Such minds are the overflow of the frothy brook, and live only in their effervescence.

But we have seen efforts to carry on a conversation, or an address, with the hope that words of beauty would make a lasting impression.

What are words of beauty?

Flowers are beautiful, gems are beautiful, colors are beautiful, the gentle moods of nature are beautiful, and that is about the limit. So the speaker or converser who would win favor from his hearers, or the novelist who would acquire fame by a richness of style, will search through the realms of flowers, of gems, of colors, and of nature in her dainty moods, and these will bloom in innumerable places in the diction.

If such words carry thoughts or feelings of beauty, they are magnetic. As mere words they have no standing. Arranged so as to be the bearers of value in the thought, they stand forth as magnetic in diction. The same may be true of words that are virile; they have no value when not portraying virile thoughts. We recall reading a cablegram that came across the Atlantic about two years ago telling of the manner in which the oarsmen of Philadelphia were rowing in English waters. It said that their stroke was magnificent, their energy seemed stupendous, their chances of success were enormous, and their zeal almost superhuman. Not one of these words has any value in the place where used, and the diction would be regarded as flat.

It is a universal rule that, where words are used in their fine shades of meaning, their magnetism is increased. When the listener is compelled to give the word a slightly different meaning from that which it carries on its face, in order to know exactly what is intended by the person speaking, it loses some of its power. Most persons use words out of their real meaning. They say things that have to be completed in the mind of the listener.

It is well worth while to learn all the words that are common to the educated public, not the technical or professional public, and then employ them with exactness for weeks in imaginary conversation or speeches, until full control of them is attained, and their finest shades of meaning are known, not by memory, but by the faculty of actual vocal use. Your own ear then becomes a channel of information to your mind, and you have the double advantage of hearing and speaking at the same time. This gives each word a much stronger hold on the mind and nervous system. The person who reads words, and never speaks them, knows no more about them than he does of the neighbors whose pictures he sees in the papers.

Chapter Twenty-three

++

A SECOND COMPARATIVE PHASE
IN THE
MAGNETIC CONTROL OF OTHERS
IS IN THE LIFE BEHIND THOUGHT

++
SPIRIT OF THE ALTER EGO
++

 VERY DEPARTMENT of the being which is known as human is involved in the study of magnetism. In the chapter before the last we dealt with the value of thoughts and ideas. In the last chapter we took up the question of diction as the agency of thoughts. We bring the work now up to the gates of the emotions. In order to understand the value of this part of the work it must be remembered at all times that the life of a human being begins in what it feels and so ends, as far as conscious existence is concerned. We have stated that the mind does not live in words, but uses them for the purposes of communication with others.

If there were no one else living on the globe there would be no words, for the one being on earth would have no occasion to use them. If there were animals that associated with him, the result would be a language that accommodated itself to both species. The dog would arouse in his master the tendency to speak in growls, barks, whines, yelps, and tones of pleasure, hunger, and so forth. Such a condition has actually arisen where a man was left his dog as the only life about him.

The man would make all the sounds that the dog could produce, and had words of his own invention that applied to things and conditions that the dog came in contact with. Both understood each other; and the remarkable fact is that no other words were spoken, after the lapse of time, than those that each could interpret.

All language is invented as the means of communication between living specimens of the animal kingdom.

But the man had his feelings that the dog could not understand and need not know. The real transactions within the brain are beyond the scope of words. *They are feelings and they live on and on until they assume a shape and form apart from the life in which they dwell. This is the emotional* ALTER EGO.

We call it emotional because there is no other word in this or any other language that will express it.

We know what it is in our own mind. We hope to make it clear to you. But words do not exist that tell its meaning and status. It has never been described in the dictionaries, but has stood out before many an individual in the hours of the night when there came the necessity of speaking to one's own self. Here are two laws:

1. *You live in the feelings that possess you, and in the moods that are the offspring of the thoughts or experiences that influence you.*

2. *Such an existence is a complete self in and of itself.*

We stand now before the real ALTER EGO.

It is this second self that controls you when your mental self is not able to hold the mastery. Therefore we find the third law as follows:

3. *Every human being has two personalities; one the direct self, and the other the* ALTER EGO.

Under this division we find that the mental self is not the ALTER EGO; but here again comes the complex nature of the proposition; and another law is necessary:

4. *The direct self is that which is composed of the thoughts, feelings, moods and emotions that are capable of being framed in words and speech; while the* ALTER EGO *is the other self, which is interpreted without the aid of words and speech.*

The reason of this rule is a natural one. It has been under way in its development ever since man reached out toward civilization. Like the horns on cattle that were compelled to fight with their heads, or tails on horses that found it necessary to keep flies away, these extra departments of life have been developed under the stress of necessity.

If you take any animal that is suited to one clime and one set of conditions, and place him where the conditions are different in one or more important particulars, you will be enacting a new episode in the race of that species, as far as that individual is concerned. The fingers on the hand were induced by efforts to make use of just such part of the body. The arm itself came into being as the slow process of an effort to use the part of the body where it is attached for the very employment to which it has been put.

Teeth came in the mouth because it was necessary to bite and tear the food; and the growing loss of teeth that is now in evidence is due to the character of the food that is eaten. If there were no other food for humanity than the mush kind or breakfast foods, humanity would have a mouth like a jelly fish. Give the jelly fish the necessity of masticating a tough diet and it will set in motion the ramifications that will bring hard teeth with enamel that will be the envy of all dentists.

So when humanity came to the front with its native being wrapped up in feelings, moods and emotions that had no words to speak with, the very fact that words came to meet another line of necessity, gave rise to a second being. But that second being, using itself solely for the purpose of communicating with its fellow beings, became the primal or first being in evidence to others.

That individuality that is in communication with other individualities must of necessity be the personality that is seen, known and met in human life. The only use or necessity for words is to communicate with other people. The knowledge that other people have of one is in their communication with that one.

To put these facts in other words, we will say that the side that is outward, or front to the world is the self that exists in words and speech; and any other self that exists in the individual is the ALTER EGO. There can be no doubt of the accuracy of this proposition.

One man lives in deeds and not in words, so we are told. But his deeds live in words, and as no man can achieve anything by himself, his commands to those who were his aids must have been given in words. When you separate a man from words you ostracize him from history.

All that the world knows and records of a man or woman is told in words.

This individual is blind, but he can talk. That individual is deaf, but he can read. The third is deaf, dumb and blind, but he can feel. Any sense that can convey an idea to the brain is talking. It is the fact that there is communication by what is termed the natural senses, such as those involved in sight, hearing, touch, smell and taste, that makes words signs, and signs words. It is the outward evidence of the inward being that constitutes the primal self. The ALTER EGO is that being which dwells by itself and has no dependence on the means of communication. It is that being that would have existed had no necessity for communication arisen.

Nature brings forth her offspring to suit the conditions in which they live. As the presence of other individuals in the world made communication necessary, the primal self came into existence. But as man has a life that is wholly independent of such uses, he must be considered in the light of that nature which is summed in the other being.

The question at this stage will arise, What kind of ALTER EGO is that which is involved in the use of the mind through words and speech, in accordance with the statements made in the preceding chapter?

The answer is this: The mind of the person controlled by an idea is emptied of its own primal self, and whatever takes its possession is the ALTER EGO in that case, but not the ALTER EGO necessarily of the person who exerts the control.

To make this clear, let us suppose that you are completely swept away from your judgment by the ideas of another person; that you enter the state of lapse that attends such loss of the primal self; and that you see or feel the ideas or emotions of another person. You have allowed your primal self to step aside, and you are beside yourself in the sense that you are not that primal self. The other person may cause you to feel certain emotions at will, or to accept certain ideas at will, these not being your own except by adoption.

That was the scope of the preceding chapter.

Here we follow out the control of the second self of the controlling party. There we followed out the laying aside of the primal self in the party controlled.

The point now to be made is quite different. It is summed up in the following general fact:

The second self of an individual is an actual being, not an idea or a feeling, not a thought or an emotion; but a real self; and, in our opinion, THE real self. This lessens the value or status of the primal self. The latter term is used because the public or those who see us, know us only by some method of communication. Hence it is the most prominent being and the one that seems to stand in front to keep guard, as it were, of the real life back of it.

These ideas will be repeated in different form in order to allow them to be the more readily grasped. Let us suppose that we are to ascertain by investigation which is the real self; that we have come to the conclusion that the being that is made manifest by the use of words, speech and other means of communication, is necessarily the real person; but that there is evidence that all such means of holding intercourse with other persons might be cut off and still another being would remain, which would compel the belief that the one that felt, that enjoyed and suffered, was in fact the real self; and therefore the primal or front personality was not by any means all there is of the individual; what will be the standing of the latter? The more we think it over the more decided will be our opinion that this last-named being is the more important.

Yet the man is what he proves himself to be by the means of communication with others. Your senses see and know of him, but only of this part of his existence. He walks before you a live man, but it is only in that one self. While this may seem involved reasoning, it is an important distinction to understand.

The second self is much more real than the body of flesh and bone. It is not dependent on senses for it disregards all such means of communication. This we know to be the existence that feels, that enjoys and that suffers. It is the existence that embraces the full scope of all the moods and feelings that have been so fully set forth in earlier chapters of this work. For the present we wish to call it the second self until certain facts are made clearer. This leaves our terms as follows:

5. *The primal self is that being that employs means of com-*

munication with other persons, such means having their uses in the senses.

6. *The second self is that which feels, enjoys and suffers.*

7. *As the primal self is a form of life in fact, so the second self is a form of life in fact.*

The first step in this department of our work is to learn to recognize the two beings that make up the individual. How shall you know one from the other? What good is to be gained by doing so?

The great men and women of the past, all those who have won either fame or substantial rewards in life, have lived in their second self to themselves, and chiefly in their primal self to others. Magnetism has its origin in the second self. Ideas that are called mental magnetism, are born in the second self. The fact that they have the moving power to control some one, or to change the current of some life, is evidence of the fact that they are not mere means of communication.

In its true sense magnetism lives only in the second self. If you witness the great work of the actor, you see the second self only. The orator who speaks from the primal self only is dry, dull, uninteresting and commonplace, and few are above that estimate. The great achievements recorded in history had their origin in the second self. The powerful sermon that is something more than noise or vehemence, is born in the second self. All art, all poetry, all fancy, all inventive genius, and all that distinguishes the human type from the animal is produced by the faculty of the second self.

All these facts have been stated in other works, and are accepted generally as true.

But to know and to recognize, and to be familiar with each self, is a most important part of training, and may be classed among the grandest of all means of culture. We know of nothing that is superior to its rank in useful value.

8. *The mind is the agent of both the primal and the second self. It seems at times to stand aside and look on while one or the other of these two personalities is holding the boards.*

9. *Each self has its good and its bad sides.*

10. *All that is heavenly and all that is pernicious may be found in the primal self; and the same is true of the second self.*

Every man and woman is made up of two opposing forces, one

working heavenward, and the other working hellward. No one is free from these counter influences. One source gives rise to the moods that are heaven-born; and the other source gives rise to the moods that are hell-born. Thus we see the workings of the full second being under these two-fold influences.

In those moods we find the second self.

But life on earth has forced a third set of moods to respond to the aroused nature that is built on the senses and contact with humanity. These are earth-born, and have their origin in the primal self, but pass over into the second self.

Look, then, at the list of moods and feelings that may be found in an earlier chapter, and note the constituent parts of the second self. As you have been studying them you have without doubt made them live in the colors that you have developed, and they are now a part of your very life. We wish you to look at them in general review in order to know what is meant by your second self.

Having done this, and realizing the meaning of this fact, you ought at all times to know when your second self is in control, and when your primal self has the ascendency.

It is not possible to separate them in normal conditions, as they are harnessed together. The orator who is relating facts, as when he reads or states statistics, is in the primal self; but as soon as he speaks from the source of the feelings, even though he relates facts, he is making the second self the master of the primal self, using the latter for the purpose of expressing the former.

The man who gets up in the morning, dresses, attends to his duties, eats his breakfast, reads the papers, goes to his work, reads more papers later in the day, attends to more duties, and spends the evening with papers and books, is giving himself wholly to his primal self, and he is building a prison house about all that is worth living for in the inner development.

This is the kind of existence that ninety-five per cent of all men and women are living. They are perfunctory employees or else routine workers in some department of life, or pass through the same old mill day after day, whether it is in doing business, running a bank, attending to professional duties, or carrying on the social functions that form the whole thought of most women. They find variety in what they read, or in cards, or in chatter, or in a humdrum existence; knowing nothing about their second self, and having no special goal or prowess in their careers.

All this kind of occupation or mental interest is of the primal or outside self.

The second self is aroused and brought out by many different kinds of influences, a few of which may be named. In the first group are the moods and feelings that have already been stated.

But we see this self paramount in the presenec of art if there is a genuine touch of real art in the humanity of the individual.

Painting that opens up a world of inner appreciation in man or woman is enjoyed in a sense that the primal self cannot understand. It reaches beyond the card player or cheap reader of sensational literature.

A statute is full of inviting power to such a person, or to one who is awakened by that line of art. Grand or beautiful or effective architecture makes a deep impression on one whose second self is awake, and is only a pile for criticism in others.

The inspiring sentences in books, essays, and lofty composition are magnetic forces to those who love them. So with music; if the primal self appreciates it, there is slang in the song or jingle in the tune.

Poetry is another element in the life of the second self, and is ridiculed by the millions who prefer card playing or big-type news. It is rare indeed now-a-days that we find a real lover of true poetry; it is looked upon as wholly impracticable in the present era. Yet, to offset this sordid feeling, the other fact stands out that no man or woman ever was magnetic or ever will be magnetic who has not read and been held in raptures by the art that frames thoughts in the rich diction of poetry. The trouble is that most people do not know that they like poetry.

We saw a coarse and hardened fellow of business mold take up the story of Little Nell in Dickens; he had never read a line of poetry in all his life; but when he came to the death of the little girl he felt almost as bad as if it had been his own offspring. Again and again he would revert to the story until the words were memorized, and he could repeat the swing of movement in that prose style that was all poetry but the rhyme. This proved that he did in fact love poetry. All he lacked was an introduction to himself. So it is with countless millions.

The love of flowers, the inclination to cultivate a garden for something besides vegetables, and the fellowship with nature not merely to drink in her pure air and get out of the office or store, are indications that a second self is seeking to force its way to the front.

There are thousands of things in the world that appeal to this inner and deeper individuality. They are passed by unnoticed by the millions who know nothing but routine drudgery of a humdrum life or who are cast in the practical mold of strict business or professional duties.

That greatness is born only in the second self has been proved countless times. It can be seen in the first third of most lives, as in the case of young Daniel Webster who pleaded for the life of a worthless animal that was caught and about to be killed at his home when he was a boy. He saw in his mind the little family that this animal was rearing somewhere in all probability; he felt the loss of the mate who would look in vain for the home-coming of the captive; and he pictured in the minds of those about him the needless cruelty which was being put upon that group. He not only had a sincere pity for the victim but made his hearers see and feel as he did, and the result was that freedom was granted the animal.

It becomes a difficult matter to separate the soft sentimentality of the primal self, which is so often in evidence, from the genuine sympathy of the second self. The startling fact stands out quite clearly at this juncture, and tells us that the second self does not and cannot make a mistake; while the soft sentimentality of the primal self rarely if ever escapes one. The silly custom of feeding tramps and of giving to professional beggars, as well as the effort to shower bouquets on men who have committed wanton murder, are born in the primal self, and have no place in the category of judgment or mercy.

The second self does not make mistakes.

It is not harshly cruel or needlessly relentless. It sees the necessity of exercising mercy and forgiveness where they are merited, and it divines their merit. It is just on the side of justice. The fact that this self does not and cannot make mistakes is the basis of the many lesser lines of influences that are to be discussed in the later pages of this work.

We wish at this time to have the fact kept well before the mind of the student, in order that what is to follow will be understood.

The entire portion of the remaining study relates to the second self, and the consideration of this part of the course should be made thorough.

Let the full purpose of this step be examined.

It is necessary that the distinction between the primal and the second self be understood. That there are two such selves is admitted. This is not a discovery, for such distinction has always been made. We are not referring to the spirit as that life is generally expressed. Let us see if the two following laws are helpful:

11. *There is in every human being a life that would go on in any planet and under any conditions, regardless of this world.*

12. *The orb on which one dwells determines what shall be the development of the life that is formed amid the surroundings of such existence.*

From these laws the conclusion is to be drawn that the inherent life will be the same wherever one may dwell. Assuming that there is one great Father of the germs of all life throughout the universe, or one Godhead over all, it is consistent that the inherent life in each individual should be the same in its basis.

But as the earth is only a mere dot in the sky, and not all that is in the universe, there must be life elsewhere in some form, and this is the generally accepted theory and belief of all intelligent people. The inhabitants of earth are identical in their inherent nature with the inhabitants of the general universe; or, in other words, they are the same everywhere in their second self. This ought to be called their first self, but the latter term is used because it represents the self that is first seen, most known and always to the front in human existence.

Taking the term, second self, for convenience only, we say that it is the same wherever there are beings, great or small, in this or in any other part of the sky.

The more you study this proposition the more firmly convinced you will become of its truth. Take time to think it out. Do not discard it on an offhand reading. Think of the origin of life, of the central source somewhere, of the purpose of creation, and of the return of the soul to its fatherhead; and then apply all the true philosophy that you can collect from any and all sources, and the more you think and study the more forcible will the truth become. We ask this in the cause of a fair investigation and against a hasty judgment. Most persons throw away the great pearls of knowledge and they remain hidden for centuries before they finally come to light.

But we believe that it is a generally admitted fact that there is a universal self, living as an individual in each and every human being on this earth and yet common with all life everywhere.

This second self is imperishable as is shown in the greater study of universal philosophy. It does not make mistakes as is also shown there. It is capable of communicating with all other life of its kind, not only on this earth but everywhere throughout the whole heavens, as is shown in Universal Magnetism, as one of its great divisions or estates.

It needs development, and it also needs a channel of recognition between the primal self and its own nature. These two phases are denied it. If we can show in this and other works the way to achieve these two ends, the labor will not be in vain.

A sensible view should be taken of this dual proposition. We do not believe in spirits, ghosts, and other paraphernalia of life, but we do know that this second self is separable from the primal, and that it can be projected more or less under the will of its owner in almost any manner and under a variety of circumstances. But this is not dealing with the doctrine of the spiritists. Fear and an abnormal love of the sensational draws many persons of weak mind into the belief that the souls of the departed come back to earth or linger here, or do other things at the bidding of the cheap mediums who practice upon the credulity of the primal mind. We teach exactly the opposite.

We state and will prove that the souls of the dead do not return, that there is no such thing as the wandering spirit, and that the whole fabric of spiritualism is a misunderstanding.

On the other hand we do teach that one or more persons are so constituted that they may be made subject to the ALTER EGO, and in this state may be the recipients of the second self of another living person, but not of one that is dead.

Any person who has read the work of Universal Magnetism can realize the methods we have adopted to secure the truth. There has been almost nothing but sensational treatment for this sacred and vital subject. Tricksters, charlatans and schemers have preyed upon the minds of their followers for centuries, and in large degree during the past fifty years. It is time that a sensible and honorable study be made of the subject in order that the truth may be had and appreciated.

That there is the so-called second self must be taken as admitted. It can be so easily proved that it should not be held in doubt except by those who are not capable of being convinced, and they play no part in any genuine investigation.

That the primal self is a necessity is seen from the fact that the conditions of earthly existence make it what it is, and develop it in proportion as it comes in contact with the experiences of this life. The size, shape of the body, knowledge of the mind and the development of the brain are all due to the conditions that attend life on this earth. If the same second self were to be born on the planet of Jupiter, the size of the body would be many times greater than here, and the specific gravity so much lighter that one of the inhabitants would seem to float like corks in our waters. And the terms used, the words employed, the ideas expressed would all be different. The face would suit the influences under which life was born, as the face of a fish is made to meet the contingencies under which it is evolved.

It has been justly said that if all the histories of a nation were to be destroyed, they could be restored in sense by the words of the literature of each epoch in the nation's progress. You can see something of this fact in the language of fifty years ago before there were electrical inventions in number, and the language of today when there are countless terms applicable to this one phase of business alone. Then twenty or thirty years ago you could not find in the literature extant any references to automobiling; now there are scores of terms in use. Thus the march of history is marked by the march of language.

The shape of the body suits itself to the conditions in which it lives. For the air there must be wings, for the sea there must be fins, for the land there must be legs. The occupations of man require arms, hands and fingers; and, in the four limbs and their terminals we have the basis of human life, and the ten digits that make up the numerical systems of the world. What these hands and digits can do is the bulk of all language and all mental development. Here we have the outer or primal self developing.

Deny a child the opportunities of communicating with other human beings or of using the limbs and digits, and you check its mental and primal growth; it will remain wherever these opportunities will. So many times has this fact been manifested that it is a settled law that all the intelligence that shows itself in the growth of the brain and in the learning and knowledge of the world, is the direct result of contact with the world.

Here is one self.

Back of it is that other self which existed before the primal self began to develop. This substantiates the statement so often made by scientists that the child knows as much as the grown adult but lacks the means of expressing it. The real fact is the same, but is told in more exact language as follows:

The second self of the child is the same at birth, during growth and at death; but the primal self is the result of gradual unfolding of the brain and knowledge of life that begins in infancy and proceeds up to maturity. This self breaks down, while the second self never loses its powers. For this reason the insane person who has lost his hold on the uses of the brain and faculties of the primal self, seems to have his identity obliterated; and the question has been asked thousands of times, Shall the individual who dies insane live again? Shall the born idiot who never has reason live again after this life?

The answer is this: The insane person is insane only in the primal self; and the born idiot is an idiot only in the primal self. The second self can have a perfect condition at birth, all through life and at death. Some of the grandest thoughts ever expressed have dropped from the lips of idiots; and the king's fool has often given the most wholesome advice. This is the second self forcing its way through in intervals at openings of the primal self; chinks that let some light through and then are dark again.

The primal self may be born an idiot, but we do not believe that the second self is so born; yet it takes on the conditions of moral insanity under the control of the means of expressing itself.

The child fresh from the hand of God is closest to its second self, and it loses that closeness as it develops under the influence of life in the world, which of necessity is compelled to place the primal self to the front. No wonder that the Savior said, "Of such is the kingdom of heaven." This means much when we know the facts that underlie the statement.

We have now gone far enough in these explanations.

If the student does not by this time understand the difference between the self that is born, and the self that is developed by life on this earth, it will be useless to seek further discussion except such as may come from repeated review of the past pages.

The moral and religious sides of the question are not to be brought into this work. They are always associated and interwoven with every faculty of man and depend on laws that are much the same; but our purpose in this course of study is to get at the laws of power and apply them to the conditions which exist about us on every hand.

CHAPTER TWENTY-FOUR

THE THIRD
COMPARATIVE PHASE
IN THE MAGNETIC CONTROL OF OTHERS
IS IN THE CREATIONS OF THE SOUL

PROJECTIONS OF THE ALTER EGO

EADERS and STUDENTS of this line of investigation will, by this time, realize that the course of progress is going into deep water. It is to keep it simplified so that any mind, even of slight intelligence, may get good from the teachings, as well as those broader and more subtle thinkers that love deep studies, that we have taken so many seemingly rambling illustrations of the laws and facts stated in the preceding chapters, and placed them before all classes who are pursuing this work.

We cannot take the space here to sum up the many propositions that have been laid down; but we take it for granted that it is well understood that there are two parts to the individuality that dominates human existence; that one part is inherent or born in the body, and the other part is outward, and to the front, having been developed by the experiences of life on earth.

What you are in the minds of others is what you have developed by contact with the world, unless you have risen out of the commonplace by the use of genuine power.

It is not probable that the primal self can change the second or inherent self, but it has wonderful influence over it in the line of unfolding or exposing it to the gaze of this world; and the strange fact is that, in proportion as the primal self breaks down, the second self comes through the openings made by the fracture. This is seen in the life of Edgar Allan Poe who shone through these great rifts in his mental nature. It is even more seen in the life of Lord Byron who was nothing but a patched-up primal self, and yet wielded a most magnificent power in the inherent realm of his nature. And it is true in hundred of other cases that are familiar to the readers of history and biography. What little we know of Shakespeare does not laud his primal self. He was certainly lacking in schooling, and in the usual means of acquiring education; his moral impulses were weak if we take his life, and not his works for proof; for, although we know but little of his life, that little is most uncomplimentary. Those who judge a man by his works must not always connect his primal self with those works.

The biography of Shakespeare, as far as known, is as follows: As a boy he got in trouble and wrote a scurrilous note to an honored and respected citizen, whose name was Lucy and whom Shakespeare terms lousy in a pun. He seduced Anne Hathaway, as the records show, for she gave birth within a short time after their marriage. He deserted her and ran away to London; making himself both a deserter of his family and a run-away. His Venus and Adonis, and his Lucrece, were poems that would today be crimes for their obscenity, and were the extreme of vulgar even for a vulgar age. His death was due to a drunken carousal, as local tradition states. His will is a direct insult to his wife, as it leaves her nothing but his second-best bedstead.

On the other hand his works are not only immortal, but stand forth as the best literature and poetry of any and every age. In his works he preaches the highest moral code, the grandest intelligence and the most sublime truths. His admirers and worshipers have taken his measure from his works, not from the man; from the second self and not from his primal self. So, finding in his productions evidences of a most lofty character, they proceed to explain his faults on the following theory: When he insulted the honored man of his town, he was a boy and not accountable. When he married Anne Hathaway he did so probably under compulsion and may not have been as guilty as the records make him seem. When he ran away he did so in order to see more of the world, and thus be more useful to the world. When he deserted his family, he may have had a real grievance. When he left his wife nothing but the second-best bedstead, he knew that she was provided for by the law, as she was sure of her dowry in his real estate. But it must not be forgotten that the law and not Shakespeare awarded the dowry; he himself being powerless to deny her that. His obscene poems were set forth as the reflection of the vulgarity of the age in which he lived; but Milton wrote in the same age and his more lofty but less sublime works are wholly free from the slightest suggestion of the obscene. And the same is true of many other writers. That age was not as obscene as the era of Dante, or the era of Virgil or the era of Homer; yet they wrote but little that was of that class of thought, and Shakespeare in the poems mentioned, was brimming full of nastiness forced in by extra efforts.

We are not belittling the products of this thousand-souled genius; they are unapproachable in all time; but we are showing that the primal Shakespeare did not and could not create the works that came forth from the inherent self behind him.

The story of Jekyll and Hyde is an outburst of the realization that there are two selves within the body.

Thus the fact is evident that the second self will break through the fractures of the moral or mental parts of the primal self. The whole history of Napoleon is positive proof of this law. The lofty Milton whose verse has touched and opened the genius of millions of men and women in the centuries that have followed, was in private life a most unfortunate man. Wesley whose preaching changed the face of English history, was still more unfortunate in his private life, both here and in his native land. Charles Sumner, the grandest of statesmen, and whose soul, as stated by Emerson was the whitest he ever knew, was unfortunate in his private life, walking out of his bridal chamber in a few hours after he entered it, never again to return. Aaron Burr, whose genius and patriotism might have been as great as Washington's was predominated by his primal self, and so fell into shame and obloquy.

We turn with admiring thought to the greatness of Alexander, and find a most brilliant power shining through the wreck of physical, mental and moral weakness. Even Daniel Webster was a libertine and a drunkard, as any Washingtonian knows who has lived there for the past generation or more. Although he has been dead for more than half a century, his career in the city is fully understood. Blessed with a vitality that might have carried him on for a much greater age, he was described while yet in the prime of life as the "grandest human wreck ever witnessed," and that by one of his friends and followers.

It may be true that, in order to let the genius and power of the inherent self break through, the primal self must give way at some place. This is in accord with the oft-repeated statements of investigators that every genius is either insane in degree or else is morally or mentally out of balance. Some go so far as to say that genius is impossible in a sane mind and a moral nature.

But this last statement need not be accepted as true, unless it is to be applied to acute genius.

Certainly Longfellow was a genius, and most certainly be combined a sane mind with a high moral nature. The same is true of Tennyson and of many of the sweet-lived poets of America and England. Macaulay was a genius, yet had no defect of mind or morality.

Gough was, perhaps, the greatest of all geniuses in his line, that of a grand dramatic orator; but his erratic nature broke open when he was a young man, sending him almost to a drunkard's grave; and, when delirium tremens had nearly conquered him, he turned about and shone from the second or inherent self all the remainder of his life. No greater exhibition of moral power or mental ability could be found than in his career after he threw away his primal self.

Beecher was the noblest of all pulpit orators in any age. Although he was charged with immorality and was subjected to court proceedings the most noted in all our history, it was the general belief that he was the target of newspaper sensationalism and free from blame. The less intelligent public still believe him guilty. We believe him innocent, for we knew him well and were in a position to judge him by evidence that could not be doubted. The fact probably is that he was a man of innocent purposes and gave himself up to the free expression of his affection for humanity without taking into consideration the appearances that are thus created. The lower status of the public mind cannot understand this manner of dealing with others, and so sneer at the suggestion.

Edwin Forrest was the greatest actor the American people

have ever seen, yet his life was a wreck in all other ways except on the stage. Edwin Booth was the next grandest of all American actors, and was in turmoil at all times after he reached his prime. He had no home except upon the stage, and died almost with the harness on. His father was almost the equal of Forrest, yet was so erratic as to be charged with all than can be hurled at a human being; and his son, Edwin, issued a biography which was intended to defend and explain his father's nature.

These are the stars of the world, not the lesser lights, not the run and average of humanity, but the loftiest names in all history.

Contact with the world teaches all the sin and all the crime that can be found in the world. Were we born on some other planet where the conditions are not favorable to the necessity of sinning and committing crimes, there would be neither a moral code nor a religion, for they would be superfluities.

Yet in life upon the earth it is necessary that all human beings should come in contact with the conditions and should meet them as best they can. Our position in this line of teaching is to maintain that, while the inherent self breaks through the wreck of mind and morals, it nevertheless comes through and makes itself apparent, proving that it exists. We see the other being, and know what it is like.

Our next position is to teach the value of cultivating that other being. It cannot first be cultivated in ourselves, but in the study of others. This means that the way to become familiar with what we ourselves possess as an inherent nature, we must first find it in the lives of the greatest men and women who have lived.

To read of this inherent nature in another and to see the work it has accomplished, biography is necessary. It must in the first place be the biography that depicts the inherent life, not the worldly schemes and business success or the financial progress or the executive work of a mere executive giant; but the struggles, the rise and the supreme success of those men and women who have achieved greatness by reason of their inherent powers.

It has always been said that the reading of biography will inspire the inner impulses within the narrow shell of the primal self, or the commonplace self. The career of Henry Wilson who rose from ignorance and poverty to the position of Vice-President of the United States, solely by reason of the power that came from reading biography, is typical of the law that works out the hidden genius.

Select one or two great biographies.

Select them well.

Do not expect to find their heroes or heroines perfect, and do not be discouraged because they are faulty. Their sins and crimes did not make them great. Read for evidences of the breaking out of the inherent self, and cling to all that is accomplished by that power.

Select with regard to your life work.

If you are a lover of the art of painting, you will find a few great mountain peaks that loom far above all surrounding mountains, and these names, like that of Angelo, will bring you into the inspiring influences of the story that is unfolded. Indeed hardly any person could read the biography of Angelo, the sculptor, the painter, the architect, the poet, without finding the full measure of inspiration.

Do not read and drop the book.

Read it once, then review it, then drink it, then take it into your heart and brain and soul, and make it yourself. This is the way in which you absorb, and are uplifted by, the nobler thoughts of the world.

If you are a lover of war you will find some similar mountain peaks looming up in every age. One or two well selected biographies of the conquerors will give you power.

If you love poetry there are hundreds of biographies that will make you feel the subtle and gentler sweep of the breeze that waves over the fields of their genius.

If you love statesmanship, there are such lives as Gladstone, Bismarck, Webster, Sumner, Clay, Calhoun, Washington, and countless others that will serve you. The life of Andrew Jackson is inspiring, even with the glaring defects in his primal character. Parton and Kellogg have written biographies that are well worth reading. The sketches of Macaulay in his history, and the similar sketches of other lives by George Bancroft in American history, are the best in all their line. They are interspersed throughout their writings and can be selected by one who cares to work in this kind of delving.

Wherever Macaulay and Bancroft take up the personal triumphs of men and women, there shines forth the rays of brilliant biography. So great was the work of the latter that he was honored as no historian has ever been since the world began.

To read history for the facts accomplished is not to drink in the inherent power that has made such deeds possible. The better way is to find what made great men and great women successful. Find out that charm, and the secret is yours. So recent a life as that of Beaconsfield is a source of inspiration.

Let biographies be written by the friends of the great.

Enemies in their desire to be partial spread too much of the primal self, too much of the faults of the body over the page; while friends seek the mainspring of power, the inherent self. We place no value on the faults that have dragged men down.

You cannot read any biography without finding yourself uplifted by its power. You will be a different person. The influence that made a person great will arouse in you the same inherent nature that was at work in that other person. This has always been true. It has always been recognized as true, whether under the terms we use or those of other writers.

Having laid this foundation for awakening in yourself the inherent part of your life, you must keep it in harmony with your mental and your moral character. Do not let your second self run in one direction and your primal self take another. If you do so, you will be making the same old history with which the world is filled.

It is possible to select from the history of the world more than a hundred great names where this harmony prevailed. The tendency is almost toward a religious life, as in the case of Moody, Whitefield and the giants who have helped hold up the ethics of life.

There is no reason why religion should claim one who has made his or her primal self a harmonic power with the inherent self. It is well that it should be so, and it is better that all who are doing the work of religious leadership should be thus in harmony in both their departments of being, and it is best that no others should be allowed to perform such duties; but the world in all its lines of business and professions, needs geniuses who can do something more than count profits or plan schemes for wresting wealth from others.

Business and professional life can be made levers for uplifting all the race and presenting to the next historian a grander civilization. The primal self can make money, can ruin or upbuild hundreds of other lives, can take good from the earth and corrupt it, can commit all the crimes of the moral and penal codes and do countless other things that seem like the exercise of power, but which in fact are the opposite. The value of an achievement is the addition it makes to civilization, not the gain it brings in horded wealth to one man. Nor can one man draw to himself by unfair methods a mass of accumulations and make amends by doing good in wholesale charity. His offering is on a par with his gaining; it is the work of the primal self; Christ blesses the charity that is born in the inherent self, and not the alms that are figured out in the brain.

Under the plan suggested in this and the last chapter, there will be a new life springing up within the student of this course.

This is based also on the magnetic training of the first book, on the early training of this book, on the development of the colors under the moods and passions, and on the after work that leads up to this stage.

Let all these steps be taken in their order, and each will be found to be a logical and natural successor of the one that precedes, until the next work is ready for your skill.

The climax of this order of development is the creation of a recognition of the fact that you do in reality possess two distinct natures or departments. You will feel and know both your primal and your second or inherent self. From this time on we will refer to the latter as the inherent self, having used the term second to show how it stands with relation to the primal nature.

By inherent is meant the born self; and by primal is meant that self which is first and most often seen and experienced in dealing with others.

We wish you to arrive at that stage where you can recognize that you possess these two natures, and we wish you to have so clear a recognition of them that there will not be the slightest doubt of their existence.

Then they must be separated.

This does not mean that they are to be put at variance with each other, but that they are to be known and used as two steeds in a team driven by the same individual. Like two steeds they should be capable of being driven singly or in double work. If driven singly they need not be made competitors or antagonists.

The practice of separating them is one of recognition.

It is performed easily and need not be difficult for any person who is in earnest.

To recognize one from the other all that is necessary is to know the work that is done by the primal self, and the work that is done by the inherent self. This is accomplished by the suggestions of the last chapter and of this as well.

Having come to a recognition of the two natures, the next thing to be done is to use them at will. If you chose to deal with another person in matters that are commonplace, use your mind, your speech, your methods of communication, your common sense, and all that is a part of your primal self. You may go through all the duties of the day in this manner. You may read for mere information, and may write, talk or otherwise keep up the work of the hour, in the same way. But when you come to conditions where moods and feelings are to be summoned, as in the grander or the finer influences of life, then your inherent self is to be employed. You will soon see how this is to be done, although you can readily ascertain what is meant by going back to the chapters on the moods and feelings and following out all the suggestions and instruction there given.

Finally the inherent self will separate itself from your body and become a creation apart.

This seems a bolder assertion than you are prepared for. If we do not make it clear at this stage we will fail later on to have our meaning grasped.

If you will read the lives of the great actors you will find that they played to ideals and not to reals.

There is hardly any life of an actor or actress where this statement is not made. And it is everywhere acknowledged as a fact and one that is necessary to the genius.

Here is a traveling star; he goes from one city to another, there finding a company awaiting him; they being known as the home or stock company. They have learned and rehearsed their parts and he fits his in with theirs, has one or two rehearsals for business, and then the plays are given at night. He is too great to be tied down to one city, and goes from place to place, drawing a large salary and avoiding the heavy drain of expenses that comes from taking a whole company with him, as well as a carload of scenery, or more.

This was the custom, and will again prevail, although it is out of favor at this time.

This star is greater than those of the same company. He may be cast as a lover, as in the play of the Lady of Lyons, or may make love as in the case of Othello in that tragedy, or may be a Romeo, or otherwise find it necessary to play to the part of some beautiful woman of the highest ideal creation. No such woman may be available. Yet he plays to her, and she is his own offspring, born of his genius and present before him.

It was said to the author by Lawrence Barrett, what is well known in the history of the stage, that he always saw his ideal woman standing before him, even in rehearsals. "I often put so much feeling into my rehearsals that the form and face of the woman would be there in the room before me as real as when I saw her on the stage, and she would surpass the flesh and blood actress in all the requirements of her parts except the voice which was absent." In the career of Edwin Booth, also known to the author, that actor often declared that his Macbeth would summon up before him, whether on the stage or in rehearsal, the real Macduff, and if the Macduff of the company were there, he would be enveloped in the actual ideal of the more powerful actor.

"How do you play to that ugly man?" was asked of Mary Anderson, also known to the author. The inquiry related to her part of Juliet, wherein she was supported by a Romeo that was a better actor than he looked. He certainly was not the kind of man that would have inspired the real Juliet, had she lived to see him.

"The man is not ugly," replied Miss Anderson. "He is most attractive and lover-like. You see it is this way: When I feel the part as I try to do with all my might and with all intensity, I see before me the Romeo that I would like to make love to, and the actor disappears to my vision. The picture is real, not fancied."

It may be true that this is the secret of love, wherein the sense of sight is blind, and the person who receives the devotion is lost in an idealized form. The impossible becomes a candidate for the holy flame, and the outer world is amazed that so much of sense could be so wrapped in so much of ugliness in another.

The awakening may never come in this or the next world, but, if it does, there is chaos and a wild stampede to undo the error.

Love is blind.

"What do you see in that woman to love?" has been asked many a time of the lover.

"Everything. She is beautiful; in fact, the most beautiful woman that I have ever seen."

We wish that we might be privileged to publish the photograph, but it would not be discreet, and a friendship of years standing might be endangered.

These forms are ideals born in the soul of the person who is thus enthralled. The actor creates his counterpart and projects it out upon the air. The Macbeth projects his Macduff, enemy though he be, and his ideal of that character lives before him. This feat has been performed millions of times, and any intensely magnetic person can accomplish it at will and under any circumstances.

Sometimes an intensity of magnetism will be aroused on the spur of the moment. It may live in one mind so strongly that it will pass to others. There are innumerable accounts, verified and authentic, of groups of persons seeing the same ghost. Give them the details they are to expect, and give them the conditions that will arouse their intensity, and also give them one of their number who has this power of projecting his inherent self, and you have the combinations which will make the same ghost live in the minds of a number of persons, yet it is but the self of one of them, unless there be the intent to make it common to all.

This inherent self has stood out in all history in one way and another, generally giving origin to religious fervor and helping to substantiate religious belief.

It is not a false method. It is as true as any process in the laws of the universe. It is not supernatural. It is one of the operations of the great silent principles of the whole system of control that pervades the sky and has its presence here on earth.

If the Creator wishes to meet humanity in an unusual way, He will not make use of a law that is denied to those to whom it is manifested. There is no fact that is beyond the analysis of the natural, although they may be classed as a part of the supernatural. This is seen in the visions that are recorded in the Bible. Christ appeared to His Disciples after His death. When

He was living He met some of the men that had been dead for many centuries. They came down out of heaven. They appeared to none except on the occasion when they appeared to Him, and were consequently not wandering ghosts. His own body, with the wounds, appeared to the Disciples, thus showing the retention of the physical form in association with the inherent form. Any other view would be a film of a disordered brain.

Visions have come to men and women more often than they have been willing to acknowledge. The founder of the greatest of sects, Mahomet, was a man that had a bad primal self, and yet a grand inherent self. He claimed to have seen visions that excelled those seen at Patmos; and his claims were accepted as true by countless billions who have since lived. They may be charged with ignorance, but no other form of religion was suited to their barbaric minds, and the great leader must be judged by his teachings and deeds, as far as he and they are connected with his inherent nature. We have already stated that no person should be judged by the primal nature when there has been a mighty influence going out from the inherent nature.

Could this latter self be developed to an average degree it would place an individual within communicating reach of other forms of existence in the universe, rather than holding him confined to earth. That this proposition can be proved and worked out is seen in the larger volume of Universal Magnetism, and is there shown in its full light.

Most persons live in their primal self, and therefore have no opportunity for widening the scope of their influence. The animal nature is wholly primal. The inherent self comes into being within the race of humanity. But there is so much descended from the animal that it clings to its influence at all times and under almost all conditions. Humanity is made up of the earth and is charged with the life of other realms, as the earth alone will not furnish the fullness of man. So the laws of heredity are at work in his being. In temperament and in make-up he is the sum total of all that has gone before him on this planet.

It is not then to be wondered at that he is inclined to give the majority of his attention to that part of his nature that is derived from the earth.

We have several times described the individual who lives only in the primal self, and reference may be had to the preceding pages for the account of such a life.   But where a man or woman has come to the fore rank in this world, the inherent self has been working out the problem.   The Heaven-born moods and feelings that have occupied so much of our earlier pages in this work, are active in that life, and magnetism is added by the processes shown.

In this system of development we have portrayed the actual conditions as they exist in the lives of all men and women who have lived for advantage to themselves and to others along the lines of an exalted progress.   This portrayal has been not only exact but also founded upon the principles that prevail throughout the universe.   We have described people as they are, and have not gone outside of their true habits in order to present a system of training that would assist all others to develop this power.   The humanity that saturates this treatment of the most remarkable of qualities, is the chief characteristic of the method employed.   We say this because we wish it understood that it is our purpose to reflect the conditions as we find them.

The power to project the inherent self or ALTER EGO, as it will now be termed, to go back to the first portion of this subject, is the summing up of the conditions that have gone before. This power may be given to one who lives wholly in the moods and feelings; but such a life on earth would be un-suited to this planet.   To dwell wholly in the moods and feelings would require a cessation of the duties of life and the abandonment of all the common place relations in the world of work and toil, and this would not harmonize with earthly existence.

But the individual who has time to himself each day, as one who labors where thought is hardly required in the details of the work performed, and also the individual who takes his hours of solitude and employs them for the development of this great nature rather than for the purpose of amusing his mind with reading idle trash, is sure to unfold the inherent self.   To this let him add the development of the colors of the moods and feelings, and he will find himself a power wherever he comes in contact with other human beings.

Take the case of one of the grandest men the modern world has known, a carpenter who thought as he worked, and who felt as he performed his tedious and monotonous daily duties, until there opened within him the impulses of his inherent nature, and he threw his plane across the shop declaring that he was through with that and all his tools. So it proved. Solitude, biography and the fellowship of the inner self, all make a force that cannot be put down.

When the Creator wishes to show Himself to a human being He gives to that individual the power to project His own image and the man walks and talks with God. In lesser degree this same power is employed by the geniuses whom we have described. It is all founded on one law.

Thus there are three of the great wonders of the Bible shown to be based upon universal laws, and the more one becomes acquainted with those laws, the grander will be the life so affected. Mind, heart and soul will all be quickened and strengthened. These three manifestations as set forth in the Bible are:

1. Christ knew the moods of others.
2. He cast out devils.
3. Holy men saw what others were not able to witness.

The sacredness of these exhibitions of power is not lessened by an analysis of their process. On the other hand God seems greater because of the creation of laws that are eternal and universal. There has never been a great religious teacher who has not upheld the doctrine that all men and women whose lives are drawn toward God in the highest degree are given more light than those who are farther away from Him. It is natural and right that this distinction should be made, and that the same avenue of approach should be open to all who come within the conditions granted to the few.

It was to secure this exalted state of the character that men and women went into seclusion, and sought to separate themselves from the world. It is true that such separation is good, if balanced by the duties of life; but it is not beneficial if made absolute, and this fact has been admitted in recent years by the advocates of the system of separation. Life on earth means more than a mere preparation for life beyond; each step is important and no person can be counted sane or a safe adviser who will adhere to worldy separation. It is going to the other extreme.

The man or woman who lives wholly in the primal self must, of necessity, be sordid, using that word in its true meaning of base; and, on the other hand, the individual who has no use for the primal self, is challenging the fact that there is a planet called the earth and that it contains created life that is here to work out a divine purpose. It is never good logic that what is, is wrong.

Let character be exalted as high as you will, but do not set it forth to wander in a cold atmosphere like a balloon that cannot come down to earth. Work in the valleys and on the plains, and along the mountain sides; but keep the face upturned toward the beauties and glories of the risen sun.

The trouble with the ALTER EGO is that it is Hell-born as well as Heaven-born. How this condition came about through natural laws is one of the duties of Universal Philosophy to explain; it has no relation to the present study except to sum up the general fact.

If you give yourself up to the baser moods you will be able to project the ALTER EGO just as powerfully as you would in the case of the nobler moods. Neither errs. Hatred is just as accurate and inspires the soul to just as much ingenuity as love. It is the impetus of war. The savages had as great a method in their diabolical plans as the more cultured people. Indeed it is supposed to be the part of skill and deep strategy to outwit a fellow being in schemes both good and bad.

The universal conditions of fraud that prevail in all branches of business and especially in the manufacture of goods, are proof of the deep laid plans of wicked men.

There are twenty persons in this world who project the evil ALTER EGO to every one who projects the good.

We are not now supposing that these people have the full power to bring before them the good or bad visions that full intensity of magnetism will summon, or that a sudden creation of powerful emotional feeling will arouse. Such uses are extreme and rightly so.

But the ALTER EGO has all degrees of use, and its common degree is the possession it takes of another's will or purpose. This was practiced in the days of witchcraft, and succeeded simply because the people were worked up to such a high state of nervous emotional feeling that they were susceptible to its use.

Under the head of distant control we will consider the subject.

The present day readers of history do not believe that there ever was such a thing as witchcraft, but suppose it to have been the result of a highly charged imagination.   Then if that be so it did exist, as the ability to capture the belief is the great goal of the ALTER EGO, and no one doubts that such a belief was once widespread.   The letters of olden times, the books of the day, and the authentic history all prove the fact that the belief in witchcraft was universal.   And that is enough.

If you can make a person believe in a thing that is not so, it is the use of the ALTER EGO, and if you can make a person believe in a thing that is so, it may be done in no other way than by the ALTER EGO, although such uses of the power ought not to be sensible among intelligent people.

Let it be stated, merely for the argument, that there was no such a thing as witchcraft, the fact that it was the subject of full belief and that no person could be found who did not at one time believe in it, is proof of the power of the ALTER EGO, which plants a belief or another self in the minds of others.

But that witchcraft was a genuine practice is amply proved at the present day.   Let the conditions of long ago be restored in a group of people who live surrounded by dangers from every side, and whose nerves are super-sensitive, and let some skilled magnetic individual prey upon this receptability, and the result will be the use of the ALTER EGO.   The power to receive it is something necessary.

The lawyer who has a bad case and is determined to win it, must study through the long hours of the night seeking some theme that will arouse the feelings within the jurors.   He must know enough of human nature to find what will move them.   He must ply that theme until every man on the jury is in full accord with it, and then he adjusts the facts of the case, not to the law, but to their state of feelings, and the result is a victory.

One of the most common methods is that which seeks to uphold the honor of a woman.   The following account has just been sent to us and is verified by persons who know it to be true:

A man was charged with an offense that meant a long term of imprisonment to him, namely, entering and robbing a home. The lawyer who undertook his defence could not see any way of escape.   He was promised a large fee if he could build up a defence, but the man was caught in the act, and there was not the slightest hope.   They might have proved an alibi, but for the fact that the culprit was taken from the house and lodged in jail, and therefore must have been where the crime was committed. Some lawyers do not hesitate to build up a defence out of manufactured testimony, and all judges know this. There was the willingness to make the defence of an alibi, but it was impossible.

"In this part of the country no jury convicts for any crime where the honor of a woman is at stake. If we could bring that in, we could so work on the feelings of the jury that they would be sure to convict."

This was the dictum of the great lawyer.

Little by little the method dawned and rose on his mind.

The home where the supposed burglary was committed was a house to which his daughter, then thirty years of age, was known to have visited. She never went there, and was in no way connected with the affair, but the fate of her father and ever-lasting disgrace to the family name were hanging in the balance, and surely she could be forgiven at the bar of heaven if she told a lie in a good cause, a lie that sent no one to jail but saved her own flesh and blood from conviction.

Here the astute lawyer projected the ALTER EGO into her very being and she actually believed it a duty in the sight of her Maker to perjure herself. Many a daughter would be likewise influenced. What wife would hesitate to save the man she loved, if in her wrong she did no one harm? It is a hard position to place one in.

The case went forward, and it was proved by other witnesses that the girl had been enticed by some person not known to this house. The lawyer used this argument with three witnesses who were his very close friends:

"It seems that this girl did go to that house and that she was seen going there. To tell you the truth I saw her go there myself. But a certain man, a client of mine, whose name I cannot mention now, told me that he had known of her going there, but that he did not want to get mixed up with the case, and he has left the town. What I want is to prove the facts. I do not wish to make up any supposed fact, not for the world, but I wish you to go on the stand and tell the truth; not the truth as you know it; but the truth as it is. You do not happen to be the person who saw the girl go into the house, but as long as she went in, you are satisfying your own consciences in stating the fact. You did not see the sun rise this morning, did you? No. But as long as you know it did rise you are honorably justified in saying that it did rise. To save the honor of this girl and to defend this man who is unjustly charged with another wrong, you will do the world a service by swearing to the facts. Everybody will applaud you for your chivalry."

The fee was large and there was much at stake. The lawyer knew his men or he would not have dared to approach them. He had been with them in other matters that required skillful manipulation.

It was proved that this girl was enticed to this house, that the father learned of it and was so overcome that he could not resist the temptation to follow at once, but that he restrained himself till such time as was most suited to the discovery of the culprit, and that he has ever since suffered the ignominy of arrest until the trial, in order that he might save too great a public scandal, especially as it would drag the fair name of the daughter in the mire.

When the trial began the great lawyer knew that the first intimation of the defence must be put in at the outset, for the leading impression generally sways the minds of the jurors. Accordingly he announced that the case of attempted rape was ready. No one seemed to know just what was meant by that. The case was the State versus Smith, as we will call it. But he termed it the case of "attempted rape." The jury were forward in an instant. The great lawyer did not allow his opponent, the prosecutor, to start the talk to the jury until he had made the rape case a still more apparent affair, as he addressed the court in the following manner:

"If your Honor please, I do not think, and the general public is of the same opinion, that the ends of justice are to be served by dragging into this court a case of this kind. It is apparent to everybody except my learned brother, that the defendant has done only what a father ought to do, enter any house where his daughter's honor was at peril and seek to rescue her at all hazards. He knew when he broke into the house that he was taking the onus upon himself, and that he would have to stand trial for it. But what is the disgrace of a father to the dishonor of a daughter?"

Here the ALTER EGO was projected at the start and all the prosecutor could do was in vain. The verdict was anticipated and the case was won.

Having been familiar with many of the cases of General Butler, and having worked in some of them, we are prepared to state that he won his great cases on this principle. It is being worked all over the world. Dickens made a travesty of it in his account of the legal methods employed in Bardell versus Pickwick. Read that case and you will see the exact process that is employed, and will be able to follow each turn in the management of the facts until they stand out like a mountain against the defendant.

Or, if you wish a still more skilled presentation of the same process, read the address of Antony in the play of Julius Cæsar, where Shakepeare makes that astute orator, who was in fact only an actor-at-large, sway a hostile mob into a frenzy of friendship.

The world is full of instances of this kind or in which this principle is involved.

As it runs in courses of danger to all who are capable of being moved, as most men and women are, we propose to follow it out to the ends where the greatest harm is possible, and much of what follows in this study will be presented for that purpose.

CHAPTER TWENTY-FIVE

✛✛

INDIVIDUAL POWER
IS NOT LIMITED
BY TIME
OR SPACE

✛✛
❧ ❧ *DISTANT CONTROL* ❧ ❧
✛✛

 ARTH AND SKY are one in plan and purpose. This fact is hardly disputed by any intelligent person. Where there is unity of plan and purpose there is always a common source of origin and a common destiny. These laws must be taken at this time as true as they require the processes of a philosophical mind to work them out. We know that the dust of the earth gave us our bodies and that it will receive them back again. We are likewise justified in believing that the vital forces of mind and soul are taken out of the great sea that sweeps onward in an ever silent rush through the boundless realms of space.

Be that as it may, there should be no hesitancy in believing that all life has a common interest. The individual can be separated or ostracized, but the life itself cannot be segregated. The primal self may be imprisoned, but the inherent self is as free as the vast deep above us.

The question has been many millions of times asked by children, how God who is so far away can hear the prayers of those who are on earth. When a child touches a proposition in philosophy the inherent mind is seeking to break through the confining shell of the primal self.

This question must not be answered by any attempt at the

289

spiritual or supernatural; for the laws of the universe step in and give the full explanation.

That there is a universal ether that occupies all space, and all solids and liquids, is well established. That it reaches to the farthest realms of the sky is also a logical deduction. Any other conclusion would be open to attack. When you stand in America and place your ear to the radio that picks up messages from Europe, as you will be sure to do some day, and you hear the voice of one who is seated thousands of miles away from you, the feeling comes plain and strong that there is some supernatural law at work, just as the Indians were led to believe that the Great Father was talking in the guns of the Pilgrims.

But as soon as the law is explained you will rest more calmly if you understand the explanation. If you do not, then you will still maintain your theory of the supernatural. Superstition melts gradually in the sunlight of investigation.

That there is an ether is well proved. That it extends from us to all the orbs of the sky is well proved. That God may send an immediate message from the remotest part of the heavens to your own little home and there be present is also well proved. The error is in supposing that it is due to a law in which you cannot participate.

This same ether-sea is in your brain, in your body, in your thoughts, in your heart, in your existence, and is moved in its waves by the intense magnetic moods which you are able to summon to your aid as agents of transit.

For this reason, and also because the facts show it to be true when employed, the power is effective between two or more persons regardless of distance. In this work we will not deal with the question of universal control, as that belongs to a larger work. Our purpose now is to speak of the laws that give one person some degree of control over another, where the two are not present.

It may be set down as a general proposition that there must be some degree of reciprocity between the two persons. It is not necessary that the recipient should be thinking of the other; but where there have been relationships of feeling, and kindred hopes, wishes and desires, the magnetic person is able by intense waves to arouse them again. Then comes the fact that they are not interpreted in a primal self. There are cases where the

ALTER EGO has been sent to the other side of the earth, from England to Australia, but they are rare. There are countless thousands of other cases where such projections have occurred and have remained unexplained. It is not at all unlikely that you may have seen forms and faces, or other visions in half sleep, or possibly in the waking hours, and have allowed the matter to escape your further thoughts.

Such occurrences may be figments of the brain where it is not normal, or they may be the influence sent out by some other person either willingly or unwillingly.

In the full waking hours, the primal self is in control and it rarely ever receives impressions from other persons, although it may see the film creations of its own abnormal brain, if such condition exists, as in the case of the victim of delirium tremens.

But during the period of sleep the mind rests and the inherent nature knows no rest. It has no need of being recuperated as it is not actively engaged in the undertakings of this life. In the moments of transition from sleep to waking the mind passes from the inherent to the primal self, and the latter then sometimes catches glimpses of the inner nature. The latter is there all the time, and the former knows but little of it. In the periods of transit from sleeping there is a film of view, and it can be made more and more vital with practice. This is done by instantly rising as soon as the mind is fully awake and writing down as much of the transaction as possible. What is written must be the exact details. Any guesswork or supply will ruin the whole power. Collect as many of these as possible, and then memorize them so clearly that they are always in the mind the last thing at night and the first in the morning. This presence of the details will stimulate the mind and it will be able to develop an almost unlimited degree of intensity which, coupled with magnetism, will place the inner self within your control.

It is in this practice that you may secure direct mastery of the ether waves, along one line of use.

When any person has been in accord with you, and especially in the use of moods and feelings, as where love has existed between two, or where the parent has held the esteem and affection of the child, it is not a difficult matter for the user of magnetic waves to impress a mood upon that person. But to carry ideas by the primal self would involve a use of the waves of thought, known as telepathy of the mental class. This is not in the range of magnetic study. The methods that influence are those that carry moods and feelings.

Many a time has a son on the eve of battle in war, hundreds of miles away from home, felt the influence of a mother's longing or the love that she has sent out to him from some intense hour at home. "On last Wednesday night at ten o'clock I was almost asleep when I felt that my mother stood near me," wrote a soldier. "I got up and remained absorbed in thought for a full hour." The letter bearing these words was sent to a friend; and, while it was on the way, it was passed in the mails by a letter from the mother to the son, bearing these words: "At a few minutes before ten on last Wednesday night I longed to see you, and I could not retire, but sat watching the moon and thinking of the days when you were a boy and we used to sit out and look at the moon and talk of what you would grow up to become when a man. I was so wrapped up in my thoughts that I fell half asleep and my hand was in yours and you were here with me. The impression was so vivid that it could not be a dream." This is one of thousands of similar experiences.

To go into a repetition of them would simply fill a book with a list of cases that are represented in one alone.

The use of the moods under great magnetic intensity is common enough to be an understood fact.

Having such moods well developed under the laws already taught in the earlier chapters of this work, all that is necessary is two things: First, there must be magnetic intensity as shown in the chapters relating to vocal undulations and intensity in this work; Second, there must be some prior relationship between the party controlling and the party to be controlled.

If it were possible for a person at a distance to influence a perfect stranger, no one would be at ease, and all would be made to suffer the interference of others who might be undesirable intruders. No law contemplates this.

What the relationship must be that will bring two persons within the rule of control when one is intensely magnetic, we will see as we take up the Episodes that follow herein. They will show, among a mass of other facts, the interwoven law of distant control, although the more common condition known as "control in presence" will be discussed as the paramount influence.

CHAPTER TWENTY-SIX

+++

CRYSTAL COLLECTIONS
OF
MAGNETIC
EPISODES

+++
EPISODES IN CONTROL
+++

ESIRING to apply the laws of magnetic control to the many conditions that arise in life, we have taken the most important of all the relationships that arise in the world, and have made them the subject of Episodes. Each of these is presented in such small compass that they may be said to be crystallized, and so called crystals. The usefulness of this plan will be seen when we state that the practical working out of the laws of magnetism are the best victories that can be attained in this line of power.

If the only use that could be suggested were that which the genius might make of magnetism, or that which some great men and women would employ, then it would fly over the heads of all the masses, and even escape those who are in the middle classes.

While it has made the great greater, and has made commonplace lives exalted, it cannot always find the earnestness and ambition among its students that would be required to reap so large a harvest of results, and therefore seeks in this stage to meet the needs of the several classes of humanity that stand most in want of help from an all-powerful influence.

The frequent reference to the sex relationship is not intended as an aid to the functional conditions on the sex side, but as a means of help to those who are in danger because of the fact

293

that they are weighed down by the nature that is in them. For the other line of study the reader is referred to the course entitled the "Sex Magnetism," which may be found in this series of training courses.

A large field must now be covered in our effort to apply the laws of magnetic control to the sex conditions; but as much information as possible will be included in each and every page, so that the condensed facts may in truth be known as the

CRYSTAL VOLUMES.

There will be no attempt to make actual separated books or chapters, under the name of Crystal Volumes; but each episode will be so regarded.

"THE YOUNG WOMAN UNDER FIFTEEN."

What has she to do with magnetic control?

If anything, has she to do with a power that she can use toward others, or toward herself, or a power that may have a bearing against her?

The young woman under fifteen has no occasion to use influence that shall affect another, unless she is developed faster than her years would warrant. In that case she will be considered in the episode that relates to the girl's age of temptation.

She is not yet fifteen, which means that she is fourteen or under. In no respect is she, or ought she to be, a candidate for either marriage or betrothal. The approach and establishing of the habits of womanhood, do not mark the era for love-making. Graver questions are at hand. These propositions will be stated at this place, and enlarged upon as the course advances.

The first proposition is that the young woman under fifteen needs a woman friend.

If she has a mother, that woman ought to be the friend of the girl, and if she has no mother then some method should be adopted to bring her under the guiding influence of a woman friend. We believe that there should be a society organized for this express purpose of molding the life of every girl who is left to herself, and the society should, as its first step, secure the friend for the girl.

If she is religiously inclined, that is well; but a girl with religion and no one to take the place of a watching mother, is not cared for in body as well as in soul.

The church should be one that has a Sunday School attached to it, and the child when quite young should be put in the school and taught to love to go. There are two ways in which to compel a child to attend such a place; one is by making the duty irksome, and the other is by making it attractive. The influence of the Sunday School is far reaching. The child is closer to God, and Christ said that of such was the kingdom of heaven, showing that the younger person is more at home in a religious place than the adult. Indifference at such a period of life as that which precedes puberty, bears the heaviest penalties.

We received from a reliable source a record that had been kept for twenty-two years, including the habits of forty families in which there were girls. Twenty families were selected where the girls were not sent to Sunday School during their early years; and twenty other families were selected where attendance began when the children were under nine years. In the latter case the girls all grew up to be good women and all became wives; two having died.

In the families where the Sunday School was neglected, the majority of the girls went to the bad, eighteen of them becoming prostitutes, and some of these entered professional houses of ill fame.

Similar estimates have been made in other localities, and it seems to be the general rule that the girl who is developed under the influences of the Sunday School, or in some manner that is its equivalent, will be safer than the girl who has not had such influence.

The reason is this:

The inherent self makes no mistakes.

The child that gets its ideas from the earth alone, is not developing its inherent self. In the Sunday School the whole appeal is to the inner nature. Little by little this is stirred and it becomes the strongest factor in the world for protecting the young woman at an age when she needs moral shelter.

Argument does not save the girl.

Most parents are told that she must be talked to and advised with; but talk and advice are evanescent, and the opening of the inherent or God-given nature is fixed as the eternal stars. There are countless books and articles telling the mother to talk to her girls, and the father to talk to his sons, so that the facts may be known ere it is too late; but talk is from the primal self, and we lay down the law that:

The girl can find no genuine protection except under the influences of her inherent self.

There is no substitute for this. What is meant by the inherent self will be known at once to all who have read the preceding chapters. To develop it is the crying question of the hour. How shall this be done?

The Sunday School performs this work. The parent can do much in the same line. There never was a child who saw something die who did not wonder if it would live again. Inquiry after inquiry will be made until the heart and mind of the parent burn with a desire to smooth the matter over with some reply that will appease the child. But the time comes when the truth must be told. Then is the period when the inner nature should be unfolded not by the base-born mood of fear, but by a sense of love for the Maker of life and all that attends its path.

This is placing the mind of the child in close relationship with its inner nature. Too much of this wonderland cannot be unfolded as long as it runs along a normal road.

We all know that the child that is taught the miseries of drink or the results of other evils, if its mood of pity or sympathy is touched, will fight such ills all though life. It took a generation to make a North that was willing to go to war to free the slaves; and it is a fact that at the mother's knee all through that North the lads were told of the wrongs of slavery. If mothers were to take their children in early years through the study in simple form of the great curse of drink, the next generation would settle the question.

It is not enough to appeal to the mind of the child; that forgets. The feelings must be worked upon, gently but with all the silent might that is possible, and the time will never come when they will outgrow it.

We trust that this distinction between appealing to the mind and to the heart of the child may be fully understood.

Arguments and reasoning are better suited for older persons; the young mind is swayed more by the heart. It is true that excess experience in one direction deadens the feeling of the child; the death of a pet cat may cause it the most intense anguish, and the repeated deaths of cats, dogs and other pets will deaden the suffering until a loved parent will not be missed one-tenth as much as the first pet that died. It is for this reason that the noblest of the gentle emotions should be taught in variety.

This plan is not to be a substitute for proper development of the primal self; but the latter alone is not sufficient for the molding of the child's character. That which is counted intelligence is the result of education based upon actual experience in the world; but it is not the kind of influence that impresses the child mind. The latter is mostly susceptible to the moods and feelings.

The female child is in every respect a different being from the boy. She has little or no thought and duty in common with him. The studies outside of those of common education, should be of a different character from those given to the lad. Her mental interests should be different. No greater mistake can be made than to allow the idea to prevail that the young woman is to fit herself for the duties of the young man.

In so far as the parents are able to separate the thoughts and activities of one sex from the other, to that extent will they build the best character for each.

The mother should think up and plan in her own mind the work, studies and duties that are best suited to the girl; and should seek to establish a complete difference between the sex of the young woman and that of the young man. Nature has made them different, and so should humanity. The lessons that are taught by nature are the most useful guides for men and women, especially in their application to the young.

To sum up the teachings in this little lesson, we will state that:

1. The young woman under fifteen should have a woman friend who should at all times maintain a watchful care over the little miss.

2. She should be developed along the line of the most useful and noble of the moods, beginning at the most susceptible age.

3. She should be made a separate being from the opposite sex in duties, studies, tastes and activities.

This does not mean that she is to be separated from the boys of her own age or environments. It is an excellent custom for both sexes to meet, but not in promiscuous play or work. The girl holds in her body the tendencies to opposite lines of development from the boy, and these tendencies should be encouraged at all times.

Boys and girls should be taught to dance at a very early age, or as near five years as circumstances will admit. In this graceful exercise, under restraint, they are taught to respect and to admire the other sex. The boy has his part to take in the dance, and it is not that which belongs to the girl. From the very beginning he learns to note the difference in the importance of the partner whom he escorts through the movements. He is taught to show her deference, to be courteous to her and to play the part of a little gentleman, until this treatment of the girl becomes a second nature with him, provided refinement prevails in the teaching.

This influence is of the greatest importance.

Not only is dancing as taught to children a very essential part of their education, inasmuch as it teaches grace, ease, refinement, and respect for one another; but it is also the preventative of error in the later years of youth.

Most persons take up dancing after they have reached their teens, and then they are most susceptible to its baneful influences. We have noted thousands of cases where children under ten or eight years of age have been taught to dance until it is a regular part of their lives; and we find that all the evils that are most to be feared in after years are avoided under these circumstances. There is no newness to the young man or young woman who comes up out of the youngest period of life with knowledge and experience of the other sex gained through the function of dancing.

On the other hand the young man who takes his partner for the first time in his late teens is laboring under excitement that often dethrones his cool judgment, and moral training goes to the winds.

In some families there is a strict disapproval of the art of dancing and of this decision we do not propose to make criticism. It may be for the best and it may not. If the children are denied the privilege of dancing, and can be kept from it all through their teens it may be possible to exert an influence over them after they have gone out into the world; but it is not likely that such power can be wielded against a fixed desire for the pleasure.

The history of fallen girls is written in its first chapters in the dance hall. Of this there is no doubt. Not all girls who fall have been in the dance hall, but those who have been there and have fallen have in most cases set going the toboggan of character in the round dance, and the peculiar fact is that they have found the embrace of the opposite sex most exciting under the general thrill of the dance.

The strangest of all facts in this connection is the safety of girls who have been taught the art when under eight or ten years of age. We know of no girl who has gone to the bad who has had this advantage.

The reason is based on the nature of the dance which is learned in those early years. To the girl the touch of the boy means nothing, and his holding of her hands, or guiding control is as empty of meaning to her as the silent wall she faces. Let this art be developed to its full at such age if at all, and then the girl will come up into young womanhood with the same feelings at all parts of the journey, and there will be no moment of transition when the young man will be more than the boy.

This is not theory, it is actual fact, and is known to all mothers who have passed through the experience.

We respect the views of those who will not allow their children to dance. In our own case we would not permit our daughters to begin to learn the art after they had passed the age of fifteen. So we had them taught when they were five and six years of age and we have encouraged their dancing all through those early years.

It is then free from all objections, and is so beneficial in all ways that the best results are secured. Having a positive advantage at the ages mentioned, it is sure to escape all the disadvantages of later years.

As far as a man has influence over his wife, if she has never learned to dance prior to marriage, he could not make a greater mistake than to permit it after wedlock. The most deplorable estrangements have followed the practice of beginning to dance in middle life.

Dancing, like music, appeals to the inherent nature and this is too much neglected in the training of boys and girls.

Music is essentially a girl's accomplishment. Boys are inclined to it as a born taste, and the greatest composers that have ever lived have been found among men; but the talent for creating music and for performing it are not always united. Of those who play, not one in a thousand is a composer. And of those who love music not fifty in a hundred can play.

The love for music should be encouraged in all persons, and no man or woman can be considered normal who lacks this love.

As the art of music is most natural to the female sex, it should be taught as early as possible. The age of five to eight years is not too young for the lessons to begin.

The most magnetic quality that a woman can possess is that of being able to take charge of a home; not to do the drudgery if she does not wish it; but to know as much of every department of her home as those in her employ know of it; to have as much knowledge of cooking as the cook possesses; and to remain interested in each and every detail of management, just as the captain keeps in touch with the movements of the ship, although he does not do the work of those below him.

A home is like a ship at sea. It cannot be left to the conduct of mere menials. There should be no moment of cessation from watchful care. There if anywhere the adage applies that eternal vigilance is the price of safety. The kitchen holds in its control the lives and health of every member of the family; yet the head of the home despises the kitchen and lets it run itself. This is far from good policy.

There is no magnetism in all the world so great as that which tells a man that there is a woman who can take charge of his home and make it successful from the standpoint of health and comfort. This knowledge will draw men when beauty and even wealth will not. There are in this country tens of thousands of bachelors who are wealthy and who will not marry the kind of girl that is set before them, and who will not go out of their class to take the kind they want. They prefer to remain single. Never before has the prospective candidate for wife been so ignorant of the duties of a wife, and so willing to live in a boarding house or a hotel; and never before are so many well-to-do men remaining single.

The daughters of the rich are gradually being taught the knowledge that makes a wife a good manager of the home; just as the sons of millionaires are learning the work of the industries from the lowest rung of the ladder to the top.

This sentiment is beginning to grow.

It is a part of the nature of a girl to learn the many duties of home work in all its departments, and the girl who is taught them in her younger years, will not hate them in later life. She will exert the most powerful influence over the best man, and other girls will find that men who do not appreciate this power will not make good husbands. The man who is willing for his wife to waste her time in empty activities spends his in the same way. Home will mean nothing to him, and so he will roam to the club or seek the society of other men and possibly of other women. There is no unity in the home, no chord of harmonic tone to sing the music of love, and the lives drift apart.

The very fact that a woman can manage her home and is ambitious to do so, and not leave its various departments to menials, is so much appreciated by the true husband that he will give his own thoughts and attention to such departments as come under his supervision; and thus the home life grows more and more sacred.

Let, therefore, the little girl be taught that it is noble to prepare for the office of queen of home. It is a part of her nature, and will fit into her great ocean of likes, if taught early enough. In fact the wise mother will make this duty grow into a pleasure by the tempting manner in which she teaches it to the child.

It would be well for the parents to sit down and prepare a plan of the life interests that are peculiar to the girl's side of existence to ascertain how many lines of duty there are that fit into her nature apart from those that belong to the boy's. A written list of these should be made and they should be posted up in the private room of the parents where they may be seen and acted on from day to day. It is a sort of campaign that lasts until the girl is no longer under fifteen. Let it begin in the first years of childhood and gradually grow as the days and months fly by.

Then take the list of the best moods as set forth in an early chapter, and find how many will suit the nature of the girl. Inculcate them not by recitation, but by little sessions of talks and explanation, and by the actual experiences of life, until the girl is responsive to a variety of heart interests.

"THE YOUNG MAN UNDER FIFTEEN."

Many of the things that have been stated in the little treatise just ended, will apply to the youth if reversed. The boy is susceptible to all kinds of impulses that are not so easily aroused in after years, and the foundation should be laid long before the age of temptation is approaching.

The world has not yet awakened to the fact that geniuses and great characters have been persons of a largely developed inherent nature, and that this characteristic is the opposite of the primal nature. The schools and colleges of the world can educate only the latter; never the former. Look to the boyish history of most great men and you will find the untrained, uneducated lads.

It is the old story of Walter Scott, a dullard at school, but a genius in spite of his ignorance. Boys who are taught knowledge only, never win fame in after life; the unfolding of their primal selves having nothing to do with the bursting forth of their inherent selves. In the latter alone are the seeds of greatness.

This fact rules the world.

Let the friend of the boy be the father. If not the father, then some man of fine character. The mother has more love and less training qualities than the father. The latter can see, if he looks, the future man in the growing lad, and he can shape the unfolding nature at will, like the bending of the twig that inclines the tree.

What you want the boy to avoid you can drive out of him when he is still in his very early years; but not afterwards.

Now what is it that you want your boy to avoid?

Cigarette smoking is near the top of the list. It will be too late when he is past fifteen and possibly when he is past ten. Begin as early as you can and make the habit hateful to him, by appealing to his sensitive nature. The evil that grows from it, the horrors of the weak brain, the half-imbecile outlook for his mind, the sorrow of the parents to know that they have reared a child that will fade away into a helpless slave to his frailty; these and other considerations can be pictured in his brain with effect, if they pass through the realm of feeling. Argument is not effective; there must be well told experiences.

Then the use of tobacco should be made unattractive to him, and this can be done with skill by the parent of good judgment.

The power to resist drink is derived during childhood, and cannot be driven home in the life of one who is in or past the teens. In a family of eight children, of whom six were boys, whose parents were both victims of alcoholism, the four youngest were made to feel the awful consequences of the habit of drink, and they all grew up free from the bondage, while the four others were all drunkards. No amount of urging or influence or dreadful experience could turn their habits about.

The great training school of the world is the home influence that is shown around the boy in his earliest years.

Let this period be neglected, and it is too late when other influences have entered the soul of the lad and he has done a large amount of thinking and feeling of his own creation or others have secured first attention.

The law we lay down is that he should have a male friend when he is in his early years, say from five to ten, and this friend should be the man of all men to whom he looks in full confidence.

This friend should open up the inner nature of the boy, so that the child will feel as well as think; and the feelings should be such a variety of those better moods we have enumerated, as will most suit his years and conditions.

Then the deepest impressions of right and of wrong should be made in this inherent nature of the boy.

These become giant factors in after life, and are rarely if ever eradicated if they are followed up with a consistent spirit as the boy grows toward the age of temptation.

It is desirable that he should learn to hate drink, cigarettes, tobacco, swearing, stealing and lying, as well as the wrongs that are quickly engrafted into these little lives. To be told that a thing is wrong, does not appeal to the boy, except as censure; but to be made to see the wrong in such a way that the feelings are aroused, the sympathy touched and the higher nature stimulated, is quite a different process. Scolding and censure appeal only to the mind or primal nature and die at the first relaxation; while the feeling, taking hold as it does of that department of the being that was in existence before the mind was born, is sure to retain the impression.

What we have said of the girl is true of the boy, but in reverse order. The lad should, soon after he is five or six years old, be taught to meet little girls in a way that will impress on him the first doctrines of chivalry; not as companions in making mud pies, but as gallants under conditions of the best refinement. It pays to do this, for the impression made upon the lad will be life lasting. We are not insisting on the use of the dance for this purpose in case you are opposed to that form of social entertainment; but if you cannot find another function as effective, you will never regret having the children learn to dance. The training will be over by the time the age of temptation is reached, and then there will be a much less inclination to engage in dancing. In fact there is a disposition not to pursue the pastime to excess.

It pays to arouse in each mind a deep respect for the other sex, and there is no influence so powerful as the restrictions and exactness of the dance movements. Then they take away the crudities and the embarrassment that are so much in evidence when the first love spell is weaving its charm in the nature of both sexes.

Parties are also effective to the same end.

All roughness, all unfairness, all disrespect and all coarse remarks on the part of both boy and girl may be controlled, with the result that they will grow up recognizing the great difference in the status of each other, which is one of the things to be sought.

The mental interests of the boy should be as different from those of the girl as it is possible to make them. It is not right to allow the same kinds of playthings to the small boy as to the small girl. The latter should be made to know what are hers, and the kinds that are suited to her sex, young as she may be; while the boy must see as though by his conscience that it is not intended that his playthings should be of the same sort as the girls. This separation is not by any means difficult and it adds to the interest in the things used and to the idea of difference between the two sexes.

While it is true that boys and girls sleep together up to the time they are ten or more, it is never the best arrangement. There is nothing immoral in it, even if they are as old as twelve or thirteen, but the question of morality is not under consideration. It is a question of framing the nature of the boy and of the girl, so that they will fit into the place designed for them by the Creator when youth is entered upon and the perspective of mature years is seen over the edge of the horizon.

As the twig is bent so the tree is inclined, is not original in this era, but is as old as the best thought of man.

The time to bend the twig is when it is a twig.

To wait until it has gathered self-strength is too late.

Playthings are educators of the mind of the infant. The most deplorable fact in the life of the child is its lack of a variety of interesting playthings, given into its care almost as soon as it can observe them. To arose the mind at the very start of life, and to keep it growing in interest in the early years, is the sure way of building a healthy brain. To accomplish this purpose there are everywhere in some parts of the world, organizations established for the purpose of distributing playthings among the poor families. It pays a large dividend in after years.

Of course the child of two years can hardly see much difference between the articles that suit one sex better than they do another. But it is time to begin to make the separation. Parents ought to have enough ingenuity to make plans to meet this distinction; and then can carry out those plans in the purchases. Asking questions at the store or of other parents who have had more experience will help in securing a different line of playthings for the boy from the kind that suits the girl.

Never allow the same kind to be used in common.

When the boy grows up he will want larger and more manly articles for his boyish taste, for he knows that some day he will be a big man and will go about in the lordly dignity of stern manhood; at least he hangs to this idea for some years.

The girl that has playthings in common with boys will incline to the habits of the tomboy. The boy that has playthings in common with girls will have a tendency to become a sissy. These are reverse conditions that interfere with the respect that the world must some day pay the youth if power and success are to be attained; and that which detracts stands as a perpetual barrier to magnetism, while that which attracts is always magnetic. The best single idea for magnetism is that which attracts, no matter what it is and how it wins. The womanish man is always out of place, and the mannish woman is equally out of place. The world admires a manly man and a womanly woman.

As the twig is bent so the tree is inclined, and the best time to bend the twig is when it is a twig.

Keep this dual law in mind at all times.

The friend of the boy, whether it is his father or not, should draw out of him the feelings and tastes that make a manly fellow in after years; one that loves fair play, justice, honor and the good qualities; but particularly one that is full of manly enterprise. The opportunities for station in life are best seen in the years under the age of fifteen. What profession or what ambition is to attract the lad might be partly hinted at in those years. There are biographies that tell the story of the struggles and victory of many a young man, and there are editions that suit the youthful nature. Let the boy have this kind of reading as much as possible.

Cheap reading should be shown in his earliest reading years to be bad for him, and the sad experiences of bad boys who have been led astray should be brought home to his feelings; and all before he is too old. What he reads in secrecy will mold his nature faster that all the good influences of his whole career up to that time.

Maintain constant respect for girls, young women, and women, and see that this respect springs from his inherent nature, not from the drill processes of his mind.

Let him go freely among girls but always under circumstances that will uphold such respect.

As he is approaching fifteen years of age, he will require still greater demarcation from the tastes and mental interests of the opposite sex if he is to be kept in the line of manly development. Some one else should do the thinking for him as much as possible. It is most wholesome to show a personal interest in his tastes and wishes, to ask him about his little world of purpose, just as though he were an object of importance. This is healthful to his mind and heart. He will look up to one who looks up to him. This experiment has been tried many times and has always brought about great success.

It is carried on by appearing in an off-hand manner to want to know what is going on in his plans, what he is doing and why he does certain things, and so let him know that he is not a mere nothing that has to be coaxed and ruled.

Obedience should be insisted on under all conditions. There should never be an attempt to bribe a child to be good. Let it be understood that obedience is a part of his very life, and that not the slightest act of rebellion will be tolerated. The parent cannot be too severe in enforcing this rule, nor should there be malice in it. Temper is the weakest of all weapons. Let the child know that love is ready at all times when there is obedience, and that things are mighty unpleasant when there is not.

An act of disobedience should never be allowed to acquire momentum. It should be nipped in the bud, and thoroughly nipped. A few lessons of this kind will change the whole method of the child and he will soon connect obedience with love, and disobedience with an unrelished state of the feelings.

Both the boy and the girl are now ready for the next great steps in life.

"THE GIRL'S AGE OF TEMPTATION."

When the organs that are designed by nature to bring other beings into the world are taking on their enlarged functions, a change comes over the mind and body. Long before this there have been feelings of love, and it has gone out towards a much older person than the one that should become the husband of the girl. It is one of the peculiar freaks of nature that she will inspire in a boy a love for an adult woman and in a girl a love for an adult man.

The best time in which to win a very young wife is when she is between fifteen and seventeen, if the suitor is a man of mature years. After the age of seventeen the girl begins to look to those who are closer to her own age.

The thought of marriage comes to most girls about the time they are ten or eleven years of age, but it is largely a play-thought. It is half a joke and they enjoy speaking of it. In the next few years it is a serious, earnest thought, mis-placed, and they are prone to keep silent about it. In the early hours of the night they lie awake and think of some man whom they have seen and who is to them the most attractive being on earth. His form, voice and conduct fill the whole horizon of their fancy.

Of all the marriages that have occurred at such disadvantages in age we know of none that have not been happy. It is not true, we presume, that all marriages of the kind are filled with content, and there ought to be some that have ended in separation; but those of which we have personal knowledge, where the couples have actually made homes and lived together, not one has ended in unhappiness.

We have records of the following discrepancies in age, the girl being the younger in each instance. A man of forty to a girl of seventeen; a man of thirty-six to a girl of seventeen; a man of forty-five to a girl of sixteen; a man of fifty to a girl of fourteen; a man of sixty to a girl of sixteen; and others along the same line.

In one case which we followed very closely as it seemed too much out of the ordinary to be productive of happiness, the girl was thirteen years and ten months of age and the man was sixty-three. He was a manufacturer, and had in his office three sisters, his future wife being the youngest. She fell in love with him, and told him so after a little inquiry. It was the case of first fancy. He was quite small for a man, and she was and still is under the average size for her sex. He was a widower and had great wealth. His life was in every way exemplary and no fault was ever found with his conduct toward women and girls unless in this case. His own account of the proposal was as follows:

One evening after the office was closed, when the two elder sisters had gone home to get ready for a party, leaving the child in the office alone with the man, she was seen to be crying to herself. The man asked her the cause of her grief, and she said she could not tell him; but said later that he was the cause. On further inquiry, she said:

"I love you and I am not happy."

"It is a child love and will soon fade."

"It will never fade. I can never stop loving you."

"What can I do? I have not encouraged it, have I?"

"No. I want you to marry me."

"Perhaps I will some time, if you do not think me too old when you are old enough to marry."

"No, no, I cannot wait. I want you to marry me now, this week, and not wait."

"But it will be illegal. Your parents will not consent."

"Yes, they will if you ask them."

The situation was novel and full of romance as the girl was pretty and very attractive in many ways. He could not summon the courage to ask the parents and spoke of waiting for a few years. She would not consent.

"I will ask them if you will give me permission and if you will let me tell them that you love me."

There was more hesitancy and more pleading for delay, but the girl persisted and he consented. That very evening after the hour of nine, both parents called with the child upon the man, and had a long conference with him. The man did very little talking for a while; but at length said:

"I have never known of so young a girl getting married, although I have heard that such is sometimes the case. I am very old, but still active and energetic, and feel no approach of decrepitude. This child is to me very attractive. Since she persists in believing that she loves me, I find that I am closely drawn to her in affection at least. I will not marry her without the consent of both her parents; with their consent I will become her husband."

The wedding took place in three days. Nearly a half century separated the man and the child-wife. She was eighteen when a child was born. She is now forty years of age and he is nearly ninety. He is active and has never been absent from home a night, nor away from a meal in all these years. His love for her is so great that he writes this: "I am studying every principle of longevity in order that I may be able to live to be a hundred, and then I shall be loath to go."

His health is remarkably good, and it is said that he does not show his age by thirty years, and that she is rapidly overtaking him along life's journey.

We traveled many hundred miles to meet this remarkable wife, and we got the story from her lips as well as from his letters. She said to us:

"It was whispered when we were married that I wanted him for his money and that he would not live many years and would leave me rich. I just set my teeth and resolved to show that this was false, and it is the solemn truth that I do want him to live, for I love him."

The first deep fancy of the opening years of her young life had never been effaced.

The explanation of this fact is this:

When the functions that reproduce life are taking on their growth during puberty, the nervous system is thrown into a mist of feeling that clouds mind and even the dictates of good sense. Things are done and said that the older woman would blush to repeat. The whole being cries out with a pain that is half joy and half suffering. It is inexplicable. The girl knows that something is transpiring within her but she does not feel able to make it known even to herself.

The boy has more attraction for her than the man. The boy could not make much headway with her in the line of temptation, while the man might lead her to ruin in a few minutes.

There used to be a theory that some medicines or powders were able to create within a female such intense excitement that she could not resist the solicitation of a man; and most girls are now prone to accept that theory as true. Mothers say to their daughters: "Do not eat any thing that is given you by a man unless you know him to be all right." The girl gets a vague idea that she will be thrown into a vortex of intense excitement that can be allayed only by the services of the man.

Whatever this claim may amount to in fact, it is true that many girls, between the ages of fourteen and eighteen, are made by nature to pass through just that torture; the purpose being to impel marriage and perpetuate the race. Women in after years deny this fact, for they see nothing specially model in having been victims of sexual passion to such a white heat. Others forget it, for memory is evanescent in affairs that are not creditable. Others wish to forget it and succeed. But there are many ways of securing proof of the truth, and we can assure you it is as we have stated.

The most surprising fact in all modern history is the falling into temptation of such a large proportion of girls during their teens. If they fail to be tempted and caught then, and have had their chance, they will not begin after they are twenty. The girl who has resisted a man until she is twenty will not be controlled by him after that age. Lost honor falls its first step in the teens and generally in the years between fourteen and seventeen.

Given a girl of moral development, and the full opportunity to yield to the man who solicits her, with no early training such as we have described in the preceding episodes of this chapter, and there are one hundred chances out of every one hundred that she will fall. That is if she is normally developed and has the opportunity, the place and the unrestrained liberty to do as she pleases, nothing will save her but the years of early training that have awakened her emotions in the right direction.

This does not imply that the man will force her, or even urge her excessively. All normal girls want the other sex; they cannot help it, for they are children of nature.

So intense is the passion at times that there are girls who have declared that they would sell their very souls to get relief. In a seminary, the principal, who was a most conscientious woman of the highest moral standard, suspected that something was wrong with two of the very best of her pupils. They were room mates and one was then in her catamenia, while the other was lying on the bed in agony. The partition was thin and their voices were intensely loud at times. The first girl was soothing the one on the bed, telling her not to cry, as all would come out right.

"I cannot help it, dear. Why are girls made this way? I am not to blame. Why is nature so cruel that she will throw me into this state when I hate the very thought of it?"

"If you had a man now you would be ruined," was the reply.

"If I had a man now I would not care whether I was ruined or not. I would not resist him, and then I would kill myself."

The lady entered the room and sought to ascertain if the girl had ever been in love, if she had been disappointed in that, or what was the cause of her special excitement. Had they been reading suggestive literature? No cause could be found but the plain impulse of nature which was driving the girl into a state of passionate frenzy.

The foregoing facts are cited to show the real condition of the young girl. The younger she is the more she is addicted to the sudden impulse of excitement peculiar to her sex. The heifer that first feels the need of the bull will give more trouble than the sedate cow of experience.

This fact should be taken advantage of in order to save this country from the fearful avalanche of ruin to which the young girls are going by millions every year.

The first step in prevention is to impart the early training already spoken of in the preceding episodes. This lacking, the next step is to give the girl as soon as she is fourteen a thorough course of training in anatomy. Not only should this be well taught by a woman of ability who should make it her profession to secure young girls for such training; but there should be the most thorough study of the sexual organs before the time when the girl is ashamed because of her peculiar feelings to discuss such parts.

Every girl should be trained in the knowledge of obstetrics, not for the purpose of practicing that branch or any branch of medicine or surgery, but to gain knowledge. Mystery is held over the young woman long after she should know all about herself. She solves it in part year by year; but most young women about to be married go to their mother and ask for information, or the mother goes to her daughter with the self-remark that, since Julia is now to be married, it is time she should know all about some things. That is the very reverse of good judgment.

As soon as Julia or any other girl is approaching puberty, she should know the full story, and not as women at home tell it, but as science puts it, in exact form. Not one woman in a thousand knows that the process of catamenia is the loss of the membranous lining of the uterus, nor that the fallopian tubes are the seat of impregnation in a majority of cases. These are mere incidents, but the proper treatment of the girl who is some day, perhaps, to become a wife, and who if she is normal will soon be exposed to all the perils of temptation, is to let all mysteries be cleared away long before she is tempted.

Most mothers frighten their daughters by saying in the most mysterious manner, that if they allow a man even to touch them, pregnancy is sure to follow. The girls sooner or later learn that this is not true and then they discredit all they have been told. They do not like to be held up by the fright route.

A teacher of private anatomy should be secured for classes of girls about the age of fourteen and older, and charts should be used, and the whole subject made clear just as is done in classes in surgery. The idea that the modesty of the young women will suffer is wrong; the facts and experience are quite to the contrary. Woman must pass through more trying ordeals in marriage and no one makes the claim that she is less modest after contact with herself and her husband than before; and surely a knowledge by charts and lessons of her own structure would be much less trying to her. That she is made more womanly has been amply proved.

Then comes the objection that it is too soon, that the child is yet but a bit of innocence that could not stand the shock of the disclosures, and so it is argued that they better wait a few years. There is where the evil comes in and the mischief is done. After the impulses are at work in the sexual organs nature makes quick strides toward love and toward temptation. She is impatient and she is impetuous.

That it is too late is seen in the havoc made with young girls by men who are able to influence them.

You may take all the pride you please in the virtue of your own daughters, but we reply that you know nothing in fact about their virtue. Love and passion are sly and are fine actors, and the doting contented mother may be so firmly assured of the safety of her daughters that she would resent as an unpardonable insult even the slightest hint that anything wrong could occur. "How could it? How could it? Now tell me that. How could my Jenny get the opportunity for doing wrong? She is with so and so, and so and so, and so and so, and they are all right. They are girl friends, and girl friends are not blessed with the means of robbing my daughter of her virtue." Yet Jenny was at the time engaged in wrong as the mother afterwards found out. "I never had the least suspicion, and my own girl would have been the last to do such a thing, I am sure, etc.," are the usual explanations.

Here is a fond mother with a nineteen-year-old girl, who is a perfect beauty. Her mother introduces her as the sweetest and the most dutiful of daughters, a breath of heaven, as pure as purity itself; and the man who has been wronging her sits within hearing distance and smiles to himself.

The normal girl is the natural prey of the man who is endowed with animal magnetism. If he has the right kind of magnetism he will be able to control himself and he will see the awful nature of the crime which he is planning for the girl. A man who is truly magnetic will hold in check the sexual impulses that arise in him; he is his own master, and therefore he saves the girl as well as himself.

But there is an animal magnetism that goes out after the girl, and the mature man possesses it in stronger degree than the boy, although the latter is more cyclonic in his display of it at times. The man of twenty or thirty is more to be feared by the young girl of fifteen and sixteen than the lad of the girl's own age; and it is a strange fact that the old man of animal magnetism will draw the young girl to him if all conditions favor the engagement for criminal purposes.

So easily is the girl tempted that the law says she cannot

legally consent to the thing that she does consent to and even asks for. It is made a crime to have intercourse with a girl against her consent; and as she cannot give this when she is under fifteen or sixteen years of age, the offence is therefore rape even if she is the solicitor. Thus the law recognizes the fact that she is quick to yield during certain years. It is in this period that a majority of the girls are ruined.

But they learn from other girls of a few years more experience how to hide it and how to avoid pregnancy; and it is for this reason that girls prefer older men, as they think the man of experience will save them from pregnancy. "I am no fool," said a girl, "I know too much to go with a boy. The married man will not get me in trouble."

Who told her that?

In the case to which we now refer a married woman who was bad and who wished to cover up her movements by having the companionship of a girl of fifteen years of age, had gradually led the girl into wrong, and liking it she kept up the practice for seven years, when she was married to one who has not even to this date the slightest suspicion of her previous doings. The ability of countless thousands of girls to escape pregnancy gives them the opportunity to carry on their wrong-doing for many years, and finally to enter wedlock with men who deem them innocent.

This in France is called the practice of the demi-verge; or the girl who has had intercourse with men and has not been pregnant. It is claimed by French investigators that such a condition is well nigh universal. In America the demi-verge is present by the million. The same epidemic of crime prevailed in the days when Sodom and Gomorrah were destroyed, also in the days when all the population was swept from the earth except the eight who went into the ark; and in the time of Christ when fornication was unlimited. In these three great eras the sin was universal. Christ knew what was in men's hearts when he said that the man who was innocent of the crime of fornication or adultery could throw the first stone at the poor prostitute before them, and all refrained. "All men are bad," says one philosopher; and another puts it this way: "Most men are bad," which is probably closer to the truth. Some men cannot commit fornication and consequently are virtuous from physical necessity. "All normally built girls who have the opportunity unrestrained are sure to fall prey to the tempter," is asserted by investigators in this country and is denied by the girls themselves.

There are more than one million girls and women now plying their trade of prostitution in the United States. This figure is not large enough. In the city of New York alone, there are close to a quarter of a million of such women, and the police say there are more. Chicago, Boston and Philadelphia will make up almost the million; and San Francisco is even more crowded with prostitutes and demi-verges.

Whence comes these girls and women, and how is it that they keep up an unlimited supply, which seems never to give out or to decrease?

This brief outline is stated to show the necessity of beginning at the right time, and not making the mistake of assuming that your own daughters can never be among the fallen. It is better to be safe than to be sorry.

Love is magnetism. Pure love is noble magnetism. Low animal love is animal magnetism. All affect the opposite sex. The love of the girl will often set the man on fire sexually. The love of the man will reach into and affect the opposite sex. No person in love is denied the power to send forth into the very air a sensation that must reach and influence those who are susceptible to its influences.

A girl who is in her fifteenth, sixteenth or seventeenth year, and has not yet become demi-verge, is the most susceptible of all beings to the general love of the man who is near to her, or who may come in the range of her own feelings.

The kind of love that is general is that which has no specific individual as a mark, but wants any one of the other sex for a counterpart. If it is the man he seeks any woman or girl. If he is hardened to it, he will take any female so that she is a female, regardless of almost all other considerations. He seeks relief and can take it gladly whenever it is offered him. It was the wise act of a young man of twenty who felt that he could not restrain himself longer to select the aid of a woman of seventy, simply because, as he stated, he could not then be wronging anybody. He remained pure as far as his conduct toward his fiancée was concerned, and when marriage came, he was in the presence of one whom he had not wronged.

It is to resist the general love that the girl should be trained at every step of the way.

Men await every sign and indication of a girl that is willing. The miss of sixteen or thereabouts, may be effervescent and thus appear to be what she is not, and the man, thinking he has prey at hand, will carry the test farther. The girl should be taught the human nature of the approach of temptation; and the rule fits the case when some man with a general eye open for his victim is on the lookout, or when the lover is pressing his suit.

The first step is in touching the hand.

It is well known to every man the world over who wishes to see if he is to succeed. When a girl is close by, as at a table, or sitting within reach, and her hand may be touched ever so lightly, as though by accident, she is in danger. The man looks off as though he did not know he had touched the hand. The girl, not wishing to give offence, allows the two hands to remain. This is the second step, and the next is either to be an insult or a victory for the aggressor. It is to partly grasp the tips of the fingers, or the edge of the hand, and so lightly hold it. The pure girl can now know for a certainty that she is in danger, and the action cannot be mis-construed. It is quite a different case from that of the man who takes the offered hand of a girl or woman and holds it in his an unconscionably long space of time. He may have no motive whatever other than to be cordial, although it is rude, and should not be permitted. The squeeze of the hand may be an insult or a cordial indiscretion, depending upon the circumstances attending it. In any case it is wrong and should be discontinued.

The girl should not come within reaching distance of the opposite sex, except to greet him. The art of hand-shaking is old time etiquette. The very best society disapproves of it. As the meeting of the hands of the two sexes gives the chance for signals or advances that are not easily possible in other ways, the practice should not be encouraged.

The girl ought never to be left to herself, or in the presence of one of the opposite sex without a chaperone. There are several reasons for this rule.

In the first place the girl who is alone or who must go alone to any place is not able to contest with an antagonist. The man is stronger on the average, and he may readily gain control of the girl. To leave one or two young women where they may be in danger from attack is not wise. The chances are slight of any harm coming, but there are chances, and they should not be invited.

Then, when the days of courtship arrive, it is not good judgment to allow girls or young women to be alone with their lovers. This rule is not accepted in America in the great majority of cases, but it is a uniform custom in England, and has shown its efficacy in the increased percentage of virtuous women.

Temptation comes from the animal magnetism of the man, which has the advantage of working upon the high strung sexual condition of the young woman, and success in effecting the ruin of the latter is only a matter of opportunity. It is a case where both are drawn to each other by mutual animal magnetism.

The power that comes from personal magnetism is not the same as that which comes from the animal kind. It is nobler and of a much grander character. The man or woman who is gifted in personal magnetism will have little or no inclination to do wrong, as respect is the basis of this class of influence, and there can be no respect where there is a desire to commit wrong with another.

It is for this reason that we ask all persons to take up the study of the higher grade of magnetism in the hope that it may be taught to the young women and the young men at a time when they most need it. This very course of training would prove a help of the most important kind to both sexes.

Animal magnetism falls down in shame in the presence of personal magnetism. It does not even contend with it. This fact has been seen at work in a number of surprising cases where girls who had mastered the common principles of personal magnetism, were approached in every kind of way by their lovers, and quelled the impetuous efforts to seduce them. A magnetic girl knows no sexual excitement whatever. She will make a good wife but not one for the sensualist. She may be alone with any man except the brute who would strike her to the ground, and she will throw power against the most intense sexual excitement and lead the aggressor as a farmer might lead a calf.

But on general principles, all girls should be kept as far away from temptation as possible.

They should see to it that no man, even the lover, can make the first step, the approach of the bodies.

They should always be chaperoned, not in a perfunctory manner, but in serious earnest.

They should cultivate as much personal magnetism as possible so that they may put down all animal magnetism that may be exerted against their virtue.

And they should lay as the basis of all this, the foundation already described in a preceding episode of this chapter.

"THE BOY'S AGE OF TEMPTATION"

We have seen the nature of the temptation to which the girl is subjected. She is sought after by men, and is in constant danger from her lover, from her friends, and from newly made acquaintances who seek her as their prize.

The boy is in danger from himself, and also because he seeks his relief in the use of the opposite sex. It was a much more frequent occurrence in the days gone by for a girl to use herself; but now this evil is done away with in almost all parts of this land except in remote districts where the world is not alive. It is a rare condition now in towns and cities; although most girls who fear pregnancy are tempted to commit the offence. In seminaries for young ladies there are methods that are part-abuse, and they will probably never be wholly obliterated.

But with boys, especially when they are about fifteen or sixteen, the case is different. It is so easy for them to commit the sin that they fall readily into the practice, and soon show it in their faces. There are but few exceptions to this condition; the most careful physicians claiming that more than ninety per cent of all boys have been guilty of the fault. If men would tell the truth, their confessions would surprise the world of women.

The best means of cure is prevention, as the Irishman would put it. Prevention is found in a number of ways, the best of which are as follows:

1. The full study of anatomy, and sexual uses, to begin before the boy of fifteen.

2. The full discussion of the sin before it is begun; for it always commences gradually and in ignorance of what it means or leads to.

3. A very low meat diet in the years preceding. This has been found to almost always prevent the offence, and there are

some persons who go so far as to claim that the absence of all meat is sure to take away the temptation to use the organs under the stress of excitement. One great physician has this for his motto: "No meat, no sexual abuses."

4. The cultivation of personal magnetism as a power that will uphold the will at all times.

5. A variety of duties and activities that will absorb the attention and wipe out all morbid influences.

6. Keep the boy at work, and do not let him idle his time away from home.

7. Keep him away from older boys who would lead him astray. If he is to go around with other boys keep him with those who are a year or two younger. It is the older boy that teaches this vice to those he comes in contact with.

Boys who are taught the nobility of work and who are kept busy all the time, except when they can play in groups, are less likely to fall. It is the pair of boys, and sometimes the small coterie of three that plan this mischief. The sons of the rich are prone to the fault, because they are always idle. It is rare to find a boy of wealthy parents who is not guilty of this vice.

Most of them, even at fourteen and fifteen years of age, are advanced far enough to know all about it and to gild the sin with embellishments of their own contrivance. They are old enough to buy and to study obscene pictures; and what town or city does not have the villain who sells fancy cards and books of this sort, preying upon the sons of the rich?

When these tender roues are another year older, say about sixteen, they can afford to buy girls for their use. Some have been bold enough to trade with the mothers; and we have been told by doctors that there was a practice in a certain part of a great city, in which women who had girls between the ages of fifteen and seventeen would take large sums of money in exchange for the privileges requested, and would look after the methods of preventing pregnancy. A boy may fall in love with an older woman, but he does not take much interest in her for animal purposes. The young girl is by far the best. There are many cases where a group of boys have allured a young girl into a building and made assignments with her for months before a discovery was made.

In all such cases the boys were allowed to idle away their time with each other.

The father should know every minute of the boy's activities on each day of the year until the lad is well in his eighteenth year.

Keep him busy, either studying, working or playing.

Idleness is his most crushing curse. The practice of boys chumming in twos, is a bad one. There is but little need of the boy going off by himself or with others into the woods or long distances away in order to find amusement.

Last of all, let the parents spend more time with their children. The father is too much engrossed with his friends to give up time to the boy; and the idle gossip of the mother in her rounds of calls, is the death blow to the companionship of the daughter.

Let parents take an account of their hours, their days that were spent selfishly away from their children, their evenings that were squandered at the club or in the store, or anywhere but with their family, and they will amass an accumulation of time that will stand like a grim shaft of accusation on which may be inscribed the words:

"Here lies the cause of the ruin of my children."

CHAPTER TWENTY-SEVEN

NO MARRIAGES ARE BLESSED
UNLESS
HUSBAND AND WIFE
ARE ATTRACTED TO EACH OTHER

✛✛
✤ MAGNETIC MARRIAGES ✤
✛✛

ROWTH IS RAPID in the changing years of youth, and the child is soon the adult. There is no stage in its progress when it is not passing a crucial period. The troubles that come in after life are due to the fact that parents do not realize that children cannot train themselves, and they are left to become their own masters. It is not best to interfere too much with the proclivities of the young men, provided they are on the right side: but to let them run as they will, is not wise, nor does it bring the best type of manhood. Let us see what this is.

"DEVELOPMENT OF MANHOOD."

A boy becomes a youth; the youth becomes the young man; and the young man enters upon the realm of manhood, stepping over the threshold of years so quickly that all is accomplished ere the parents are aware.

What makes the man?

It is not education, although that influence has much to do with the outcome. The right kind of knowledge is not imparted to the boy to make the right kind of man.

Yet it is the first thing that the fond father will contemplate.

He wishes his boy to go through all the public schools, and that is right. Let the lad go as far as there are public schools for him to attend before he thinks of going to a higher institution where he must pay for his tuition. It is not the money part of the transaction but the character of the education that is to be considered. The first principle is that he should exhaust the right to attend all public educational institutions, for they are planned with a desire to meet the best requirements of youth.

In those schools let him follow all the languages that are available. It is not a question whether or not he can make use of any of the languages, but it is important that he should be able to know his own inner nature better; and the rule is this: The greater number of words he knows and feels the meaning of, the closer he comes in touch with the magnetic forces within him.

Let us see how this works out.

It has been stated in this work that the inner or magnetic mind is not built on the words of speech for they represent what has been acquired through experience in living. But it was also said that the two powers, the primal self and the inherent self, are two steeds that can be driven separately but that drive better together. It is also a fact that many of the feelings are interpreted in words.

It is the latter fact that we make use of now.

There is no language on earth that is full enough to express the tenth part of the feelings; therefore there is no language that can stand for the inherent nature. The French has words that tell a better story of some of the emotions and magnetic nature than any other tongue in the world. This then should be a part of the education of every human being.

The combination of the French and English languages will make a much more powerful mind and magnetic nature than either alone; although the French is much the greater of the two for the purposes stated. It lacks some in educational value for developing the primal self, and the English excels in that respect. But the two make a most excellent pair of steeds.

The German has words that cannot be found either in the French or in the English. Their meanings are quite different, and it is difficult to find synonyms for translation. But the words that do have equivalents in English are shaded to such a nicety when standing for the moods and feelings that they add a vast percentage to the power of the mind and magnetic nature. Then there is the old Latin, and the old Greek, and the old Hebrew, all dead as dead can be, yet freighted with a value so great that no one can understand what they will accomplish in the development of an individual.

But the word dead means that the people that spoke the tongues are no longer speaking them; it does not mean that either the words or the thoughts are dead. The English of three hundred years ago is much more defunct than either the Latin or the Greek or the Hebrew.

In the history of the Hebrews when their language was much alive, they felt and experienced conditions that are common to all peoples, and to all parts of the universe. Their language opens up faculties in our nature that can be developed in no other way. the word still lives, and will endure as long as humanity feels and yearns to express its inherent nature. In those old centuries there was much less of the primal self in evidence, for there were fewer experiences; and the same fact is true of the Greek and the Latin.

Here are five grand tongues, containing, with the English, so many thoughts that belong to the inherent or magnetic nature that they will do more for imparting a genuine education in the mind and heart of the young man than all other lines of training combined.

You cannot build power on air.

You cannot make the man a power in himself by merely telling him a few of the secrets of development. The more that is genuine in the education and character of the man, the greater will be the magnetic force he will wield. Let power rest on a foundation of granite or adamant if you will.

It was the good fortune of the author to be directed when a lad into a love for all the languages we have named. It was not our choice then, and had it not been for proper guidance the results might have been different. Since then we have advised that French should be started when children are five and six years of age, and we have lived to see the workings out of the plan in unfolding a better and clearer mind in the children as they grow up.

The greatest lawyer that ever stood before a jury was Rufus Choate, and his closest competitor was Daniel Webster. Both won through their magnetism. Both were the greatest of actors, yet had no display of the stage in their work, and never took part in dramatic productions. Both ascended high on the ladder of fame and statesmanship. Both had an intimate knowledge of several languages, Choate being able to read Greek fluently when he was yet under seven or eight years of age.

When we say they were actors we mean that they could express all the emotions, all the feelings and moods with perfection, and had a repertoire many times greater than the real actors on the real stage. They also had the art to conceal their art. The real actor on the real stage shows himself to be an actor. The lawyer or orator who does greater acting, gives out no appearance of being an actor. Hence he is the greater.

The most versatile and successful of the magnetic actors of the last century was the elder Booth, and some critics place him at the head of the list of all actors. He was master of seven different languages and spoke them fluently. His knowledge of the old Hebrew was surprising and the question arose many times how he was able to find the time to acquire so much.

But the fact is that a half hour a day persisted in will enable any man or woman to master all the languages we have mentioned, the Hebrew, the Greek, the Latin, the German and the French. And there is no person so busy who does not throw away a half hour a day. The mistake is made by all beginners, of thinking that they must make up for lost time by studying hard, that a half hour is nothing and they will plunge in and study several hours. They forget that language must soak in. It is better to leave the study with a keen desire to renew it, than to leave it with a heavy head and tired nervous system.

It has been many times stated that each language carries on its face the progress of civilization and the interpretations of the feelings and heart history of the people through whose lives it has developed. As each human being has the same inherent nature, and as all magnetism has its origin and greatest power on the inherent nature, it must follow that the greater number of languages that are mastered the more the inherent nature of the man will be developed.

We know that we are talking to disbelievers, for there is a general feeling today that a language that cannot be spoken is of no use, and so the demand is for things that can be spoken and can be of use. So ignorant and sordid is the public mind that even the study of French which is the polite language of all Europe will not be agreed to unless there seems to be some chance for the student to go to Europe and talk it. It is not in the talking of it that any language has its greatest usefulness. Most foreign linguists will do well to retain their native tongue when they have talking to do.

The talker has ideas that are very limited and are born in the commonplace uses of the day. But the inspired works of poet, of biographer, of historian and of prose writer, the contents of which hold the best fruit of mind and heart, are the media for the use of other languages as well as our own.

The man who is to enter upon the full estate of the best manhood should be one who knows and loves the language under which he was born, and he should not look for his knowledge of it in the papers, magazines and novels, primarily, but in the works that are undoubtedly inspired, such as the recognized poetry of the past centuries, the great histories of human action, the biographies that are noble in their authorship, and the essays and other prose of the highest minds.

No other part of a language is worth attention from the student.

This mastery of English need not precede the study of other tongues.

Another of the mistakes that are made by the public in the estimate on foreign languages is to claim that it is time enough to master some other tongues when English is mastered, and the common thinker applauds vigorously; he calls it sense. But it is far from that.

But there is no possibility of securing any mastery over the upper half of the English language until Greek, Latin and French are studied. For every word that you take out of another tongue and put in your own, you must find one in your own that is akin to it, even if it is not an equivalent. In learning the meanings of words in other languages it is always necessary to learn more of English words, and their finer shades of meaning. No word is well learned, and few are really understood until they have soaked in. They must get farther than the mere brain. A word is a thing and has an organic life of its own and should be a companion as well as food and drink for the whole being.

When words are absorbed they exert an influence over the mind and the heart as well.

The best way to learn English is to first learn some other language; the latter is never learned except through the medium of your mother tongue.

A laborer and a business man will not be able to see what connection there is between the mastery of languages and labor or business. In the matter of toil where the man is a machine, it does not matter at all if he is content to remain a machine. In business a man may keep within mean and narrow lines, and never get out of them; and he has no need for the larger influence that tends to broaden the scope of one's usefulness and powers.

But if the business man or the professional man seeks to be more of a man he should cultivate the instincts that broaden and deepen him; and to be a master of words is the most effective of all. It will help on the work of magnetism, and the latter will feed the power that is thus unfolded. We do not recommend the learning of language by grasping definitions, for they are not acquisitions. We have seen many persons who could define thousands of words the meanings of which they knew nothing about.

The young man should also be trained to become both active and manly. To be manly is to be strong of purpose and strong of execution.

The man who would hold a woman's highest regard, who would win her respect and perhaps her love, who would retain that exalted opinion which uplifts him in her vision, must be a man. The word virile means manly. The influence which is almost magnetic of a soldier's uniform has been hard to understand except as construed under this Law; but it is not worship of color or dress that makes the despised fellow of the streets the idolized hero of the uniform. The transformation in woman's appreciation is due solely to the fact that the dress suggests the call to war; war suggests battle; battle means the willingness to face the enemy, to meet sabre-thrust, or the advancing bayonet, or the shot and shells that rain death; or the hand-to-hand encounter in which the soldier strives to kill in order that he may survive; all these are the highest types of virility or manliness. No wonder woman cannot resist the uniform.

The mimic battle of the college field likewise arouses the admiration of the fair sex. Few are the girls who would not leave prospects of wealth for the hand of the football victor. This is strange but true.

But virility is more than physical prowess. It is success in the graver battle of life. The skilled workman, the clerk rising year by year out of his first rank to higher walks in business, the struggling and winning merchant who holds the reins of success in his tight grip, resolved to climb higher and higher by dint of energy and resourceful activity; this is the virile man. His mother, sister, wife, whoever she may be that watches his progress, feels with him the pangs of struggle and hopes with him for ultimate victory. The most glorious thing in the world is not the top rung of the ladder of success but the step up from the first rung to the second.

Virility is energy of purpose. It is study, planning, preparation, looking for opportunity, fitting oneself to accept the hand of proffered chance, the eternal habit of getting ready, and the development of judgment and careful mental acumen, all of which come slowly through effort, and which, when come, are masters of the future.

Activity is a recognition of the value of small moments. "My husband never wastes a minute of time. He is learning something more every day. He says that one never knows how many opportunities there are in the world for winning success until he becomes active. He helps me at home, and is not afraid to do anything that will lighten my work, for I am not strong like other women. My girl friends who are married pity me for being poor. They say their husbands enjoy life and take things easy. But we will forge ahead in time." Poor girl! Her husband was lowly, and that was years ago. When Andrew Carnegie called him into his palatial drawing room and asked him to have a cigar, the young man said that he did not smoke, that he never had time for that pleasure. Nor had he time to learn to drink. He is now a millionaire, and the other girls' husbands work for him. And the humble wife of years ago has had health now in rich abundance; God bless her!

A woman soon learns to worship the man, however poor, who is active and strong in his ambitions, who never idles away precious moments, who works and makes his work count something for the future. On the other hand, she soon loses respect for the idler, for the novel reader, for the fellow who smokes his time away, or seeks diversion in the papers, or enjoys the magazine, or likes a social game of cards, or his chums hanging around, or is in her way, or makes himself a drone at home, or annoys and disgusts her with his bad or unclean habits.

Never cross the sexes.

By this is meant that the young man should not be allowed to do the work primarily of the young woman, nor the latter his work.

As the early years of the child were witnesses of the difference in the playthings used by each of the sexes, so the activities and interest should be separated as he grows up toward manhood.

It is our candid belief that the principles of magnetism of every kind should be studied and understood by the young man, for they will make him a much stronger being than he can hope to become by any other process. Magnetism alone is not enough; for it must be founded on something that is substantial in each and every department of life; and the attempt to draw success by throwing out a mysterious and subtle influence will not achieve great results.

Every good quality of mind and faculty is attractive and therefore is magnetic.

"THE BLOSSOMING OF WOMANHOOD."

The woman should decide whether or not she is to choose the life of a toiler in which there is no hope of being anything else; or is she to build the broad foundations of a grander personality?

We propose to look at natural principles in this discussion and not give attention to the conditions that prevail. It is a law of nature that a woman shall be constructed on different lines from man. The attempt to make the conditions the same has signally failed and will always prove fruitless.

Woman adds to her misery the more she departs from her true rank.

The fact that she was a slave in her earlier history and has been subjected to a rule that was both tyrannical and unjust does not warrant a complete adoption of conditions that will make her wholly independent of man. She should be reasonably dependent on him, and he on her. They are counterparts of each other and it is not good for either to be alone in life.

The first natural principle, then, is this: Every woman should be developed to the estate of association with men, either as wife, or in a capacity that will enable her to look to him for protection and yet be independent in her own affairs.

Conditions of house-keeping should not be such that scandal can arise, even though it is unfounded. Baseless slander built on appearances, is due to the indiscretion of parties who permit the appearances to exist. Where there is opportunity for wrong-doing, even though it is not done, there is the wholesome tongue of scandal, designed undoubtedly by nature to prevent the opportunities. It is a well settled rule that where there is no opportunity for doing wrong, there can be no wrong done; and the eternal fight against the opportunity is the best step that can be taken. Remove the opportunity and you remove the appearance, and prevent the scandal.

Purity is the first great power of woman.

Here is a young woman who went Maying with a young man. She was as pure as an angel all day long; yet there were both the opportunity and the appearance against her. Here is another young woman who dropped for a few minutes into the private room of a young man at the hotel. She meant no harm in it, and the young man in fact treated her most courteously; but scandal grew from it, because there were both the opportunity and the appearance. Never create either. Never allow circumstances to create them.

Purity in fact is not so magnetic a weapon as purity both in fact and in appearance.

Up to the time that the woman becomes the wife, from the year preceding her approach of puberty, she should be constantly under the eye of some one who can know that there has never been the opportunity or the appearance of evil. She carries with her the power to tempt man, and there are very few men who will not yield when tempted. Many men are thrown into a fever of excitement when, being alone with a young woman, she permits the least impression to go out that she is temptable. Being alone, and having some initiatory pretence to act upon, it is easy to use a small amount of strength and thus lead the innocent girl astray.

The young woman who is blossoming into womanhood has her

wealth, which is her virtue, to protect, and she cannot afford to be placed in a position where the least freedom of speech or movement will draw some man to her. If she does, he may in one strong unyielding move, throw his arm about her waist, and lift her from her feet, hardly before she realizes what is transpiring. A girl of eighteen who was small of stature and not possessed of strength, but who was vivacious, found herself in a single second lifted from the floor, placed upon a couch and in full possession of her lover. It was the truth she spoke when she said that she had no suspicion or realization of what was going on until it was too late, and her most violent struggles were in vain.

This bit of history has been repeated millions of times, and accounts for the first step in the ruin of girls. The excitement is not objectionable to them, and they have less desire than reason to object.

The purpose is to avoid the opportunity.

To thus avoid danger, let every woman see to it that she is not alone with a man; and this should be done for her good name as well as for her real safety.

The young woman who is virtuous against temptation, knows her power and her value. Knowledge begets confidence and confidence begets magnetism. She has full confidence in herself and others have the same in her.

The question of a woman's virtue is hidden from the world in a great majority of cases. But the question of her general purity is not obscured. What is her trend of thoughts? She cannot conceal them from those who know her. Herein purity is of the highest importance. She has a much stronger following in her sex if she is known to women to be pure in thought. A dirty story may produce fun for a time, but the teller of it is never the same in the eyes of those to whom she told it. No woman fails to drop some each time she does an impure thing before other women, or speaks with the tongue of obscenity.

The best method of uplifting this trait until it becomes one of the nobler feminine qualities is to cultivate it in the privacies of life. Before your own sisters or female friends, even where men are sure not to see or listen, be careful in both the subjects that are allowed to enter the mind, and in the diction employed in discussing them; and, to this, add the most scrupulous vigilance in every action so that it may be refined.

There are many girls who are known to all their girl friends as being above the practice of doing or saying anything in the presence of close acquaintances that is not refined in the highest degree. This fact cannot be concealed. Some girl will mention it to some other person and the young men will learn of it sooner or later. The prude is one who parades aggressively her distaste for every form of questionable conduct; but she is not so pure in fact as one who makes no parade of it and yet is refined. Some prostitutes are prudes; to the world they are over-exact; in secret they are criminal.

A woman who will intensify a condition that would die out of itself, is obscene in her prudish nature; as where some slip of the tongue has caused the cheek of a modest girl to pale, and the prude censures the careless individual in the presence of others. Disregard of the remark and a graceful changing of the subject were the only measures necessary.

Let the purity of thought, of action, and of word, begin at home in the bosom of the family; and then let it increase abroad in the midst of girl friends and woman friends, until it is well established that you are by force of habit clean in mind and heart.

This is the most magnetic of all traits for the fair sex.

There should be some education on which to base a thoughtful and exalted womanhood.

We have no hope to change the trend of things at this time; but the day is not far distant when all girls will be kept within the realms to which they are born. Today they are reaching out for man's work, and are rapidly becoming his competitors in all branches.

The proper education in the teens will avoid this fault of the general people.

We have laid the basis of such education in the discussion of the young woman under fifteen. There the distinction was made between the two sexes; and, if well made, it will be difficult for parent or girl to shift things about so as to fall into the prevailing error of today.

In book learning the girl should be both a good mathematician and a good linguist; she should study mathematics as far as the end of algebra, and should make that training as thorough as possible; and with it she should study French, German and Latin. These three tongues will open up the inherent nature of the woman where is found the only real magnetic power for great purposes in life.

The reason stated in the discussion of the development of manhood will apply to her.

The result is a fine mind, and a finer nature. She may never have occasion to see France or Germany, but the words that have come into her mind have carried a larger and deeper life into her whole being. To train a girl for commercial life is the greatest blunder ever made. Let us look at a few cases to see what law is at work. The faculty we have for getting at facts is summed up in the statement that we have for years sent out experiments and requests for observation and for securing reports, so that we may know the truth and not depend on theory. The magnetism club helped us to make many thousands of tests; some of the members were given initial experiments to make, and those who were energetic were retained, while others were not sent further work to do. The best reports and the most accurate have come from physicians and professors, as these two classes of men are intensely interested in the subject.

We find that the life of the girl is shaped just as she is about to enter womanhood; that is, when she has passed the first year or two of puberty and is taking on the estate of the woman.

Of ninety-eight girls who were about to decide whether to enter the classical course in the high school or to take the commercial course, or business course, as it is called, we found that nearly eighty were advised by their parents to take the latter studies; the reason being that, if anything happened to the parents, the girls would be able to provide for themselves.

Before the decision was made we sent printed arguments of the most earnest character urging that the girls be allowed to get a full knowledge of mathematics to the end of algebra, and a full education in French, German and Latin, going as far as the public schools taught those subjects. We succeeded in swerving fifty-three to our views; and we had a careful watch made of all the girls who went through the two courses; on one side the classical, and on the other side the business training.

Of all those who graduated, every girl who took the classical work, excepting two who were not sincere students, rose in life to a much grander rank. All ninety-eight girls were members of families in middle circumstances; all had fathers or relatives who worked as employees, and not one was in independent circumstances.

All who graduated from the classical course showed in after life a decided difference in every respect from those who took the business course. The latter were not of the genuine refinement of mind or body that characterized the former. They had a cheapness about them, and it came in evidence at all stages of their work. They never got out of the lower stratum of life.

Those who graduated from the classical studies were better educated and a few of them pursued their studies much farther and accepted good positions as teachers for a few years; most of them entering wedlock, however, ere long. The others of the classical graduates were married, excepting four, who are still single.

To carry out the comparison, all of the business girls who got married represented in their husband's total wealth, as estimated, a total of eighteen thousand dollars; that is, the supposed financial worth of all these husbands combined reached that figure. On the other hand, the total combined wealth as estimated of the husbands of the classical graduates was sixteen million dollars and over. Many of them married into wealthy families, although they themselves came out of families of middle rank in life. Three of them in three different States at the time, were married to men, each of whom had over a million dollars.

There is no need of a girl marrying a man who is poor or who is destined to remain poor. In one case a girl was wedded to a man who had no wealth whatever; and in ten years he has had uniformly great success, now being counted worth three hundred thousand dollars; and he pays his wife the compliment of saying that her level head has been his guide in all his undertakings.

These figures are not visionary. We will guarantee that the same results will come out in any comparative lists of girls made on the same basis. You or any one can prove the principle in your own way and it will always be the same.

If these facts are true, you ought to know it.

If they are true, you and all others ought to act upon the law that is thus proved. If they are true they are important enough to be studied for the good they will produce in the lives of millions of young women.

That they are true can be easily ascertained. Look to the history of your own community; and, if it has not been carried away by the prevailing spirit of commercialism, you will find that the girls that study thoroughly the three languages we have mentioned and are able to read fluently all the grandest works of the greatest geniuses in the literature of those tongues, and who also have mastered mathematics as far as the end of algebra, are far and away the superiors of the girls about them.

There are many solid men in this country who do not marry because they will not take the kind of girl that they must marry. They do not want the prude, nor do they want the cut-and-dried schoolmarm; but they will not marry the empty-headed girl who knows how to play bridge and can shuffle, shuffle, shuffle cards from the middle of the morning to the middle of the night. They will not marry girls who take pride in being ignorant of the duties of their servants, who know nothing of the chemistry of cooking, who can talk and make themselves nervous in gossipy conversation, but have not strength enough to plunge into the duties of overseeing the transactions of their homes.

These men to whom we refer are men of wealth.

They are deterred by this fact, as shown in an engagement that was about to be made. A young lady agreed to give her final answer on a certain night. The man called. The mother said:

"It must be understood that my daughter will not know what is going on in her kitchen. She prefers to board, and hates the very thought of housekeeping."

The man said:

"I board now. I have longed for years to get a home. I was reared in a home. I am able to conduct one in first-class manner, but I do not think that a wife should be willing to let ignorant servants conduct her household affairs entirely for her."

"If you love my daughter as much as you say you do, you will be willing for her to board," was the mother's reply.

"Love is most fickle that is based on the ideas that are repugnant to home-making. I believe that love is created by nature for the purpose of inducing two persons to make a home. To board is not to make a home."

"Well, then, it is best that my daughter should give the matter more consideration."

The man is still single. The girl married a wealthy manufacturer who promised that she should never have to look into her kitchen, and the divorce courts are now separating the parties.

The kind of training we have indicated will make the woman's mind rich and strong. Against it is the view of the general public asking the oft-repeated question, What good will those things do?

The studies of mathematics, of algebra, of French, of German and of Latin, do not on their face have any connection with the future usefulness of the woman. But the laws under which such things proceed are fully stated in the preceding discussion of the development of manhood. If these cannot be understood, then there is no remedy.

The mind that is rich is a powerful magnet. We would make our first choice of all the women of the world from those who have thus enriched their minds.

Coupled with that training, the study and practice of personal magnetism will add value and attraction of such import that the woman thus equipped will have no real competitors in the battle for the best husbands in the world.

That should be the goal of magnetism to each blossoming woman.

With tastes and mental interest suited to her sex, with activities that belong to her sex, with a rich mind, with a magnetic personality gathered from this very work, especially in the cultivation of the mood-colors of the early chapters, any woman ought to stand as queen in her sphere. The history of recent conquests proves this claim to be a true one.

Separation of interests and of activities, from those of the male sex, should be insisted on at every stage of life.

There can be no compromise in this truth.

It is the duty of man to provide the means whereby every woman who is connected with him shall have an independent income without being compelled to do his work. The customs of today are the reverse of this law.

Girls and women are doing men's work. Men should do their own work, and do enough of it to make it unnecessary for girls and women to undertake what is not in their natural department.

A woman lives for a man; and a man lives for a woman; and both live for their children or for the succeeding generation.

This is the plan and purpose of the Creator, and the prevailing denial of that arrangement will only work harm to the race and to the individual.

"WHO SHOULD MARRY?"

Every normal man and woman should marry.

Some of them do not wish to, and others have some trouble in finding suitable counterparts.

It is directly in the purpose and duty of magnetism to make it the wish of all normal persons to marry; and to provide the means whereby the suitable counterpart may be forthcoming. The power to be attracted establishes the wish, and the power to attract sets up the other condition. By this is meant that a person should be capable of being drawn into the desire to marry, and the same individual should be able to draw a counterpart out of the general fund of humanity.

There are more women out of wedlock than men.

There are countless thousands of men out of wedlock who ought to be married.

These are the normal individuals, not members of the class that should not marry.

A normal person is one who is capable of becoming the parent of a healthy child who will be sound in mind and body.

Who are not normal will be considered in the next episode.

Love is not by any means an essential of marriage. Love is guilty of more mis-mating than any other one influence in the world; and the reason is that it is the outgrowth of the mind and not of the inherent nature, as generally employed. That kind of affection that comes direct from the inner being is called the affinity, or suitability of one person for another. It is also known as love, and may be so called in its higher attributes.

But the love that jumps to the surface in an instant and destroys appetite and everything else that is useful, and that is most dejected when most satiated, is not a sane condition. Many kinds of feelings may be called by the name of love; the liking for a dog or cat, or the appreciation of a plate of soup or a dish of ice cream, or the parental love, or the love between brothers, or between men or between women, or the love for any relative, all these are quite different from that peculiar nervous affection that mounts to the brain of either sex when properly instigated by the other.

If a woman finds that a man is her affinity, or if a man finds the same of a woman, and there are no reasons why they should not marry, it is much better than a match founded on the fever of love.

There is a vast amount of sentiment about the conditions that are precedent to marriage. The first fancy of a girl for a man, and perhaps of a rich girl for a poor man, is often life-lasting; and she weeps in silence when she is led to the altar by one of her own rank, knowing that the first fancy is still alive. She yearns for him even during the hours of brightest gayety. The fever lingers in her nervous system.

Let us be frank. To pretend sentiment and to express it in the face of natural laws and facts, is not exactly honest. Take, if you will, one hundred girls and one hundred poor men who are better qualified to make them good husbands, and against these hundred men place another hundred men who are very wealthy, and ask the girls to fall in love with either class; how many, do you think, would prefer the poor men? In form, health, education, ability and all else except riches, the poverty class are the marked superiors of the opulent class. But the chances are two to one that the hundred girls will select the latter, and most of them will declare, and some honestly too, that they really and truly love them.

This supposed condition relates to those girls who have not yet been in love, or who at least say so, or are heart free.

Take as many young women who have felt the pangs of this fever, or who are not heart free, but whose words have been given to as many poor but worthy men, and let them receive genuine proposals from rich men whom they do not love, and how many, think you, would wake up to the realization that they did not in fact love the men they had expected to marry, but have come to experience the thrill of deepest love for the rich suitors?

Sentiment says that the true girl will not leave the poor man she loves, for the rich man she does not love; but the facts say otherwise in a large majority of instances. It is easy to find an affinity where proffered love and opulence appear hand in hand.

The question arises, shall one marry for love?

If other considerations warrant the match, love is no obstacle;

but standing alone it is not enough of an incentive to wedlock. It is the cause of many bad endings to the romance. It is sweet, dreamy, sad, tender and all that; but it cannot face the battle of life as will judgment and grand executive ability. It is supersensitive, and that means danger when the least thing goes awry.

In royalty there is very little pretence to love-matches; policy and many conditions of state determine who shall be the high contracting parties. Among the wealthy it is the purpose for certain kinds of family friendships to be welded by unions among the younger generation. Love is compelled to step aside in almost every such case.

The poor should marry the poor; the middle class should marry the middle class; and the rich should marry the rich. Less after trouble comes from this plan. It is not by any means good judgment for the woman in moderate circumstances to wed the man who is wealthy; she make demands on him that savor of sordid purposes, and the affair is soon clouded in smoke. Where there have been unions between a wealthy girl and a poor man or one in moderate circumstances, or between a rich man and a girl who is not rich, there have been more divorce cases than where the rich have intermarried. The least friction arises where the wealth is about equal in the two.

The disparity of wealth leads to a feeling of suspicion that is often well founded, that the marriage was designed for ulterior purposes. The rich husband, if he gets the least bit angry with his poor wife, may be tempted to charge the fact of mercenary intentions and she will go to her grave never forgiving the allegation. Even if she does not hear it from his lips, there are so many ways of acting the thought that she thinks she sees it in his glance or very move.

What she thinks intensely will become to her a sensation of fact and then she will be unable to separate the imagination from the reality.

It is a bad match that brings rich and poor together.

The man who marries for money earns it.

The woman who marries for money is a source of annoyance to the man she has secured.

It is almost a public fact, at least well known to all who are wide awake, that there are thousands of poor women, or those who may not be actually poor but who are in straightened circumstances, who are on the lookout for rich husbands. The latter are caught by the cute and ingenious wooing which such a woman can do when she makes up her mind that the man is to be won. It is this aggressive agreeableness that attracts his attention. His rich lady friend will not make herself so attractive and he is soon convinced that this adventuress is much to be preferred.

Herein the man is badly bitten, as the phrase goes.

The adventuress has nothing else to do but to make herself sweet and attractive. She lives in that one idea. In the morning every little touch of art that will add to her powers to please, are given full attention. So much as an extra curl, or the fluffing of a bunch of hair, the fragrance of the body and the breath, the dainty and delicate coloring of the bloom on the cheek, and the small but telling motions of the hands and feet, are studied and carried into reality.

The subjects that are to be discussed, the tastes of the old codger, the style of talk, and the diction that will most impress him; these are developed as only the adventuress can unfold them. Added to this is the calm, the serene, the seraphic smile that seems to be the natural position of the features when they are in repose, and the hearty but kittenish laugh that ripples from the opening in the face like a brook burbling over placid shallows; and the man is soon enveloped in a sea of warmed-over love that drowns out his consciousness of every other fact in the universe.

If the rich woman should show this amount of attention and preparation, the man would quickly propose to her; but she is adored and worshiped by a lot of adventurers, and she does not propose to stoop to the wooing act with any man, not she.

The result of this twisted arrangement is that rich men are the victims of adventuresses, and rich women are the victims of adventurers. It is easily figured out. The rich man will not woo; he has no occasion to do so. The rich woman will not woo; she has no occasion to do so. The rich man is wooed by the poor woman, although she is skillful enough to conceal the fact or the process. The rich woman is wooed by the poor man and he makes his work effective.

It is a fact that a great majority of rich men are victimized, not in the course of every decade; but every year thousands fall victims to the intrigues of the adventures which are aimed at their purses. To keep an account of these many cases would amaze one; and most of them never get into the lime-light of full publicity. Once you start to make the record you will stop in bewilderment to think that there are so many fools in the world, as they seem to you. We do not call them that; they are the victims of schemers.

What is to be done?

Let the rule be adhered to, that each class shall marry in its own kind; the poor with the poor, the middle class with the middle class, and the rich with the rich. Last year a very beautiful young miss was wedded to a man of fifty who was reputed to be worth over eight hundred thousand dollars. This young wife lost no time in nagging him until he had made a deed of his mansion and real estate to her, and it was soon learned that her relatives had coached her throughout the whole transaction. The couple are now tangled up in court proceedings.

This is a typical case, and there are thousands of others who have made the same mistake.

It is not true that a poor woman can love a rich man, or that a poor man can love a rich woman. The disparity in financial conditions is such as to make love a trifling matter.

All rich men who have created their wealth have risen from the ranks of the poor or middle classes. It is well for both husband and wife to start poor, or in middle circumstances, and grow rich together. In such case they agree better and have a satisfaction in common that will never grow less.

An educated person should marry one who is also educated. A refined person should marry one who is refined. An ignorant person should marry one who is ignorant. So often have we received letters like the following: "My husband is a coarse, common boor, ignorant and disgusting in all that he says and does. On the contrary I am an educated and refined woman." This discrepancy is a serious one. Two hogs can live at peace in the same pen; but a hog and a lamb do not harmonize.

Marriage is a contract, and its purpose is to make a home with or without children. As a contract it would be entered into with at least as much care as would be exercised in the forming of an agreement to purchase a horse; yet most men who could not be cheated in a horse trade get the worst end of the contract when they take a wife. How many persons apply the same care and caution to making the contract for marriage that they would employ in buying a house? The house costs more, but is it as important?

Love is a disturber of the judgment and cool powers of reasoning, and will bring people together in a chaos of blunders.

"WHO SHOULD NOT MARRY."

Some day the law will wake up and discard its theory of personal liberty and permit only those men and woman to marry who are capable of bringing into the world children of sound mind and body. This change will not come about at once or by a sudden uprising; but public sentiment will be quietly molded until little by little the laws will be changed.

The first move will be to prevent those who are known to be mentally diseased to a dangerous extent, to marry. The next step will be to prevent those who are criminals by instinct and carry the disease of crime in their blood, to enter the state of wedlock.

When these entering wedges are started, the other steps will follow. Then it will not be possible to saddle upon the coming generation a progeny of half-idiots, natural born criminals, and wretchedly diseased mortals who are always a danger to society and to the race.

The law of God and of nature is plain and the duty is commanded humanity to check the spread of crime and mental imbecility, by the only effective method that will ever be known; namely, the closing of the source of such offspring.

If you have a filthy river that is flowing through your house, you may consult experts who will tell you how to clean up the house and renovate the things that are polluted; but some one may come along who will suggest that you stop the flow of the river in the direction of your house. You never thought of that and it seems a good idea. It does not cost a very great effort to thus deal with it, and in a short time the offense is gone because the source no longer exists.

This is logic.

Applied to the affairs of life it is the best exhibition of sense.

The status of a man or woman cannot be judged by poverty or ignorance. There is nothing to be gained by legislating against the abjectly poor or the lowly ignorant. From these classes there may come the next generation of bright minds and well-to-do folk. The humble classes are not the meanest. In a debate not long ago which was participated in by over seventy men of the highest intelligence, the question came up as to what would be done with the world of humanity if each one present had autocratic authority to order and to compel execution of any law he might choose to make.

The opinions that seemed to come nearest to unanimity were put into definite form and expressed as follows by one of the debaters:

"If I had the power over the whole world at this moment, I would have every confirmed drunkard removed where he could not offend other human beings. With him I would have every wife-beater, every thief, every liar, every ravisher of women, every murderer, and every criminal of high degree, also sent to keep each other company. I would add to the colony every man and woman who would not do honest work in his or her class and rank. I would let this motley collection make their own laws and rule themselves."

He forgot to add that North America would not be large enough to hold the colony that he was planning.

The upper classes, by bad examples in the way of wasted time and hollow frivolities, to which may be added insincerity, arrogance and countless disagreeable traits, prove to the world that wealth and rank do not make the lady or the gentleman. In the middle classes, with a few exceptions in the upper and lower strata, are found the best type of man and woman. But they are not perfect. The serfs are a part of the plan of creation and cannot be spared.

It is not class distinction but the broad separation of abject criminals and all who cannot bring into the world sane and healthy children, keeping them out of wedlock, and so preventing the increase of unfit offspring. As the world now wags there is being brought into existence about twenty millions of criminals and mentally debased children every twelve months, and the penalty is to be paid sooner or later. Each person reasons that it cannot much affect the present generation and the next will be able to take care of itself. In the course of about fifty more years, if there is no change, the whole realm of civilization will be built upon the lines referred to in the colony-scheme of the committee of seventy.

But the principle is not thereby changed, which says that each man and woman ought to take the matter in hand for the sake of the families that may be raised in their own connection; and, having done that much for themselves, they should proceed to deal with the rights of those who cannot act for themselves.

Sickness of a constitutional character ought to be a bar to marriage if it will result in the birth of weak children who will suffer and pine away before they have seen much of the world. Why entail unnecessary misery on those who have no voice in the matter?

CHAPTER TWENTY-EIGHT

✛✛

WRONG LOVES
HAVE WRECKED
MANY
VALUABLE LIVES

✛✛

❧ *MAGNETIC AFFINITIES* ❧

✛✛

EVERY MAN AND WOMAN who has passed into the changes that denote the age of puberty has been in love. You could no more stop that fever than you could check the onward rush of Niagara. It is nature. It is oftimes animal in its characteristics. The birds thrill and squirm under its tender and exhilarating impulses and the sad-eyed animals all feel its throes. It is more than likely that the spider, the fly, the gnat, the flea, and all that mate in life, have their respective experience, even if they may fail to attach poetry to it.

To birds, a day is a month; and in the few days in which they woo and win their sweethearts, they pass into a large era of history making. With them the love episode is deeper and more passionate than that with human beings. The male is true. Loyalty takes the place of the fickle character in our own race. When the male bird, as is sometimes the case, will sit on the eggs and keep house while his wife hunts bargains, he is not chargeable with lack of domesticity.

Thus we find this little species setting an example to the human family.

The more we study life about us the more we are convinced that nature intends that the two sexes shall come together by the

344

strongest kind of attraction, lest the race shall fail or grow less. Under the most favorable of circumstances it is possible for the increase of offspring to crowd the earth with population in a century; but this tendency is offset by sickness and other causes, until the increase is very slight. In bringing the two sexes together by the strongest impulses, nature creates an unrest in the nervous system that is sure to manifest itself until it is either satisfied or else is conquered by the power of self-magnetism.

Puberty does not dawn suddenly. It is years making its approach felt although it is not fully understood until well established. This phase of human life is responsible for the first of the three loves.

It is the object of magnetism and has no influence over the other sex. It is also overcome or held in check by self-magnetism.

Later on in life, and it need not be very much later, the animal love follows, in case the first love is lost.

Still later on there comes the third love or the affinity, as we wish to call it. Thus we have the three loves. We find that each has a place in the study of personal magnetism, and each must be considered in the light of the rules that apply to human influence.

These rules we will now consider.

"THE THREE LOVES."

These three loves are summed up as follows:

The First Love is the *Fancy* that is created by puberty.

The Second Love is the *Animalism* that is created by sexual desire.

The Third Love is the *Affinity* that follows the union of judgment and profound regard.

Each one of these loves has more or less magnetic importance, and plays a great part in life.

The peculiarity of the first love, which we call fancy, is that it cannot endure disappointment. In some cases this disaster means the ruin either of the mind or of the whole after-career. Many a person has gone into an insane asylum never to emerge again, as the consequence of this misfortune.

This fancy builds the unreal. It sees what is not, and if it is gratified it will continue all through life seeing what is not.

While it is the creation of the approach of puberty, there are many cases where it is delayed for ten or twenty years.

Some persons are bachelors, male or female, because of the slowness of development of the full nature of puberty; the sexual organs and their functions being actually dwarfed during the slow process of development. In persons of this class the fancy may not come until late in middle life.

But when it comes, all the world seems to be different during the period of its existence. Fancy creates a much purer love than animalism, as we shall see. The latter seeks sexual gratification, while fancy never does.

The peculiar fact about the latter is its freedom from any exhibition of animal interest in the opposite sex, no matter at what stage of one's life the feeling may arise. This does not mean that fancy is free from sexual interest after both parties are married; but it does mean that purity of thought and interest will remain as long as it is morally wrong to do otherwise.

So many kinds of testimony have come to hand to sustain this point that we wish to sum them up in the following extracts from evidence that has reached us from thousands of sources:

In one case the fancy dawned when the lad was fifteen years of age and had for its object a young woman of twenty. She agreed to wait for him to grow up, and they were married when he was eighteen. They have both lived in harmony and apparent happiness ever since. Their first child was born when she was thirty.

In another case the fancy originated when the lad was fourteen and had for its object a girl of fifteen. They were always true to each other and were married when she was nineteen. The first child was born when she was twenty-three.

In another case the fancy was not known to exist until the young man was twenty, as he had been ill for several years and his development was delayed. It had for its object a girl of fourteen, and they were married before she was fifteen. They lived happily together, and have had no children.

In another case the fancy originated when the lad was seventeen, and had for its object a woman of twenty-eight. He inherited wealth, and the woman married him before he was twenty, although he had not yet come into possession of the inheritance. No children were ever born. She was a widow before he fell in love with her. When he was twenty-two she secured control of his property and left him. His fancy for her was deep-seated and genuine, and he never took action against her. Later on when she had met reverses he shared with her the little that he had.

In another case a girl of fourteen took a fancy for a man of forty and they were married the same year. He was wealthy and she came from the ranks of the middle classes. He had neither love nor fancy for her and his conduct made her life unhappy. Through his subsequent reverses she was faithful and nursed him back to health when there seemed no hope of his recovery, although there was no merit on his part. Her pathetic regard for his worthless frame after he was unable to support her only confirms the steadfastness of the first love, known as fancy. The object of it may be impelled by the animal love, and therefore not hold the position of the true lover; but the one who has been drawn by fancy to another rarely ever breaks away voluntarily.

In another case a man of nineteen who claimed that he had loved a girl of his own age, courted her for ten years, and they were then married. She died in giving birth to a child. Both husband and wife were thin, and wrinkled. He never paid the slightest attention to any other woman. The child did not survive. The two graves were marked as one, and the man devoted his thoughts to keeping them in grass and flowers in the summer time, and had an expensive monument erected after the lapse of a few years. In his home where he keeps house by himself, he has every evidence of the former presence of the beloved wife. Before her death he had given no attention to religious thoughts, but now is earnest though not demonstrative in his study of matters concerning the world beyond.

This case is not by any means extraordinary.

We know of no instance where any other kind of love except the first love or fancy has ever wrought so deep an impression on the heart of either sex.

Could it be possible for the boys and girls to know each other in the gallant way suggested under the earlier episodes, such as those that relate to the young woman under fifteen and the young man under fifteen, so that the sudden bursting out of the fever of fancy would not come too early nor find them unprepared to meet it with marriage, there would be dearer ties on earth.

It has been truly said that, if there were some way in which the first dawning of love, the fever of fancy, could be delayed until the parties were of marriageable age and condition, it would bless the whole world. But there are the following objections and advantages to be considered together in the study of this question:

1. The fancy of one person may not be responded to by the fancy of the object of such love.

2. Where it is not responded to it is sure to lead to some kind of misfortune.

3. Where it is not responded to, but is met with animal love, it will enslave the person who has originated it; for the other party will know the secure hold which is thus given and will never feel the true appreciation of it.

4. The fancy may be denied by the other, which means that the one who originated it must fight it down, or go through life in disappointment, as did John Greenleaf Whittier. This is a frequent experience.

5. Where the fancy of one person is met by the affinity of another the parties always live most happily.

6. Where the fancy is at first met by animal love, and courtship follows, with a breaking off of the engagement, the fault is always with the party of the animal love. Such a breaking off has been followed by a pining away and death of the one who originated the fancy. We have a record of many such cases.

7. The only solution is in the meeting of two persons each of whom will hold first love for the other; or in the meeting of one who has the fancy and the other the affinity.

It is because of the blending of these several propositions that we find it necessary to study the three loves under one head.

We are firmly convinced that, where there is an exchange of fancy between two persons, there will never be the slightest feeling or thought of sexual interest until marriage comes. This is not true where one side has the fancy and the other the animal love or the affinity. If a girl has the fancy for a young man who has been through his period of fancy with another girl and has met disappointment, he will not give honorable response to the girl of his second choice, and it is of the highest importance that this fact be understood.

Natural magnetism is the instinctive means of defense furnished and maintained by nature for the purpose of securing the happiness and welfare of both sexes in this relationship. It is summed up in a few propositions:

1. *A girl who has never passed out of her first love or fancy will not go wrong with her lover or with any man.*

2. *A girl who has passed out of her first love or fancy is in special need of protection and watchfulness during the period of her teens, for she is easily made the prey of animal magnetism by any man.*

3. *A lad who has not passed out of his first love or fancy will not go wrong, either with his sweetheart or with any other female.*

4. *A lad who has passed out of his first love or fancy will be in special need of protection until he has passed out of his teens, for he will take advantage wherever he can of the other sex. It is this kind of young man that furnishes the bad men of the world.*

5. *The influence of the natural magnetism of the first love is so strong that it awakens every sense of morality and ethical development as well as fidelity to the obligations of life.*

How often we have had some such statement as the following made to us in letters from our students: During the three years from the age of fourteen to the age of seventeen that I gave my love half in silence and half in quiet conversation to the little girl for whom I thought I was created, I never wronged her in thought or deed. Once I was alone with her all through the dark hours of the night when a slight accident compelled us to remain away from home, and she lay in my arms asleep as though I were her mother instead of her lover. Several times we had been together for many hours where the opportunity for wrong doing was most inviting, and no thought came to us of such a thing. It was my sickness and poverty that drove me away a long distance and that gave to her parents the disposition to break the engagement. With tears and struggles she was forced to promise to marry another man, one who was ten years her senior and who had wealth. She since told me that, from the first moment of their engagement, this man was continually trying to ruin her, and that she had to fight him with all her strength. I came back and found that I had lost her. In my desperation I took another girl, one that that was sweet, and pretty, and I found that I did not respect her chastity. To me she was only an animal love. My first fancy never died out, nor did the fancy of that little girl for me. We ran away and got married, and now we are happy. She came to me pure as when she was born, but I cannot say the same of myself.''

As long as the first love has the opportunity for holding its own there will be no disposition to do wrong, and the moral standard will remain at its height.

Because of this fact the parents of young men and women should know something of what is going on in their lives. The father should be the companion and the close personal and confidential friend of his boys, and the mother should be even more in touch with her daughters. It is the best plan to talk freely and fully in all seriousness with the young people and find out what they are doing. Have the talks before there is the chance for fancy developing. Try to shape its direction and select its object.

This may seem difficult but it is not so very hard. There is no such thing, as far as this one relationship and experience are concerned, for a person to be wholly fitted by nature for one other only. Thus a budding fancy that has not yet taken hold may be diverted to another object; and skilled parents have succeeded in doing this. When once it has taken hold, there is the end of all effort. The greater the opposition then, the greater will be the resistance, and the more deplorable the inevitable disaster.

It is like tempting fate.

Talks and training preceding the approach of puberty, with all the preliminary influences thrown around the boys and girls in the tender years within the future is mostly molded, will serve to delay the final blossoming of fancy, and there may be time enough for the direction of its influence.

Fancy is natural magnetism that sways the heart, the mind and the nervous powers of the young man or the young woman until they are made slaves both for their own good and for the good of the world. It is a serious matter when this force of the mother of us all is fought down by those who are not in the direct focus of its purpose. Let time and thought be devoted to the study until it is better understood.

The term fancy as used in our other courses of education that relate to this subject is taken to mean, not the magnetic influence of nature, but the mental flight of the individual; just as the word love may apply to other views taken of the matter. Herein we are studying magnetism and we are looking at the magnetic side of the subject.

There is no magnetism that so securely binds a person as this form.

It may come late in life, but that is not to be ordinarily expected.

There are women who do not have their fancy till they are out of the teens or the twenties. They may declare that they have been in love but have outgrown it, but this is due to the fact that they do not know themselves. There are men who have never had a fancy until they have reached their twenties or their thirties.

But it is true that the first love is either a fancy or it is animal love. In ninety-nine instances out of every hundred, the first love is the fancy or true affection. Normal individuals have all experienced it, and some have had it before they were ten or twelve years of age.

This is rather a dream. The boy will have his day dream, and the girl will have hers.

But the deep-seated fancy is real love that plans marriage and the building of the home and all that.

The dream is sometimes called the fancy, and we have often referred to it as such, but it is really only the first signal of the coming love. It finds the most extraordinary objects for its flights, such as great disparity in age, and wide departures from the exercise of good judgment. It never has resulted in marriage unless it has deepened into the true fancy. As a rule it is willing to let go and take up a new conquest, which the fancy will not willingly do.

The first love will not magnetize the object on which it is exerted nor will it be able to impress itself on such party. The only hope for it is the reticence of the maiden and her steadfast endeavor to keep from making any demonstration of her feelings. She should confide at once in her mother, but the latter must not crush out the opportunity where the young man is heart free and is sincere and capable of making a good man; for this kind of help is the most wholesome that can come to him in all his life.

A typical case that was well managed was the following:

A boy of sixteen who had been constantly in his father's charge during his spare time, was the object of the fancy of a girl of fourteen who had seen him in church. His father was a carpenter, and the girl's father was a machinist. The young folks had both learned to dance when they were under ten years of age, but had not taken much interest in it for several years since. This accomplishment had made them familiar with the society of the sexes, so that the morbid embarrassment that so often attends young people, had not marred their conduct.

The girl at once went to her mother, and the latter went to the boy's mother. It was agreed between them that the two young folks should be brought together. The result was that the boy awakened to the fancy that was the first impulse of love in his nature. They were then friends for four years, and afterward were married.

Delay after there is an exchange of fancy is an advantage, as it will show the fact of sincerity on the one hand or the mere dream on the other.

This dream condition must be looked after, as it is most fickle.

When the fancy has not met response, or has been defeated, as by death or interference, or by other cause, the party who had originated it is pretty sure to go to the bad in greater or less degree. There is no longer an object to be respected, worshiped, adored, exalted, but only one or more to be hunted down like prey and taken advantage of. The girl who has thus passed out of her fancy is either set and sharp in her disposition, with the prospect of becoming an old maid, or as is often the case she will go to the bad on the first magnetism of the man who comes her way and pleases her.

As it is a difficult thing for both sexes to come together on the first love, there are more than seventy-five per cent of them adrift in the stream catching at straws, making marriages of policy, or of convenience, or in any way they can. Adventurers and adventuresses are thus given to the world. It is a search for prey in which both sides are engaged.

One of the most common remarks is that which says: "You are the first person I ever really loved." The word really implies on its face that there has been love but that it has not been real. But the fact is that if there has been any love whatever it is, in a hundred cases to one, the fancy which we have described, and the party has walked out of it. To be forgiven for making the statement that "you are the first person whom I ever really loved," there must be a belief that the teller of that falsehood has been deceived by a genuine sincerity in the assertion. The fever of love often clouds the memory, and the summer girl who accepts a promiscuous betrothal may declare with the tears of the actress in her deeply lashed and softly flashing brown eyes that each and every subject of the moment is her first, her only, her last and her eternal love, and so pass on to the next.

Animal love is desire to be with the other sex.

It is magnetic and has immense influence over both the party suffering from it and certain others who may come within its reach. Given a reasonable prospect of being agreeable, or persona grata, a man who has passed out of his fancy, who meets a female who has likewise passed out of her fancy, and there will be wrong-doing at the very first opportunity unless the female is keen from past experience and wishes to lead the man on. She has the mood to yield to his magnetism. He is swayed by his own impulses, she by hers, and each by the other's.

On the other hand the woman who sets up an intention to work upon the sexual feelings of a man who has need of companionship with the female, will make havoc with his moral and physical being, and leave him a wreck in both. Properly managed by a knowledge of man, the most repulsive of women sexually may claim great victories and wear many scalps. There are women who do not allow men to do them wrong in this respect, who are able to pass as ultra virtuous and yet seem to be passionate, by which double charm they secure a firm hold on the will-power of the man.

Many cases of such control and the laws by which it is worked have been related in the course of training, called Two Sexes.

All we have time to say in this work is to warn both sexes against every display of tendency toward the development of animal magnetism.

If you have passed out of the mood of fancy, do not stop in the mood of animal love.

The only destiny for you if you wish happiness and safety is in the realm of the affinity.

Before we take this matter up let us warn you against the

magnetism of animal passion. It will engulf you from your own condition, as your feelings soon become your master; and it will lead you to the power of others who will even more seriously harm you. That kind of magnetism is the hardest of all to resist. You can see it everywhere.

There are concerns that sell obscene books and pictures because they know that there is always a market for such things. There are playwrights that produce just as bad plays as they can to be within the law, knowing that a cleverly constructed drama of the obscene type will draw better audiences than if the bad quality were omitted. Theatrical managers often like to have it known that their play-houses are to present such plays. One of the most advanced methods of advertising a play is as follows:

The Monday performance is the general introduction to the new city, except where Sunday theatres are allowed. On the next morning the public, including those who may go and those who do not expect to go, look in the papers for the review of the play, which review is supposed to be written by the papers themselves but which in fact is in type before the play is presented in that city. In the review there are hints about a great and powerful drama, interlarded with remarks that the play, despite its great value to the dramatic world, and its tremendous interests, is too suggestive to be permitted by the authorities. Here is an exact quotation: "The author has done the art a splendid service by writing what is probably the strongest and the most important play of the last ten years, and his work speaks volumes for American skill in this regard. But we must, in all frankness, state that he has unnecessarily dragged into the play a number of exciting incidents that are not to be tolerated on this side of the water. Suggestiveness is at home in Paris but not here. Fair women all over the fashionable audience blushed a deep crimson at some of the situations, the truth of which they recognized only too clearly. Let the police but see this performance and it will not fare any better than did Sapho some years ago." The result of this notice, which was varied in the several morning papers, was that the theatre was packed on every occasion during the week. Women and daughters came forth, wondering where the fault was, and men who had gone to see more females blush, were sorely stricken because the play was highly moral and extremely commonplace.

On what principle did thousands of people flock to the playhouse if there is no magnetism in the suggestion of the sexual nature?

It is this very magnetism that will dethrone the most astute mind, whether of the business man, the banker, the financier, or the shrewd woman.

Not long ago a man wrote to us saying that he had knocked around long enough; he felt the need of a companion; and he was to be married to the first one he could find, and he would not lose any time finding one and marrying her. He made a business of finding one at once. During the hunt he remained virtuous so that he would be more vigorous on the honeymoon; but, while he found a woman who, like him, felt the need of a companion, and some one to provide a home for her, he and she were brought together solely by animal magnetism. There could be but one ending for such an arrangement.

And that is the history of ninety-seven or ninety-eight per cent of all the love affairs today, where the law of the affinities is not observed.

As the fancy is too uncertain of meeting its mate with a fancy too, and as the second love is merely animal passion, the third and last of the three loves is of necessity the only one that can abide or that should be considered when the fancy-mood has passed.

We are now to speak of the bodily affinity.

The spiritual affinity is treated of in Universal Magnetism, and the affinity of the higher sexual being is dealt with in the book of Sex Magnetism.

Here we are speaking of the magnetism that brings two bodies together, including the mind and all the attributes that make earth a pleasant abiding place because of happy marital relations.

The affinity is the third love. It is magnetic in that it sends out influence and ever is self-magnetized.

In the first love there is self-magnetism with no power whatever over the object. Such a love cannot win.

In the second love, the person who has the fever is magnetized by it and is also capable of exerting a vast amount of power over the opposite sex. Aaron Burr, one of the most magnetic men ever known, but who lent his powers to all that was good and bad as his whims directed him, was able to overcome a woman by the first touch of his hand, and never had to use his strength in so doing. Unless a woman was specially magnetic herself, or was true to her husband by reason of holding a first love for him, this remarkable man had only to approach her to make the conquest sure. So daring was he that he would step behind a curtain in a crowded room, and there wrong the woman who went with him, when the mere act of lifting the corner of the curtain would reveal the crime.

In both the first and second love, there is self-magnetism; in the second and third loves there is outward magnetism, which means that others are influenced by the power. In the third love there is no self-magnetism.

These three distinctions should be kept in mind. They show the characteristics of the three loves, and also hold each one up as being different from the others. Thus, to sum up:

The first love magnetizes the possessor, but has no outward power, which means that it has no power over others. It is fancy.

The second love magnetizes its possessor, and has power over others. It is animalism.

The third love has no self-power; but wields a great influence over others. It is the union of the deepest regard with the greatest judgment. It is an exalted love.

Now comes the peculiar fact in relation to each of the three kinds of love.

The first comes but once and abides forever if there is a prospect of winning and holding its object. It is not transferable.

The second is like the love of the cow, the horse, the bull, the hen, the rooster, and most of the animal kingdom. It is a cat and dog love; and yet is almost universal. It is the love that makes divorce possible and even probable.

The third is transferable, as is the second. But the third is true wherever it finds its mate. If that mate dies this same love can take a new partner, unless there is some sentiment in the blood to the contrary.

Now how is the affinity originated and how does it differ from the first and second loves?

In the first place human judgment comes into play.

This is a necessity.

More and more in the era where the spirits of adventure, blackmail and mercenary gain are not involved, the tendency is to set up marriages founded upon the exercise of the judgment. This is well, and should be encouraged.

In the second place the deep and respectful regard for the object of the affinity is being cultivated and taken as a necessary basis for the union. This is still better.

Here we have two qualifications for marriage, good judgment and deep regard. They have been employed a long time, but only in rare cases. Certain axioms should be kept in mind. They will stand the deepest investigation.

A wealthy man should marry a wealthy woman.

A millionaire should marry a millionaire.

A person in middle life should marry one in middle life.

A poor man should marry a poor girl.

A slum fellow should marry a slum woman.

A criminal should marry a criminal, if married at all.

A coarse and clumsy lout should marry a woman of his **exact** calibre.

An un-refined man should marry an un-refined woman.

A refined man should marry a refined woman.

An educated man should marry an educated woman.

A home-lover should marry a home-lover.

A boarding-house-lover should marry a boarding-house woman.

A hotel-lover should marry a hotel-woman; that is one who likes to live in a hotel.

A club man should marry a woman who regards home and the society of her family as bores.

A literary woman should marry a literary man.

A super-sensitive woman should marry a super-sensitive man.

A lover of nature should marry a lover of nature.

A lover of the city should marry a lover of the city.

A brawny, muscular woman should marry a brawny, muscular man.

The tale about marrying opposites is very good until it comes to harnessing two horses together who are not in any way able to pull together. The same judgment that is used in getting horses to pull alike is required in greater degree with the marriage problem.

Opposites in tastes do not agree; but opposites in many other respects are an advantage. Thus the young girl is often happier with the man of mature judgment and more years. The short girl often likes the tall man. The stout woman often likes the slim man.

A literary woman in a house where the husband expects to find the home functions at their best estate is both a nuisance and a discord. She should either not marry or should make arrangements to meet the tastes of her husband for home life.

The educated and the ignorant will not pull together, any more than the racer and the draught horse will do well in double harness. This law is without exception. Wealth and poverty sometimes blend, but it is unnatural, unless one has earned the wealth during the era of marriage, in which case the other may or may not be a coadjutor.

Judgment must be cultivated. It will not crop out of itself. If there is an attempt to run counter to its dictates there will be trouble sooner or later, and the man will learn life's lesson by the throes of bitter experiences, while the wife will go often home to her mamma with tears and tales of woe.

Judgment should be cultivated until it becomes the best of the fine arts; for it is the doing of the best things in living and the taking of the most exalted steps in these solemn associations, that averts errors.

In addition to this excellent quality of the mind and soul there must also be a deep and lasting regard for the object of the affinity. This regard must be well founded, not temporary. Study the woman or the man and know just how the mind and the habits are constructed, so that there will be less that is disagreeable to be found out later on, and at a time when it will entail sorrow to learn the lesson. Regard must have something substantial on which to be founded. The kind of man that a woman will appreciate is one who is very active along useful lines, one who is progressive along conservative lines, one who is manly and chivalrous, and one who knows how to show supreme respect for her sex.

The kind of woman that a man will appreciate is one who knows the chemistry of food, the art and the science of wholesome cookery, the care of the house from one part to another, and the methods by which home is made attractive and beautiful. He likes a woman who is active but not strenuous, one who can find duties that are real and substantial and who has not been reared to think that work and interest in the action of the day are solely ordained for menials, nor the woman who hates to rise at a reasonable hour in the morning, and wishes to have all the world bring her a round of satisfying pleasures up to the very hour of retiring.

Here is the kind of woman who may or may not marry. She is right where we can analyze her life. She has a very wealthy father, and she thinks that his wealth will some day come in large share to her. Many men think so, too, and they pay all the attention to her that she will permit. Several of these men, thinking that a little display of money will move her, have gone to the last dollar they can borrow to effect this flashing triumph. But she has been trained day after day to regard the men as seeking her for her money. Her father says that he will not support an idle son-in-law, and so the impecunious must stand aside for a number of years.

There are many worthy men of her own rank in wealth who would make excellent husbands for worthy wives, but they know her and they have known her for years. The town in which they live has less than twenty thousand inhabitants, and so it is not difficult to know a girl. And she has some brothers who are friendly with these men; a sort of friendship that counts value.

Why is it that these wealthy bachelors will not propose to her?

Let us see what they are to get if they win the lady. She is about thirty years old, and should have been married long ago. But she went to a seminary and came out of it with affectations that a sensible man wishes to tide over until time has had an opportunity to iron them out. So there was waiting on that account.

Having graduated from a seminary, where she acquired these affectations and a diploma which she has framed, all her mental progress came to a full stop. A feather colliding with a stone wall could not be more effectually checked than was her mind's improvement from and ever after that graduation and that diploma.

It is true that she looks sometimes at the daily papers and absorbs the sensations when there are any. It is true that she has a long list of magazines that she culls over and reads when she is not too tired to hold them in her hands. It is true that she can play many different games of cards, and thus entertain her friends with a splendor that would have dazzled the Queen of Sheba had that personage been brought within the dominion of this mass of laziness. But her mind stopped growing when she got the diploma and that was a long time ago. The paper on which it is printed is yellow as an indication that it keeps in touch with the brain energy of the woman who is described on its face.

She does not get up early in the morning; to be at the breakfast table before nine o'clock is to her a most annoying incident. From the time the sun is up until after the morning meal is ended, nothing is doing in which she is interested. From the time she finishes her breakfast until the period of the noon meal, she is waking up to the fact that there is busy life all about her on every hand. She has nothing to do with it however. The afternoon is spent in attention to her personal embellishment and some social duties; she calls them duties, but they serve no usefulness to any one, not even to herself. Then she must eat again, and the evening is at hand. If nothing has been provided for her pleasure she is discontented with life

She has an appetite when she is not taking drugs. She can eat, but she can be dainty, too. She never uses a spoon for a liquid that can be induced to poise on the tine of a fork. This, in fact, is her chief accomplishment. She can be dainty when there is some one looking at her who may learn to admire her. But she can eat. She stuffs three times a day regularly and at odd intervals between. Then she must have her sweetmeats, and all sorts of other things to eat at, lest the digestive apparatus have a rest, and her medicines might also have a rest.

In all her career the long year through, she does no work, and has no ambition. Because it is the style to be charitable she makes a great fuss over some such work, and knows absolutely nothing about it. If it were not the style she would not do it. Knowing in her innermost nature that she is a blot on creation and that she carries from morn till night a lazy carcass, she feels that there must be some way of atoning for the crime of sheer idleness, and so she makes the greatest sort of an enterprise over the least attempt to do a stroke of good in the world.

What does a man want of this acme of laziness?

What service would she perform for him except to grunt and to moan and fuss and demand attention that he loathes to give, and get in the way of honest people who seek to do some worthy duty in life? She is the typical woman, not in the ranks of duty-performers, but in the mass of lazy wealth.

Charity may cover a multitude of sins, but it cannot conceal from God the hideous wrong of the time waster. People are not put in the world for the purpose of being waited on. There are duties everywhere, and they are not the work that is called charity, but the greater work of looking after the home and those who wish to live in it in peace and comfort. The word home is the earthly word from the same source and meaning as the grander word heaven. The latter is the home hereafter, and the former is the home on this planet. The three noblest words in any language, are mother, home and heaven.

The woman who will make a worthy mother, a genuine mother, not a lazy time-killing mother, not a card-playing and gambling mother, but a mother who loves her home and its duties and who is at the helm of her little dominion at all times, having its success and prowess at heart above all other considerations in life, is the magnetic woman. Let the man of position, of wealth, of honest love, be convinced that such a woman is awaiting his offer, and she will not be left long without an earnest lover.

Take heaven out of the universe and you take God out of all religion. The Creator is made the personification of the bridegroom in the Bible and the bride is awaited in heaven. No other marriage occurs there. The sexes will consist of God and nature, not of men and women. But the idea of home prevailing everywhere is not to be denied. If there is no heaven there is no hereafter, and no happiness beyond the grave.

What heaven is to the soul, home on earth is to the man and woman who are worthy to inherit the home beyond. The home-hater here is the hell-lover there. Everywhere in and out of the realm of religion, in nature as in the great books of teachings, we find the instruction to make the home, and to maintain its sacred character, not in a religious sense, but in the serious phases of existence. Out of the home come the ties and the blessings that make age acceptable and all the duties of life attractive.

The world today is full of lazy women of affluence. They are of no value to their husbands and to the world. As we have said they make a social display with more or less of cant and bustling activity when there is a charity function to receive their attention; but this is the slimeiest mockery at that true charity which, as the Bible says, should begin at home. Such mockery offends God.

The woman who would be magnetic cannot be lazy. Nor can she deceive a man by her pretenses to useful activity. One of the first questions that a man will ask himself is this: What would I have to contend with if I were to marry this woman? And then he proceeds to find out.

From the experience of other men who have met their Waterloo in marriage, he would find the woman before marriage making every possible show to convince him that he is getting a bargain. She dresses in the richest style and has a variety of gowns that amaze him. She is as attractive as art can make her. She is pleasant, and all that. But he is a bachelor or nearing the age when he will be so termed, and therefore gowns and smiles are not meat and drink to his heart. He wants a woman who will be his life-partner, who will be in sympathy with his ambitions, who will advise with him, think with him, and give time and feeling to his cares and responsibilities.

This woman who, before marriage, is pleasing, dainty, eats soup with a fork, plays cards brilliantly, smiles at him and uses coaxing tones when he talks to her in private, who is full to the brim of the pretence of activity and sounds the keynote of many a grand idea, is just a lump of helpless beef after marriage. Merely this and nothing more.

The fact somehow leaks out.

Not long ago a man told his business partner that the greatest mistake he had ever made was to get married. And the partner came back with the question:

"But why did you not find that out before you took the step?"

"I did not know. I wished a home. I wished a woman who would be to my home what I try to be to my business, helpful and interested. I have a wife who gets up in the morning because she cannot lie abed all day. Instead of being a helpmeet, she is a helpless woman who must be waited on. She has females come into the house at night and they play cards till it is near one o'clock; then my wife goes to bed with a raging headache after berating me for my lack of interest in the game; and she must be waited on in the morning to such an extent that I am late at my office and my business suffers. If I had this thing to do over again, I would never marry unless I could find a woman who, to my perfect knowledge, is willing to share with me the duties of life."

The partner did not exactly follow the advice; but he did something better. He ascertained the habits of the woman to whom he was about to engage himself, and refused to be trapped, as she was the common type of woman who hates the duties of home-making. He then followed this experience with more than a dozen other women, discarding all chances that seemed to him to be of the same character; and at length came upon the one particular affinity that he felt sure was destined for him.

It was no easy task.

His method consisted in the employment of a private detective who was sent out by a concern that could be trusted. The detective was a woman who was introduced, through influential friends, into the best of the local society, and was vouched for. In her growing friendships for the young women of her own age, she was able to learn the private habits of those in whom this man might be interested. The sentimental world will call it a cold blooded bid for a wife. But any man of wealth can enter a city where there are thousands of young women who are candidates for marriage, and he can deliberately study them by the hundred and make his selection in his own mind, and then woo and win the one that seems to him to be his affinity. This is both legitimate and divorce-saving; and, in these days, a divorce-saving device is most important in social economy.

The partner found, by the aid of the detective, a woman who was three years his junior. She had been in love several times, and had been betrothed twice; once because her affianced was a drinking man; and the second time because her lover sought to effect her ruin in preference to marrying her. It was believed and is probably the fact that she was sexually pure. She loved home life, and helped her mother in the care of the house. It was one of her self-imposed duties to make the tour of every part of the house once during the forenoon, once during the afternoon, and once during the evening, and to know what was going on. She studied the house and the home life in it, not only for her parents but for the three brothers she loved; and it is a fact that has since been investigated and proved true that her father and all her brothers were in love with the home and with her, and spent their evenings there almost the year round. Few homes have such attractions. This young woman was not afraid to do any kind of work, although servants were employed and she was above the necessity of labor. She was in perfect health and enjoyed life to its utmost.

The partner sought out the girl in such a way as to make his appearance seem accidental. There was no cut and dried method in his wooing. He lost no time and did not hurry. He was bent on having her for his wife. No one was taken into his secret. Her parents both knew him and thought well of him. After the introduction and a call or two, he found that she had abandoned all thought of marrying, owing to her two broken engagements; and he spent a full year in breaking down this prejudice.

She then told him that she had no love in her heart and never could have. To him she appeared so worthy, so noble, so frank and so true to all the finer instincts of her sex, that he would not allow her to say no; nor would she say yes; A second year passed, and she had grown to like him. Her tastes were somewhat different from his. He ascertained what they were; he studied and created in his own mind similar tastes; and finally he went so far as to buy her a ring. He put it on her finger, and during a rather long visit that evening, which began early and lasted till late, she did not remove the ring, although she declared that she could not become his affianced wife. The next time he called, she still wore the ring but persisted that she would never be engaged.

One day he secured a marriage license and a clergyman, with the quiet consent of her parents, and a marriage that was almost as much of a surprise to her as to some others, took place. When the usual question was asked, if she would love him, etc., she said: "I do not love this man. I respect him. He respects me. I esteem him as highly as any woman can esteem a man she is willing to marry, and this to me seems higher than love." And they let it go at that.

The man said to his partner: "This woman who has now become my wife was selected because to my mind she was the most worthy of all the women I have ever met. I really do not love her in the sentimental sense, but I shall be true to her, and my first, last and eternal thought night and day will be to make her happy."

Four years later, when the elder partner had been divorced, he was told by this younger man: "I selected my wife with all the care and judgment that I could employ. She has made a home for me and every minute of the past four years has been a heaven-on-earth.''

This case was an instance of affinities.

The affinity is the result of a combination involving the exercise of judgment and profound respect. Let that judgment be as nearly perfect as possible, and let the other party be one for whom the deepest respect and regard can be entertained, and the only remaining thing is for the two parties to meet and establish the affinity.

To win a woman whom you do not know, let all the methods be those that are usual in the grade of society to which you belong. Attempt no other style of conquest. When once you have the right to address the lady, do so as a social acquaintance. Do not presume that she will say ''yes'' in response to a proposal made within a short time after you have met her on terms of familiar friendship. The oft-quoted charge that a woman's no means yes, is based upon the fact that the masculine gender is privileged to make the proposal, and does so at too early a stage of the acquaintance. Her no would not be necessary if the man were to wait until there has been established between them some evidence of an affinity.

A man ought to know the bent of a woman's mind well enough before he proposes to make the formal question superfluous. The men who win the best suits rarely if ever ask any question. Matters shape themselves without the use of a catechism.

''THE FIRST STEPS IN MARRIAGE.''

As the chances are so slight of a fancy ripening into marriage that is mutual, owing to the difficulty of finding the fancy originating from both parties, it may be safely asserted that the only betrothal that is to be approved of is that between affinities, or where the choice is made with the most excellent judgment and is attended by genuine regard and respect by both as well.

Such a union with time enough between the betrothal and the wedding to enable the two to determine if the judgment has been correct, will be fruitful in happiness.

There is no time in the whole history of marriage when the husband and wife should do more planning and preparation than in the first steps. These are the first twenty-four hours after the ceremony, and the first month following, and the first year added.

It is said that marriage is a great revealer of human nature, that its freedom gives rights that cannot be had between any two other human beings, and the familiarity breeds all sorts of new conditions in the mind and the affections.

What these are we wish to see.

There is never a time when restraint is so necessary as in these periods following the ceremony. The restraint should be exercised by both the husband and the wife.

Many things should be known before the marriage, such as the physical health of the two; but with this we have nothing to do. A person lacks in magnetism who is a sieve; that is, who will tell over the details of earlier life. The grounds for divorce have been laid in a large number of cases in the first few hours of wedlock.

To begin with, most men, if not practically all, have episodes in their past that should be kept to themselves. If there are confessions to be made, they should all be made before the minister was engaged to unite the parties, not after the curtain has been drawn on the first night. Many a couple tell over their past faults with the other sex. It causes a distinct feeling of horror in the mind of the listener and the respect that is necessary to the establishing of the affinity is lost and may never be recovered.

There were over three hundred marriages brought to a termination in this country in the year 1904 within twelve hours after the knot was tied; in eighteen of them the woman refused to live longer with the husband, and in the remaining cases the husbands secured confessions from their wives to the effect that they had been guilty of wrong with other men.

Magnetism means poise of mind, and the power to retain a secret forever and forever. Some persons claim that there should be no secret between husband and wife. If this claim is well founded then the confession should be made prior to wedlock, and the other party given the opportunity of withdrawing from the compact. But what has occurred between one of the parties and some former person, if not known in time to cancel the engagement, should not be made known at a time when it will weaken the knot and possibly break it.

The refusal to make a confession need not be point blank, as that will excite suspicion. Thus where a person says that she will not tell, it may be presumed that she has something to tell. On the contrary if she asserts her womanhood in the proper manner the husband will not follow the inquiry.

It seems that many husbands use promises to forgive if the wives will speak frankly, and they pretend to make light of the matter until they secure the confession; after which there is a coolness that never is overcome.

The true husband will ask nothing of the past and will not allow himself to think of it. The true wife will also take her husband for what he is and is to be to her, and not for what he has been in his past. Let the dividing line be drawn from the time of the ceremony, and allow no thought or remark to bring up the shortcomings that may be hidden in the preceding period of each life.

This is one of the first steps in marriage.

Another step is to avoid the familiarity that tends to breed contempt. Flesh is property, but let it not be usable at the wanton will of the other party. Study to pursue the most exalted refinement during all the years of marriage, consistent with the privileges; and let this step be taken at the outset, never to be abandoned.

Then the next thing to keep in mind is the fact that the wife is the closest of all relations to the man, and she should be so considered at all times. No one on earth is to be preferred to her. Under all circumstances let her be first and most prominent in thought and in deed.

By the same rule the wife should prefer the husband to all other living beings.

A firm resolve should be made by both, not only at the start, but daily as long as life shall last, to the effect that there must be an abiding loyalty each to the other at all times. This will not be an effective resolve if it is made at the beginning and then is salted down for a life time. It will be forgotten, and inch by inch there will come a willingness to let this grand character of marriage be lost in careless methods. What is contained in the idea of loyalty is the cultivation of a firm belief and faith in each other. Doubt, suspicions, jealousy, and fault-finding grow rapidly into great images that obscure the horizon of happiness. The loyal husband will not entertain under any circumstances any doubt, suspicion or jealousy of his wife, nor will he do or say anything that will cause her to have any doubt, suspicion or jealousy of him.

A loyal wife will never entertain any doubt, suspicion or jealousy of her husband, nor will she ever give him cause by her conduct or speech to be doubtful, suspicious or jealous of her.

This is loyalty.

It embraces more. There must be no fault-finding. What she does that is wrong, let him overlook; and she must not see in him any fault whatever. Stand up for each other, think there are no such people in the whole wide world as the two, yourself and your counterpart. Let this feeling of pride be cultivated.

Whatever nature you choose to develop toward each other, will come as a matter of cultivation. By encouragement you can learn to admire and to exalt each other, or to put down and despise each other. It is all a mirror of the heart.

These efforts are magnetic.

You cannot uplift another person in your opinion without doing so to some extent in fact. This law has been well tested and will always prove itself.

If you wish to magnetize your counterpart, the best step to take is to really begin to believe in him or her, and let that faith grow day by day. It will show itself, and you cannot conceal it. You need not say one word on the subject, for there is something that will carry the story better than words or action. All we ask is that the feeling of loyalty and of pride and of high opinion be cultivated and increased, and the results will come about by the law of magnetism.

These steps should be taken in the beginning of the marriage experience.

"ASTRAY."

If the wedding has been the culmination of the second love, there will be very little chance to save it, unless the laws of magnetism can come to the rescue.

The second love is animalism.

The body of the woman fascinated you, or the form and passion of the man drew you to him. There was the temptation and perhaps the feeling that it was better to be married than to be paramours, so you consented, with the result that the aftermath is loathing of the situation.

You would give all you have or ever expect to have if you could be free again; and the chances are ten to one that you would soon be in the same kind of chaos.

The animalism in love is the falsest of all inspirations. The cow is as willing for one bull as for another to visit her. The bull even prefers a variety. Husbands and wives who are brought together by the sexual passion are merely legalized prostitutes and the children of such a union cannot be sweet and affectionate, nor be held in restraint as they grow up.

But as such a wedding has occurred, the remedy is not separation or divorce, but to apply the laws of magnetism and come out of the animalism into the affinity. That this can be done has been many times proved, and we are positive that you can do it. The law of affinity is one of the grandest and the most effective of the principles of magnetism.

The first thing to do is to get together. If you cannot do this, then get ready to get together.

You know the tastes of your counterpart. Study them. If there are some that can be adopted by you, adopt them. Do not drop from your disposition to be refined and conservative, but take your mental interests along the same road as those of your counterparts.

The union of the better tastes is magnetic and has done more to maintain the peaceful trend of married life than any other one cause. It applies to those who are not astray as well as to those who are.

Sometimes the union of one preferred taste or mental interest will of itself bring about a more harmonious feeling.

If you are a man, do not show an animal interest in your wife. Let her sway your conduct and do not seek to influence in the least. Hold yourself in full restraint, for restraint is one of the great laws of magnetism, as you will see by referring to the early pages of this work. True enjoyment is deeper than the animal nature that knows only play, quarrel and sleep.

If you are a woman, show all the attention that your husband can ask or wish, and be gentle and refined in so doing.

Read all that has been stated under the first steps in marriage and apply them all. If your pride is sensitive, let that suffer quietly. Humility shows itself in words and action, but loyalty shows itself in the regard that may be wholly independent of both. It reaches the other party by the process of magnetism, as has been explained.

The next step toward bringing together the hearts that are astray is to build up affinities. Read what has been said under the third love, and apply it. The hub around which the affinities revolve is home life, and this must be studied as a high science. Cultivate a genuine interest in establishing and maintaining the principles of home life. A thousand ideas might be suggested at this point, for there are countless things that can be done, one at a time, and all little by little, to make the home attractive and the methods of enjoying it inviting. These must be left to your own ingenuity. But the home must not be neglected. The husband who loves to stay in it during his spare hours, will find a wife who will not leave it, and who will make it more and more attractive as he evinces an interest in its many details of comfort and lets her know he appreciates them.

The wife may remain in evenings while her husband goes out; but the husband will rarely remain at home if his wife forms the habit of going out. If she is to be left alone, she will shrink to the narrowest compass in the house and seek to find enjoyment in her half-prison. On the other hand, if he spends all his evenings at home, she will enlarge the scope of living existence, occupying more rooms, and having the house a home instead of a cold and cheerless room barren of even one aspect that is inviting.

The initiatory rests with the husband in most cases, and he should make any and every sacrifice, no matter how great, to remain with her every evening. It is here that the first astray occurs. Some husbands induce their wives to honestly believe that they, the males, are in the way. The cigar smoked in the house is not only not agreeable to the woman despite her claim that she just loves tobacco smoke, but is positively injurious to her health, as is all smoking in the house. But she encourages him to spend the evening out so that she need not tell him that the cigar hurts her lungs.

This is not right. The woman will have some difficulty in setting up an affinity where her husband must either smoke indoors or else go out for the whole evening. She should control him and thus influence him to adopt different habits. In seeking to establish this control she must pass through the course in magnetism that precedes this book, and must also adopt the methods taught all through the present work. Failure cannot be possible if she does this.

With the husband influenced to take the initiatory the wife will then have in her hands the success of the undertaking.

Assuming that you are the husband and that your wife is refractory, the process is to make yourself not only magnetic but attractive as a man under the plan stated in the study of the third love. In no case will the estrangement continue. It is much better to heal the wound than to cut off the limb.

"AFFINITIES, REAL, IMAGINARY, NATURAL AND CULTIVATED."

A real affinity is the third love.

As has been repeatedly stated it depends on the union of correct judgment, formed after full analysis of character and habits, with the respect that the dearest and most exalted friendship will inspire. If these elements do not combine, the affinity is not real.

It is imaginary when it is impelled largely by the second love.

The second love often drives a person who wishes to be moral into marriage for the purpose of gratifying an animal passion. It is full of disappointment and regrets. The true affinity is never touched by either of these debasing influences.

The natural affinity is one that exists between persons who are alike in tastes and in all physical and mental characteristics, as far as semblance is possible between two persons of opposite sexes. Under the influence of a natural affinity both husband and wife come to look like each other, or to show signs of a tendency to be alike in lineament and mannerisms. There are thousands of such affinities, and we have never yet known of trouble between the parties. Harmony seems to be the watchword.

To establish the natural affinity, the ages should be nearly alike, the husband being slightly older. A difference of five or ten years is not by any means a discrepancy in the age. It is so close as to be regarded as about the same age for both, if the husband is the older.

It is natural for the man to be about six inches taller than the woman, and this helps to establish the natural affinity. The case of the tall woman and the short man is a wide discrepancy. It is much better for all tall people to find their affinities among themselves, and for short people to combine with each other. There are many cases where the husband and wife are quite small of stature. Against this claim is the argument that two small parents will produce dwarfs for offspring. This might seem true, were it not for the fact that some of the tallest men and women living are born of parents both of whom are small; and some very small children are born of tall parents. We have an instance at hand where a child weighing less than two pounds was born from a woman who was unusually tall, the husband being nearly six feet high.

But it is often true that small parents produce small children.

The sameness of age and of size should also be met with a sameness of weight or breadth. This tendency is the result of temperament, and a union of temperaments is an advantage.

The most common illustration of the natural affinity is that which is included in the real as far as rank socially and financially is concerned, as well as status in education and refinement; and in the agreement as to size, age, weight and physical endowments are involved.

Stupid people get along much better with stupid people in marriage. To wed an ass is not good judgment if the other party is intelligent, and the fact that the former has plenty of money does not lift the alliance from a case of adventure.

There are many unions of persons who are almost idiots enough to enter an asylum; and it seems strange that these people get together by some hook or crook. It is probably due to the fact that there is nothing else left, and no choice remains.

Cultivated affinities are most excellent and include some of the best romances in the history of wedlock. We have given one instance of this kind of affinity in the case of the partner who sought out a first class girl by the aid of a detective and ascertained what were her tastes so that he might cultivate them in himself.

It is possible to create an interest in anything that is worthy and sensible; and if the man whom you would like to wed is of far different tastes and habits from your own, it is not a difficult matter to select some few of the most prominent characteristics that invite the attention of your sex, and bring yourself into the habit of liking them and actually adopting them.

We will suppose that he is fond of art, of paintings and the works of the great masters. This is not generally a born taste. It can be cultivated. But it will not do to merely talk of the art, for that will bore the man much more than silence. A lady who thought she would win a man who was regarded as an expert critic in art, said to him on every occasion of their meeting: "Oh, I do so love a beautiful painting. I just dote on the art, etc." This was not a cultivation of a taste, but a mere falsehood, apparent on its face. To cultivate a thing it must be studied, analyzed, adopted in one way or another, and made an intelligent basis of appreciation. It is not necessary to be a painter or to be the thing you admire.

All persons have a decided liking for some particular method of living. Some prefer the city, some the country, some the free and open life of the country in or near the city, and some the life of the city in the surroundings of the country. Some dislike the solid comforts of home, and others crave them as a thirsty man craves the water from the cool brook. Pretences are deception that will re-act in every instance. The genuine taste and preference should be really cultivated until it is really liked. This is not a difficult result to achieve.

In summing up this part of the present work we do not wish to leave the impression that we are opposed to the doctrine of a marriage founded on love. Most contracts are made with such care that they are sustained by the parties and by the courts; but the contract of marriage is so disjointed and chaotic that it is easily broken by the parties with the aid of the courts. These facts point to something that is radically wrong, which means that the root of marriage, supposed to be love, is the cause of much misfortune in the making of what should be the most solemn and most permanent of all agreements and compacts.

When a tree shows decay on its trunk or in its branches, the first place to seek the cause is in the roots. Love is the root of marriage. If there is but one kind of love, what kind is that? But there are many cases of happy love-making in this relationship that never ends until death comes, and there is no animalism in the affection. This is not the general character of the love that brings hasty and repentant wedlock.

It is a fact that animalism plays so important a part in love-making and marriage that the wife is made the tool of her husband and is not appreciated in any other use. Such a compact is a misfortune to the woman. In such cases she is almost always the one who must pay the penalty.

Yet on the other hand, she does not bring to him the fitness and preparation for the higher home duties that he has a right to expect. She may be a household drudge, and may work from early till late, but that kind of faithfulness is not the best. Thought and intelligence are better qualities than the ability to do a good day's work. The wife who goes to a husband with no other preparation for marriage than a willingness to work hard, is not fulfilling her mission. Toil is energy, such as that pent up in the locomotive; it may be expended in a skillful manner, or may run into routine channels that never produce results beyond those of the menial.

The wife of a man who is in or above the middle classes should not be a menial. She should aspire to something beyond labor. Yet she should know every detail of home-making and house-keeping, and thereby make her services valuable to the home without being compelled to enslave herself in the toil that deadens all interest in living. She must possess attractions that draw those around her up to a loftier plane of existence. Then she becomes lovable.

A cultivated affinity implies that there is something to be cultivated.

That which is worthy of cultivation is attractive.

That which is attractive is magnetic.

That which is magnetic is sure to win and to hold.

CHAPTER TWENTY-NINE

+++

ALL LIFE
IS THE PRODUCT
OF
ANCESTRAL HABITS

+++
  MAGNETIC PARENTAGE
+++

IGHT AND WRONG are so prevalent in every part of this world that all that transpires must be placed to one side or the other of the ledger of life. It seems that everything is right or else is wrong, or has elements of both qualities mixed. Much of the tendency in human nature to run to weeds is inherited, and for this inheritance the parents are responsible. The relationship that incites parentage is one of attraction. If this were not so, there would be few people left on earth fifty years hence.

As the world is held in place by the magnetism of the sun, as the solar orb himself is kept upon its mission through the sky by a superior influence from the great center, as the tree and plant are drawn by magnetism from the soil and made to lift their leaves to the sun, as animal life is perpetuated by the magnetism that brings the two sexes together, so every human being who is normal is attracted to some other human being of opposite sex, for the purpose of carrying on the race.

The strongest magnetism in existence that reaches earth is that which thus impels the sexes toward each other. The man is the positive power, and the woman is the negative; but, better expressed, the man is the affirmative, and the woman the acquiescent; or, still better, the man is the giving and the woman the receiving agency. In animal magnetism the sexes play equal parts in wielding the influence, with the keener power of attraction resting with the woman. So strong is this influence that a woman, known to be virtuous and pure, would sway almost any man by the merest hint that she was ready to break down the barrier in his particular favor. Few men would be able to resist the power thus thrown over them. On the other hand the common female would repel men who were not abject slaves of passion in its lowest form.

All this is animal magnetism; not all there is to that power, but there is no other kind of influence involved.

Personal magnetism does not think of the sexual attractions of either sex. It is able to absorb all that accumulation of desire and turn it to better uses. A man who is truly magnetic in this better kind of power, would not only take no advantage of the opposite sex, but would not think of attempting. His thoughts would seek to avert such relationship, to save her and to save himself. The same rule holds true with woman.

The promiscuous and careless manner in which legally married parents will bring their children into the world, is evidence at once of wrong and of animal magnetism. It is wrong because it does the world a wrong and is not best for the child in most cases. It is animal magnetism because there is a yielding to blind impulse in the transaction.

The world has always been governed by the law of personal liberty. There has never been a disposition to interfere with the right of any man or woman to become a parent or to bring into existence any kind of offspring that chance might dictate. In recent generations the law has begun to look into one phase of the subject, the prevention of parentage. It has made it a crime to kill the unborn fruit of the womb; and still later there are some parts of the country where the sale of appliances for prevention of pregnancy have been forbidden and made a crime.

As these steps are innovations, the time will come when the law will go farther and prevent the bringing into the world of defectives.

But there can never be any law but conscience that will deal directly with the control of progeniture.

We are not now discussing the right to prevent conception, but the right to enter into the transaction in a hap-hazard way. To control progeniture is to direct the result, not to shut it off. To control the water course that supplies water for a city, means to assume charge of its movements and its direction with a view to securing the best results, and does not imply that the water is to be cut off entirely. That would be the suppression of it.

"CONTROL OF PROGENITURE."

The first law of magnetism is absolute self-control, or the ability to recognize a faculty and to use it. The lack of this ability leads to hap-hazard living, and hap-hazard living leads to loss of power in the world. All animals were illustrations of this fact, until the intelligence of man came in and made them bring forth improved species. Very few horses, cattle, sheep and other valuable animals are allowed to use the hap-hazard method. And the same is true of the valuable flowers that have come to the front in the past thirty years, as well as the fruits, vegetables and other products of nature. During the countless centuries that preceded the advent of man all other forms of life and vegetable growth were awaiting his coming, and had only the law of the survival of the fittest as the guiding impulses of progress.

In an age of intelligence this law of the survival of the fittest would work a gross injustice to the weak, and artifice has come into use as a means of partly off-setting it.

But the accumulation of artifice today is so great that it cannot long endure, and there must come a new phase of living if the race is to be saved.

Under existing conditions the only law that can be of value in the solution of the problem is that of conscience, founded upon the magnetic principle of self-control.

A person of good conscience will not permit a child to be born that should not come into the world; but the steps of prevention cannot be taken after the child has been conceived. Conscience should see to it that conception is not begun. After that event has taken place the whole duty of the parents is to bring the child into the world and make it as strong and as intelligent as possible. Everything should be done to increase its vitality, and to make its position in life as great as care and attention will permit.

The sex of the child is determined at the very climax of conception, and depends solely on the greater magnetism of the one parent over the other. This has been variously stated in different books, but the law is well fixed and can be proved by any parents who care to test it.

It is a common remark of some man or woman who wishes to raise a family, and who desires to do so with deliberate planning, that a son is wanted, or a daughter is wanted. In the Ralston Club many members write letters in confidence, and this desire for one sex or the other in preference to the hap-hazard method, has been expressed many thousands of times by would-be parents; that is, a man may wish a son, while another man may wish a daughter; or the wife may have a preference. Two days ago our attention was called to a missive in which we read, "I am fond of children; but, although we have been married six years, my wife and I have avoided parentage because we both wish to have a son. All our relatives have raised girls and we wish to be exceptions." Then followed a request for suggestions and advice.

One book of leading authority lays down the rule that whichever parent has the greater degree of sexual vitality at the time of conception will control the sex. What this means has been difficult to understand. It has been proved in a large number of cases that the woman will stamp her sex on the child if she is sexually the fresher; and the man will stamp his sex on the child if he is sexually fresher. The same law has held good among animal breeding. The male that is tired from too much association with females, as among cattle, will not stamp his sex on the offspring. This fact has been seen of late by several persons who have caused the experiments to be made on this basis; as in the case of a fresh bull that served several cows on the same day; the one cow that was first served produced a bull calf; and all the others produced heifers.

But this law has not always worked out this way, and there needs to be some modification of the statement. It is not always sexual vitality so much as sexual magnetism. This is resolvable into the question of the orgasm. If the latter be wholly lacking in the woman, and the man be magnetic at the time, the result will be a male child. If the woman have her orgasm, and she be more magnetic at the time, the result will be a female child. If both have the orgasm simultaneously, the one that is the more magnetic will control the sex.

This is not a haphazard guess, it is a proved fact.

We have collected thirty-six cases of men who have had two or more wives, who have invariably raised boys by their first wives, and girls by their other wives. These men were accounted magnetic, and were so in fact, but they had women for their first marriages who were weak in this respect, and who died from loss of vitality due to too much magnetism on the part of their husbands. They married more vigorous women, and the latter controlled the sex. In seventeen cases the husbands died from loss of vitality; after eight to fifteen years of wedlock with their later wives.

Size and physical prowess do not play a part in this control. Sometimes a small man will have a large woman for his wife, and the children will all be boys. The reverse is also true.

The test is in the power of the sexual magnetism, which means the influence that will draw one partner to the other at the time. The wife who is indifferent will be pretty apt to produce a boy, unless the husband is weak from too much indulgence. The husband who is drawn to the wife by her influence will be likely to become the father of a girl.

We can state with certainty this proposition: Let the husband refrain from the act for some days or possibly for two weeks, and come fresh in every faculty, having the magnetism to make the wife desirous; and let her refrain from her orgasm; and the child will be a boy.

Reverse these conditions except as far as the orgasm is concerned, and the result will be a girl.

Magnetism is the fine edge of desire created in the partner, and any person who has cultivated this power in a general way as in the first course of training, will be able to exert it effectively in this matter.

"DUTIES BEFORE BIRTH."

After conception there are many duties; the first of which is to help the child from the very first. To wish that the condition might be otherwise, is wrong. To try to make it otherwise is a sin. To seek to destroy the life that is hidden within the woman is a crime against nature.

Let it come. Do not let it come as a thing that is unwelcome, but throw into its development all the interest, care, attention and love that you can summon to your command.

The child knows your intention towards it. It is a life in the inherent state that feels and interprets and has knowledge. From the moment of conception the life is made; it is really an act of creation in which the two parents take part, and are creators, acting as agents of a higher power. While the child will inherit the sum total of the influences of past generations, its inherent nature may be brought in close connection with its earthly career if the parents do their duty.

In the early part of the course of training much space is devoted to the consideration of the Heaven-born moods and feelings, as well as to the others; and their influence in magnetism has been fully shown. The duty of parents is to develop in the unborn child as many of these noble moods as possible. Under the plan of control of progeniture both parents, being quasi-creators, should come to the act of conception with the better moods in the ascendency in their own dispositions. This can be accomplished by self-culture, which is largely composed of self-watchfulness, accompanied by the restraint that is evidence of magnetism and its most potent proof.

But under the plan of duties before birth both parents, and especially the mother, can actually develop in the child the magnetic power that comes from the nobler moods. The husband's part of this is to throw around the wife all those influences that serve to make it easier for her to maintain her own control. He should resolve to assist her in every moment of her pregnancy, to keep a peaceful disposition, and to preserve the better moods. He has the opportunity of fretting her, or causing her to worry, or of making her life burdensome; for, as her own condition tends to make her restless and irritable, so his methods may increase those evil characteristics, until she gives way.

Each moment of such depression counts against the disposition of the child. We recall the case of two sisters, whose ages were twenty and twenty-one at the time they became pregnant; and it so happened that they began this condition in the same month. They lived in the same house. It was a double dwelling, and was in fact two residences joined in one, with a partition wall that made them separate. One of these sisters allowed herself to give way to every influence about her. As it always happens, it is easier to float down stream than to pull up against the tide, and the nerves of the woman who exercised no control over herself were finally distracted. This was nearly eighteen years ago. Her child, a little girl, is practically a nervous wreck, and has been examined by the authorities for insanity.

The other sister resolved to never give way to her feelings. She pulled up stream against the tide. All through her period she was calm and full of peace and sweet nature. The better moods possessed her. Her child, a beautiful girl, is one of the most attractive and most magnetic of young ladies.

These two children were made by their mothers.

The laws that were at work in the two cases cited are always at work in all cases. There is no escape from them.

Thus the parents can transmit to their unborn children the grandest principles of magnetism. It is starting at an early stage in the career of the child, but it serves the parents as well as the offspring; for they find a happiness that will not depart readily for a lifetime, in the perfection of their children. To raise ugly boys and girls and to impart to them an inherent nature that is sure to grow worse as it develops, is to be a constant source of grief for the parents when they are old and dependent.

These better moods are not only magnetic, but they are in the most exalted form of attractiveness which is the glowing and dazzling sunlight of magnetism.

If they can be transmitted to the young, there is every reason why they should be so directed; and, if the children can be given these magnetic qualities, no steps should be omitted to accomplish this end.

"SHAPING HUMAN LIFE."

The duties before birth have a direct influence in the shape which will be given to human life. For instance, if the pregnancy comes as a disappointment to the mother, she will not fail to impress that fact upon the fœtus. If it comes as a sort of surprise and is accepted with resignation this influence will show itself in the deadened powers in the later life of the child. If she is glad of the pregnancy, this joy will sweeten and brighten the coming life. These are facts that have been amply proved.

Most mothers, especially those who are able to employ the service of skilled physicians, seek to lose the fœtus by some kind of treatment which he knows how to give for a consideration. In a majority of cases this will fail and the child will go on to development and birth, carrying in its nature the inherent, although untranslated, knowledge that the mother had been engaged in a conspiracy to kill it. There is no escape from this conclusion. The shape given to that life can be easily imagined.

But the ambitions of the child may be trained better before birth than after. While it is yet in the womb it is part of the life of the mother, and her life is influenced by those she loves. If her husband is in this category, he has the power to shape the life of the child at that period.

If on the other hand no effort is made to direct its ambitions or impulses during the period of pregnancy, the opportunity is lost for a number of years. Not until the child can be given thinking and reasonable faculties can it be argued with; and not until it has grown to an age when its feelings can be made sensitive will its life-long moods be touched. Thus years are lost between the time of birth and such development.

But before birth the whole career of the child can be shaped, if not fully directed. The mother who wishes her boy or girl to be a lover of music should turn her thoughts and feelings to that art as early as possible after conception. Every day lost makes it less potent as an opportunity for influencing the unborn being. If war is the theme, the study and the analysis of the methods of great warriors should be given as much attention as possible. Stories of battles, and the movements whereby victory followed the crisis of conflict, should be deeply impressed at this time. Merely thinking of it will not do. The most effective method is to give deep study and thorough analysis to the matter; but it should go far enough to arouse the feelings. The mind has some power in this stage, but the feelings have tenfold more.

There are numerous instances where this plan has been put into use in the past fifty years. But the number of parents who, in the past twenty years, have adopted it is surprisingly large. Any profession or any calling may be implanted in the child during pregnancy if the plan suggested is made a thorough one. Half way efforts are not valuable.

Some parents wish their children to become orators, some statesmen, some physicians, some ministers, and so on all through a long list of avocations; and these dispositions may be made supreme influences in the coming life if they are adopted as part of the thought and feeling of the mother.

It must be remembered that she will unavoidably reflect the conditions that surround her. She is moved by the very atmosphere of good will or of malice about her. What she is, may be often charged to the husband who has her in charge; for he should mold her thoughts and her moods at all times. Thus her own purposes and will are helping him, and he is helping them at the same time.

But the theme of shaping human life rises to higher ground when we consider the fact that the moral nature of the offspring and the lofty impulses that should possess a grand character, are given their direction in this period. Most parents live in a humdrum way; they are commonplace under the belief that they are practical, and to them what is practical is sensible. But their commonplace existence is death in the body. It is death of the mind, death of the heart and death of the faculties; for where there is no progress and no stepping upward year by year, there is a no real life.

In this commonplace, humdrum plodding along the highway of life, they give no care and no thought except for their own convenience and for their own routine methods of doing things. The child comes into the world a dried piece of commonplace clay, and it will be that all the way through unless some flame of genius is touched by a random spark which will fire it. The commonplace children and families are seen in the homes where there is the grind of duties from morning till night, doing the same old work over again and again, and getting the three meals a day, washing the dishes, making the beds, reading the papers and some books that interest but do not improve, and then sleeping till the next day shall be on hand, and so going through it all with endless sameness until the funeral takes one away, and another funeral takes another away, and so on, without relief and generally without desire for relief.

When even one thought leaps the bounds of this imprisonment and soars to a higher atmosphere, something is gained. It may not be anything more than the planning of change, of a house or home perhaps, or the hope of something better. Hoping and wishing are excellent qualities of the heart if there can be found some chord to connect them with the execution of all or some part of them.

The world of nature is boundless in its opportunities to please and to uplift. In that realm there is no limit to what you can plan and execute. This will draw you out of the commonplace. The making of a beautiful garden will add greatly to your value to the world, for he who makes the dull surface of the earth to smile with blossoms or with foliage, is doing his race a good deed.

There are boundless realms in architecture, in art, in poetry, in history, in literature, in the professions, and everywhere. Let the inspiration of any of these seize the mind and take hold of the heart and it will exalt both. It will pass on with a rapidly increasing influence to the unborn child. It will shape the life long before it has come into the world, and at a time when it can be controlled better than at any other period for years after.

If it is true, and it is, that there have been born into the world many great men and great women who are not only geniuses, but more than geniuses, then it must be true that they have drawn their impelling tendencies from the blood of the mother. It has sometimes, and many times in fact, been asked by what law commonplace parents have been able to bring into being children that have towered above their fellows like the great peak above the plain; and the answer is that, in some way that may not be seen in after years, the mother and perhaps the father also, must have drawn into the life that was forming, some exalted influences caught from sources that served to bring about the result.

The meanest of minds, the plainest of lives, may seize upon ideas and catch feelings that will take strong hold. The outside public has no opportunity for beholding what is going on in the quiet hours of the day or with what prayers and thoughts the mother lays her head on the pillow by night. The morning may bring resolves, or earnest hopes may mold desires until they live as realities in a super-sensitive organization. If the cravings for food are strong enough to make the child, the yearnings of the heart should have still stronger influence over the moods and feelings of the fœtus; for it imbibes what dwells in the mind and nervous system of the mother.

Why not seek the highest goal? Why not aspire to the most exalted condition of the soul in thus shaping life? The answer is that the commonplace people do not see any advantage in it. We once said to a married couple: "At this time you may perhaps give to the coming human being one of the grandest characters that the world has ever known, if you will build up within your own minds and hearts the ambition and the resolve to train yourselves to this purpose." And the wife made this reply: "I shall be too busy making clothes."

This is the commonplace cast of mind that holds down all the great masses of humanity. There is no cure for it in most cases. The very fact that it cannot be cured by advice or suggestion gives to you your opportunity; for if there is a bag of gold ten miles from you and all your neighbors and acquaintances start for it, you will stand less show of securing it than if they all remain dully idle and indifferent while you have the road to yourself.

You who have gone through the preparatory course in magnetism in the first book, and have gone through the present course up to this stage, and have a desire to make your own acquisitions count in favor of your unborn child in case you are a prospective parent, will find this opportunity a great one. You are more likely to adopt these suggestions than one who is commonplace; for the very fact that you are reading these words is proof that you have exalted hopes and ambitions.

You can give to the child that is yet unborn as great a character as you choose. It is not necessary for you to be what you study, and you may study of great accomplishments and inhale the spirit of tremendous achievements if you so desire; and what you cannot execute in your own career, the child will find easy to put to the test of realization. This law explains why such mediocre parents as those of Shakespeare brought forth so grand a man, taking him on the side of his inherent character.

CHAPTER THIRTY

++++++++++++++++++++++++++++++++

MAGNETISM
IS A CONSTANTLY ATTRACTING
FORCE THAT DRAWS
US TO A GOAL

++
❧ SPAN OF A MAGNETIC LIFE ❧
++

ET US NOW ACCEPT the fact that the magnetic influences of the parents have gone out in favor of the child and that it has come into the world and must act for itself. In the preceding considerations we have taken the student into the secrets that are working out the destiny of greatness, for we have carried you through the age of development of the lad and of the girl; we have shown you the era of temptation for both, and the opening of the temples of manhood and womanhood, as well as the ties that bind and do not bind the hearts even though the bodies are bonded by the thread of matrimony; we have analyzed the loves and the affinities that play havoc or bring bliss into the lives they affect; and the natural end of all these steps was the production of new beings to come on the plane of action and take up the reins of rule.

One generation thus has passed on into another generation.

"PURPOSE IN LIVING."

What is all this for? We cannot look at the philosophical side of the study, for that is too deep for this kind of training, and is reserved for the much greater work of Universal Philosophy. But we can discuss the relation of life to its purposes and see if there are laws that should serve as guides for human conduct.

On the philosophical side, which we briefly refer to in a mere line, we seek to know why there is a race of human beings, and what part each generation plays in the plan. On the magnetic side we are to search for an answer to the inquiry why any one particular individual is born and what end is to be sought.

There are in this world, to say nothing of what may be obtainable from the next, both abundance and variety of wealth of every conceivable kind. Money is only one of the agents of wealth. The latter may consist of property or of rights or of pleasure, or of opportunity for happiness, or of many other ideas that make life a great success. The test is this: When a man is dying and asks himself what he is at that time, he has an inventory of his wealth. Or when he is too old to earn money or property and seeks an account of himself, then his wealth is what he is in fact, not what he can sum up in books.

Taking the word wealth to include all such things, money, property, rights, enjoyment, freedom, opportunity, health, clearness of mind, grasp of nature and of knowledge, the whole idea will be classed as the fund from which each individual has the privilege of drawing according to his or her talents.

This fund is in bank. God and nature are the keepers and the distributers.

There is but one key to open an account in that bank, and that key is magnetism, for magnetism is an attracting as well as an attractive power. It draws on the fund in favor of its owner.

The purpose in living is to draw as much as possible from this great and exhaustless fund of universal wealth. The more you draw the more there is for every other human being. People seem to have wrong ideas of possession. A man may own a hundred million dollars worth of buildings; and the more he owns the more there is for others.

A man with money who did nothing with it would be useless to the world. His spending what he has or changing the nature of his wealth always makes wealth for others. Thus if he were to put one hundred millions of money into the same value in buildings, he would have the full amount of wealth when he had completed the transfer, and he would at the same time have distributed the same amount among others, with the result that there would be several wealthy men where before his transfer there were none, as far as he was concerned.

As activity is life in the body, and as no person is natural or happy who is not very active, the first purpose of living is to be active to excess. This does not mean to strain the faculties or injure the mind or body by breaking down the channels of use therein; but it does mean that the more active you can be and still maintain your health of mind and body the more successful and the more natural and happy you will become, provided the activity is along lines of usefulness prompted by the best judgment. We intend to include only the better moods, and they contain the incentive to the greatest possible activity; that is, some of them do. They are an all-round, wholly practical, complete presentation of every phase of human life on its better side.

We know of no magnetic person who is not ultra active.

This question has come up in many forms for more than a third of a century, and it has led to the assumption that excessive activity of itself creates magnetism. This is undoubtedly true, but there may be losses attending such activity that should be conserved under some guiding principles of a training course like this.

Thus mistakes and the loss of half a life time of experiment and costly experience will be saved.

Combine, if you will, the noble or Heaven-born moods that admit of great activity, with the highest use that can be made of them balanced by well-planned and unremitting activity, and the results will be acquisition.

Under this double principle all wealth should be kept moving. All money should be made active, except that a certain percentage should be laid aside each week for the sinking fund, which will stand against want in old age. This sinking fund should never be attacked.

But it need not be more than five per cent of one's earnings. In speculation, the curse of healthy business, this fund should be held against it as sacred and untouchable. So in all ventures. Let this law be a secular religion. No matter how much you earn, or how little, save five per cent each week and let it stand where it will not be drawn upon in any event until the battle of life has been won.

If all the people were to keep their movable wealth moving, there would be in every two years a doubling of all the wealth of the country; and this would mean the accumulation of vast property that would serve as the means of helping up all who are in a position to take advantage of the activity.

Figure this out.

It does not look reasonable on its face, but figure it out.

If a body of men have one hundred millions of dollars, and do nothing with it, what benefit is conferred on the world or on the public?

The accumulation is absolutely dead.

If they spend it in the erection of one hundred million dollars worth of buildings, they own the buildings and thus have the full value in useful property; but the money has gone out in so doing and has become the property of many different parties who were engaged in the work and the business of furnishing the material, and somebody now possesses the one hundred millions of money or what it buys, while the original owners possess the buildings.

It is a clearly proved fact that the wealth has fully doubled itself by being used. This is activity.

All activity gathers additional value as it moves.

Wanton waste is the expenditure of money for work that produces nothing that can be called property after it has been attained.

The example is but one of many scores that might be given to illustrate this principle. Wealth is not altogether in the form of property. Life, liberty and the pursuit of happiness are all forms of wealth. The enriched mind is much more opulent than the enriched pocket.

To gather from the fund that is everywhere abundant is the purpose of earthly life. It does not conflict with any dogmas of religion, for the latter teaches the wealth of ethical acquisition as the grandest of all ambitions. The fund is limitless in all directions; but humanity must draw from it; and in so drawing it has only to take what it will, and the fund grows larger in the use. It is like some of the miracles of two thousand years ago, where increase came in the need.

The opposite of this purpose is the commonplace condition that nearly all men and women accept and never challenge. They may think it is conservatism; but on this principle the non-progressive savages are the most conservative folks on earth. The dead are conservative.

In the preceding chapter we discussed at length the conditions that favor the commonplace and showed the disadvantages of the fate that thus hangs over most all humanity.

As the fund is directly the source of every kind of blessing to men and women, it is necessarily the expectation of nature that it will be drawn upon by the energetic classes. Gold, lead and rock may all weigh down the scales, and the ignorant or indifferent mind would be as content with the rock as with the gold. The fund that contains all the wealth of the universe offers nothing but the richest gems and metals, nothing but the most valuable of jewels for the mind, the heart and the physical being; yet commonplace people care nothing for it, and so it is the same old case of proffered blessings disregarded.

One of the most magnetic of all treasures is home life under the influences of marriage. But this sweetest of all blessings is turned to dross by commonplace uses. Not in one instance in a thousand is it rightly studied and rightly enjoyed. It is one of the many forms of wealth that can be drawn from the great general fund of nature; but it is as important as any.

A man recently said that he had all the power and all the opportunity that great wealth would buy, but he was utterly wretched as he lacked a home, and it was too late to begin one now. He had proceeded on the principle that he must first earn the means whereby the home could be secured, and then when he had achieved that end, it was too late in life to procure the home. This teaches that the two sub-purposes of living, or at least two of the many sub-purposes, the founding of a home and the attainment of wealth in money or its equivalent, should proceed side by side instead of in succession.

The reason why the unmarried men did not marry has been stated in earlier pages of this course. The reason why unmarried women did not marry has not been stated, as the cause rests with the unfitness for the position and duties of wife.

Of all the women now married not one in ten is qualified in the highest degree to take charge of the home, and of all those who are unmarried not one in a hundred is so qualified. As a result the number of men who do not marry is to go on increasing and the body of bachelors will be an ever growing one.

The true bachelor is a man or woman who is by nature and not by necessity or choice constituted such.

"BACHELORS, MALE AND FEMALE."

To be a true bachelor, of either sex, there must be an exclusion of the other sex. The cause of this condition is the lack of magnetism. The latter power is an attraction, and the first object that it naturally exerts its influence upon is its opposite. A magnetic man attracts a woman. A magnetic woman attracts a man. This is one of the purposes for which the power was created and given to humanity.

Not every unmarried man is a bachelor, for the rule requires that the other sex must be eliminated, and many men who are not inclined to take upon themselves the burdens of matrimony are almost as fully associated with the other sex as though they were in fact married. The same may be said of a large number of unmarried women.

The true bachelor wishes to be free from all entanglements and all companionship with the opposite sex. The thoughts and feelings do not run in such direction. There are a large number of such men and such women in the world; but they are either abnormal or else are carrying a lifelong disappointment in some former affair of the heart. A man like Whittier was a bachelor from such misfortune. A man like Sumner was a bachelor from natural inclination; and, although he was united by ceremony with a widow, he lived with her but a few hours, and became in effect a bachelor. Here are two common types of men.

There are also men and women who are actually married and who have been in wedlock for years and yet who carry with them all the characteristics of the bachelor. They take no part in the rights of marriage, or else do so in a perfunctory manner, and care nothing for affiliation with the opposite sex.

In all such cases there is a lack of the sexual attraction known as one of the phases of magnetism. Sumner was repellant in every way except his dignity and his power of mental oratory. He was not a magnetic speaker. He did not draw people to him as an individual. He had commanding ability and was pure in purpose and in action. But he lacked that magnetism that is necessary in order to make friends and secure happiness; and so he walked through life by himself.

The bachelor can be detected in the first years of puberty. If the boy is to take on the nature of the bachelor he will not be addicted to the peculiar habits of the boy whose sex magnetism is being developed. The latter, all unconscious to himself, begins as soon as puberty is established to show signs of carefulness in his appearance when he is to approach the other sex. Whereas, before the dawn of that condition, he never cared how he dressed or looked, now he is growing to watch his own clothes, to see that they are neat and tidy, that they are free from stains and daubs, that his shoes are clean and bright, his face washed and his linen unsoiled. The vigilance comes on very gradually and he does not see it in himself, but his friends notice the carefulness in all matters that relate to personal appearance.

In the same way the young male bird, before puberty, is rough of plumage and harsh of note; but in the after weeks when mating becomes a possibility, he keeps his feathers clean and he tunes his voice to a tender sweetness, not even then being in competition for a wife. It is the sign of the marrying bird.

With the boy it is the sign that he will not become a bachelor. The girl takes on the same extra neatness and carries an air of attractive longing when she gives her thoughts to the other sex. The line of separation in the girl is not difficult to find as she passes from the condition of a child to that of a woman, although it may not require three weeks to make the passage.

A man of keen observation may detect in the face of the girl the fact that she has entered upon her mating condition. The philosophical reply of a prominent man as to the age when it is no longer proper to kiss a female child, is true in fact as well as in theory. He said: "You may kiss her during the age that gives no satisfaction; but as soon as she is old enough to cause you pleasure in the kissing then she is too old to be kissed."

No better illustration could be given of the power of this

class of magnetism than this reply. A man may be friendly to a family and may have formed the habit of kissing the girls while they are children. There comes a time when the touch of the lips carries with it a thrill of magnetism, and then the whole character of the act is changed. The girl who thus imparts the feeling of magnetism in her lips is not inclined to become a bachelor girl. If she fails to wed it will be due to circumstances over which she does not have control.

We recall the following incident told us by a lady school teacher who was under thirty when she related it: A boy of twelve was in the habit of greeting her with a kiss as he came to school. He formed the habit of his own accord, and it was told of him by his parents that he was an unusually affectionate child. As he grew to thirteen he continued the salute, and even into his next year; but one day the school teacher felt an unusual thrill in the touch of the lips, and she thought it over day after day, while the salutes continued. One afternoon they were alone in the room after school was over, and he threw his arms passionately about her neck and would not let go, nor would he take his lips from hers.

Hardly knowing how to treat the matter she permitted the custom, and it went on until the summer vacation. He was the only child of parents of wealth, and she was wholly dependent on her income as a teacher; so she could not resign her position to avoid the salute, nor did she wish to give offence to the boy's parents.

There seemed nothing left to do but to allow the matter to take its own course. During the summer vacation the boy did not see her, but he addressed several letters to her in which he called her "dear teacher" and ended with a formal phrase "lovingly yours." But he showed discretion in the correspondence. She replied in terms that would be usual between teacher and scholar.

One more year of school remained, and his kisses became more and more passionate. After graduation he went to college and yet never seemed to care for any girl. He wrote occasionally to the teacher and she replied. To her surprise she found that she was in love with him, although he was about fifteen years her junior. When he was of age and had come into wealth owing to the death of his father, he proposed to her, but she declined. He then declared that he would never marry any person if she would not accept him. But his nature was not hewn for that of a bachelor. She moved far away and married a wealthy manufacturer with whom she lived unhappily. He married a young girl with whom he lived unhappily. And so the romance ended.

But the fact that he was magnetic as a boy passing over the line of childhood into the realm of manhood, was evidence that he was not designed by nature for a bachelor.

Had he selected an affinity he would have been very happy with her. Had the teacher selected an affinity she too would have found happiness, and the dream of the first fancy would have proved evanescent.

The study of magnetism has changed many lives of bachelors, both of the male and of the female sex, and led them into marriage.

You cannot imagine an animal that lives in an unmarried state from choice. What would you say of a bird that had no mate? Wedlock is the necessary result of the condition of the sex. If there were no distinction of sex, there would be no suggestion of marriage. But as long as there are men and women so long must the only normal condition be marriage.

"CHANGE OF LIFE."

Everything that is born dies, and everything that is born and dies enters upon the state of maturity and ripens as the climax of such condition. There is nothing that does not ripen provided it lives. Hence there must come a time in every life, both male and female, when a change ensues that corresponds with the determination of puberty. In the early teens the boy becomes the man, and the girl becomes the woman. In the late forties the woman becomes the senile, and the man in the late fifties enters upon the same state; although sexual magnetism is not lost in either case. The woman ceases to be potent because the number of ovaries has run out and none remain to carry on the function of pregnancy. The man never ceases to be potent for he is always the man unless, being exhausted, desire shall fail.

The woman who is passing through the change of life should

substitute for the youthful buoyancy that is natural to her years prior to that time, a large fund of magnetism which will serve to hold her juvenile character, and retain the impulses of the girl.

If she does not do this she ages very fast and the old saying will prove true that after forty a woman ages two years to a man's one.

As the period of the change comes on, which generally begins in the early forties, the woman is a being of organs rather than of flesh. Heart, lungs, stomach, liver, kidneys, and the lower organs all undergo changes. Two or three great essentials are necessary to counteract this altering of the plan of nature.

The blood should be cleansed and all the tissue of the body should at all times be kept free from the accumulation of clogging material.

Rest is the most hurtful of all habits in the years from the late thirties to the late forties. This does not mean that excessive activity should be indulged in, but that there should be no decaying rest. The latter comes from lying down too much, too much sitting and too little action. Long walks are not good, but a great many brief walks are especially helpful. Do not get unusually tired, but do not let the body accumulate its material which results from the stagnation of all the functions at this time of life.

The faculties also should be given a full variety of activity. The inclination to take life easy is the deadliest foe of either man or woman. As a guide to the methods to be adopted, the following rules and laws are given here:

1. *The functions set in motion by the approach of puberty, run out at the time of the change of life.*

2. *When puberty begins, a new epoch in human conditions is inaugurated in the body and all its functions.*

3. *When the epoch inaugurated by puberty runs out, a new era is instituted in the body and all its faculties, and this is known as the third era of life.*

4. *With the dawn of the third era the remainder of human life may be shaped at the will of its owner.*

5. *The shaping of the remainder of life must be done during the process of change from the second to the third era.*

6. *The current of thought, action and ambition that sets in*

during this process of change, will shape and control the whole of the remaining years of life.

These guiding laws and facts are of the highest importance. They are in many ways related to magnetism. In the first place this is the time in the life of every man and woman when the natural magnetism runs out and must be renewed or decrepitude will begin its work of debilitating the purpose and the will of the mind and the high tension of the nerves, and the result will be a dumpy condition in every department of life, or a strong tendency in that direction.

In the second place the individual should be self-master which is the greatest of all magnetic powers, and thus there will be control over others. There will be some leadership, or even great leadership at a time when the younger generation with all its superfluous activity will drown out the man or woman of advancing years.

The change of life begins with the woman, generally speaking, when she is about thirty-nine and ends when she is about forty-nine. The ovarian function may be through its work at forty-five or sooner, and sometimes much later; but the effects of the change are quite sure to terminate before the age of fifty.

In a man the change begins at about the age of forty-nine, generally speaking, and ends at about the age of fifty-nine. His sexual powers may be strong even then, or may be weak; but they are not closely associated with the change of life in his case as with the woman.

The era which passes with this change is that of maturity, and the epoch that is inaugurated is that of senility.

It is the turning point when the fact is to be determined whether or not the body and the mind are to turn toward decrepitude or are to escape it during the years of the third era.

To be dependent on others is not relished by any person and there are many men and women now living who are past eighty and yet are fully able to take care of themselves. They are many in a country where ninety-nine per cent of all men and women are helpless or seriously dependent on others. What is the use of living and be thus made a member of the class of second childhood?

It is a fact that a man who is past forty-nine is not able to find employment or to initiate a new line of venture whereby to gain a livelihood. The great concerns of the country, the interests that employ assistants and clerks or workmen, will not engage a man who is thus advanced in years, if he has had no experience in the work, and the chances are that even if he has had ample experience he will not find a place open to him. The man who has had an independent income for many years and who suddenly finds it cut off, will not secure employment no matter how hard he tries, if he is past the age named and is without experience. A young man would be given the chance to learn the work or the duties, but the man of fifty would be barred.

The case came to our attention recently of a business man who had laid aside over a hundred thousand dollars made in the dry goods business, and who lost it all in speculation in stocks. He was forty-eight years of age. He had a family to support. Having no capital and being obliged to close out his business to meet his debts, he found himself without employment. The dry goods business was all that he knew anything about. There was no store in his county that could give him a position. He went away to a large city and was turned down at every store. One man had the unkindness to say: "We would not think of employing a clerk who was as old as you, no matter how much experience he had." Then he went to another city, using money borrowed from his sister who could ill afford to lend it to him. He offered to work for two dollars a day in any store, but there was no opening for an old man.

He finally engaged himself as a laborer at twenty-five cents an hour, but he was not used to the shovel and the pick and he broke down completely, becoming at length an object of charity.

We recall being in the office one morning of a great manufacturing concern that had advertised for *girls* at seven dollars a week, ten hours a day. It was in a city. Several hundred females called, and fully one-fourth of them were women past forty years of age. The head man who selected the help for the company paid no attention to any applicant who was apparently over twenty-five years old. The others had no chance whatever.

This condition is natural, yet it is a sad reflection on the fact that the body must ripen and go to seed, and the further fact that the matured body is no longer a magnet for any purpose. Men of any age who have lived long enough to have their eyes opened, are not prone to seek the association of companionship of mature women. The younger the girl the more she draws and attracts.

When in rare instances a woman of forty or fifty carries herself with the attractive qualities of a young girl, without the simpering imitations of senile women in their forties or fifties, she fascinates men with ease. There are women as old as seventy who play the dickens with the hearts of sensible men, who are drawn with wonder into their little kingdoms and are content to be the subjects of so delicious a lot of sovereigns. These women are not plentiful, but they exist. We met by the request of a Judge of the Supreme Court, a remarkable woman who was not wealthy, but who was most intelligent and vivacious without being flippant. She did not have the fussy activity that old women affect in order to seem young and energetic; but she possessed the charms of a miss of twenty, despite her gray hairs. She had taken wonderful care of her health and was without sickness or debility. Her eyes were bright, her voice tuned to a pleasing key, and her manner easy and full of quiet, strong dignity.

In motion she was surprisingly graceful. We saw her at a ball and danced with her. There was no suggestion of age in any respect.

The face had some wrinkles, and she assured those whom she took into her confidence that she had done nothing to keep the wrinkles away. But at the length of the ball room she seemed to be smooth of feature. A man who had reached his thirty-fourth year and who was wealthy but without a wife, declared that he would rather marry that woman than any other in all the world. She refused to enter into an alliance at her time of life and this showed her excellent good sense.

One of the most remarkable conditions noticeable in her case was the smoothness, fullness and solidity of the flesh of her arms and neck. This could be seen at a glance, and indicated the presence of that renewing process in the body by which the old material is daily changed for the new, with the result that the flesh is kept as good as the food of which it is composed.

This law gives to every person the opportunity for renewing the youth that has fled, if it is taken advantage of at the right time.

The body dies in part each day and is renewed in part. If the food is of a perfect character, the new portion of the body will tend toward the greater vitality that abounds in youth, and the buoyancy of that period will be secured.

The time to take advantage of this law is when any new era is being inaugurated. The boy or girl who is entering puberty, and is between the years of twelve and sixteen, is much more pliable than at any other time as far as the tissue and organic construction of the body is concerned; and this pliability is again present in the ten years of change; that is, in the case of a woman, between the ages of thirty-nine and forty-nine, and in the case of a man between the ages of forty-nine and fifty-nine.

In those ten years the chemistry of the body and the chemistry of food should be studied and put into practice in order that perfect flesh, bones, muscles, nerves, organs and vitality may be given to all parts of the body. It will be found that there are fourteen chemical elements that make a perfect body, and that these are useful in seventeen chemical compounds. Wherever they have been adopted as such, the result has been a remarkable increase of vitality and the renewal of the powers of the body.

Then the cleansing effect of such an aid as viteau or perfect water which washes out all accumulations of old age material and makes a direct attack upon the germs of senility or advancing age, should be sought and applied. These things are within the reach of every man and woman and cost nothing.

In this pliable age, known as the change of life, the faculties may be turned to youthful tendencies or to decrepitude, according as they are used. If they are dulled by lack of test, they will take on the latter condition. The brain and the memory are now beginning to soften and weaken, and they should be made vital and strong by special training lest they throw their owner into a state of dependence.

Use of all the leading faculties, hard and energetic use, not resting and rusting, must be sought, for the time is opportune and all the powers are supple and pliant.

The two ages in the life of a man or woman when the body and faculties may be given new impulses are puberty and its running out; or during the years from about twelve to sixteen, and in the decades mentioned in the foregoing discussion.

The things that do not favor the coming conditions are the following:

TO BE AVOIDED.

Too much rest.

Weak influences over the body such as languor, too much sleep, too much sitting, disinclination to walk or take exercise, love of reclining positions during the day, lounging, placing the feet above the floor, throwing the torso back as in easy chairs, and the desire to have someone else wait on you or do your errands or otherwise relieve you of the activities that should keep you moving. These influences take the vitality out of the muscles and lessen the vigor of every part of the body.

Weak influences over the mind are equally injurious; and these are light reading, light conversation that idles away the time, light thinking as in lifeless pondering over useless subjects, light reading as of novels and sensational trash, games of chance where a lucky turn will decide, as in cards and other forms of amusement; and all wasteful indulgences.

TO BE ENCOURAGED.

Constant but not straining activity of all the physical body.

A protection of all the membranes of the body by the use of the most wholesome food.

The development of the highest state of nervous vitality.

The inclination to spend much time out in the sun and light and fresh air.

The support of the poise of the physical parts of the body so as to prevent the loss of alignment in the carriage of the whole body. The first evidence of physical decrepitude is in this loss of alignment.

The relief of all pressure on the spinal column either in walking, standing or motion of any kind.

Special attention to the vitality and growth of the chest.

Daily bathing of the lower half of the body from the waist down to the feet, the night being the best time for this.

The skin of the whole body should be kept hard, vital and active at all times, so as to allow the changing poisons to free themselves, as they are particularly injurious at the time of the change of life.

Peristalsis should be regular and free, for the reasons just stated. This may be maintained, if the general functions are about normal, by eating an apple every morning before breakfast for 365 days in every year. The effect of this one rule is so great that it has been claimed for it that it will do more to maintain perfect health than any other one rule of conduct in life.

Plain food, moderate eating and slow mastication.

The mind and memory should be given tests of strength at this time, for the tendency to lapses of these faculties will quickly age the individual.

The love for children and the participation in their forms of active muscular plays should be adopted; for the mind and body are colored in the spirit of renewed youth, which is the most important of all results.

During the age of puberty, and especially during the period when life is changing, there should be a fixed time each day that is to be devoted to the study and practice of magnetism. It will pay for the reason that this line of culture will hold back all the ripening agencies of mind and body, and maintain the conditions of middle life instead of allowing the down grade to begin.

The change of life is the threshold of this down grade which all sensible persons dread and seek to avoid.

The use of chemicals and treatment for the face, the hair, and the general outside appearance, which has been employed for many thousands of years as a veneer of the age that is fast creeping on, is the worst of all kinds of dependence, and this veneer will so soon rub off and show the depleted youth underneath that the penalty is greater than one who is so ambitious deserves.

The remedy is in the steady and persistent employment of the principles of magnetism.

At the age when life is changing there is a growing disposi-

tion to have a good time, to take things easy, to indulge in
rich foods and all kinds of palatable stuff, and to coddle the
mind and faculties.   This plan of living soon makes the inroads of ill health seen and felt, and the man or woman who
indulges in it will fall by the wayside much sooner, overtaken
by the grim hand of disease or the dark messenger of death.

Let the pliant period be an era for the re-kindling of the fires
of ambition in whatever sphere of life you dwell, and let it also
be the time for holding the body and the faculties under the
controlling mastery of the will according to the first chapters
of this course.

Life will take on new hopes and new coloring and there may
be guaranteed then a long span of enjoyment and keen satisfaction in well living.

CHAPTER THIRTY-ONE

CONTROL OF OTHERS
DEMANDS
FIRM
CONTROL OF YOURSELF

♣ ♣ SELF-MAGNETISM ♣ ♣

++

EARING the end of these higher studies in magnetic culture, we wish to give you a key, the possession of which alone insures you the rewards you crave. The pages that follow present a complete system of aid intended to correct DISEASES of the WILL-POWER, IMPATIENCE, IRRITABILITY, INABILITY to resist TEMPTATION and WEAKNESS OF PURPOSE. They are presented here in recognition of the necessity that everywhere exists among humanity for psychological aid in moments of impending failure.

We call this Department Self-Magnetism. We always use the word magnetism as the synonym of control. This would indicate that the present Department is one that teaches self-control. But time and experience have abundantly shown that the power which is so-called cannot be awakened, developed and maintained by words of advice, or even by the pangs of adversity that follow its lack.

Something more is needed. There must be a course of treatment that goes directly to the root of the diseases and builds a substantial condition in their place.

Disinclination is the most common symptom of a diseased will-power. It shows itself in the inability to make up the mind to do the right thing; and this acts as a perpetual barrier to recovery in sickness, especially when the malady drags itself along through a course of chronic ailments. Will-power has done more to pass the crisis of an acute illness than the doctor's remedies. Nothing will help the physician so much as this determination on the part of the patient to get well.

Self-Magnetism is something more, however, than self-control. Magnetism is influence of a positive nature. It is not a mere act of the thinking brain, but a condition of life within the soul, the mind and the nerves. It is a substance, not a rule of conduct.

Some persons dread to think about magnetism, ascribing to it some mysterious power which they fear. It is nothing of this kind. On the other hand, magnetism is a healthy operation of a healthy will, living in facts and results, not in theories and alarms. Because we have always regarded it as the most important of all studies, we have for more than a quarter of a century maintained an organization that has devoted itself to the task of securing all the facts, laws and principles that had genuine value and practical sense.

This chapter deals with a very limited part of the study of magnetism—a drop, scarcely, in the great bucket; but as far as it goes it is supremely important. And each idea is presented in simple language, free from technicality, so that every reader may understand.

While it can be encouraged and taught by others or by books, it cannot be acquired without a serious effort on your part. It is a kind of self-education that depends on the purpose and ambition of the user of it.

It is most serviceable in many ways in maintaining health or in getting through the crisis of disease. Some of the few instances in which it is advantageous are the following:

1. It saves the hysterically inclined woman, and the womanish man, from the approach of the malady.

2. It saves the irritably inclined man or woman from the terrors of nervous breakdown.

3. It saves the mind of the person who is likely to fall into paresis, softening of the brain, or forms of insanity, where the lax hold of the will-power lets the tendency increase, unless over-mastered.

4. It furnishes a dominant will that has judgment and yet strength in every crisis.

5. It enables a person to follow out a line of practice, regime or other course that is beneficial to the health or to the mind. Herein it saves weaklings from themselves.

The FIRST LAW of Self-Magnetism is PATIENCE.

This is not a homily, nor a sermon, nor an ethical treatise; but a campaign of practice in magnetism. Yet to advise a person to be patient looks like preaching. We have no such intention.

All development and all progress in the world is born of some idea. A strong idea, once well established in the mind, will sweep the past out of existence and open up a new future as bright as human possibility can make it. It is the sudden birth of a thought that has made wealth flow in an endless stream into the lives of thousands. The idea has reformed the bad, raised the lowly, sent the sinner to better conditions, and moved the whole world like a lever.

Let us see what these laws are:

LAW Number 1.—*The cultivation of PATIENCE is the basis of Self-Magnetism.*

LAW Number 2.—*The first complete idea of the day is the ruling power of the day.*

LAW Number 3.—*The last complete idea of the waking hours is the saturating thought of the night.*

LAW Number 4.—*No person can fail in anything who builds on Laws 2 and 3.*

LAW Number 5.—*Ideas should be made worthy of supreme effort.*

It will be seen that the foundation required is of the highest importance, and the purpose is such as not to attract a dead mind. Ideas should be made worthy of supreme effort. This will not appeal to those who do not care for a grander life on earth. Yet there are many who will welcome the aid which we tender in these lessons.

The laws all help each other. The cultivation of patience is the basis of Self-Magnetism. The question arises, how can one cultivate patience? Then comes Law 2, which says that the first complete idea of the day is the ruling power of that day. The last complete idea of the day holds control in the night; but how? What kind of an idea is it that will assert such power in life? It must be an idea that is worthy of supreme effort. You see that these matters all work in a circle and are parts of each other.

A supreme effort is one to which you are willing to throw all your thoughts and determination for the time being. It must be a constant effort. Applying it to the second Law we find that the first complete idea of the day is the ruling power of that day; thus coming back to the original process.

The supreme effort must be directed toward whatever idea you choose to build upon; and, in this case, it is the idea contained in the first Law, the cultivation of patience as the basis of Self-Magnetism.

No person can think long upon any subject without being under the influence of the subject. This is a universal law, and is fully shown up in the great work of Universal Magnetism. The lover who gives his attention to the girl of his heart is sure to color all his daily life with the feeling he entertains for her. The man who allows his mind to dwell continually on sensual topics will color his conduct in that line of feeling, and his habits will be in the same channel; he will see in what he hears and reads only the drift of his mind. The same law holds true in the nobler lines of mental activity.

While the best minds are well balanced, and take in a great variety of subjects, the predominance of one above all others is sure to fill that life with its influences. The basis of Self-Magnetism is patience; because this quality is needed more than any other.

If we were to set up a school of training that would yield the best results in the career of every man and woman, we would at once start with this basic quality.

Patience is not endurance. We do not use it in that sense. It is instant suppression on its affirmative side, and instant courage on the negative side. In suppression it checks you at the very moment when you are about to give way. You suppress the display of anger, of petulance, of complaint, of exclamation, or of irritability. These are the enemies of happiness. The most common of them is irritability. A thousand little things each day may go wrong and you are fretted by them. Stop. Be patient. They will grow less in proportion as you are patient; they will grow more in proportion as you give way or let go. Self-Magnetism is self-power, and you have no power if you fail to rule yourself.

Then other persons soon understand your weakness.

The habit of giving way to little things, or to big ones, will soon grind out the exalted character of a man or woman, and what is left is dross. The latter is scoffed at in the world; but the commanding character is sure to attract and lead thousands of others.

On the negative side you must be patient because it will give you the courage to face all assaults from the shafts of enemies and misfortune. It will show the reverse side of every condition in life.

How is this commanding quality obtained?

It is planted like a tree in the garden or forest. But it is that kind of a tree or plant that is sensitive to attention or neglect. It needs little acts of care and thought, as well as the big determination to make it thrive.

Let the first attention of the day be given to it. This is done by placing the mind upon it as soon as you are awake in the morning. Say to yourself that you are determined to be PATIENT all day long. Say it as you arouse out of sleep. Say it as you jump from the bed with the spirit of a new-born day. Say it as you dress. Say it as the little vexing details of the morning's duties begin to come in your path. Say to yourself, "I'll be patient."

This is culture. It is training. It will engraft the principle in your very blood, in your nervous system, in your mind, and in all the avenues of your life.

Let us see what are some of the powers you will attain in your relations to yourself and to others by Self-Magnetism, starting at the basis, which is patience.

You may be so situated that you can take advantage of another; if so, think it out, and see the final disadvantage to yourself; then be patient and let time and fate lift you up to a higher realm of purpose. To conquer the disposition to wrong another is Self-Magnetism.

Someone has done you a wrong, or you fancy that such is

the case. Be patient. Let time work out the matter for you. If the wrong is in progress at the time, or if you are in danger from the evil acts or intentions of another, defend yourself at once. But the fancied wrongs, the misunderstood remarks, the injury that your over-sensitive nature imagines; these are mere vapors, whether they be true or not. Be patient and let them alone. Never let your feelings or fancies have control over you. They may be schooled in time.

Revenge is the basest of all motives. It has made the wars of earth. It has set up the standard of private enmity everywhere. It is the reason why feuds, lawsuits and slander exist. Be patient. Allow no such ghost to walk in your life.

If the tendency to set yourself or your opinion against some person or project shall appear at any time, be patient; remember that obstinate people are shadows in the world that cast a dark gloom over themselves and all others. It is noble to yield, especially when you feel that you ought not to do so.

If any form of temptation shall seek to control you, hold still for a while; think it over; be patient, and the impulse will soon be conquered. People who plunge into things without sufficient thought are usually sorry afterwards.

Do not deny to others the generous acts that well up in your heart on an occasion of true inspiration. Then it is that your better nature is at work in you; but your acquired disposition will soon control it. It is generous to speak well of another, but in moments of meanness the impulse comes to say the wrong thing. Be patient; let the ill nature vent itself. Try to never be guilty of hasty speech or act to the injury of another or the lowering of your own standard of nobility.

Apply Laws 2 and 3 to your daily life.

On what ground you please to explain the phenomenon, it is nevertheless true that the first earnest, vital thought of the morning will have a large share in controlling you all day. But the greater mystery is found in the fact that the last vital thought of the night, just as you are ready to drop asleep, is sure to saturate your being, and make you really what you are.

"MENTAL MASTERY."

We come now to the use of this principle in self-control, or the power over your own mind. Select any brief period just before you fall asleep at night; a few minutes will do; and then put the force of your thoughts wholly on the idea which you wish to control you; and you will find that the thought will live on in the brain and nervous system long after you have fallen asleep. The test of it is this:

Fixed inclinations rule every intelligent person. Some individuals are willing to tell falsehoods; others could not be induced to. In one make-up the inclination is ever present; in another the nature of the mind refuses to state an untruth. Conscience is the same thing. It is the result of inclination.

If a person is inclined to be discouraged, the tendency may be thrown off by the practice of Self-Magnetism. Let the mind just before sleep each night start on a search for the possibilities of success in the near future; let a hunt be made for everything that is bright or that may be turned to brightness and encouragement, and you will be surprised to learn how many pleasant prospects there are in your future. But you must hunt and search with the determination to find all that is bright in the possibilities of events; and you must not allow yourself to think of the dark side of anything. The habit is quickly formed, one way or the other.

The custom of worrying, of looking at only the dark side of the supposed morrow, or of seeing the possibilities of failure, is one of the forms of Self-Magnetism, by which it is seen that, if you do not take positive steps toward the better view, your own nature will take negative steps, and you will drift along the current of disappointment.

Very few people fail who are optimistic; very few succeed who are pessimistic. Caution and preparation must at all times be cultivated, but they are but the reins by which we drive the steeds of our inclinations.

The mind is conscious when we are not conscious of its operations. It goes on in its work while we are asleep, as is shown in the higher steps in the study, Seven Realms of Mind. This organ of life is active even when we are felled by a blow, a drug, or otherwise lose consciousness; but there is an immense difference between knowing and not knowing what it is doing. The mind is like the operation of circulation; sometimes we are able to detect what the heart is doing, and later we have no knowledge of its activity. We may feel the operation of the intestines, or may have no sensation in that direction; but our lack of consciousness does not prove that the intestines are inactive. So it is with thought, and with mental purpose.

You can set the pace of the mind's work for the next twenty-four hours by giving it the last suggestions of the night.

Did you ever stop to think that the mind is like a steed at play? If left to itself it will wander and drift and play and go on aimlessly, and be of little service to you; but if held subject to the rein it will lead you as you direct, and become your slave. The reason why so many persons cannot sleep at night is because they are being driven by their own steeds, the trains of thoughts that run adrift. The reason why so many people are made the tools of others is because they do not drive their own steeds of thought, but allow themselves to be driven by them.

In magnetism, one person is the controller, and another person is the subject. In Self-Magnetism, you are the controller and the subject; your mastery of yourself gives you the double office.

The reason why we select the last period of the waking hours is because, during the activities of the day, it is not so easy to divert the attention from what is going on; as many duties demand your thoughts. But at night, just before going to sleep, the mind should never be in the controlling part of its action; then of all times it should be made to do as you wish and command. Let it control you and you will be restless and adrift, not only during the night, but all day long after the morning has come. If you control it, you will find that the next day is a part of your thoughts of the night before. So true is this proposition that it has shaped the lives of the most successful men and women.

We have seen it work out the better inclinations of all classes of people, and in almost every age from infancy to maturity. It is a mistake to let children go to sleep at night thinking of the day that has just passed, unless there is much that is pleasant. The purposes of the morrow are what should be put in their little heads. We know of many discouraged boys and girls who could not learn their lessons, and who were disposed to take it to heart; but they were sent to bed with pleasant thoughts of the triumphs that they would achieve on the morrow, and they were shown the way of possible success in their studies, with the result that they awoke each morning with the victory nearer at hand.

Let the hand of the mind be pointed always ahead, never backward, when the time comes for sleep. This will give the thoughts a new power. We recall the case of a young man who had been hard at work for a long time on a matter that was too deep for him, and he was losing sleep as well as health in the struggle to conquer it. We suggested that he stop thinking of it during the day, and take up light reading and outdoor exercise for a week; but at night put himself to sleep thinking that there was some way of solving the tangle that would come to him of itself. He was able to understand the meaning of the plan, and he schooled himself to go to sleep at night with a certainty that there was to be triumph in a few days. At the end of a week, he was to give the first hours of the day to the matter, but should rest his mind the rest of the day, and at night should continue to put himself to sleep by taking the rosy view of the subject. Then he won, and his mind became all the stronger by reason of this kind of habit. In referring to the crisis, as he called it, he wrote to us the following explanation as it seemed to him: "I am convinced that the mind works out our desires without our aid, and that it can do better work when left alone, provided we hold the reins, and make known our purposes. It is like a team of horses that is struggling up an incline; we should keep them going in the right direction, but otherwise should let them get up without our interference." The simile is very helpful, for it is known that free rein is necessary when horses are struggling up a difficult steep. Yet how many persons lose their grip on their mental powers by nagging and fretting this great organ.

A little study of your nature will reveal to you the fact that there seems to be a power somewhere around that takes a special interest in your success. The mind is the portal of entrance for the good offices of this attendant angel; and you put up the bars when you drive out the pleasant prospects that wait your summoning. This friendly power is born of sunshine and basks in it. Darkness drives it off. There are two sides to everything; even the earth has two; and one is always in darkness while the other is always facing the sun; but the revolution of the earth gives all parts an opportunity to bathe in the sunshine. So every fact and every detail and every prospect in your life has two sides, one bright and the other dark; and you can turn them over in your mind at will, selecting the sunny side or looking only on the gloomy part. How will you present these details to your own mind? You can find what you seek in this world. Dr. Talmadge never said anything truer than this: "You may take any joy, and by turning it around, find troubles on the other side." Likewise you may take trouble and reverse it.

It is not easy at the very first trial to throw the mind into just the channel you wish; but the habit soon forms. We do not speak from theory, but from the experience of many tested trials in many of our followers. Of course it is easy for some preacher to tell his people to look on the bright side of things; that is advice, and nothing more. Advice is rarely ever accepted and acted upon, for humanity has had that kind of mental diet for thousands of years. Advice is abstract; Self-Magnetism is concrete, tangible, and effective. This power which we are now dealing with is as far from advice as the sun is far from the center of the earth. We may advise a person to do all the good things of life, but there must be some helpful action by which it is possible to take up a definite line of practice. The common remark, "I will be optimistic," is mere air in most lives, for the nervous forces of the brain have nothing to grasp.

But just as the mind is entering into its night's sleep, it is ready to take up given directions, which it cannot do as well at any other time; but the next best opportunity being the first waking period of the morning. But night is by far the best. If you go to sleep, and someone awakens you, and tells you certain things, you will adopt them, and in time they will control you, provided you do not fully awaken and throw off the suggestion. That this is a well established psychological law cannot now be doubted; it is so easy of proof that no one has a right to doubt it. Nor is any charm or other notion needed; it is plain, natural fact founded upon the known operations of the mind. You can do as much with any person whom you can approach upon the conditions named; and the only chance of failure is in the clumsy way in which you may go at it.

What you can do upon some one else, some one else can do upon you; and what some one else can do upon you, you can do upon yourself. But, you will say, you do not get into the half-sleep state when you try this upon yourself. You should start as soon as you begin to get sleepy, and you should keep up the practice until you drop off to slumber; thus meeting exactly the other conditions named.

The almost uniform success of this practice in the past few years gives perfect certainty in its usefulness. *We know that it cannot fail.*

Now let us advise you to read, and again to read, and still read ALL that has been stated on all the pages of this treatment or treatise, until you understand it. You may think you understand it, from the first reading; but what is the use of getting only a faint idea of the power, and letting it rest at that, as far as the reading is concerned; plunging ahead with the practice in a wrong way, or with only half of the spirit of the instructions in your mind? We strongly advise the reading of these pages, or some of them, just as you are about to retire at night, so that your thoughts will be absorbed in the right idea.

Suggestion must take actual form; it must live in language; it cannot be a wish, unless words and sentences are constructed in which that wish may dwell. The mind has some tangible place in which to live; and so has the soul. The frail human body is a constructed abode. In like manner the sentence is the house of a thought. A wish, an idea, a hope, if vague and unframed, will vanish to nothing. Therefore, it is of the highest importance that you have some sentences in mind; not the following, but some made after them, suited to the trend of your thoughts that will give strength to the structure of your wishes and hopes:

"I know there is a chance of success in everything."

"There is no doubt whatever that I can succeed."

"I will surely find the bright side of this matter."

"I will think and act with courage."

"My thoughts are fixed on the certainty of doing just what I have in mind."

"Let me see if I can count the number of things that I will accomplish tomorrow."

"This trouble looks dark at first view, but I KNOW there is a blessing in it; and I will find it."

"I am going to sleep tonight with the idea fixed in my mind that I shall find the right way in this difficulty."

Thousands and tens of thousands of such sentences may be formed, and as they are uttered silently the mind should see the words of the sentences very clearly. This is like setting an automatic phonograph to a certain idea and letting it keep repeating it all night long, as the mind will surely do.

Now just see the danger of allowing this mind of yours to set its own tune for the night; to make its own pace, and saturate your nervous system with its weakening and discouraging results.

Think over the two ways.

They are not new things; but have been practiced by the noblest men and women of all ages. Some allow themselves to drop to sleep between their better hopes and their solid determinations to win; and this is the grandest form of the habit; it is the most exalted example of Self-Magnetism.

"PUTTING THE POWER INTO RESULTS."

Self-mastery and perfect control of the forces that are marshalled in your life, must be shown by a new line of conduct in all your waking hours. Let us see what this should be.

In the first place you should take the deadness and flabbiness out of your nerves. Vital weakness is the opposite of magnetism. It is a sort of nerve-relaxation, and not muscular ease. The two are not the same. The muscles may be weak, and the nerves strong; and magnetism follows the character of the nerves. Many people have enough muscular energy, but wholly lack nerve energy; and they are not magnetic.

When energy is changed into muscle-setting, it is no longer

evidence of magnetism, but of physical exertion. This distinction is very hard to teach. On its being understood depends all success in this one branch of habit-culture.

This study has been covered in Chapter Seventeen in the section "Self Containment."

The beginning of this habit is in the perfect control of the body and all its parts. If you lack grace, ease, good poise, polish and the traits that outwardly mark the lady and gentleman, try to attend some school where expression is taught, or seek a graduate of such a school, and obtain all the training possible. It would require hundreds of pages to teach it by book, and that kind of teaching is not effective. The schools of expression are everywhere increasing in numbers and they are doing a grand work. They teach the best use of the faculties, which is so essential to success. Among these are the development of rich and pleasing voices, the mastery of the art of modulation, and the attainment of perfect self-control under all circumstances. Thus expression and magnetism go hand in hand.

Habit-culture is next best as a means of securing control of the body. It does not require practice, but will claim attention during the period that you are passing out of old ways into new. It is necessary to form the habit of observing yourself, to see what are the faults that are likely to mar your usefulness or lessen the respect that others may have for you. There is no personal magnetism that is strong enough to overcome the disgust that follows certain defects of judgment. The man who sucks his teeth in a drawing-room is doomed in the opinions of all who have been offended by the breach of etiquette; and likewise the individual who is in need of a bath, or whose breath is fetid, or who is nasty at the table, or who performs any one or more of the animal characteristics that still cling to our race, is certain to drop so low in the judgment of others on whom these faults are inflicted, that no amount or kind of magnetism will offset the damage.

But there is another class of faults that affect the person guilty of them more than the observers of them, and yet are handicaps in both ways. The most noticeable of these is physical restlessness. It wearies the eye of the beholder, but it also weakens the vital centers of the person who is restless. There can be no self-containment where this fault exists.

While it requires several volumes containing many private lessons for learning the art of controlling others, it is however true that the habit-culture of this chapter will develop in every person who adopts it as much magnetism as is obtainable by natural gift, and as much success in using it. The fact that there are many intricate arts employed in the use of this power should not discourage a person. The study of magnetism in human affairs is almost as limitless as life itself. A careful adoption of the suggestions of this treatise will bring ample reward; and progress will be most decisive.

Chapter Thirty-two

EVERY HUMAN LIFE
MUST HAVE
A FIXED DESTINY
AND DEFINITE GOAL

ADRIFT AND ASHORE

OU SEE THE MAY morning creeping up over the ocean's edge, and you hear the airs of countless birds that carol their joyous strains on the breeze. It is a time of hope and of preparation. At the dock the great boat is showing signs of an early departure. The hands are everywhere active and the steam is thrumming in the pipes. The noise of countless voices is heard above the rolling of freight and the stir of passengers. Soon the order will be given for letting loose the lines that bind the giant vessel to the wharf, and the sea will open its wide expanse to the ever-seeking view.

Within the hold of the lower decks the merchandise and general stores are rich in value and full of usefulness to those who are embarking on the long voyage.

The ship itself is qualified to sail by its own power in any sea and to any port. The earth is not too large for its movements over the surface of the deep. In fact if there were another orb attached to this and if connection were possible, this great vessel could make its way to the farthermost parts of the annexed world and still have power and supplies to carry on its enterprise.

Now comes the order to let go.

The last line is taken in and the monster craft begins to move, although so slowly that she seems yet to be standing still, and the land appears to be receding, pier, dock-house and all. Down the glassy bay she winds her stately course, while all the lesser shipping stands aghast at the splendid display of power.

No freight could be more precious than the stores of value she upbears on the bosom of the deep; no lives could be more useful to the world than those that are borne along with this mighty structure that the genius of man has created out of the forest and the mines.

From the city's edge to the outer banks of earth and landscape the boat moves, and comes upon islands and rocks that stand aside to let her pass. Salutes are given and exchanged and all the world seems to wait the message that is being carried onward by this noble agent of an unseen power.

At last the shores seem to lie low and then to fade from view, as the round surface of water rises to make a new horizon. The day droops and twilight with its chill and yet its soft winds is coming down as though from the overcast sky. Colors float about the west and the dark east grows black, while the ship makes it its goal and plunges into the night without thought of fear. Some master hand is in charge of the craft and there is composure and calm in every mind and heart.

The sea is no longer glassy.

Gentle waves are tossing white caps that fret about the boat and show a desire to beat hard against the iron hull; but they fall away discouraged and nothing comes of their tiny onslaught. The clouds join the miniature battle but also give up the fight and break for hiding places in the deserted north, while the moon peers forth in her queenly beauty. Golden bars cross the water and stretch from the ship's side to the untraveled realm that leads away to heaven.

Few of the passengers care to retire as long as this scene is being enacted. Silently they watch the growing glory, resting now by the very edge of the boat or pacing the deck with clasped hands and upturned faces. On goes the great ship without halting or slack of speed. She sails through the night with ease and pride, and other craft pass her with signals, or, being too distant, allow her to go on her independent course.

From the gray east where not a cloud has built its airy palaces, the light brightens and the sleeping hosts give it no heed, so beautiful was the night before. Their tired bodies still rest below.

One by one after the orb of day has climbed to a lofty place in the sky, the men come out and drowsy women follow.

The day is bright and attractive. The ocean is all its own, for not a trace of land or island can be seen, and other ships are scant and far away. Steadily the voyage proceeds. Meals come and go, night gives place to day, and weeks flit by, while all is content on the ship. At length a port is seen far off to the front but the ship ignores it.

Who is the master of this great vessel?

He comes forth on the highest bridge and gives commands at times, and again his officers attend to the duty of directing the floating home.

As he stands at times within sight of the passengers they wonder how one so young as to seem a mere boy could have attained to so great a rank as master of the ship. Yet in the boyish face there are lines of mature thought that indicate the weight of responsibility. These lines show promise of deepening as the voyage proceeds.

Months more are spent and ports have appeared in sight again and again, but the boat has never headed for them. Whence goes she?

The youthful master has indeed grown older, and the lines are now deepening into furrows.

Whence goes the ship?

"We do not know," is the response from the passengers one and all.

"I do not know," is the admission from the young man who has the ship in charge. No one knows. The supplies seem to hold out, and there is hardly any prospect of their becoming scant. The power is not as great as at the start, but still it suffices. On they sail never landing, never making port, and never showing knowledge of their destiny. A few of the passengers have grown old or sick or feeble and have died, only to feed the ravenous fish in the deep below. More have died, and more are weak. The crew has thinned out to such an extent that they are not able to yield the service that so strong and powerful a vessel demands, and signs of slowing speed and disintegration are everywhere becoming manifest.

The hull is weighted down with decay and barnacles.

The wood and iron are without paint and creak with loosening joints and parting beams.

Now all the passengers are dead except a few who cannot creep upon the deck; and the crew is too feeble to do its work. The boat must float under other power than its own; winds and waves beat it to and fro, and shoals are ahead. It would seem strange if so noble a ship should strand on a barren shore where neither city nor inhabitant will give it welcome or help.

It is adrift.

Of what use is the grandest structure that the brain of man can conceive, with its freight of supreme value, with its load of passengers and its trained crew, if the master has no port to which to steer its little world of power and of opportunity?

Of what use is an abundance of useful faculties if they are allowed to take us on pleasure trips across unknown waters never to return? No man and woman is so poor in this world as to be without the same relative powers as those described in this great ship. But they set sail without goal and seek no shore until the weakening forces become the prey of wind and wave, and then all is stranded on distant and inhospitable sands.

"CONTROL OF THE USEFUL FACULTIES."

These are the equipment of every life.

They are abundant in all who have the slightest ambition, and are standing ever ready to be employed. But the ship, grand as it may be, sails on under the fairest promises and seeks no shore nor has in view any port or destiny. The faculties are allowed to run away with the vessel, and all falls to ruin when, as is almost always the case, the heart yearns for some fruitage for having made the voyage.

The powers that are given to humanity are capable of bringing results that will not cause the soul to quail when the curtain is falling on the last act of this drama. "I have lived without result," is the thought and often the language of the man and the woman who has achieved nothing but the securing of a living. To win a little money is not enough. To wring from the earth the food and the means of shelter is not enough.

Most drifting masters of the ship of life look upon the attainment of wealth as the one goal of earthly existence, with the promise to themselves that, after this has been attained, then the other departments of the being may be considered. So the boat drifts without port or shore.

The accumulation of wealth can bring nothing more than the house for shelter, the clothing for the body, and food to sustain it; unless it topples to the other extreme of adding luxury, and here ruin enters. There has never been a time in the life of any human being, and there will never yet be such a time, when luxury, or excess of comfort will not weaken both mind and body. The hardihood of the great men and women of the world has been the staying powers of all their faculties. Comforts are intended to lessen the depressing influences of living on a plane below the necessities of existence. They bring us up to the high water mark of useful activities and become partners in all wholesome enterprises; but luxury is decay, for it takes the place of effort and destroys the need of energy.

Given what powers you know you possess, you should turn them to the most exalted usefulness all through life. Do not make the mistake of thinking that charity or parting with your possessions is the key to usefulness, for this is not true. The rich men and women of this land are doing more to injure and weaken the sinews of industry and ambition by their indiscriminate giving, than all the tramps and lazy idlers can show to their credit on the reverse side of the ledger. When Christ said that the woman who had given the mite had out-classed the rich man who had given from his abundance, He struck the keynote of true charity. The poor should learn the lesson that God will not do for those who will not do for themselves; and, when they have learned this lesson, they will become producers of their own income instead of entering into a general conspiracy with defunct rich folks to be fed and cared for.

The truly needy require the care of those who can help them, but they do not grow thrifty and industrious when they know that the pinching fingers of poverty will not be felt as a result of studied neglect and indifference. Penalties must and should be borne by those who have invited them. Poor people who accept charity with annual regularity are the most extravagant spendthrifts in the world in proportion to their incomes, and the most indifferent to consequences when, through a "handout," they have a little with which to gratify their tastes and whims.

The peculiar force with which a man or woman who has lived in vain will undertake to atone for it and do something that can be called useful by indiscriminate giving, is a mark of the wreck of the soul that is about to strand upon the hidden shoals.

In this country alone it is reckoned that one hundred billions of money has been given away by the rich in the past four years; the rich who have accomplished nothing but to receive or accumulate money. They cannot purge their souls in this way. Such giving as is now on the increase is a mental and ethical disease.

Far better would it be to establish a government fund to be sustained wholly by private giving, for the support of men and women who have gone through life with ambition and zeal, who have been willing to do a fair share of their work, who have lived decent lives, and who are now unable to support themselves. If we were to be blessed with the billions that are thrown to the winds of fickle charity every year, we would make homes for the homeless who would maintain them. Indifference to good living and the duties of citizenship would not be rewarded by support after years of laziness and the gratification of beastly tastes. If a man will not work he shall not eat, is the word of God. But the weak rich controvert this doctrine and set up their edict as follows: If a man or woman who can work and will not, becomes desirous of receiving money and food and clothing and luxuries, we will provide them.

Penalties must be paid.

The penalty of allowing useful faculties to run to waste should be paid by suffering and poverty.

As we go to press we have heard of a family with whom we have been acquainted for years, who are all on the verge of starvation. The father at one time received a salary of three thousand dollars a year under the United States Government. His hours of work were ridiculously few and his actual services were worth about fifty dollars a month. But the United States Government is engaged in ruining the faculties and powers of usefulness in thousands of its so-called employees, by short hours and an insufficient requirement of services. It cannot be true that the work done in the clerical departments of the government is harder than similar work done in mercantile establishments.

By this weakening sinecure method of employ this man with the salary of three thousand dollars a year became useless to himself. He went through with the routine work day after day, consisting mostly of sitting and opening and shutting papers and documents, and drew his princely salary of three thousand dollars a year. This went on for twenty years. Before he was appointed to the government position he had succeeded in earning from five hundred to eight hundred dollars a year by long hours and hard work; and he had saved up two thousand dollars.

After he became a government employee he saved up three more thousand dollars in the first two years, and had five thousand dollars invested. Then his useful faculties having weakened, he began to spend more than his salary. His investments were sacrificed in high living, and his wife and two daughters assisted in the wild wastefulness. They became arrogant, looked down on their neighbors, were saucy and indifferent to suggestion, and defied fate.

Then came the loss of the position attended with debts that could never be paid, and finally poverty.

Their poverty became so abject that it was the subject of pity. But somehow the people who knew them would not lift a helping hand, and they now plead in vain. One man who had been as close a friend as such a fellow could have under the circumstances, said in a letter: "I have four hundred dollars that I can spare as well as not, and this man was my friend. But I fear that if I give it to him it will set so bad an example to others like him and his family, that it will do no good although it may afford a temporary relief. I have therefore made up my mind to give this four hundred dollars to a poor man who has been working hard to pay off a mortgage on his little place." This was done and the arrogant government product was left to his penalty.

Find out what are your most useful faculties and seek the means whereby you can control them and turn them to advantage in life. Do not wait till it is too late. The time to save the ship is before it strikes the rocks.

"CHOOSING AN AVOCATION."

By the law of magnetism and of destiny an avocation chooses the individual, and the individual never successfully chooses the avocation. The deliberate selection of some calling is as absurd as the decision of the fond father before his son is born, to make him a lawyer or a preacher or some other thing, before the sex of the child is known.

No parent can choose an avocation for a boy or a girl, and no boy or girl can do this either. As has been stated under the law of magnetism the avocation is bound to choose the individual. If this process of nature is interfered with, disaster will follow, as has been the case in millions of instances.

Look back over the life history of any person for whom an avocation has been chosen, and get at the facts that lie hidden often in the debris of failure or mediocrity.

When the avocation chooses the individual there can be no failure.

Do not study theories, but come in touch with the hard facts of life. Men and women will talk with you, and they will tell you freely the facts in their own careers.

Nothing has been to us a more interesting theme than the line of conversation that deals with this one great and vital law of fate. We have had the expressed opinions of the most successful people and the rule still is always the same, that, under the law of magnetism and of destiny, the avocation will surely choose the individual.

It may come late in life, but what does this matter when failure would have occupied the whole stage of life even to the seventh and last if one endured so long?

What shall be the avocation?

Shall it be that of an employee or of an employer, of a professional career or in the pursuit of art?

The story of choice must begin in general preparation. There is no such thing as special preparation until the avocation has made its choice. Let this fact be kept in mind.

Genius or youthful precocity often manifests itself early in life, and sometimes before the child has reached the age of ten; but this is unusual. If, however, the avocation has then actually called the individual, the selection is over, and all will be well. But mere precocity is not a sure guide. There must be substantial evidence of sound genius; and careful watchfulness is necessary to save the youth from himself.

Until the facts are known to a certainty the life of the boy or girl and of the young man and young woman must proceed along the lines of general preparation. This subject will be found fully discussed in the description given to such themes as the young man under fifteen, the young woman under fifteen, the development of manhood and the blossoming of womanhood. There are many facts and laws there which will bear studying and reviewing scores of times. Do not depend on a single reading of them; nor upon one or two reviews. The facts there stated are so potent and so applicable in this connection that they should be absorbed and made a part of one's acquisition. Not one statement should be omitted from the most serious attention.

General preparation is, then, the law at this stage of the study. We know of no calling in life where general preparation will not be of help. No person has ever been successful who has lacked it, for the very idea of a specialty is the current of wisdom that runs through it. To be nothing but a lawyer, in the sense that the knowledge of law is all sufficient, would make a man so narrow that he could not deal with the rest of the race. He would be all in all to himself and the law books, but he could not connect his acquisition with helpfulness to the world or to himself.

It might be thought that the painter need know nothing

but his art, yet his art is the reflection of a vast realm of knowledge in which human nature is paramount.

The same law underlies the whole consideration of the subject. General preparation is the basis. Without it the rule of destiny will be paralyzed.

"FITTING ONESELF FOR A LIFE CALLING."

The suggestions just made fit now in this and the final theme of the present course of training. The purpose is to connect the powers that are derived from magnetism, with the highest attainments in life. Let us see if this can be done.

The basis is a general preparation, and what this means has already been stated.

In this preparation the effort should be made to discover the faculties that are most easily developed, and then give them the greatest amount of attention.

Having too many irons in the fire is not helpful to any person. To be ground under conflicting and discordant interests will make diamond dust of the qualities that are given to all persons. Avoid floating. To roll from place to place will gather nothing worth having.

On the other hand it is not good judgment to remain the same thing all the time. The commonplace is the humdrum style of living.

What is meant by the commonplace has been amply described, and it should be understood in its true meaning. Do not get out of the duties that make up the commonplace, but add to them enough outward reaching to destroy the humdrum conditions.

There are two great influences at work in every human life, and they are molded by the training that unfolds the larger vocabulary of which so much has been said in the earlier of these episodes, and by the inherent power that is developed by the acquisition of the colors in the analysis of the moods and feelings. Go back to the pages where the power of education that comes from the study of language has been described, and find out what is meant by the unfolding of the magnetic realm through the greater hold on the natural thoughts that are universal throughout all created life.

This development will place a man or woman in touch with the whole gamut of avocations. All that is in the being will come into action, and the line of life-work for which one is most fitted will take its place in the foreground, claiming attention.

Another and simpler way of stating this fact is this:

If you are a graduate of the first book of practice in the course of magnetism, you will have made your powers of attraction keen and strong. This will render the present course of training a rapid and splendid success. All the directions of the teaching should be grasped to know what is insisted upon. This will fit you for the most advanced stage of self development. An all-round progress is necessary in the use of the moods and feelings, in order that you may know yourself and all those who come into any form of relationship with you.

We now have the following steps in the make-up of the individual who is ambitious to ascertain the life-calling that is most to be desired:

1. The development of personal magnetism by the use of the course in the exercise book, known as the first course. The present work is not allowed to go to any person who does not first have that course, so that it is certain that you possess it.

2. The development of the full colors of the moods and feelings and the many uses that are suggested for them in this work.

3. The acquisition of the largest possible vocabulary of words that reflect the powers of the inherent nature, such as suggested in the episodes in the preceding chapters of this work, referring to the young man under fifteen, the young woman under fifteen, the development of manhood and the blossoming of womanhood.

4. A general all-round preparation in the shape of knowledge on all the subjects that are useful in a practical life.

5. Then add the inspiration that comes from the reading of biography. At this stage of the progress such inspiration may touch as with magic the very chord that may vibrate against the line of life-work for which a person is designed.

In all this plan not a minute is lost. No time can be wasted.

The thoughts will run along the best channels, and will be tending toward the goal of fitness. Every part of the way will show progress of the most gratifying character.

Whether a person be magnetic by nature or by cultivation, the result is the same. There is a natural fund of personal power in most lives that are active, and it sooner or later draws from the greater fund of opportunity. But words, words, words are the agencies of development if they are absorbed and made living realities in the inherent being. A man who had no education but a strong natural fund of magnetism in the crude state, did not find his development until he acquired words. Then all was easy. The more words he added to his usable and living vocabulary, the more he was drawn away from the humdrum existence with which he was weighted down; and soon his ambitious soul was ready to soar to the greater things of life. He was past thirty when he first stepped out of the commonplace conditions into the work for which he was fitted.

This same rule will apply to every man and woman.

Activity is magnetism; but useful and result-producing activity is a thousand times more magnetic than hap-hazard or commonplace effort no matter how energetic it may be.

Trying one thing after another grinds away the hope of reward. Whatever is entered upon should be pursued until it has crystallized into some useful attainment; then it need not be pursued further if there is a distaste for it.

One person will take up the study of French; stick to it for at least three years, at the rate of not less than three hours a week, and then drop it; but do not begin it and withdraw from the study. The same rule should apply to all studies that are undertaken. Either do not engage in them, or cling to the work until some good has been achieved.

If you must earn your own living, do so under any honorable circumstances; but, wherever you begin work, do not allow a minute to be wasted, for you can add to your general knowledge by training courses, which are the only genuine help that can be sought. Reading for the purpose of becoming well informed is wasted time. Biography, poetry and history are the three lines of general reading open to one who wishes to advance. To these add training courses.

We have for thirty years advised young men and young women to thus improve their minds; and we are glad to note the fact that some have done so.   The following case is typical of thousands:

A young man of twenty had been advised by his father and his uncle to take up the study of law, while his mother favored the ministry. He attended the law school and found that the whole profession was unattractive to him. Later on he sought the ministry. After two years of this preparation he abandoned it. At twenty-five he was adrift, sailing on unknown seas without rudder or compass.

Under our suggestion he accepted some position where he could earn some part of his living. While in this employment he followed a plan of mental improvement, accepting the motto: "Let no moment be lost in idle talking, idle thinking, idle reading or useless activities." This precept was hung where he could see it and also was carried in his pocketbook. Still acting under advice he made the business in which he was engaged the most important theme of his life during the hours that belonged to his employer. Another motto was given him which read as follows: "Think hard, plan hard and work hard to ascertain in what way the business may be made more successful." It must make no difference if the good to be accomplished cannot be seen. Do not let the idea prevail that such extra effort will bring advantage to no one but the employer. Good will somehow come to reward earnest and sincere efforts that are made solely for the advantage of another. This seemed like a hard doctrine, but it was lived up to.

All the while the man was making himself valuable. He took up the study of magnetism and thus made his powers greater and his energy of execution a leverage for success under the most trying circumstances.

Soon he was too valuable a man for his employer to let go; but he did not like the business and never had a thought of remaining. His salary was increased several times, yet he chose to find more congenial employment or activity.

His uncle was a man of wealth and his father was in moderate circumstances. A certain secret process had made the uncle rich. The nephew at times, almost involuntarily, wondered what it was, but he did not care to ask, even if he had thought he might be told. Not even his father knew. At the hour of retiring he found his thoughts centering on the idea, and this condition of his mind would last for an hour or more before he could get asleep.

His uncle who had wished the nephew to enter upon the study of law, found him surprisingly appreciated in the place where he had sought employment, as all thought for the time being only. But he did not know that the nephew had made himself valuable by the exercise of the strongest will-power and severest application, both of which were naturally not within his temperament. The uncle however wished the young man to come into his business and perhaps to inherit it as he had no children, although he was blessed with several nephews and nieces. The man thought he saw the chance to step to higher things and accepted, as the salary was double what he was then receiving.

But the wary uncle did not choose to tell him the secret process that had made him rich. He contented himself with writing it down in full description, sealing it and placing it in the safe of a deposit company, directed to his executors in case he should die suddenly. The wife was not taken into the secret and would not have understood it had she been, for it required a technical mind to understand it.

The nephew had thought hard and long and for many months. In the new sphere of activities he saw how the process worked out, and his mind was ripe for a discovery. It came in such form that he was enabled to couple it to that which his uncle possessed; and the two together produced a new result that achieved the greatest success yet attained. The income from the combined secret processes was enormous, and the nephew came in for his due share. The strange part of the matter was that the nephew and the uncle both became necessary to each other; one knew part of the process, and the other knew the culminating part of the advanced method; but neither would disclose the secret which each held.

The nephew is now worth millions and is still active in business.

Had he entered the law he would not probably have accumulated ten thousand dollars by this time, and he would have been engaged in an avocation for which he had no taste or liking.

His acceptance of the position of clerk after he was past twenty-five years of age and when he should have been well on the way to success in some chosen avocation, seemed to him a still more wanton waste of time. But he was accepting advice and he did not know what else to do. In that position he had the opportunity for making himself exceedingly valuable. As he grew in value to himself and to others, he also improved his own mind and accumulated powers through the study of magnetism that made him a keen and deep thinker. It was a natural thing for his mind, during its imprisonment in narrow environments, to seek the opportunity to unfold its wings and take new flight into other zones.

But at this point the only thing for him to do was to keep on with his plan of self-improvement, and bide his fate. This came to him in the silent hours of the night when he could not sleep until he had done some important thinking that seemed to him to be in the line of curiosity. But it was destiny at work.

Each step was necessary to every succeeding one. There could have been no leap from the condition of idleness that confronted him at twenty-five, to the solving of the problems, for he was yet unprepared to enter the business house of his uncle, nor would the latter have been attracted to him until he had made his value known in the first position.

The whole story is told in this one account.

If you can read between the lines you can understand how a person can fit himself for a life calling. The man now admits that the avocation which is his at this time is his destiny, and that it called him.

Thus the law holds true that the avocation will seek the individual and not the individual the avocation.

To be called, one must be ready for each opportune step in the process.

"THE LAW OF DESTINY."

To every magnetic man or woman there is a destiny waiting to be fulfilled.

This law has been recognized in every age for thousands

of years. It has been applied to every person above the rank of the commonplace. The biographies of great men and women show that they were and are believers in the law of destiny. Napoleon judged himself by this standard alone. Frederick the Great plunged to battle under full belief in the efficacy of the law. Wellington said, before Waterloo, that his star was about to rise. Grant, after Vicksburg, said: "When the surrender was a certainty I knew that I must end the war." In one way and another there has been a belief in the destiny of the individual. But who ordains it and by what law is it worked out?

In the first place it must be fully understood that the whole universe is a clockwork of interchangeable influences that have no limit and no end.

In the second place it must be understood that this clockwork is telling the progress of all parts of the universe in and through all the orbs that spin their courses in the sky.

In the third place it must be understood that progress is possible only where there is constant activity.

In the fourth place it must be understood that each and every part of created life is involved in the work that is going on. Nothing is too small to be of service. Indeed the very basis of all change is located in the tiny cell so small that billions of them can stand on the point of the finest needle. By these minute organisms the grandest results are achieved. Humanity, then, is not too insignificant to be considered as highly important in the process.

Activity is the strongest magnet that exists.

Humanity, in order to be included in the work of advance must be in harmony with the unceasing activity that is urging on every step of the way.

In the march of events the same material is used over and over again. The commonplace returns to the earth or whatever fund it came from, and this is the process of nature. We do not believe that God or nature will assist those who refuse to lend a helping hand to the great cause of universal advancement; and, for this reason, we believe that all persons who persist in living commonplace lives are shut out from the law of destiny.

This law is one of the most difficult to understand on a casual reading, and yet, after it has been well considered by the thinking mind, it is the plainest, most simple and most far-reaching of any principle in the whole universe.

The culminating reasons for its establishment are fully stated in the most elaborate manner in the greater work of Universal Philosophy.* Such discussion has no place in this work.

Nor, on the other hand, can we leave the student in the dark as to what is meant by the law and how it is able to affect the destiny of a man or woman.

One of the basic rules is this:

There is a fixed general purpose in everything, and there is a special design in each and every detail of life.

This rule is so completely proved, and its operations are so held up to the light of investigation that not the slightest trace of a doubt is left in any class of intelligent minds, no matter how humble. If this rule cannot be sustained by proof beyond the vestige of a dispute, then there is no sun and the earth is a myth.

Something tangible must be known to rest investigations upon.

Surmise and theory are not wholesome to the brain and stand as images of vapor in every scholarly mind. In dealing with the propositions that affect the most vital interests of the soul and of life on earth in particular, the most unsatisfactory of all plans is to admit suppositions, probabilities and possibilities where it is possible to find absolute conclusions. The latter are not so numerous as to crowd a book, and therefore should be hailed with welcome when they appear in any garb.

It is a proved fact that there is a fixed general purpose in everything.

It is a proved fact that there is a special design in each and every detail of life.

Nature is trying to uplift all life, and is exerting herself as best she can to this end. Everywhere can be seen the marks of the struggle to advance the conditions of the face of the earth and each species of value that dwells thereon. Man, being the most valuable and important of all the species, is the natural object of this purpose to improve life.

---

*Referring to our giant system ''Future Seeing and Destiny'' (1,000 Lessons in Philosophy).

Breaking through every condition that exists, there can be found the impulse to better it. Progress is the religion of nature. It is the first law of God, both in and out of the Bible. The goal is summed up in the one word perfection; and, while it is not attainable in this world under the burden of the present evils, it is nevertheless the only word in the vocabulary of nature and nature's Creator. It is the direction in which all life is tending.

As has been aptly spoken, it matters not how fast you are traveling, the important fact is the direction in which you are going. Nature's goal is in the right direction; and, if we do not reach that end, we are safe as long as we are moving in that direction.

To be born, to grow up, to survive the ills of life, to keep the body alive for many years, to get enough to feed it, to clothe it, and to shelter it: these may seem the chief purposes of existence to the individual; but nature gives such details no heed at all. In her sweep onward the inefficient soul is a pigmy in a flood of fire. The end only is in her view.

Out of a thousand buds that form upon the fruit tree nature can spare nine hundred and not miss them. Those that bear the impress of staunch value are her special and only care. For them she has a destiny and a reward.

To be in harmony with the spirit of advancement is to be the petted and loved child of nature. To find some means of making yourself better because of living, and of making some one else still better by reason of your own existence, is to stand in line with nature. Her impulses all go out toward you, and her hand is held to yours to uplift and sustain you in a new and higher rank in the world.

Nature has no present purpose but to connect the weak past with the strong future. If you are dead to this purpose you will become but the stepping stone on which others will march to victory; for it is a triumph to be able to add one jot to the small advancement of each era.

While the fact is an old one, it has never before been brought to the attention of the public; and what is hidden up to the time of its discovery may be regarded as new when found. For all purposes this law is new.

It is new to the people to study the plan of nature's progress, and to seek to fall in line with it. Nature has in her mind the carrying on of her great work of advancement, and she will have equally in her mind the man or the woman who comes into harmony with her purpose.

Taking as the basis the greater series of facts that are established in Universal Philosophy, and accepting as true their perfect demonstrations, we find that general and special design are everywhere manifest. We also find that each person may be the object of specific care in the guardianship of nature; by which is meant that an individual may be guarded and cared for as well as uplifted and advanced by the direct mind of nature.

For countless ages all things have been coming up through the night into the light.

The tendency is still upward and will not cease until the goal has been reached. This goal cannot be attained in the present generation, nor is there any person now living who will come within hailing distance of it; but it is in sight and nature is moving toward it with unremitting energy.

The belief that one person cannot accomplish much in the plan of nature is error. Through humanity all will be achieved. The grain of sand might withdraw from the mountain on the same plea so often made by indifferent people: "Oh, there are enough without me."

In the law of destiny each individual stands and acts alone. It is to be assumed that such person is all that is necessary. The fabric of progress cannot fall because of others' neglect if the individual who is inspired to act does the best that is possible to such unit.

Imagine yourself nothing but a grain of sand, if that is your estimate of your value. God works out all His problems with particles.

But, having made up your mind that you are something, even if only a grain of sand, do the best that you can under the circumstances and conditions that frame your existence. This best consists of two lines of duty: One to yourself, and the other to the world. This is rightly called

NATURAL RELIGION.

We do not wish to suggest any new sect or new denomination of religious interest; for there are too many of these subdivisions now among the people. We would be the first to oppose and to fight down any new branch of the church, as the old established sects and denominations are already too numerous. Natural religion fits into every man's creed like heavenly raindrops into the parched earth. Its creed is very plain and straightforward:

1. *The highest duty to self.*
2. *The highest duty to the world.*
3. *Constant activity in the exercise of each duty.*

Here we have the trinity of belief, and there is but one rule in the penal code of natural religion:

Time wasted is the greatest sin.

The first law is that of the highest duty to self. The question may be asked with the fervor of deepest earnestness, what shall such duty consist of? And the answer must always be the same: "This course of training in Advanced Magnetism, which is now drawing to a close contains the whole story."

We believe in codes. They are wholesome to the mind and helpful to the art of living. If you will take the first ten pages of this work as the beginning of a private code which we wish you to make for yourself, you will find in them certain ideas that should be written down on separate paper, or in a small book, putting their subjects only in writing, and then reviewing them until you understand their value to yourself. Having done this, then proceed to the next ten pages, and note down the helpful suggestions, and so go through the whole book. To your surprise you will have a mass of guiding facts and principles that will serve you for a lifetime.

They show you the highest duty to yourself.

In the matter of education much has been stated under the episodes relating to the development of manhood and the blossoming of womanhood. These fit the mind for the great battle of life; and, through the mind, they reach all the faculties and make them stronger and better in every useful way.

It is not likely that all the suggestions and training methods of this entire course could be adopted by a person who was very busy; but they contain the essentials of self development and some of them must be absorbed into one's life or the duty that is the highest of all will not be fulfilled.

The debt of care that the progressive individual owes to

the world at large, is not paid by helping aimless and useless people to bridge over the misfortunes that result from their own neglect and indifference. Such people are valueless to nature and are in the way of her advancement; and for you to reward them with unearned advantages and blessings will serve only to increase their shiftlessness without exciting their gratitude.

Your highest duty to the world is to help those who are trying to help themselves, to encourage them in their efforts, and see that no fatal stumbling block is placed in their pathway. Under the training of this course in Advanced Magnetism, you will find ample means to ascertain what is needed in the performance of this duty.

Constant activity is the most magnetic charm in all the universe.

It is a magnet that draws from all directions and from all sources. But the kind of activity should be selected with the greatest of care. There must be an object in all that is done, and some final goal in view. This object need not be your life avocation, but the attainment of some grain of usefulness that will be of service to life.

Certain kinds of activity are wastefulness of time, and here a sin is committed in the very act of effort. Play is helpful as a dessert to work; but the best play in the world is variety of useful work; for the change from one kind of duty to another is a relief to the faculties that were wearied by the sameness of action. Still the greatest men and women of every era in the history of the earth have had their terms of play in almost every day, but they have not been prolonged into wastefulness and excess.

Play should not appeal wholly to the mind; when it omits muscular participation it ceases to be play, and hence is useless because it is un-hygienic.

The woman whose only accomplishments are music, exercise, social functions and dressing, is a waster of the time that God has placed in her hands, and she suffers sooner or later from the sin, for the law of destiny makes a mark of her. There never has been a case of a time-waster who has not been the special victim of the shafts of revenge hurled by this same nature.

Specific design is one of the greatest facts in the universe and there is no fact that is more readily proved.

Activities that are aimed at pleasure and amusement or in the gratification of abnormal tastes are likewise sins, and under the law of destiny the only goal is the penalty. Chance and luck are never waiting on those men and women who live only for the pleasure they can get out of existence. And there are millions of people who not only waste time, but also try to invent methods of killing it. Over their lives, ere the years are spent, the clouds of gloom, despondency, melancholy and despair hang dark and heavy, until the penalty is all they see left of their careers.

Stated in another way the law of destiny may be made to read like this:

Develop within yourself any lines of usefulness that you please, be judiciously active, and avoid time-wasting, and nature will show you the avocation for which you are fitted and lead you on to your true destiny.

You cannot be the choosers of your own destiny, nor do we believe that you can be the choosers of your own avocations. The avocations must choose you, and your destiny must draw you on.

There has never been an instance in all the history of the world where a man or woman has successfully chosen an avocation that did not make the first advances toward that individual. Those who doubt this law are ignorant of the facts that have prevailed in the lives of the great. These facts are read under the process and with the aid of the searchlight of strict analysis of human nature. They cannot be guessed at or set down as mere conclusions of the judgment.

We have seen this law of destiny at work in a large number of lives during the past thirty years; and, when we say that out of an organization that we founded even longer ago than that, comprising two hundred young men all of whom were pledged to adopt the rules of this very law of destiny, not one has come up into manhood who has not been a direct proof of the workings of the principle. Over and over again it has been said that nothing so wonderful has ever been witnessed in human life, as that there should not be an exception in the entire list.

Boys who were supposed to be aimless in life, many of them wholly uneducated as far as schooling was concerned, and others who were graduates of such universities as Harvard and Yale, while a large group of others occupied a middle ground in the matter of education, all bent to obedience under the same rule, and all found the law of destiny working out their fate, It was this society that gave to us the impulse to toil and to accomplish the tasks that have since been achieved.

Many and many a time have we been solicited to advise young men, young women, and adults as well, on the problems of their drifting lives. They have chosen and failed. We had but one line of advice to give them, and it was this:

Make yourself as much better mentally and in all your faculties as you can, develop within yourself any lines of usefulness that you please, be judiciously active, and avoid time-wasting, and nature will show you the avocation for which you are fitted and lead you on to your true destiny.

You may be the architects of your own fortune, and the makers of your fate, but you cannot choose either. To be such an architect you must make the most of the ever-present, add to your value in every way, not necessarily financially, and be prepared for higher steps on the plane of life. Just as sure as you draw breath you will find nature placing her hand in yours and drawing you up, higher, higher and higher all the time.

It may be claimed that this theory does not agree with the claim made in Universal Magnetism that a man may will or decree a certain ambition in life and win the end sought, even against the most unyielding obstacles. Cases are there cited of great victories achieved against the decrees of fate. One notable example is the career of Beaconsfield who was a Jew and who determined to prove that the Jews in England were as powerful as they chose to make themselves. He resolved to reach the highest rung in the ladder there, the rank of Prime Minister, and he succeeded. Another great example was that of MacMahon of France who, when as a poor boy, resolved that he would one day rise to the highest position in the army, that of Marshal of France.

All these cases are based upon the exercise of a much higher power than that of Advanced Magnetism, and this exalted influence is that known as Universal Magnetism. It has never failed where it has been employed in the manner there taught. Beaconsfield became Prime Minister of England and Mac-Mahon became not only Marshal of France but its honored and popular President.

Great souls are born in humble bodies sometimes, and they are admitted to partnership with fate and destiny, becoming makers of the law of success. It is magnetism in the highest degree and there is no greater phase of it anywhere in all the universe. But who will attempt so much? Who will ride in the chariot with the gods?

Who has the power of execution—to actually DO?

Day dreamers and "castle builders" seldom execute. Once in a while they make the attempt and more rarely still they succeed. To build castles in the air is not such an idle occupation as we would think. All great men have indulged in this happy occupation, but have turned their dreams into realizations. There are few castles of this kind that cannot be made realities, for they are founded upon desires, and these desires are inspired by what has been accomplished. "What man has done man can do."

Many persons make plans which they know they can execute, but never enter upon the doing of them; or, if they do, they lose interest in them, or have not the energy of completion.

To go about a thing is a refreshing element in one's character. You are sitting now in the memory of some task that you have left unperformed. It would have been done but you could not summon the energy to start about it.

"Decision" is akin to this, but quite apart. It takes a decisive character to know *what* to do, and *how* to do it. To make up one's mind firmly to do or not to do a certain thing is "Decision." To execute a thing is to go about it at the proper *time* and *place*, without delay.

So we say—you have come thus far in the study of Advanced Magnetism, and have shown commendable persistence. It should be an easy step into the higher realm where you put into execution the laws of this art.

In the biography of a successful man, we find that he was accustomed in the morning to write down the tasks of the day, especially those that did not come under the usual routine duties; and at night he would check those which he had performed. In this way he formed the habit of doing everything that had to be done, and by this pleasant method achieved great success in life.

"Never put off until tomorrow what can be done today," is the spirit of execution, and seems to have been made a very essential element in the lives of many great men.

Executive ability is so necessary is every successful life that you ought to cultivate this power by special practice. This you can do by making up your mind that you will undertake something difficult and persist in it to the end. The quality grows by using, and no person need fail ever who is not lamentably weak. One success leads to another; one failure paves the way to its successor. No more marked evidence of a lack of character can be found than the inability to carry into execution what has been begun or what should be undertaken.

Everywhere in the world the demand is for men and women of executive ability.

In the present course in Advanced Magnetism we seek to make the adoption of the principles of power an easy matter in every case, and to include every grade of rank among the people. When, therefore, we state that the law of destiny decrees that the avocation cannot be chosen at will, and that fate is the master and not the tool of men and women, we refer to all those who are not makers of destiny. The best laid plans of men and women go astray, as we are told by the poet-philosopher, who also includes mice. Man proposes, but God disposes, is another form of the same rule.

The gratifying principle, however, is behind it all, and tells us that some grand destiny awaits every man and woman who will perform the great duties we have mentioned, who will improve self along the most useful lines of life, even though it is done blindly, who will help others who are trying in all sincerity to help themselves, who will adopt a career of constant activity based upon good judgment, and who will avoid a wanton waste of time.

These things you may do and do blindly, and they will bring you through the darkest night of discouragement into the light of the brightest day of success. Let the night be as gloomy as it will, let the heart bend beneath the yoke of discouragement, let tears of sadness and sorrow run down the cheeks ever so fast and so hot, this line of active duties well performed and executed with no apparent aim, will bring you through the night into the light.

The commonplace will not elevate a person. The drudgery of humdrum life will not bring reward. Hard work, having no ambition and no hope, unattended by increasing knowledge and improving faculties, will end where it begins, with hard work. Destiny has nothing in store for these classes.

The practical is eminently inviting to all minds of solid common sense, but it is not enough. In a world where mysteries are everywhere surrounding the conceited mind of man; where he knows nothing beyond the telescope and nothing beyond the microscope; and where his familiarity with the earth is cut short a mile below its surface, and hundreds of miles this side of either pole; this man cannot resolve all processes of nature to the rules that he has invented for his own guidance.

The practical man does not choose to believe what he cannot see, and he sees less than one-millionth part of what God has created about him. He is the child of more than a hundred forces of nature which he tries to harness and which fell him as a straw is crushed beneath the avalanche of rock and ice.

There will never come a time when man will master any of the elements or any of the forces that give him their usefulness for his inventions to play with. As mysterious as electricity will be the over-hanging influences that uplift him or allow him to drift down stream to oblivion. So simple a power as gravity is wrapped in the profoundest of all mysteries. Its operations are understood in part, but no one knows what it is or by what means it can control matter through dead space. And so it is with all the forces that surround man.

When we say that there is a specific design at work in every human life that is in harmony with the activities of nature, we draw from a higher course of training than this for our proof; but when we say that such a power knows, understands and participates in the individual life that is so in harmony, we find our proof in the working out of this principle. It does not have a religious basis, for it has been in evidence ever since life has found an abiding place on this planet. Religion is subsidiary to this grander law. The latter uplifts and enobles religion itself.

Rank, fortune, worldly success, achievement in the open field of opportunity, fame and all that it implies, are not measures of the man or woman who is the special ward of the law of destiny. Down in the humblest strata they may be found; through the thronged paths of the middle grades and occasionally on the heights of human ambition, these favored people dwell and work out their triumphs in obedience to the light with which they are inspired.

They are watched and are guided.

The highest power that rules the universe may know very little of them as individuals but there are countless forms of subsidized powers that not only know them and can see deep down into their inmost hearts, but that live with them and breathe with them the wish of the day and the hope of the morrow.

Nothing is in vain that is in earnest, and all that is in earnest is active and energetic. The least thing that is done should be done as well as the greatest. Sincere efforts for self-improvement and for the performance of duties of every character will draw one up to some of these subsidized powers, and so a charm will fall upon the life that is thus uplifted.

Such a person cannot fail, nor will the ground slip beneath the feet. The earth and the sky are full of energy, of power, of mighty influences that are made to unite their potency with the will of man and command the fate of every life that suits its purposes or those of the great Ruler of us all.

CPSIA information can be obtained at www.ICGtesting.com
Printed in the USA
BVOW081414090212

282456BV00001B/13/A